NORTHWESTERN WISCONSIN

OUTDOOR RECREATION & CAMPING GUIDE

Gary Kulibert

Published by:

Explorer's Guide Publishing
4843 Apperson Drive
Rhinelander, WI 54501

All Rights Reserved. No part of this book may be reproduced in any form or by any means, electronic or mechanical, including photocopying, recording or by an information storage or retrieval system without written permission from the author, except for inclusion of brief quotations in a review.

Copyright ©   1990 by Gary Kulibert
Printed in the United States of America
Printed by F A Weber & Sons, Park Falls, WI

ISBN 0-962-3430-4-8

PLEASE NOTE:

This book has been designed to enrich your knowledge and appreciation of Wisconsin's vast outdoor recreational opportunities. Every reasonable effort has been made to gather the most current and accurate information. There may be mistakes both typographical and in content, therefore information presented within this book is intended only as a general guide and not as an authority on that subject. The publisher and author shall have neither liability nor responsibility to any person or entity with respect to any loss or damage caused, or alleged to be caused directly or indirectly by the information contained in this book.

TABLE OF CONTENTS

AREA 1
NORTHERN SHORE AREA

ASHLAND, BAYFIELD, DOUGLAS, 6

Recreational Waters, 7
Public Lands, 8
Chequamegan Forest, 10
Parks, 12
Apostle Islands, 15
Trails, 18
Bait Shops & Guides, 22
Campgrounds, 25
Area Activities, 30
Information/Emergency, 31
County Maps, 33

AREA 2
RIVER AREA

BURNETT, SAWYER, WASHBURN, 36

Recreational Waters, 37
Public Lands, 38
Parks, 45
St Croix Riverway, 47
Trails, 51
Bait Shops & Guides, 60
Campgrounds, 64
Area Activities, 66
Information/Emergency, 68
County Maps, 70

AREA 3
BLUE HILLS AREA

BARRON, POLK, RUSK, 74

Recreation Water, 75
Public Lands, 76
Parks, 80
Trails, 83
Bait Shops & Guides, 88
Campgrounds, 90
Area Activities, 91
Information/Emergency, 92
County Maps, 93

AREA 4
WESTERN COAST AREA

DUNN, PEPIN, PIERCE, ST CROIX, 96

Recreational Waters, 97
Public Lands, 98
Parks, 100
Trails, 105
Bait Shops & Guides, 108
Campgrounds, 109
Area Activities, 111
Information/Emergency, 113
County Maps, 114

AREA 5
TRANSITIONAL AREA

CHIPPEWA, CLARK, EAU CLAIRE, 118

Recreational Waters, 119
Public Lands, 120
Parks, 122
Trails, 127
Bait Shops & Guides, 133
Campgrounds, 134
Area Activities, 137
Information/Emergency, 138
County Maps, 139

INDEX, 142

DESCRIPTION OF EACH SECTION

RECREATIONAL WATERS

Throughout each area there are a number of lakes, streams and rivers offering many opportunities to swim, canoe, fish and explore. The types of recreational water vary with the geology of that area. Parts of the state may have many lakes while others have flowages and rivers. Still others may have very little surface water. In this publication it is not possible to provide information on all the named and unnamed lakes located in each area; however, we do provide a brief description of the more noted waters. It is important to remember that each body of water can not be all things to all people. Some will be good for fishing while others great for skiing, boating and other activities. Access will also vary. Not all landings can handle bass boats and other large boats. For more information contact your local guide, bait dealer or Department of Natural Resources Office.

Fishing in Wisconsin is as varied as the lakes and rivers. There are trout in the cold, deep lakes with panfish, northern and bass in the shallow waters; walleye and muskies are scattered throughout the state. Water clarity, weeds and depth will have lot to do with the fishery. Of the unnamed lakes, the majority are from .1 to 5 acres, shallow with only minnows present; their use as a sport fishing resource is limited.

When it comes to fishing, normally larger lakes offer more diversity in the type of fish and structure. When fishing any lake, it helps to get lake maps and fishing reports such as those produced by **Fishing Hot Spots, 1999 River Rd, Rhinelander, 54501, (715) 369-5555, 1-800-338-5957**. These minimize your time on non productive waters. It is also good to talk with the local bait dealer or hire a guide. With the number of river systems throughout the state, many of them have been dammed, forming flowages. These flowages vary in size from a small mill pond to large lakes and are used to maintain water levels to limit flooding and to provide water to downstream industries. Flowages offer many recreational opportunities; however, water levels fluctuate, sometimes by many feet, depending on the time of year and amount of precipitation. With such water level changes the character of the flowage changes, affecting fishing patterns, land forms and boating hazards. Not all rivers are suited for all types of recreation; it is best to first check with the local Department of Natural Resources office.

PUBLIC LANDS

The state has extensive areas of public lands. These are owned by city, county, state and federal governments for a variety of uses. Except for selective refuges, these lands are open for public use but may not suit your particular needs. While the local municipalities have a limited amount of forested lands, they do offer many parks and boat landings. The lands owned by county, state, and federal governments are managed for multiple use, including timber, wildlife and recreation. Lands bought for forest and wildlife management also provide excellent places for bird watching, berry picking and other related activities. Access into the larger areas may be by walking trails, logging roads, cross country ski and snowmobile trails. However, due to the amount of privately owned lands with these projects, and the new trespass law, make sure you know where you are. Please respect the rights of the private land owner.

PRIVATE FOREST

Besides the government lands, there are several large private forests dedicated to timber production. Under Wisconsin State Law, lands dedicated for forest production that receive a special property tax break, must be open for public use with some limitations. These lands, called forest crop lands, are good for hunting, hiking, fishing, berry gathering and more. The companies ask that users exercise caution and respect both nature and the company's rights. Some have established trails or are located on a desired body of water. Most prohibit the use of all terrain vehicles and camping. For information on these lands call the county forester or the local Department of Natural Resources office. The location of all forest crop lands are registered at the courthouse.

PARKS, BOAT LANDINGS AND OTHER THINGS

Whether you are planning a "major expedition" or a day at the beach, within each county there are a variety of parks to meet many of your needs. State, county, city and town park systems may offer anything from large sport complexes to a little out-of-the-way spot on a quiet brook. Space does not permit the detailed listing of all parks here, but we have included the main or unique ones. When traveling the area highways, stop and enjoy these great recreation spots.

TRAILS

The mix of forest and parks throughout the area provide an interesting backdrop for a variety of trails, ranging from the water trails of our forefathers to the modern interpretive nature trails. There are trails built for hiking, skiing and multi use. A fall hunting trail may be used for summer berry picking and winter cross country skiing or snowmobiling. Logging roads, closed after completion of logging activities, also provide good access to many areas. Trail maps, for most formal trails, are available from the property manager of these trails. If you are planning to do a lot of hiking in one area or if there are no established trails, you may want to purchase a topographic map from U.S. Geological Survey.

When talking about a ski trail, a rating of difficulty may be mentioned. This is strictly provided for general information. It is not intended to be used by anyone in picking out a trail.

Canoeing the "wild rivers" of this country can also be very enjoyable, even in the more developed areas of the state. It lets you see a different perspective of the land. Not every river or stream is suited for a good and enjoyable canoeing experience. Larger bodies of water and boat traffic can cause possible capsizing, while small rivers may be too shallow or have many obstructions like fallen trees or rocks. When canoeing a small river, the water elevation may rise quickly due to spring snow melt or big summer rains but fall during dry summers and falls. This will dictate if you will have to portage your canoe over shallow spots in the stream. Be sure your experience and equipment fits the river. Even the small streams can be deadly with a sudden summer storm.

GUIDES AND BAIT SHOPS

Area Bait Shops: Bait dealers come in a variety of sizes, shapes and services. Some offer basic crawlers and minnows while others have a complete line of baits, including the new "in thing" plus tackle, guide service and more. Listed in each area are some of the area bait dealers which are licensed by the state.

Area Guides: When fishing in a new area, a guide can minimize your nonproductive time in the field. A list of some of the people licensed by the WI DNR to guide for fishing is provided. Guiding is seasonal work; not all of these guides may be available at the same time. Fishing guides are normally hired on a half or full day basis to fish one or several species of fish. The fee is usually for one or two people and includes the use of the guide's boat. Extras, such as poles, baits, lures, may be provided for a fee. When hiring a guide it is best to first ask what is included for the fee so you will not be disappointed later. Guides are listed by address but many also work in surrounding counties.

CAMPGROUNDS

Dispersed Camping: You may want to strike out on your own to find that perfect camping spot, away from everyone. This is called dispersed camping. When you find that "spot", the question is, "Can you legally camp there?". Each unit of government has its own rules on this type of camping. The state does not permit camping on any of its lands unless it is specifically designated for camping. This includes the canoe camp sites. It is best to first call the property owner first. It may save you some embarrassment or possibly a fine.

Designated Campgrounds: The campgrounds listed in each section are licensed by the Division of Health to assure they meet minimum health standards. Included with the private campgrounds information is the location, number of sites, phone number and address and if the campground is located near water.

AREA ACTIVITIES

In each area there is a list of activities. The list will help you plan some of your fun when in the area. Included is a list of museums, water tours, rustic roads, amusement parks and more.

EMERGENCY/OTHER INFORMATION SOURCES

There are times when you need to know if the fish are biting, if a park or trail is open, or many other things when planning your trip. A list of county, state and federal and tourism contacts is provided. Also included is a list of the local sheriffs and hospitals, just in case help is needed.

AREA 1
Northern shore
Ashland, Bayfield and Douglas Counties

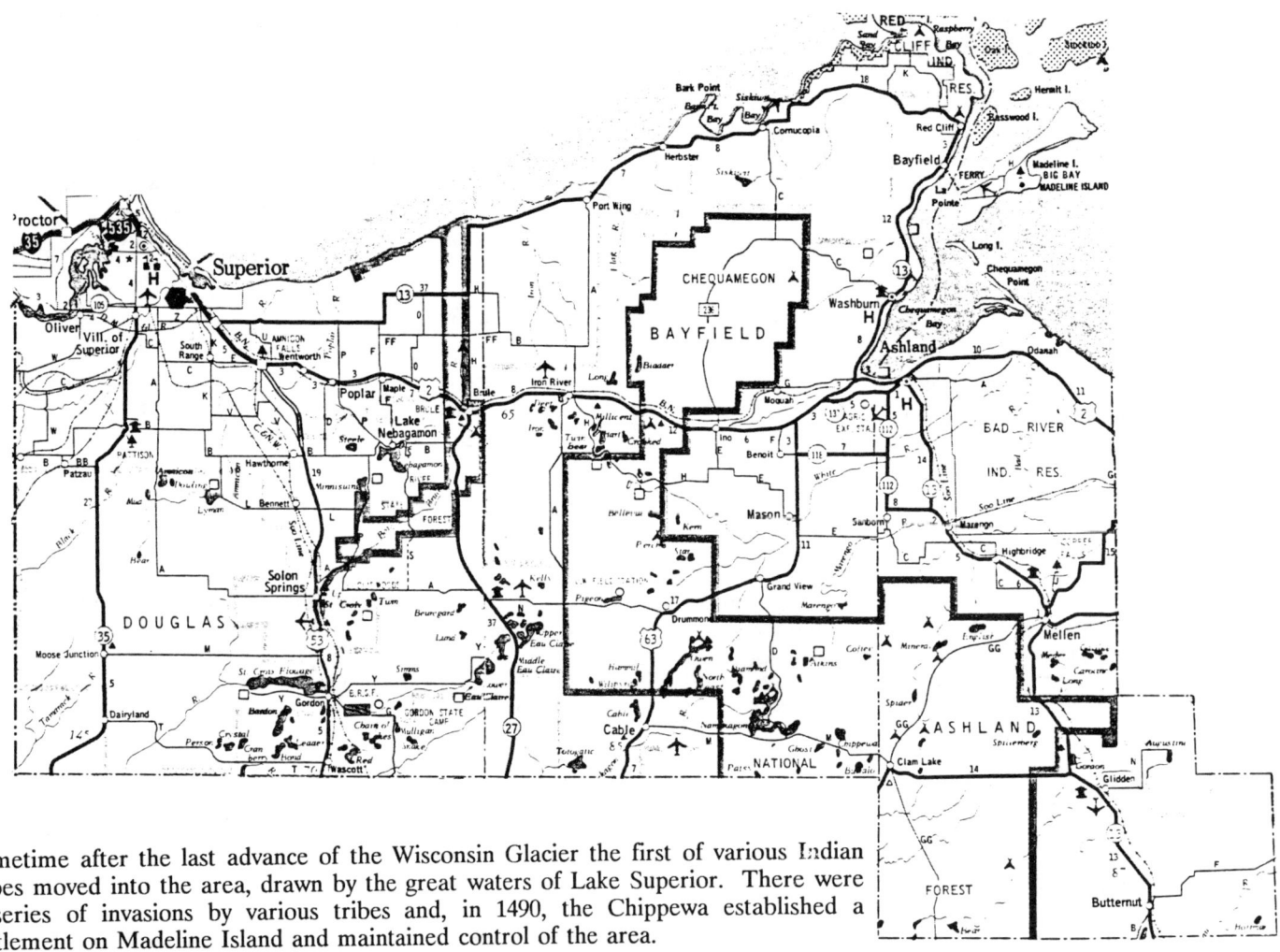

Sometime after the last advance of the Wisconsin Glacier the first of various Indian tribes moved into the area, drawn by the great waters of Lake Superior. There were a series of invasions by various tribes and, in 1490, the Chippewa established a settlement on Madeline Island and maintained control of the area.

In the early 17th century, French explorers and missionaries, such as Father Menard, Father Claude Allouez, Radisson & Grosseilliers, Nicolas Perrot and Pierre Charles Le Sueur, passed through the region, leaving their names behind. Many of these explorers also traveled the Bois-Brule River upstream to the St. Croix River, then down to the Mississippi. These men were followed by the French Canadian voyageurs, who canoed "Lac Superior de Tracy", where they bartered for pelts with the Indians. Their colorful songs, legends and tales play a large part in the heritage of the people who now live in the Lake Superior region. The area today still has its "Lac Superior de Tracy", majestic rivers, forests and prairies, which provide an excellent place to enjoy the great outdoors.

There are a number of cities plus a scattering of unincorporated settlements.
In **Ashland County**, Ashland, the county seat, is located at the northern end of the county where Highway 2 & 13 meet at Lake Superior. Mellen, Glidden and Butternut are to the south along Hwy 13. Clam Lake is in the southwest corner.
In **Bayfield County**, Washburn, the county seat, is located on Hwy 13 in the northeast corner of the county and on the shores of Lake Superior. On Hwy 63 to the south is first, Mason and then, Cable which is near the Sawyer County line.
In **Douglas County**, Superior, the county seat, is located in the northwest corner of the county on the Minnesota state line. Solon Springs and Gordon are to the south on Hwy 53.

RECREATIONAL WATERS

Great Lakes:

Lake Superior is properly named, as it is the largest fresh water lake in the world. It covers over 20,352,000 acres, 21 times more than all the inland surface waters in the state. Lake Superior touches three states (Michigan, Minnesota, Wisconsin) and Canada. The lake is used for many different recreational purposes including sea kayaking, sailing and fishing. Due to its size and its temperature (cold) the lake has been noted since the days of the early voyageur as being temperamental and dangerous. Caution is always advised. Landings can be found at many of the lake side communities like Superior, Washburn, Bayfield and Ashland. Chequamegon Bay, located east of Bayfield County, is a wide, shallow bay of the lake. Fisheries include salmon and brown trout, with splakes during the winter months. Walleye and northern pike can be found on the eastern side of the bay. Other activities include boating, sailing, sea kayaking and agate picking along the shore.

Lakes and Flowages:

There are 547 named (39,221 acres) and 953 unnamed (4,018 acres) lakes in the region, including several man-made flowages. This accounts for 10 % of the total number of Wisconsin lakes, covering 4.5 % of the state's total inland surface water. Most of the lakes will be found in the lower two thirds of the county. North of the iron ranges there are many small rivers and streams which flow into Lake Superior.

Ashland County has 77 named (5,549 acres) and 81 unnamed (463 acres), lakes. Several of the nice lakes include:
Mineral Lake, 225 acres, is located about 7 miles west of Hwy 13/77 at Mellen on Cty GG. Located on US Forest Service lands, there is a federal campgrounds on the south shore and minimal private development around the lake. The lake is noted for muskies, walleye, bass, and panfish such as crappies.
English Lake, 244 acres, is located about 5 miles west of Hwy 13/77 at Mellen on Cty GG. This lake, located to the north of the road, is partly surrounded by US Forest Service lands with some private development. Fisheries include largemouth bass, walleye and a lot of panfish.
Long Lake, 111 acres, is located about 2 miles south of Mellen on Hwy 13/77, then east about a mile on Cty MM and south 1.5 miles on Long Lake Rd. This lake is also located within the national forest and has limited development. Fisheries include northern pike, largemouth bass and bluegill.

Bayfield County has 319 named (20,702 acres) and 645 unnamed (2,455 acres) lakes. A more noted one is:
Lake Namekagon, 3,227 acres, is located 8 miles east of Cable on Cty M. Cty D passes along the east shore of the lake to the federal campgrounds. This is a large, irregular shaped lake with several large open areas and small bays. This is also the beginning of the Namekagon River which flows west into the St Croix River. The shoreline is well developed. Fisheries include walleye, northern pike and panfish.

Douglas County has 154 named (12,970 acres) and 277 unnamed (1,100 acres) lakes. A more noted one is;
St Croix Flowage, 1,913 acres, is located 7 miles south of Solon Springs on Hwy 53, then at Gordon, west 1 mile on Cty Y. The dam on the St Croix River which from the flowage is 5 miles further west. This is a long, shallow lake with several islands and bays. It has maintained a scenic and wild appearing shoreline. Fisheries includes northern pike, panfish and bass.

Rivers:
Brule River, has two different personalities. From Lake Minnesuing, north of Solon Springs to Hwy 2, the river flows through coniferous bogs with many springs. The river has a gentle fall of 3 feet per mile. However, between Hwy 2 and Cty FF, it crosses the Copper Range and begins a sharp drop to Lake Superior. In 19 miles the river falls 328 feet in 19 miles or over 17 ft drop per mile. This drop results in rapids and steep river bluffs which require expert skill to canoe. The river is noted not only for its canoeing but also for its great trout fishing.
Namekagon River, has its start in Ashland County, east of Cable. For more information please see page 47.

Trout Streams:
The area has many streams, including 223 classed as trout waters, covering 947 miles. There are 351 miles of Class I stream, 341 miles of Class II and 255 miles of Class III. Several of the noted streams include the White River and Bois-Brule in Douglas and Bayfield, and Silver Cr and Augustine Cr in Ashland.

Public Lands

County:

Ashland County, has 32,116 acres in the southeastern area of the county. The general boundaries are Cty F on the south, Hwy 13 on the west and Cty MM on the north. Hunter walking trails have been developed throughout this area.

Bayfield County, maintains 166,674 acres in 8 management units. This acreage, plus the national forest and Indian reservation lands, make up the majority of the county's available lands. The county lands can be found on the north and west sides of the national forest. There are over 96 miles of hunter walking trails through these forest lands.

Douglas County, has 267,281 acres in county forest and parks. This is one of the largest county forests in the state. There are five different forest areas but the largest covers the majority of the southwest 1/4 of the county. The general boundaries are Cty B on the north and Hwy 53 to the east. Other smaller parcels can be found in the southeast corner, east of Cty G; just south of Superior and west of Cty C and Hwy 35.

State:

Bark Bay Preserve, 625 acres, is located about 22 miles west of Washburn on Hwy 13 or about 4 miles west of Cornucopia on Hwy 13, then on Bark Bay Rd. This is a bay on Lake Superior which has a natural lake shore setting of wetland areas, sand beaches, and upland boreal forest.

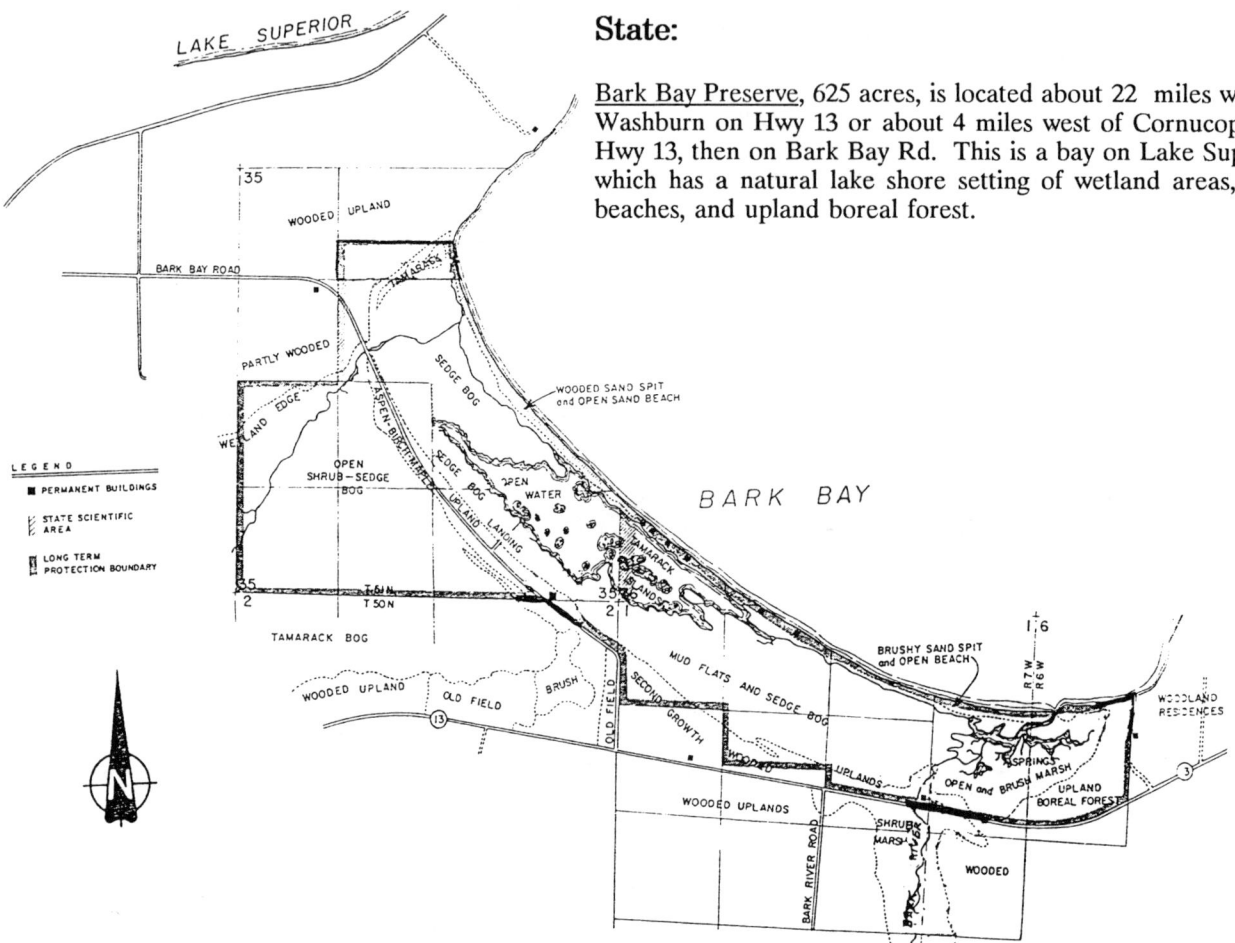

Brule River State Forest, 40,000 acres, is a long and narrow property located about 21 miles east of Superior on Hwy 2. The forest, following the Brule River, extends 27 miles from the shores of Lake Superior south southwest to Solon Springs. The forest was established to preserve the natural beauty of the Bois-Brule River. The river is noted for its canoeing and trout fishing with the slow flowing upper reaches and the sharp drop of the lower portions with its rapids and steep river bluffs. There are 10 designated access points to the river which must be used when launching or landing on state lands. These are located on Cty P, Stone Chimney Rd, Stone Bridge, Pine Tree Rd, Bois Brule Campgrounds, Hwy 2, Copper Range Campground, Hwy 13, Mouth of the Brule, Winneboujou and on Cty FF. No inflatable rafts or similar devices can be used on the river. Other recreational areas in the forest include two family campgrounds, 3 picnic areas and a cross country ski trail. Brule River Forest, Hwy 2, Box 125, Brule, WI 54820, (715) 372-4866.

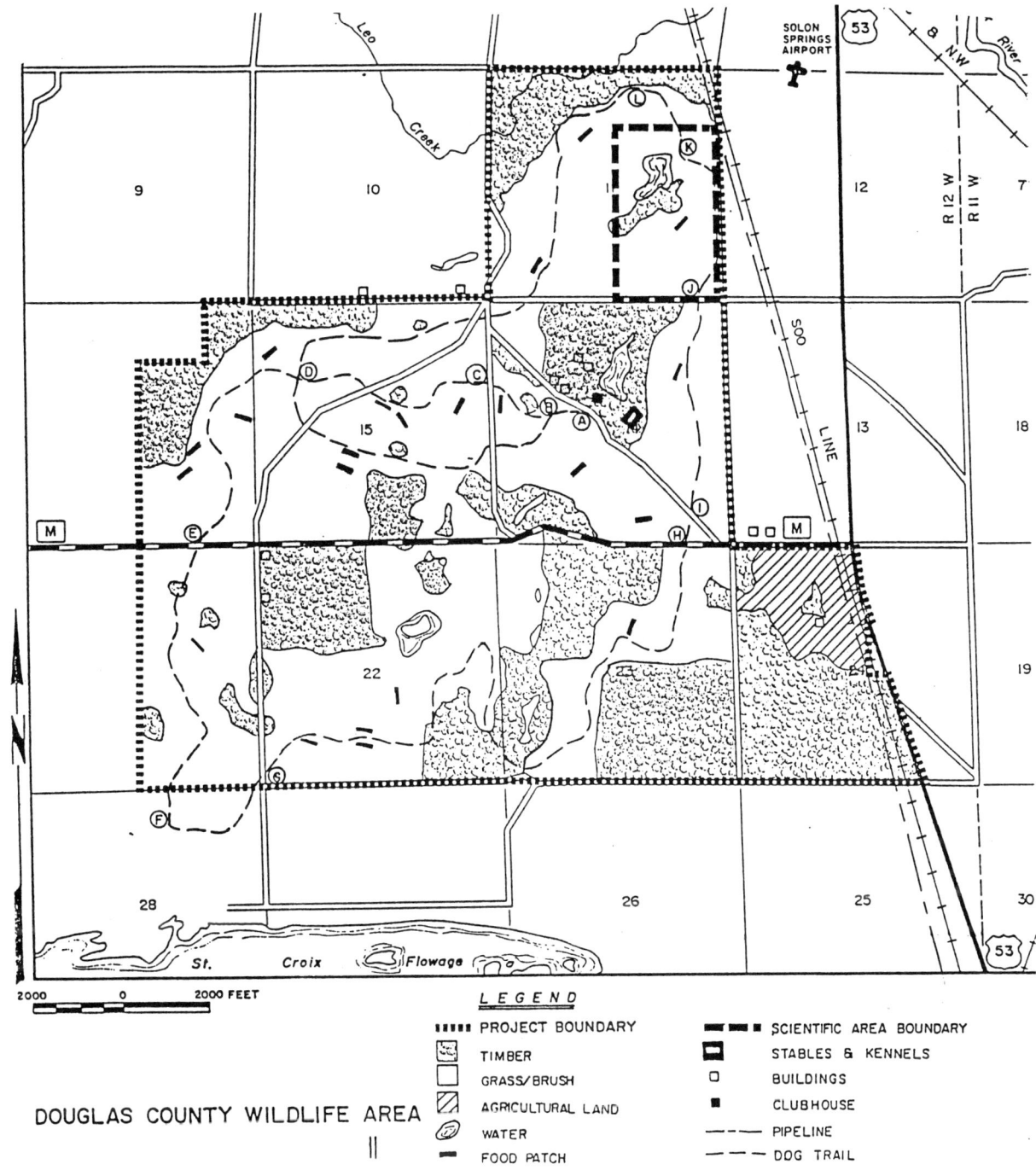

DOUGLAS COUNTY WILDLIFE AREA

Douglas County Wildlife Area, 4,500 acres, is located south of Solon Springs on Hwy 53, then west on Cty M .5 miles to the project. Cty M splits the property in half. The area is a mix of timber, brush and prairie for the management of sharp-tail grouse.

Port Wing Boreal Forest and Beach, 1,500 acres, is located on Lake Rd, north of Hwy 13 at Port Wing, which is about half way between the Cities of Superior and Washburn. This is a scientific area of open marshes, boreal forest, sedge bogs, river and sand beaches on the shore of Lake Superior.

Totagatic Lake Wildlife Area, 1,200 acres, is located about 2 miles south of Cable on Hwy 63, then west on Squaw Bend Rd, south on Sunset Rd and west on Totagatic Rd. This is a 537 acre lake surrounded by marsh and wetlands with upland ridges. It is managed for waterfowl and forest game animals. It also preserves a natural lake in its wild state.

White River, 960 acres, is located 3 miles south of Ashland on Hwy 13. The property starts at the highway and extends east. This is a stream bottom and timber uplands which provide access to trout waters. Managed as fisheries habitat, improvements are made to promote trout habitat. The lands are also managed for wildlife needs.

White River, Bayfield County, 2,406 acres, is located west of Ashland on Hwy 2 about 13 miles, then south on Cty E and west on Cty H. This is part of the project listed above.

Federal:

National Forest:

Chequamegon National Forest is one of two national forests in Wisconsin. The forest was established in 1933. One of the driving forces in the forest formation was the tax delinquent lands which the counties could no longer absorb. The initial forest was 177,000 acres. By 1935, ninety three percent, or 789,284 acres, of the present day acreage was already acquired. The naming of the forest was hotly debated within the Forest Service. The name, Chequamegon, came from the Ojibwa language. The translation is thought to mean "long point or strip of land" or "the place of shallow water" after the Chequamegon Bay area. These lands are dedicated for multiple use by the people of this country. There are three management units in this area. These extend from Lake Superior south to the Chippewa River.

Chequamegon National Forest Headquarters, is located at 1170 4th Ave, Hwy 13 South, Park Falls, WI. There are 5 ranger districts plus a number of wilderness, scientific and special areas throughout the forest. The specific districts for this book are listed below.

Glidden Ranger District, USDA-Forest Service, Glidden, WI 54527, (715) 264-2511, is located on Hwy 13 in Glidden and on the eastern fringe of the forest.

Hayward Ranger District, USDA-Forest Service, PO Box 232, 604 Hwy 27 North, Hayward, WI 54843, (715) 634-4821, is located on Hwy 27, west of the forest.

Washburn Ranger District, USDA-Forest Service, PO Box 578, 113 E. Bayfield St Washburn, WI 54891, (715) 373-2667, is located on Lake Superior and east of the forest.

There are 15 campgrounds, 2 wilderness areas, a number of ski and hiking trails and 9 picnic areas. For more information please see the respective sections.

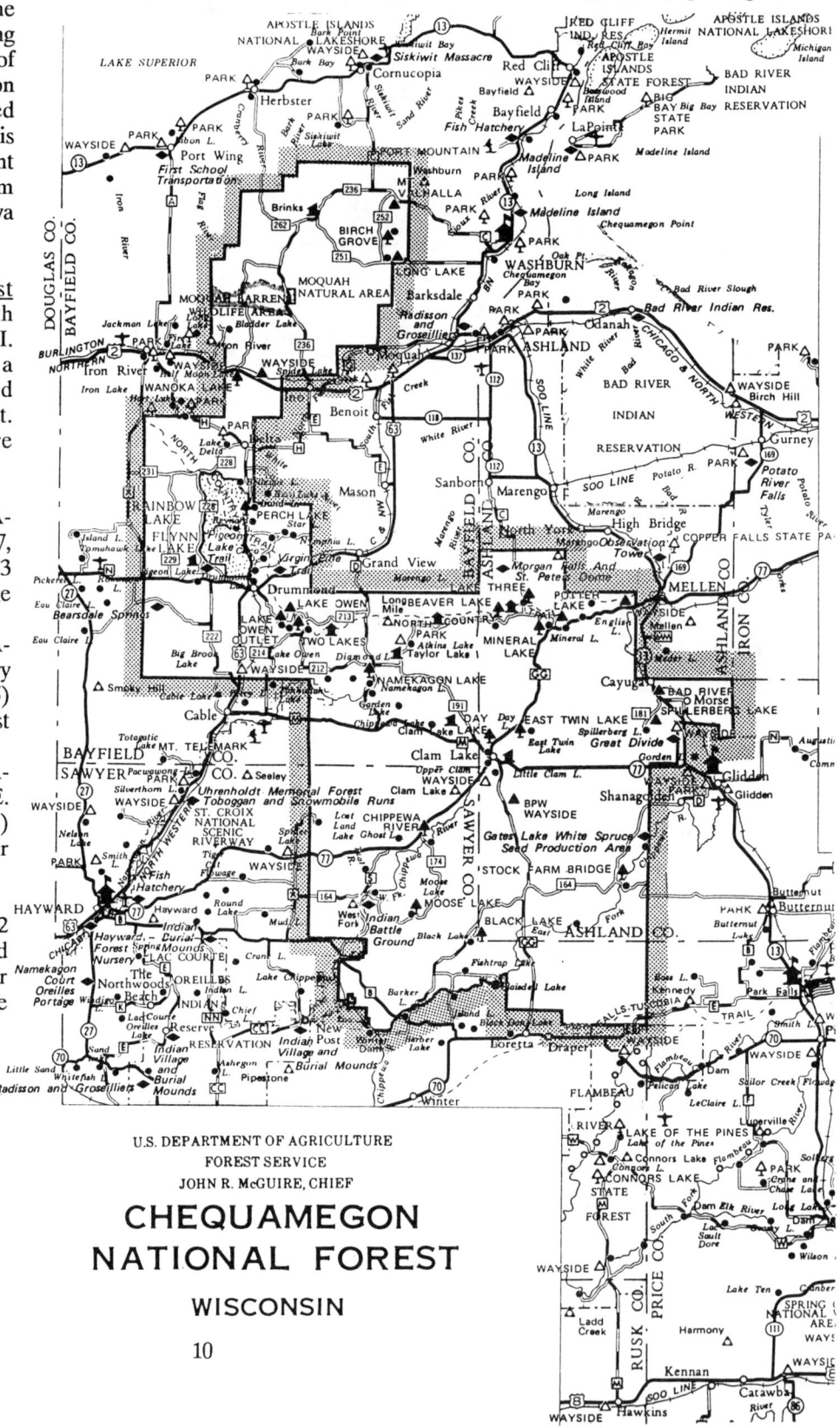

U.S. DEPARTMENT OF AGRICULTURE
FOREST SERVICE
JOHN R. McGUIRE, CHIEF

CHEQUAMEGON NATIONAL FOREST
WISCONSIN

Wilderness areas:

Porcupine Lake Wilderness, 4,235 acres, is located about 4 miles south of Drummond on FR 213. The wilderness area extends 1 1/2 miles to the south and 4 1/4 miles to the east. The boundaries are FR 213 on the north, Cty D on the east, FR 374 on the south (eastern half) and FR 214 on the west. The area is characterized by rolling hills in the west then to flat and finally swamps in the east. There is a mix of hardwoods and pines throughout the area. Six lakes larger than 5 acres can be found with panfish and northern pike. The Northern Country National Trail (4.5 miles) runs the length of the wilderness. Any camping must be 100 feet from any lake or trail.

Rainbow Lake Wilderness, 6,583 acres, is located west of Ashland on Hwy 2, then south and west of Hwy 63 to Drummond. From here go north 3.5 miles on FR 223 to the southeast corner of the wilderness. The boundaries are FR 223 on the east, FR 227 on the north, FR 228 on the west and FR 392 on the south. The area is criss-crossed with two trails and a trail head on each road. A six mile section of the North Country Trail passes through the wilderness. This area is rolling, glaciated lake terrain with a mix of hardwood and pines. Fifteen lakes in the area offers good fishing for panfish and northern pike.

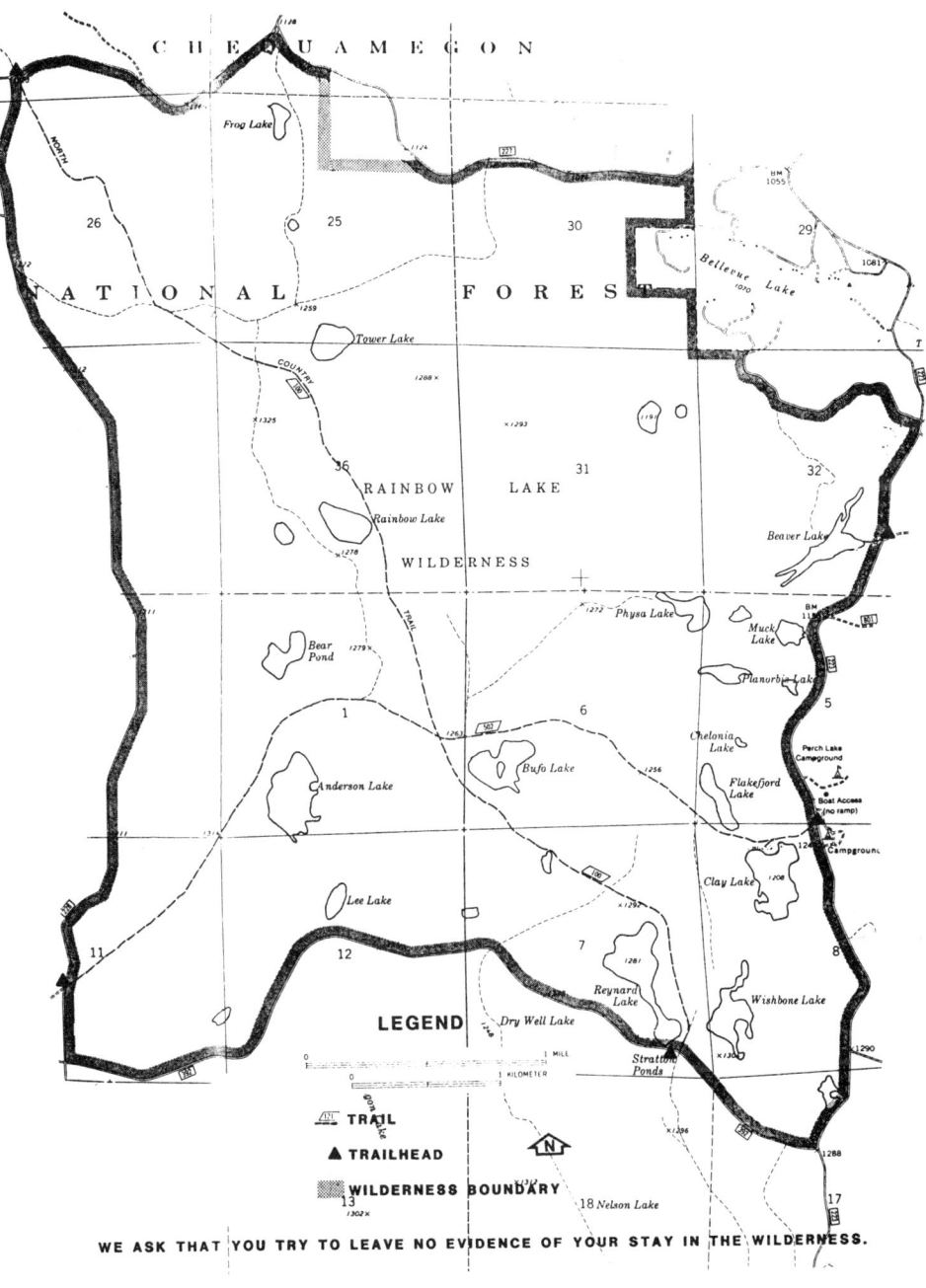

WE ASK THAT YOU TRY TO LEAVE NO EVIDENCE OF YOUR STAY IN THE WILDERNESS.

PARKS, LANDINGS AND OTHER THINGS:

Bayfield County:

County Parks:

Big Rock Park, is located 1 mile northwest of Washburn on Cty C, then north on Big Rock Road. Facilities include campground with toilets.
Delta Lake Park, is located south of Iron River on Cty H, then west 1 mile on FR 228, then north to Delta Lake. Facilities include campground, beach and boat landing.
Twin Bear Park, is located 5 miles south of Iron River on Cty H to the Pike Lake Chain. Facilities include toilet, beach, camping and boat landing.

Municipal Parks:

Memorial Park is located in Washburn on Lake Superior. Facilities include toilets, showers, beach, and playground.
Moon Lake Park is located 1/2 mile south of Iron River on Cty H to Moon Lake. Facilities include camping, beach and boat landing.
West End Thompson Park is located in Washburn on Lake Superior. Facilities include toilets, beach, camping, boat landing and playground.

State Waysides:
Hwy 2, located 1 mile east of Cty A, has a picnic area, drinking water and toilets.
Hwy 2, located 5 miles west of Ino, has a picnic area, drinking water and toilets.
Hwy 13, located 3.5 miles west of Port Wing, has a picnic area, drinking water and toilets.
Hwy 63, located 1.2 miles south of Cable on the Namekagon River, has a picnic area, drinking water and toilets.

Douglas County:

County Parks:
Anna Gene County Park, 256 acres, is located south of Superior on Hwy 53, then 7 miles west on Cty L. Facilities include boat landing on Lyman Lake, picnic area, bathhouse, swimming, restroom and trails.
Bass Lake Park, 20 acres, is located about 5 miles east of Solon Springs on Cty A, then 2 miles south on Bakken Rd, Muskrat Lake Rd and Bass Rd. Facilities include boat landing, picnic area and swimming.
Gordon Flowage County Park is located 6 miles west of Gordon on Cty Y on St Croix Flowage. Facilities include camping, boat landing, picnic area and swimming.
Lake Minnesuing County Park, 30 acres, is located north of Solon Springs on Cty A, then north on Cty P about 7 miles, then west on Minnesuing Rd. Facilities include boat landing, picnic area, swimming, drinking water and trails.
Lower Eau Claire Dam Park, 38 acres, is located 11 miles east of Gordon (Hwy 53) on Cty Y. Facilities include camping, boat landing, picnic area and toilets on Lower Eau Claire Lake.
Lucis Woods Park, 41 acres, is located just south of Solon Springs on Hwy 53. This is a former state park which the county now operates. Facilities include camping, boat landing, picnic area, stand of virgin pine and swimming.

Municipal Parks:
Town of Brule Picnic Area, 1 acre, is located off Hwy 2 on Main St. Facilities include picnic area.
Radigan Park, Tn Dairyland, 13 acres, is located the southwest corner of the county on Hwy 35, then west 3.5 miles on Town Rd (opposite Cty T east). Facilities include picnic area on Tamarack River.
Louise Park, tn Dairyland, 22 acres, is located in the southwest corner of the county. Take Cty T 3 miles east of Hwy 35, then south on Rocky Brook Tr 1 3/4 miles, then south on Park Rd to St Croix River. Facilities include boat landing, camping and picnic area.
Schoen Park, Tn of Dairyland, 3 acres, is located in the southwest corner of the county. Take Cty T 3 miles east of Hwy 35, then south on Rocky Brook Tr 4 miles, then south on Schoen Rd to the St Croix River. Facilities include campsite, toilet and picnic area.
Gordon Wayside, 2 acres, is located on Hwy 53 just north of Cty Y in Gordon. Facilities include picnic area.
Efaw Park, Tn of Hawthorne, 129 acres, is located south of Superior on Hwy 53, then west about 1 mile on Cty B. Facilities include picnic area, restrooms and ball diamond.
Lake Nebagamon Village Park, 8 acres, is located in town, has a picnic area.
Lake Nebagamon Beach, 1 acre, is located south of Cty B, has a beach.

City of Superior:

Billings Park, is located on the east side of town. From Tower Ave, take 21th St. It is on the shores of the St Louis River and has a lagoon, playground, shelter and picnic area.
Wisconsin Point, a break water, which protects the harbor area, provides a great view of the area. There is a sandy beach, lighthouse and Port of Superior entry. Located at the east end of Superior on Hwy 2/53, take Moccasin Mike Rd east, then Wisconsin Point Rd.
Superior Boat Landing, is located north of Hwy 2/53 at the marina on Barkers Island.
City of Superior, Municipal Forest, 4,500 acres, is located on the southwest side of the city. There are a number of bays of the St Louis River. The general boundary includes 28th Ave on the north, Albany Ave on the east and Hwy 105 on the south.

State Parks:

Amnicon Falls, 816 acres, is located 10 miles east of Superior on Hwy 2. Here you can observe the effects of the great earthquake which occurred about a half billion years ago. The movement of the rocks has made the falls on the Amnicon River possible. Facilities include campgrounds, picnic area, scenic water falls, hiking and nature trails, toilets and drinking water. Hwy 35 S, R 2 Box 435, Superior, WI 54880, (715) 399-2115 (715) 399-8073 park; (715) 399-2115, ranger station.
Pattison State Park, 1,370 acres, is located south of Superior on Hwy 35. The falls at this park are also formed, in part, by the Douglas Fault. Big Manitou Falls, 165 ft drop, located at the park is the state's highest water fall. Facilities include campgrounds, picnic area on Interstate Lake, toilets, drinking water, bathhouse, trails and swimming. Hwy 35 S, R 2 Box 435, Superior, WI 54880, (715) 399-2115 park and ranger station.

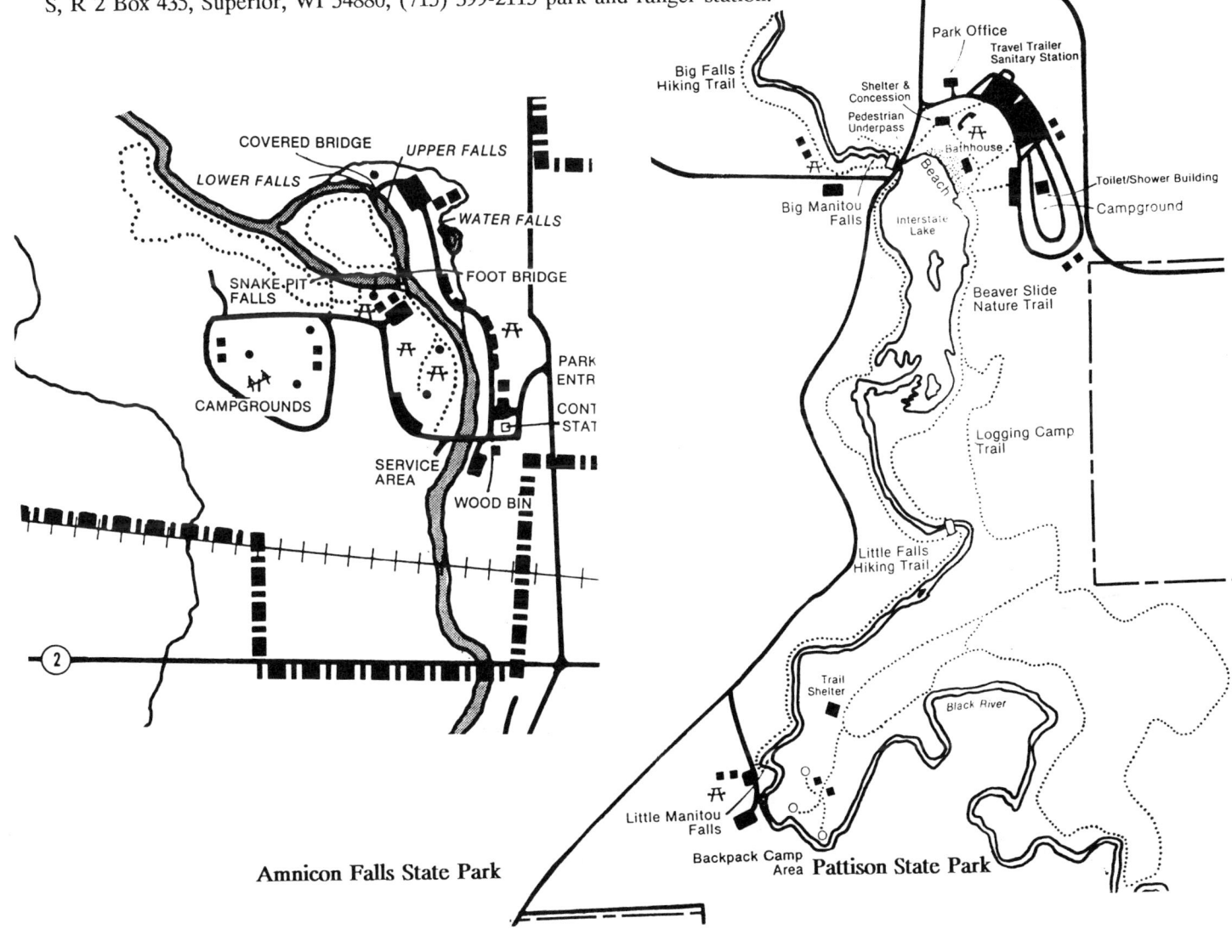

Amnicon Falls State Park

Pattison State Park

Brule River State Forest, Box 125, Brule, WI 54820, (715) 372-4866.
  Bois-Brule Campground Recreation Area, 10 acres, is located just south of Hwy 2 on Hwy 27. This area has a campground, a separate picnic area, and a landing and parking lot to the river. There are toilets, water and hiking trails.
  Mouth of the Brule Recreation Area, 25 acres, is located 9 miles north of Brule (Hwy 2) on Cty H, then 2.5 miles further north on Hwy 13 and west on Brule River Rd to Lake Superior. Facilities include boat landing, picnic area, swimming and scenic overview of the lake.
  St Croix Lake Recreation Area, 5 acres, is located north of Solon Springs on Cty A (east of Hwy 53) and just south of Cty P on the west shore of the lake. Facilities include boat landing, picnic area, water and toilets.

State Waysides:
Hwy 2, located 1/2 mile west of Hwy 27 at Brule. Facilities include picnic area, water and toilets.
Hwy 35, located 1 mile north of Cty M. Facilities include picnic area, water and toilets.
Hwy 53, located 2 miles south of Cty A at Solon Springs. Facilities include picnic area, water and toilets.
Hwy 2/53 Information Center, located at southern limits of Superior. Facilities include picnic area, water and toilets.

Ashland County:

County Parks:
East Fork of the Chippewa River, 3 acres, is located about 2 miles south of Hwy 77 on Hwy 13, then south on Cty D about 4.5 miles. The park will be to the east and has campsites and picnic area.
Cammerer's Lake, is located east of Glidden (Hwy 13) on Cty N, then 2 miles on Mercer Rd; park is to the north. Facilities include boat landing, campsite and picnic area.

Municipal:
Wood Brothers Public Beach, 2 acres, is located 1 mile northwest of Glidden (Hwy 13) on Hwy 13, then about 2 1/2 miles north and west on Gordon Lake Rd, then south on town road to the lake. Facilities include boat landing, picnic area and swimming on Gordon Lake.
LaPointe Lake Front Picnic Area, 1 acre, is located several blocks east of the ferry landing on Madeline Island. Facilities include picnic area, open shelter and boat landing on Lake Superior.
Big Bay Island Tn Park, 60 acres, is located on Madeline Island. Take Cty H east from the landing. Facilities include picnic area, camping and swimming beach on Lake Superior.
White River Town Facilities, 6 acres, is located south of Ashland on Hwy 12, continue 1 mile south on Cty E. Facilities include picnic area and playground.

State:

Big Bay State Park, 1,690 acres, is located on the southeastern end of Madeline Island. From the ferry landing, take Cty H southeast to the park. There is a campgrounds, water, toilets, picnic area, boat landing, swimming and trails. PO Box 589, Bayfield, WI 54814, (715) 779-3346
Copper Falls State Park, 2,252 acres, is located at Mellen on Hwy 13, then about 2 miles east Hwy 169, then north on town road. Facilities include campground, picnic area, swimming and hiking. There are trails to view the various falls. Box 438, Mellen, WI 54546, (715) 274-5123.

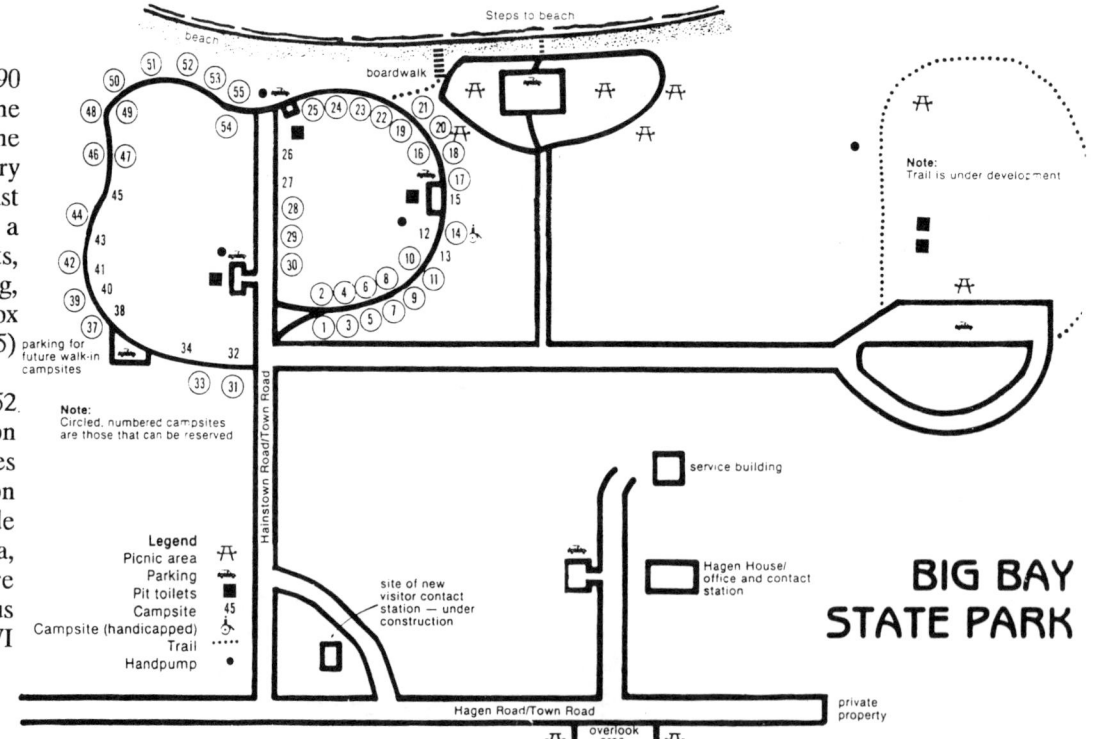

BIG BAY STATE PARK

Federal:

Apostle Islands National Lakeshore:

This national park lies at the tip of northern Wisconsin. Formed by sediments of ancient seas is was shaped by glacier's over 10,000's of years. It was visited by the first white men to enter the heart of this country, over 350 years ago. These islands became the center of fur trade and logging over the centuries. Today the park contains 21 of the 22 islands. Madeline Island, located just east of Bayfield, is mostly privately owned and not part of the park system. The park also contains a 12 mile long section of mainland, west of Red Cliff. The islands are accessible by water taxi and private boats. However caution must be used at all times, for the cold water and sudden storms can be very dangerous.

The park has a visitor center in Bayfield at the Bayfield Old County Courthouse. There are interpretive films, slides, artifacts, information and restrooms. The center is open from 8 am to 4:30 pm.

There is a second visitor center at Little Sand Bay, which is located at the eastern end of a 12 mile long stretch of National Lakeshore shore line. Take Hwy 13 west of Red Cliff, then Cty K north, then north on Park Rd. There is a long, sand beach, displays, protected harbor and a fishing camp museum. On the west end there are sea caves caused by wave and frost action over time wearing away the sandstone. These can be seen by taking Hwy 13, about 12 miles west of Red Cliff or about 7 miles west of the second Hwy K intersection to Meyers Rd. This road is on the north side and can be difficult to find. The road goes to the water's edge where sea kayaks can be launched. The caves are to the east and can be seen from shore.

Listed below are the islands with noted facilities including camping, light houses, trails, docks. The islands can be reached by water taxi, tour boat or private craft. Communications to the island ranger stations is by marine radio, channel 16.

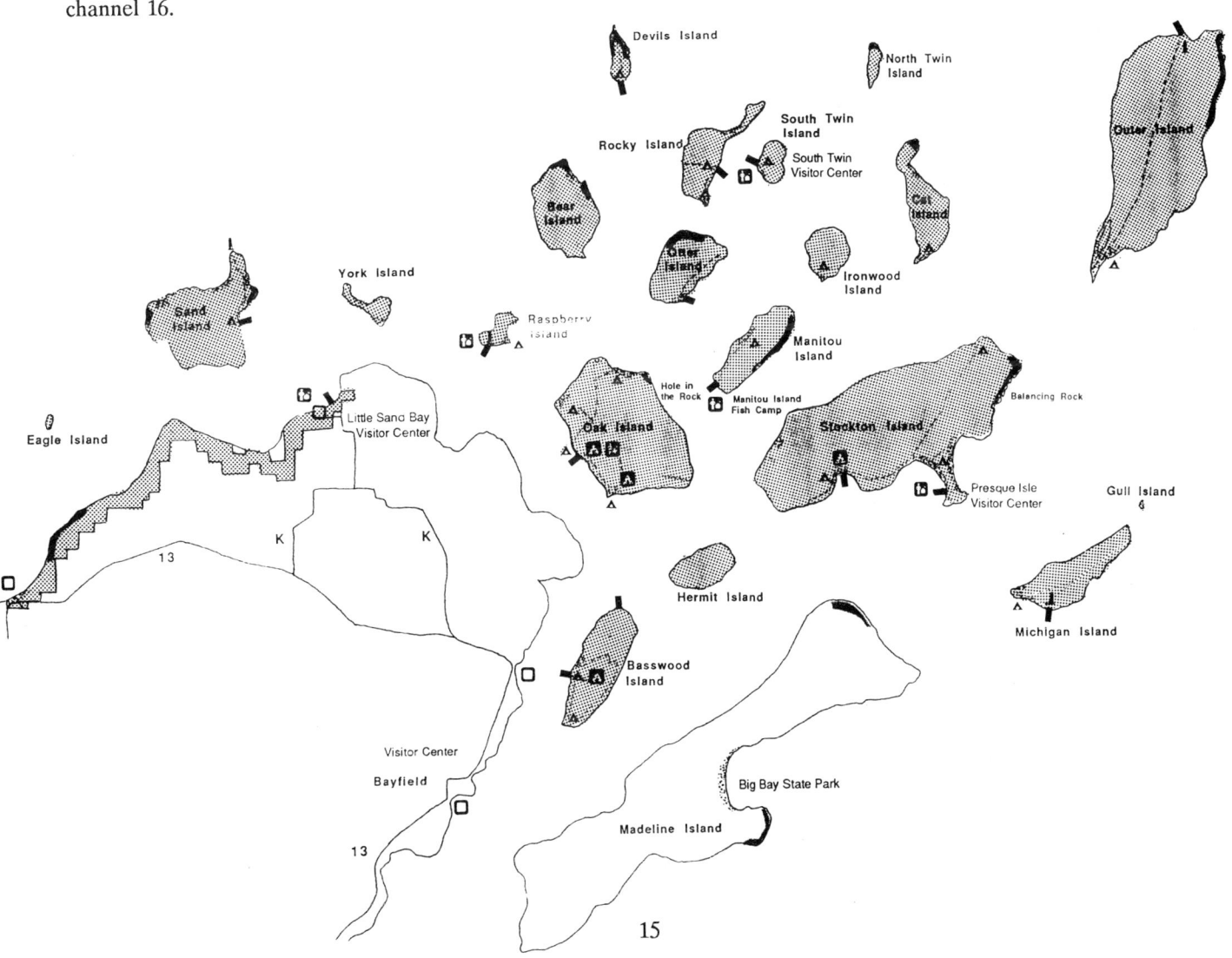

Basswood, 1,910 acres, there is a dock on the west and north ends plus a designated campground with water, toilets and a 5.2 mile trail. Dispersed camping is permitted.

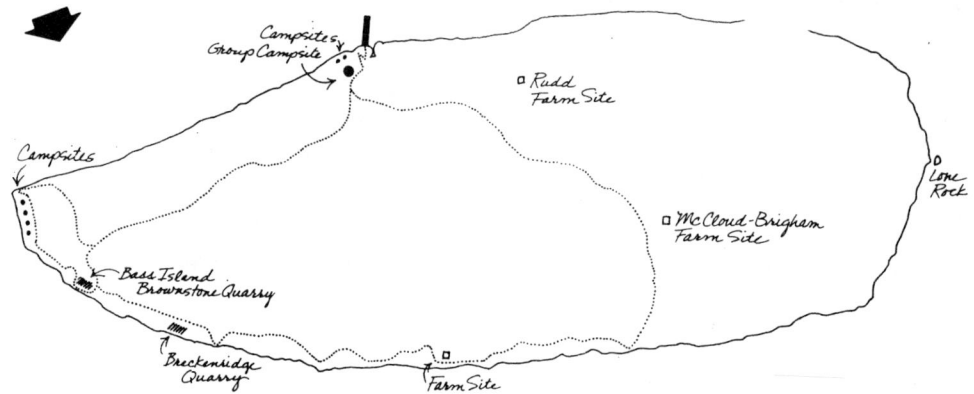

Bear, 1,824 acres, there are no facilities, however dispersed camping is permitted.

Cat, 1,342 acres, there is a common, day anchorage site on the north end with a campsite on the south. Dispersed camping is permitted.

Devils, 318 acres, there is a dock and campsite with water and toilets on the south end; dispersed camping is not permitted. There is a 1 mile trail to a light house.

Eagle, 28 acres, is a colonial nesting grounds. Boating within 500 feet of the island is prohibited from May 15 to September 1 each year. Please leave the birds alone.

Gull, 3 acres is also a colonial nesting grounds. Boating within 500 feet of the island is prohibited from May 15 to September 1 each year. Please leave the birds alone.

Hermit, 733 acres, there are no facilities, however dispersed camping is permitted.

Ironwood, 659 acres, there is a designated campsite on the south end; dispersed camping is permitted.

Long, 300 acres, there is a lighthouse and dispersed camping is permitted.

Manitou, 1,363, there is a dock on the southwest end at a restored fishing camp. A park interpreter will show you around and explain the importance of the fishing industry. There is a 2.7 mile trail to a campsite plus dispersed camping is permitted.

Michigan, 1,578 acres, the dock is on the south end at the lighthouse which is manned by volunteers. A campsite is located at the west end of a mile long trail. Dispersed camping is permitted.

North Twin, 175 acres, there are no facilities.

Oak, 5,078 acres, there is a dock at the southwest end along with 2 group and 6 different campsites. Water, toilets, 11 miles of trails and a ranger station are present.

Otter, 1,333 acres, there is a dock on the southeast end with toilets, water and 1/2 mile trail. Dispersed camping is permitted.

Outer, 8,000 acres, there is a dock and lighthouse on the north end; 8.7 miles of trails and a campsite with vault toilets on the southern end. Dispersed camping is permitted.

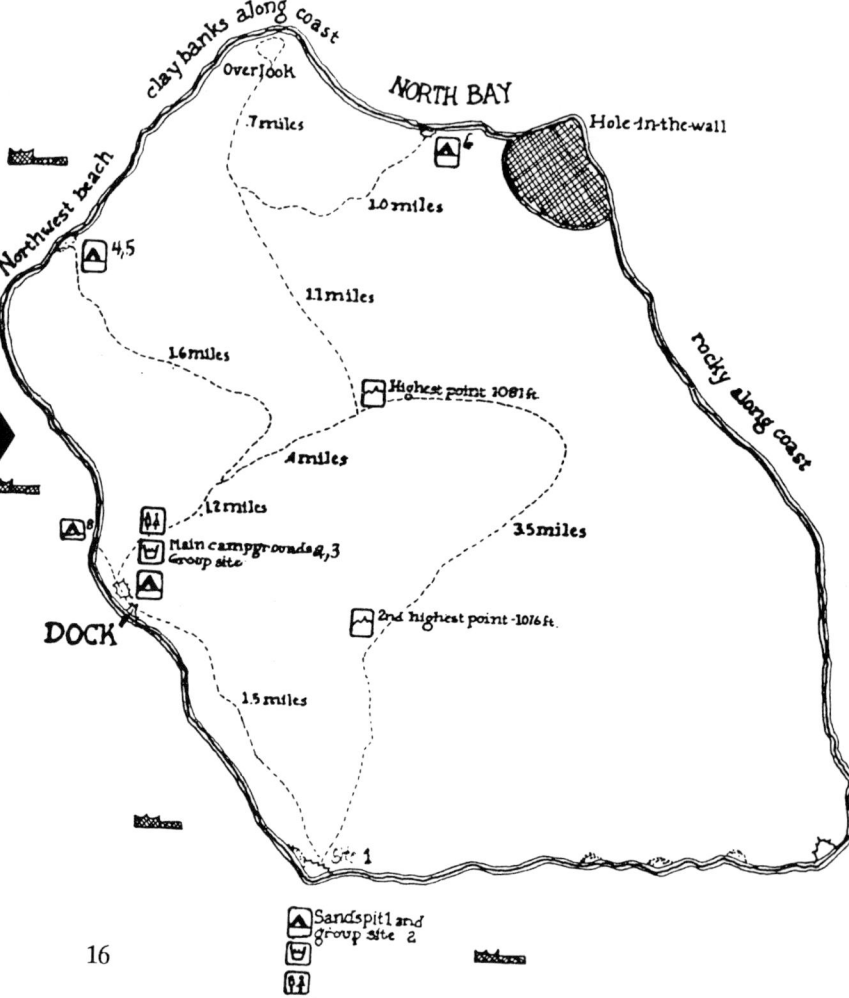

Raspberry, 295 acres, has a dock on the south end with lighthouse and ranger station. There is a campsite on the southeast end with vault toilets and 1.5 miles of trail. Dispersed camping is not permitted.
Rocky, 1,100 acres, has a dock on the east side with 7 campsites with water and toilets plus 1.9 miles of trails.
Sand, 2,949 acres, has a dock on the east side with 3 campsites, drinking water, toilets and 2.6 miles of trails. There is a lighthouse on the north end manned by volunteers.
South Twin, 360 acres, has a dock on the west side with 4 campsites, drinking water, toilets, ranger station and .25 miles of trail.

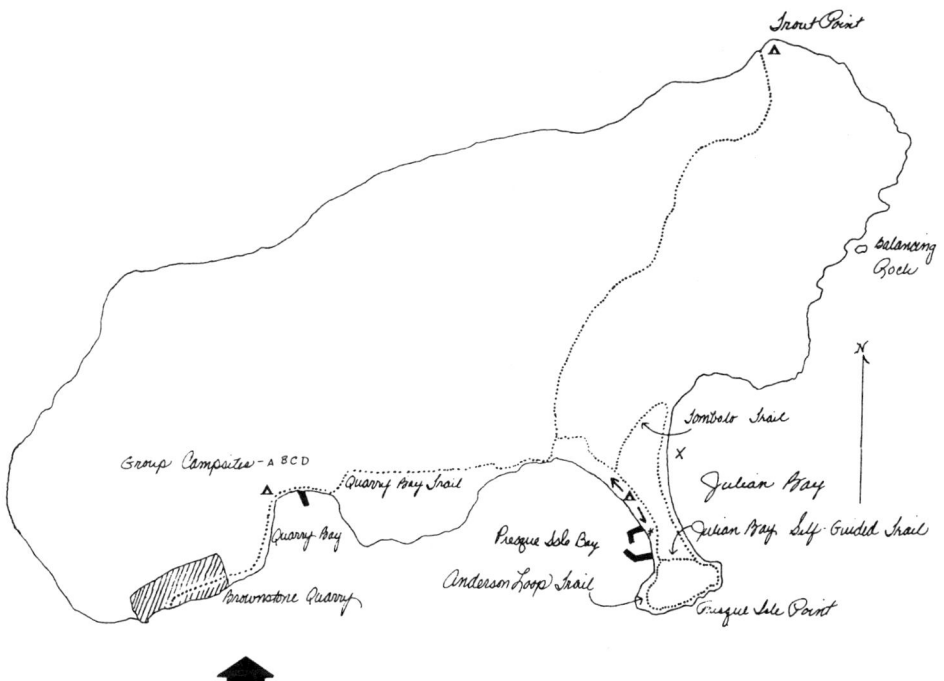

Stockton, 10,054 acres, is the largest island in the park and with the most facilities. There are two docks, one on the southwest end and the second on the southeast side. Facilities include 21 campsites, 4 group sites, 14.5 miles of trails, drinking water, toilets, visitor center, brownstone quarry and more. Dispersed camping is also permitted.
York, 320 acres, has no facilities.

Chequamegon National Forest:

Additional picnic areas and beaches can be found at the forest campgrounds. Please review the campground section.

Bad River Picnic Area, 5 acres, located 6 miles south of Mellen on Hwy 13 where the Bad River crosses the road, has a picnic area.
Potter Lake, 6 acres, is located about 7.5 miles west of Mellen (Hwy 13) on Cty GG. The picnic area is to the north and has a boat landing.
Spillerberg Lake, 3 acres, is located about 8 miles south of Mellen on Hwy 13, then south on Linden Rd and southwest on FR 181. The lake is on the south side and has a boat landing and picnic area.
Hwy GG Wayside, North, 14 acres, is located about 2 miles west of Mellen on Cty GG. Picnic facilities are provided.
BPW Wayside, 3 acres, is located about 3 miles south of Clam Lake on Cty GG. Picnic facilities are provided.

State Waysides:

Hwy 13, located 2.5 miles north of Hwy 77. Facilities include picnic area, drinking water and toilets.
Hwy 77, located 1.3 miles west of Cty M. Facilities include picnic area and toilets.

TRAILS

Mountain Bikes:

Ashland County, bikes are not permit on gated or posted trails.
Bayfield County, permits the use of bikes on gated and other trails throughout the county forest.
Douglas County, does not prohibit them on county property at this time.
Chequamegon National Forest, permits the use of bikes on all trails, with the exception of trails within Rainbow Lake & Porcupine Lake Wilderness Areas or where posted.
Wisconsin DNR, permits the use of these bikes on selected trails managed by the Department. It is best to contact the property manager to get the latest information.

All Terrain Vehicles:

Ashland County, does not permit ATVs on gated or posted trails.
Bayfield County, does not have any policy on ATV use.
Douglas County, does not prohibit ATVs on county property at this time. Presently there are two county trails.
Chequamegon National Forest, permits the use of ATVs and motorcycles on trails controlled by the Forest Service, except where the trails are posted or in the wilderness areas.
Wisconsin DNR, does not permit the use of these vehicles on any of the trails managed by the Department.

Horses:

Ashland County, permits the use of horses on county trails.
Bayfield County, permits the use of horses on county trails.
Douglas County, does not prohibit them on county property at this time.
Chequamegon National Forest, permits horses on trails.
Wisconsin DNR, policies varies with the properties, it is best to contact the property manager for the latest information.

Hiking, Hunting and Cross Country Ski Trails

State Trails:

Amnicon Falls State Park, located 10 miles east of Superior on Hwy 2. There are two trails, including the Thimbleberry Nature Trail, which lead to the falls.
Brule River State Forest Ski Trail, is located west of Brule on Hwy 2, at Afterhours Rd. The parking lot is on the south side of the road. The trail is 5.6 miles long in 6 loops.
Copper Falls State Park, is located 3 miles northeast of Mellen on Hwy 169, north on Cty J. There are several nature trails and paths to the falls. There are two ski trails along Cty J. They cover 5 miles in 4 loops and are rated beginners and intermediate.
Pattison State Park, located south of Superior on Hwy 35. There several hiking trails from .6 to 4.7 miles long to the falls, backpack camping areas and other points of interest and a 2 mile nature trail.

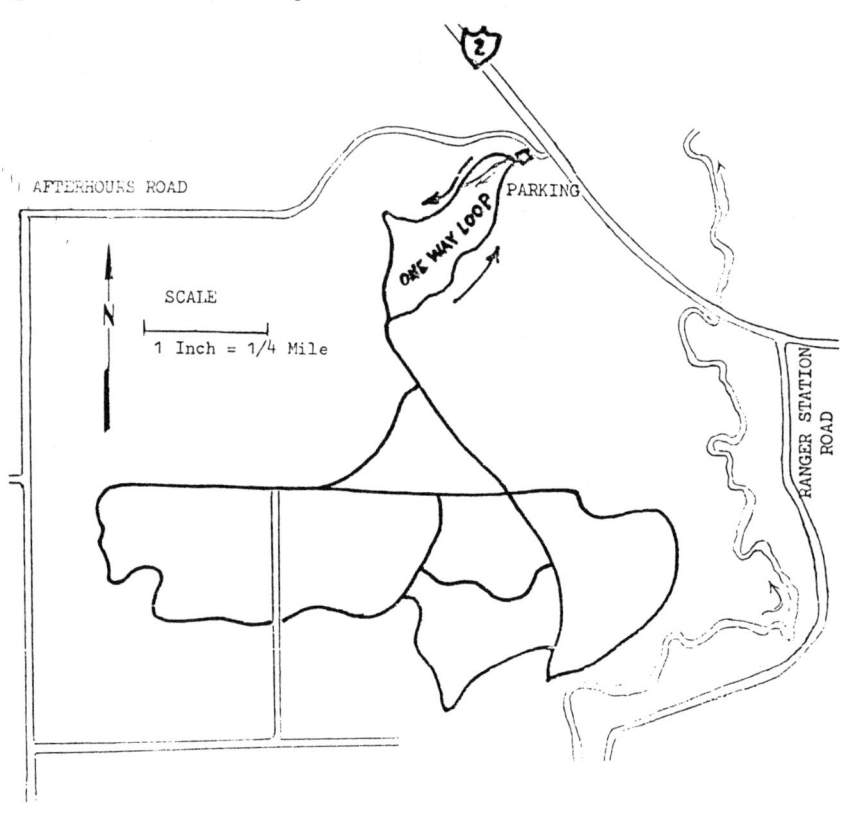

Federal:

Apostle Islands:

Trails have been established on 12 islands. They range from .25 miles on South Twin to 11.5 miles on Oak Island. For more details please see the Park Section.

Chequamegon National Forest:

Glidden Ranger District: Glidden, WI 54527, (715) 264-2511.

Rock Lake National Recreation Trail, is located 7.5 miles east of Cable on Cty M and is a non-motorized area. This 13+ mile trail system is open for hiking, skiing and mountain biking. It passes by several lakes and crosses 1 snowmobile trail. For cross country skiing, there is 1 trail rated easy, 3 rate more difficult and 2 rated most difficult.

Birch Grove Interpretive Trail, US Forest Service, is located west of the City of Washburn. Take Hwy 13 south 1 mile, then west on Wanebo Rd 6 miles, then north on FR 435 to the campground. This 0.9 mile trail features area plants and animals.

Day Lake Campground Interpretive Trail, US Forest Service, is located 1 mile north of Clam Lake on Cty GG. The trail extends from the fishing pier along the lake to a point, west of the campsites.

Pigeon Lake Interpretive Trail, US Forest Service, is located 3 miles west of Drummond on Cty N, then north 1 1/4 mile on FR 228. This 1 1/2 mile trail will be on the north side of the road.

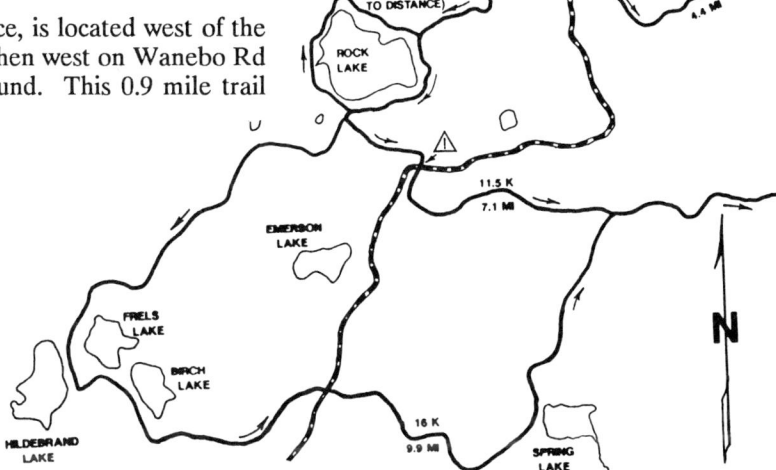

North Country Trail, is a 3,200 mile trail system established by Congress in 1980. The U. S. Park Service manages the trail system which extends from the Appalachian Trail in Vermont westward to the proposed Lewis and Clarke Trail in North Dakota. The trail enters the forest 2 miles west of Mellen (Hwy 13) on FR 390. It extends 60 miles to the west northwest to Cty A, which is 4 miles south of Iron River (Hwy 2). The eastern half of the trail passes through highlands with scenic overlooks and rock outcrops, while the western half of the trail passes through uplands and wetlands. The trail crosses many of the area's major roads. There are parking lots on FR 390, 604, 188, 187, 202, 399, Cty D and Cty A. It also passes through both Rainbow and Porcupine Lake Wilderness Areas.

The Great Divide Highway, National Forest Scenic Byway, is 29 miles of Hwy 77 from Glidden through Clam Lake to the western forest boundary. This highway, which traverses the watershed divide between Lake Superior and the Mississippi, is one of the most pleasurable scenic drives in northern Wisconsin. It is a "scenic corridor of outstanding visual, historic, recreation and interpretive forest values".

Hunter Walking Trails, 50 miles are provided throughout the area. Maps are available at the forest ranger stations.

St Peter's Dome, US Forest Service, is located west of Mellen on Cty GG, then north on FR 187 about 5 miles, then west on FR 199 about 4 1/2 miles. The trail, 1 1/2 miles, extends to the east to St Peter's Dome which is a granite knob. This is the highest point in the forest with an exceptional view.

Black Lake Trail, US Forest Service, is located south of Clam Lake on Cty GG, then west on FR 164, then 173, then east on FR 1666 to the parking lot. This 4 mile trail starts at the walk-in campsite parking lot. It extends around Black Lake with nine interpretive stops. This trail was established to interpret the logging history of the area.

Mt Valhalla Recreation Area, US Forest Service, is located 7 miles northwest of the City of Washburn on Cty C. There are two cross country ski trails that start at the chalet. It includes:
    Teuton Ski Trail, with 3 interconnected loops, 1.7, 2.8 and 3.5 miles long.
    Valkyrie Ski Trail, with 4 interconnected loops, 1, 1.1, 2, and 6.1 miles long.

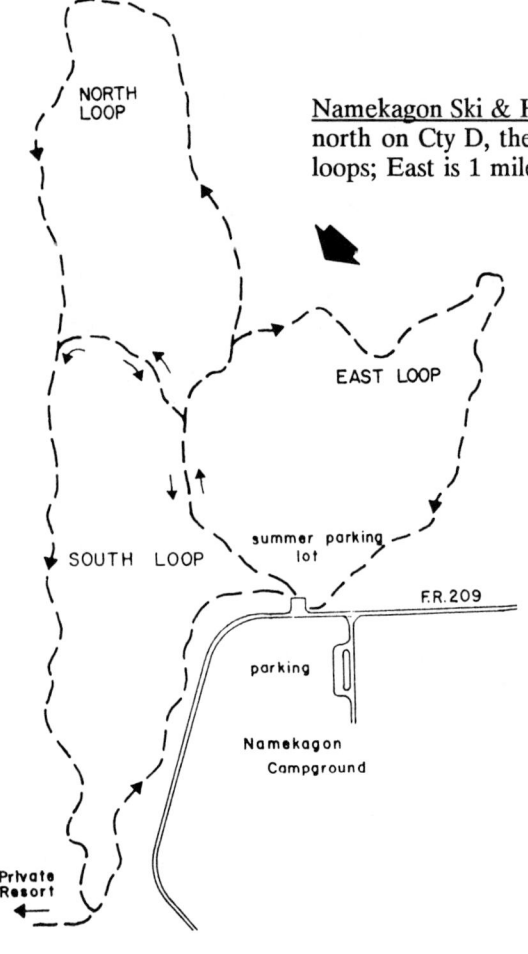

Namekagon Ski & Hiking Trail, US Forest Service, is west of Clam Lake on Cty M, then north on Cty D, then west FR 209. It is located by the campgrounds. There are three loops; East is 1 mile, North is 1.5 miles and South loop is 1.4 miles long.

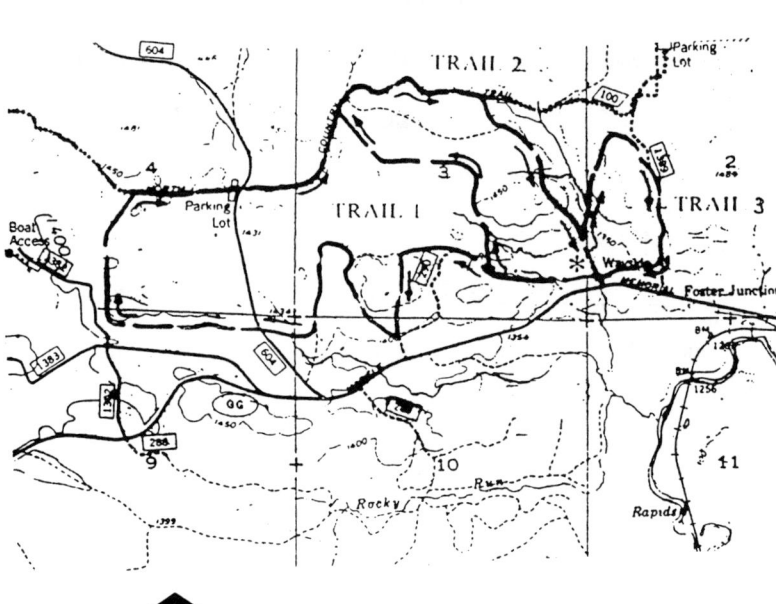

Penokee Mountain Ski Trails, US Forest Service, is located about 2.5 miles west of Mellen on Cty GG. The trail head is to the north and west of FR 1389. There are three trails covering 10.2 miles. The trails are rated from more difficult to most difficult.

Dead Horse Run ATV/Motorcycle Trail, Glidden Ranger District, is located just east of Clam Lake on Hwy 77. A second trail head can be found 17 miles south of Clam Lake on Cty GG. There are 70 miles of trails through a mix of terrain and trail types. A section of the Great Divide Snowmobile Trail connects this trail to the Tuscobia Trail, which is open to ATVs from Ojibwa to FR 161, from April 15 to Nov 15.

West Torch Lake Ski Trail, US Forest Service, is located 1.5 miles south of Clam Lake on Cty GG. It starts at the BPW Wayside and runs east to the West Torch River through 4 interconnected loops.

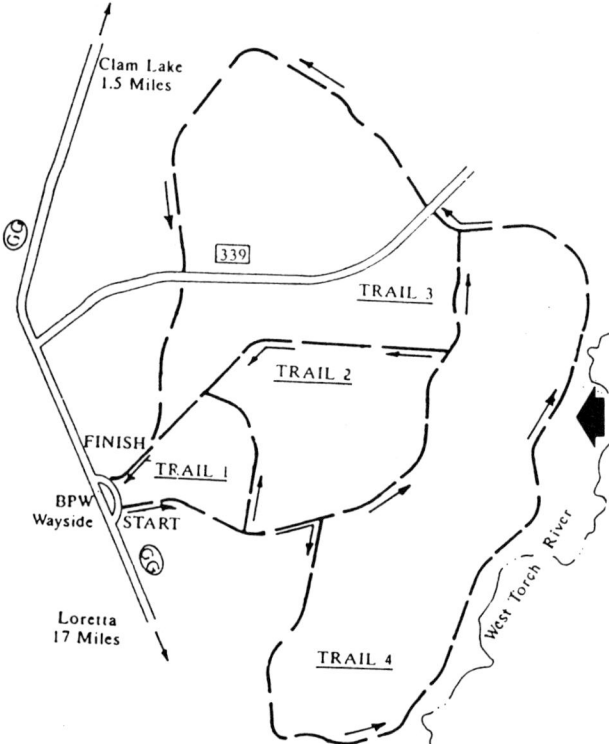

County Trails:

Ashland County Hunter Walking Trails, 16 miles, are located east of Glidden on Cty N. There are five trails off County Forest Road 8.

Bayfield County Walking/Hunting Trails, has trails throughout the county forest. The county has maps available of each trail system. For detailed maps, please call or write the county forester. Several of the trails are listed below:

    Sand River Trails, 10 miles, are located west of Red Cliff on Hwy 13. The trails are north of Hwy 13 after Sandy Point Rd.
    Spring Creek Trails, 20 miles, are located west of Red Cliff on Hwy 13, then south on Cty C. The trails are south of Mountain Rd and to the east.
    Ahmeek Lake Trails, 20 miles, is located west of Iron River on Hwy 2, then south 2 miles on Town Hall Rd. The trails are to the east. Trails heads can also be found on Pero Rd.
    Tn of Russell Trails, 2.7 miles, are located west of Red Cliff on Hwy 13, then north 1.25 miles on Cty K. Continue north on Big Sandy Bay Rd 1/4 mile, the trails will be to the west.
    Ruth Lake Trails, 5.5 miles, are west of Iron River on Hwy 2, then south 3.5 miles on Cty A, then east on Lake Ruth Rd. There are 5 trail heads along 2 miles of road.
    Hekin Trails, 14 miles, is located west of Red Cliff on Hwy 13, then south on Echo Valley Rd, west 1 mile on Gravel Pit Rd, then south on Hinkens Rd. The trails are on both sides of the road down to Star Route Rd.
    Flag River Trails, 9.5 miles is located west of Washburn on Wanebo Rd (FR 251), then west on FR 236, FR 262 and Fr 246. The trail is to the north just as you get out of the national forest.

Douglas County Hunter Walking Trails, are scattered throughout the county. For more information and maps please call the foresters office.
Douglas County ATV Trail, is located just north of Cty M at Moose Jct on Hwy 35. The trail runs 12 miles northeast, crossing Cty A. This is a section of the county snowmobile trail funded for ATV use.
Douglas County Ski Trail, is located on Hwy 53 across from Solon Springs Airport. There are three loops covering over 7 miles of groomed and tracked trails.
Tri-County Recreation Trail, has its start at Prentice Park in Superior and extends 60 miles to the east to Ashland. The trail, an abandoned railroad, opened in 1987. It is for both motorized and non-motorized uses including ATV, snowmobiles, hikers and horses. Tri-County Recreation Corridor Commission, Security State Bank Building, PO Box 648, Iron River, WI 54847.

Other Trail Systems:

Lake Owen Cross Country Ski Trails, is located 1 mile east of Cable on Cty M, then 2 miles north on Trail Inn and left on Resort Rd. There are 30 km of trails and loops which connect a number of area resorts. The mixed terrain of rolling hills and wooded level areas are rated for beginners to intermediate skiers. Cable, WI 54821, (715) 798-3833.
Superior Municipal Forest, City of Superior, is located in the southwest corner of the city by the St Louis River. The trail head is south on Tower Ave and west on 28th St. The city maintains cross country ski trails throughout this forest.
Telemark Lodge Ski Trails, PO Box 277, Cable, WI, (715) 798-3811, is located east of Cable on Cty M, then south. They maintain 100 km of ski trail which may be used for a fee.
Tomahawk Lake Park Trail, Tn of Barnes, is located between Solon Springs and Gordon on Hwy 27, then east a short distance on Cty Y, then east on Elison Lake Rd and north on Moore Rd to the park. There is a single 5.5 mile loop around several small lakes. The trail will be challenging for a beginner skier. Gene Miller, HCR 66, Box 2731, Solon Springs, WI 54873.

Canoe Trail:

The most noted canoe trail in the area is the Bois-Brule. For more information, please see the Public Lands Section, Brule River State Forest and the recreational waters section.

GUIDES AND BAIT SHOPS

Area Bait Shops:

ANGLERS ALL	2803 FRONT ST E	ASHLAND	WI 54806
DON'S BAIT	RT 4 BOX 20	ASHLAND	WI 54806
JOHNNIES BAIT SHOP	501 E 3RD ST	ASHLAND	WI 54806
MR MINNOW	2803 FRONT ST E	ASHLAND	WI 54806
TREBA'S BAITS	910 WATER ST	ASHLAND	WI 54806
BARNES RIDING STABLES	BARNES RD	BARNES	WI 54873
BLACK BEAR SALES	RT 1 BOX 180 HWY 13	BAYFIELD	WI 54814
CAMP I	955 CO FF	BUTTERNUT	WI 54514
DALY'S CEDAR LODGE	RT 2 BOX 386	BUTTERNUT	WI 54514
EAGLESGLEN LODGE INC	RT 1 BOX 127	BUTTERNUT	WI 54514
FORT FLAMBEAU RESORT & CAM	6168 DOWNEY RD	BUTTERNUT	WI 54514
HIAWATHA RESORT	1030 HIAWATHA RD	BUTTERNUT	WI 54514
MIDWAY BAR	RT 2	BUTTERNUT	WI 54514
STEVE'S CORNER		BUTTERNUT	WI 54514
WEIK & SONS	RT 2 BOX 112	BUTTERNUT	WI 54514
BIG BROOK BAIT & LAUNDROMAT	BOX 284	CABLE	WI 54821
BIG JOHN'S RESORT	BOX 605 RT 2	CABLE	WI 54821
JUNEK'S BAY CABINS	RT 2 BOX 226	CABLE	WI 54821
KRAVICKS GEN STORE	RT 2	CABLE	WI 54821
LAKEWOODS INC	RT 2	CABLE	WI 54821
MOGASHEEN RESORT	RT 2	CABLE	WI 54821
MORTENSONS SPORTSHOP & RES	RT 2 BOX 568	CABLE	WI 54821
NAMAKAGON CHIEF	HC RT 60 BOX 690	CABLE	WI 54821
NAMAKAGON CHIEF RESORT	RT 2	CABLE	WI 54821
OTTER BAY RESORT	RT 2 BOX 107	CABLE	WI 54821
PIONEER BAR	RT 2 BOX 405	CABLE	WI 54821
TELEMARK POINTE	BOX 277	CABLE	WI 54821
RENZELMANNS	MAIN ST	CLAM LAKE	WI 54517
BEAR COUNTRY	BOX 57	DRUMMOND	WI 54832
RICKS BAIT	RT 1 BOX 258	FOXBORO	WI 54836
CHOP'S NORTHWESTERN	288 GRANT ST	GLIDDEN	WI 54527
MUSKY PETE'S		GLIDDEN	WI 54527
BIG BOBBER	RT 1 BOX 209	GORDON	WI 54838
GORDON SPORT & GIFT	BOX 38	GORDON	WI 54838
J J'S HARBOR INC	RT 1 BOX 673	GORDON	WI 54838
SUNNY POINT RESORT	RT 1 BOX 192	GORDON	WI 54838
HUNTER'S CHOICE	BOX 97	GRANDVIEW	WI 54839
EAGLE HOLLOW RESORT INC	RT 2 BOX 153	IRON RIVER	WI 54847
IRON LAKE BAIT	RT 2 BOX 222	IRON RIVER	WI 54847
IRON RIVER BAIT & TACKLE	HC RT BOX 20	IRON RIVER	WI 54847
IRON RIVER MARINE	BOX 646	IRON RIVER	WI 54847
JACK'S MARKET	BOX 535 HWY 2	IRON RIVER	WI 54847
JOES BAIT SERVICE	BOX 388	IRON RIVER	WI 54847
MR T'S SPORT & HARDWARE	BOX 277	IRON RIVER	WI 54847
PINE POINT LODGE	RT 2 BOX 123	IRON RIVER	WI 54847
THE LUCKY FISHERMEN	312 MAIN ST	IRON RIVER	WI 54847
TOM'S BAIT SERVICE	RT 1 BOX 285	IRON RIVER	WI 54847
BEMIS' VARIETY & SPORT SHOP	HWY CO TR B & F	LAKE NEBAGAMON	WI 54849
LAKE MINNESUING STORE & RESORT	RT 1 BOX 753	LAKE NEBAGAMON	WI 54849
PIERCE'S MINNESUING STORE & RES	RT 1 BOX 753	LAKE NEBAGAMON	WI 54849
WASKOS CAMP GROUND LTD	RT 1 BOX 718	LAKE NEBAGAMON	WI 54849
LONNY'S LIVE BAIT	BOX 93	MASON	WI 54856
MUNSON'S	RT 2	MASON	WI 54856
ANDERSON FUELS	HWY 77 E	MELLEN	WI 54546
WALT BAITS	RT 1	PORT WING	WI 54865
JIM'S BAIT & SPORT SHOP	TOWN OF BARNES	SOLON SPRINGS	WI 54873
PREVOST'S SPORTS	BOX 241	SOLON SPRINGS	WI 54873
ALLOUEZ GARAGE	4003 E 2ND	SUPERIOR	WI 54880
CORBINS BAR	RT 1 BOX 138	SUPERIOR	WI 54880
SPORTSMAN'S CHOICE INC	721 BELKNAP ST	SUPERIOR	WI 54880
SUPERIOR SPORTS & BAIT BOX	3731 E 2ND ST	SUPERIOR	WI 54880
WES'S VARIETY SOUTH	5909 TOWER AVE	SUPERIOR	WI 54880
CHEQUAMEGON SPORT & TAXIDERMY	331 W BAYFIELD	WASHBURN	WI 54891
LEINO'S GAS & GOODS	137 W BAYFIELD ST	WASHBURN	WI 54891
WASHBURN SPORT & BAIT	331 W BAYFIELD ST	WASHBURN	WI 54891

Area Guides:

Last Name	First Name	Address	City	State ZIP
BEEKSMA	CHRIS	509 BEASER AVE	ASHLAND	WI 54806
BIETKA	PAUL	RT 2 BOX 289	ASHLAND	WI 54806
DIXON	JACK	RT 2 BOX 259	ASHLAND	WI 54806
DUNN	THOMAS	307 11TH AVE W	ASHLAND	WI 54806
HEALY	JOHN	RT 1 BOX 342	ASHLAND	WI 54806
HEITING	STEVEN	304 11TH AVE E	ASHLAND	WI 54806
LAPENTER	ROGER	2803 FRONT ST E	ASHLAND	WI 54806
LAWVER	GEORGE	221 8TH ST E	ASHLAND	WI 54806
MARSLAND	JOHN		ASHLAND	WI 54806
WICKMAN	CRAIG	621 VAUGHN AVE	ASHLAND	WI 54806
COOMBS	LEO	RT 1 BOX 180	BAYFIELD	WI 54814
YOUNG	TOM	BOX 270	BENNETT	WI 54815
BERUBE	LAWRENCE	BOX 56	BRULE	WI 54820
LEWAN	ELMER	BOX 141	BRULE	WI 54820
LYONS	MELVIN	RT 1 BOX 450	BRULE	WI 54820
BEECHLER	EDWARD	RT 2 BOX 371	BUTTERNUT	WI 54514
BLUEDORN	DALE	RT 2 BOX 445	BUTTERNUT	WI 54514
DROTT	RANDALL	RT 3 BOX 266	BUTTERNUT	WI 54514
KINNEAR	JOHN	RT 2 BOX 13	BUTTERNUT	WI 54514
LINSMEYER	MIKE	RT 2 BOX 508A	BUTTERNUT	WI 54514
LYNCH	JAMES	RT 3 BOX 268	BUTTERNUT	WI 54514
MARTNER	LEE	RT 1 BOX 127	BUTTERNUT	WI 54514
ROBINSON	EDWARD	RT 2 BOX 378	BUTTERNUT	WI 54514
SHERFIELD	DALE	955 CO FF	BUTTERNUT	WI 54514
WILTGEN	FLOYD	6168 DOWNEY RD	BUTTERNUT	WI 54514
BENJAMIN	ROBERT	RT 2 BOX 296	CABLE	WI 54821
BRANCHFORD	ROBERT	BOX 123	CABLE	WI 54821
GAIER	RICKY	RT 2 BOX 134	CABLE	WI 54821
GRAN	RONALD	RT 2 BOX 773	CABLE	WI 54821
MILFORD	RAYMOND	RT 2 BOX 731	CABLE	WI 54821
ROUSE	WILLIAM	RT 2 BOX 383	CABLE	WI 54821
SCANLON	DAVID	BOX 33	CABLE	WI 54821
SMITH	RONALD	RT 2 BOX 633	CABLE	WI 54821
MCDOUGALL	DOUGLAS	BOX 443	CLAM LAKE	WI 54517
BRENEL	ELGART	RT BOX 30	CORNUCOPIA	WI 54827
GIBBONS	GLEN	BOX 275	CORNUCOPIA	WI 54827
MEYER	GEORGE	RT 1 BOX 12	DRUMMOND	WI 54832
RICE	THOMAS	BOX 84	DRUMMOND	WI 54832
SHUMWAY	BRUCE	RT 1 BOX 82	DRUMMOND	WI 54832
MOEN	KENNETH	RT 2 BOX 218	FOXBORO	WI 54836
KUBLEY	CARL	STAR RT BOX 32	GLIDDEN	WI 54527
LAUBENSTEIN	JEAN	TYLER CT #7	GLIDDEN	WI 54527
LONG	BRIAN	BOX 253	GLIDDEN	WI 54527
SIPPLE	KEVIN	RT 1 BOX 145	GLIDDEN	WI 54527
HENNESSY	FRED	RT 1 BOX 460	GORDON	WI 54838
LANTZ	LOWELL	RT 1 BOX 74	GORDON	WI 54838
MERRITT	EDWARD	BOX 295A RT 1	GORDON	WI 54838
MERRITT	KEVIN	RT 1 BOX 289	GORDON	WI 54838
LIND	EDWIN		GRAND VIEW	WI 54839
PRIEM	ORVILLE	BOX 145	HAWTHORNE	WI 54842
KACVINSKY	STEVE	RT 1 BOX 70A	IRON RIVER	WI 54847
LINDSEY	WILLIAM	BOX 714	IRON RIVER	WI 54847
MISSLING	RAYMOND	BOX 153	IRON RIVER	WI 54847
MORGAN	RAYMOND	111 S MAIN ST BOX 172	IRON RIVER	WI 54847
WALSH	THOMAS	RT 1 BOX 285	IRON RIVER	WI 54847
CAPELLE	TERRY	BOX 187	LA POINTE	WI 54850
BEMIS	BRUCE	BOX 176	LAKE NEBAGAMON	WI 54849
SAARI	BRIAN	BOX 58	MAPLE	WI 54854
BROWN	LEWIS	RT 1 BOX 220	MASON	WI 54856
BROWN	TERRY	RT 1 BOX 142A	MASON	WI 54856
FISCHER	JEFFERY	BOX 85 RT 1	MASON	WI 54856
GUSTAFSON	LONNY	BOX 93	MASON	WI 54856
HAMANN	MARTIN	RT 1 BOX 246	MASON	WI 54856
ANDERSON	ROBERT	RT 1 BOX 727	MELLEN	WI 54546
MORTIMER	LARRY	BOX 115D FLAG RIVER RD	PORT WING	WI 54865
ALBERTS	GARY	BOX 306	SOLON SPRINGS	WI 54873
DONNELLY	JAMES	STAR RT BOX 5230	SOLON SPRINGS	WI 54873
FREID	TIMOTHY	BOX 207	SOLON SPRINGS	WI 54873
JELICH	TONY	BOX 163	SOLON SPRINGS	WI 54873
NIECKULA	JAMES	STAR RT BX 6315	SOLON SPRINGS	WI 54873

Area Guides: continued

NOGLE	GEORGE	BOX 118	SOLON SPRINGS	WI 54873
ASHLEY	PAUL	1202 OGDEN AVE	SUPERIOR	WI 54880
BARTON	JOHN	808 N 6TH ST	SUPERIOR	WI 54880
BEMIS	ROBERT	3502 E 1ST	SUPERIOR	WI 54880
FLOOD JR	ERICK	605 E 3RD ST	SUPERIOR	WI 54880
HEFFERNAN	THOMAS	1401 1/2 BANKS AVE	SUPERIOR	WI 54880
LUNDMARK	HARRY	1205 E 5TH ST	SUPERIOR	WI 54880
MOSSE	RICHARD	2017 LACKAWANNA AVE	SUPERIOR	WI 54880
NELSON	JOHN	3719 E 1ST ST	SUPERIOR	WI 54880
SOLEIM	JOHN	522 N 21ST ST	SUPERIOR	WI 54880
THERRIEN	STEVEN	1708 N 21ST ST	SUPERIOR	WI 54880
THIELMAN	LEON	RT 4 BOX 519T	SUPERIOR	WI 54880
DEUTSCH	JOHN	RT 3 BOX 3545	WASHBURN	WI 54891
DIBBELL	JEFFREY	917 W PINE ST	WASHBURN	WI 54891
WARREN	DARYL	RT 1 BOX 79	WASHBURN	WI 54809
ZIEGEL	NATHAN	115 6TH AVE W	WASHBURN	WI 54891
CARSWELL	JERRY	RT 1 BOX 142	WENTWORTH	WI 54894

Fishing Charters:

A & B Charters: charter fishing; (715) 774-3564.

Angler's All: Lake Superior charters; 2803 Front St. East, Ashland, WI 54806; (715) 682-5754.

Apostle Islands Outfitters: charter fishing on a 28 ft modern Chris Craft; Roberta's Charters, P.O. Box 841, 10 South Broad St, Bayfield, WI 54814; (715) 779-5744.

Barkers Island Marina: sailing, trawler, and fishing charters; 250 Marina Drive, Superior, WI 54880; (715) 3392-7131 or (800) 826-7010, & in WI (800) 472-7133.

Bayfield Trollers Association: charter fishing among Apostle Islands, fully equipped boats, licensed captains; City Dock, Bayfield, WI 54814; (715) 779-3330.

Dave's Charter Service: deep sea fishing for salmon and trout; full & 1/2 day charters on Lake Superior, package plans, overnight trips, scenic cruises; 414 West 7th St, Ashland, WI 54806; (715) 682-3379.

Fisherman's Cove: charter fishing on Lake Superior on a 34 ft trawler; Rt 1, Box 28, Port Wing, WI 54865; (715) 774-3886.

Leeward Charters: charter fishing on Lake Superior; Rt 1, Box 126, Iron River, WI 54847; (715) 372-4275.

Lou's Charter Service: daily charters on Lake Superior; 2914 East Front St, Ashland, WI 54806; (715) 682-5710 or 682-2646.

Pier Trolling Headquarters: deep sea fishing charters; City Dock, Bayfield, WI, 54814; (715) 779-3330.

Port Wing Marina & Cabins: fishing charters, full service marina; (715) 774-3555.

Washburn Marine: deep sea charter fishing; P.O. Box 506, Washburn, WI 54891; (715) 373-5545.

CAMPGROUNDS

Dispersed Camping:

Ashland County permits dispersed camping.
Bayfield County permits dispersed camping.
Douglas County permits dispersed camping.
Chequamegon National Forest permits dispersed camping, except in posted areas.
WI DNR does not permit dispersed camping on its properties.

Private Campgrounds:

Bayfield/Washburn Area:

Apostle Islands View Campground: located 1/2 mile south of Bayfield on Hwy 13 & Cty J, follow signs; tent & RV sites; showers, game room, water & elec, sewer hook-ups; (715) 779-5524; Star Rt, Box 8, Bayfield, WI 54814.
Big Rock Campground: located 3 miles north of Washburn via Cty C, turn right on Big Rock Rd, one mile; walking trail, rustic setting, fishing; overlooks the Sioux River; Washburn, WI 54891.
Red Cliff Recreation Complex: 3 miles north of Bayfield on the Red Cliff Indian Reservation; 40 lakeshore sites, water & elec, restrooms, dump station, laundry, beach, canoe rentals; (715) 779-5805; P.O. Box 529, Bayfield, WI 54814.
Trailer Inn: located on US 2; shady, pull through sites, rural farm setting, flush toilets, water and elec, hiking, quiet; (715) 682-4658; Rt 3, Box 353, Ashland, WI 54806.

Iron River Area:

Birch Grove Camping: shady sites, water, elec, showers; on Deep Lake; (715) 372-8879; Iron River, WI 54847.
Eagle Hollow Resort: tent & RV sites, live bait; (715) 372-4615; Rt 2, Box 153, Iron River, WI 54847.
Johnson Recreational Properties, Inc.: (formerly Anchor Inn Campground); full hookups, cabins/TV, hot showers, laundry, playground, store, dock sites; (715) 774-3658 or 774-3511; Hwy 13 & Cty A, Port Wing, WI 54865.
Top O' The Morn Resort & Campground: 40 campsites; boats and motors, hot showers, L.P. Gas, housekeeping cottages, year-round camping; a Good Sampark; on Iron Lake; (715) 372-4546; Rt 1, Box 21M, Iron River, WI 54847.
Tri Lake Timbers: located 3 miles east of Iron River on Hwy 2, 1 mile north on East Long Lake Rd (Jct FR 242); cottages and camping, laundry, beach, boat & motor rental; (715) 372-4627; Rt 1, Box 282, Iron River, WI 54847.
Wild Wood Campgrounds: located 1 1/2 miles from the Iron River; take US Hwy 2 1/2 mile to Wayside Rd, 1/2 mile to campground; 24 sites (12 primitive); picnic tables, playground, water, electric, boat and motor rental; on Peterson Lake; (715) 372-4072; Rte 1, Box 270A, Iron River, WI 54847.

Gordon/Solon Springs Area:

Adventure Campground: located 6 miles west of Gordon on Cty Y; (715) 376-4528; Gordon, WI 54838.
Bob's Tall Pines: located on Hwy 27; groceries, gas, information center; (715) 795-2551; Star Rt, Box 6235, Solon Springs, WI 54873.
Buck 'N' Bass Resort: located on Lake Rd, between Cty Hwy Y & Hwy 27 in Barnes; cabins and campground, fishing, bar, grill, game room; on Middle Eau Claire Lake; (715) 795-2718; Star Rt, Box 6525, Solon Springs, WI 54873.
Charlie Brown's Campground: located 3 miles west of Hwy 53 on N Flowage Dr.; (715) 376-4422; Gordon, WI 54838.
Conway's Bar & Campground: located 6 miles west of Wascott on Cty T; (715) 466-2710; R. Route, Gordon, WI 54838.
Golden Chipmunk Bar & Campground: located 7 miles west of Wascott on Cty T, 1 mile south on Cranberry Lake Rd; (715) 466-2414; Rural Route, Gordon, WI 54838.
Strong's Resort & Campground: located east of Gordon off Cty Y, on Fowler Rd.; (715) 376-2382; Rt 1, Box 189, Gordon, WI 54838.
Sundance Campground: located in Barnes on Upper Eau Claire Lake, 20 miles north of Hayward on Hwy 27, east on Pease Rd 2-1/2 miles; beautiful sandy beach, water & electric, flush toilets, hot showers, playground; (715) 795-2698; Star Rt, Box 5835, Solon Springs, WI 54873.
Swanson's Motel & Campground: (715) 378-2215; US 53, Solon Springs, WI 54873.
Tyman's Old Oak Bar, Supper Club & Cg.: located east of Hwy 53 on Cty Y; (715) 376-2788; Gordon, WI 54838.
Uncle Sam's Lakeshore Resort: Lake Rd and Mid Eau Claire Lk; campground, cabins, swimming beach, game room; (715) 795-2718; Star Rt, Box 6525, Solon Springs, WI 54873.
Y-Go-By Campground: located 11 miles east of Gordon on Cty Y; campground, ice; (715) 376-2231; Gordon, WI 54838.

Glidden/Mellen Area:

Northern Lure: housekeeping cottages, campgrounds, sauna, sandy beach, laundry, shower house; on Lake Gordon; (715) 264-3677; Rt 1, Box 111, Glidden, WI 54527.
Riverside Campgrounds: located just past Copper Falls State Park on Hwy 169; full hook-ups, laundromat and showers; (715) 682-3379; Rt 1, Box 35, Mellen, WI 54546.
Wildwood Haven Resort: take Hwy 13 to Cty Hwy MM to campground; 9 unit campground with elec; showers, toilets, playground, swimming beach, dump station; on Long Lake; (715) 274-6136 or 274-3584; Box 766, Mellen, WI 54546.

Superior Area:

Brule River Campgrounds & Motel: located on Hwy 2; 20 RV sites (12 w full hookup), dump station, tent sites, restrooms, showers, laundry; on Little Brule River; (715) 372-4815; P.O. Box 98, Brule, WI 54820.
Manitou Valley Campground: located 13 miles south of Superior on Hwy 35; (715) 399-8696; Rt 2, Box 383, Superior, WI 54880.
Northland Camping & RV Park: located at the junction of Hwy 13 & 53; (715) 398-5701; Superior, WI 54880.
Poplar Golf & Recreation Campground: (715) 364-2689; Hwy 2 & Co. Rd D, Poplar, WI 54864.

Cable Area:

Holz's Island View Campground: located on Cty Hwy D; RV & tent sites, water & elec, flush toilets, showers, boat launch; on Lake Namekagon; (715) 794-2461; Rt 2, Box 460, Cable, WI 54821.
Wasko's Lakeshore Camping: (715) 374-3514; Rt 1, Box 718, Cty P, Lake Nebagamon, WI 54849.

Municipal and County Campgrounds:

Bayfield/Washburn Area:

Big Bay Island Park: operated by the Town of LaPointe, Madeline Island; located on the north side of Big Bay, adjoining the state park; 44 rustic sites, first-come, first-served basis; picnic area, beautiful sand beaches; Madeline Island.
Big Rock Park, is located 1 mile northwest of Washburn on Cty C, then north on Big Rock Road; campsites & toilets.
Clover Park Campground: located on Lake Superior Beach in Herbster; boat launch, well, firewood; (715) 774-3740; Lake Superior Beach, Herbster, WI 54844.
Dalrymple Campground: located 3/4 mile north of downtown Bayfield on Hwy 13; 30 wooded lakeshore sites; city water, picnic tables; overlooking Lake Superior; (715) 779-5712.
Delta Lake Park, is located south of Iron River on Cty H, then west 1 mile on FR 228, then north to Delta Lake. Facilities include campground, beach and boat landing.
Memorial Park: located on Lake Superior in Washburn; 52 tent & trailer sites, electric, flush toilets, showers, firewood, playground, picnic tables, swimming beach, freezer service, cable TV hookup, pets allowed; on Lake Superior; (715) 373-5440; Washburn City Hall, P.O. Box 638, Washburn, WI 54891.
Moon Lake Park is located 1/2 mile south of Iron River on Cty H to Moon Lake. Facilities include camping, beach and boat landing.
Prentice Park: campground, observation tower to observe wild swans, playground, walking trails, pavilion, picnic facilities; City of Ashland.
Twin Bear Park, is located 5 miles south of Iron River on Cty H to the Pike Lake Chain. Facilities include toilet, beach camping and boat landing.
West End Park: located on Lake Superior in Washburn; 45 tent & trailer sites, dump station, electric, flush toilets, showers, firewood, playground, picnic tables, boat launch, swimming beach, pets allowed; on Lake Superior; (715) 373-5440; Washburn City Hall, P.O. Box 638, Washburn, WI 54891.

Douglas County:

Gordon Flowage County Park is located 6 miles west of Gordon on Cty Y on St Croix Flowage; campsites, boat landing, picnic area and swimming; St Croix Flowage; Douglas County.
Lower Eau Claire Dam Park, 38 acres is located 11 miles east of Gordon (Hwy 53) on Cty Y; campsites, boat landing, picnic area and toilets; on Lower Eau Claire Lake; Douglas County.
Lucis Woods Park, 41 acres, is located just south of Solon Springs on Hwy 53; campsites, boat landing, picnic area, stand of virgin pine and swimming: St Croix Lake; Douglas County.

Ashland County

Cammerer's Lake, is located east of Glidden (Hwy 13) on Cty N, then 2 miles on Mercer Rd, park is to the north; campsites, boat landing and picnic area; Cammerer's Lake; Ashland County.
East Fork of the Chippewa River, 3 acres, is located about 2 miles south of Hwy 77 on Hwy 13, then south on Cty D about 4.5 miles: campsites & picnic area; Chippewa River; Ashland County.

State Campgrounds:

Amnicon Falls: located 10 miles east of Superior on Hwy 2; 36 campsites; picnic area, scenic water falls, hiking and nature trails, toilets and drinking water; Amnicon River; Hwy 35 S, R 2 Box 435, Superior, WI 54880, (715) 399-8073 park; (715) 399-2115, ranger station.

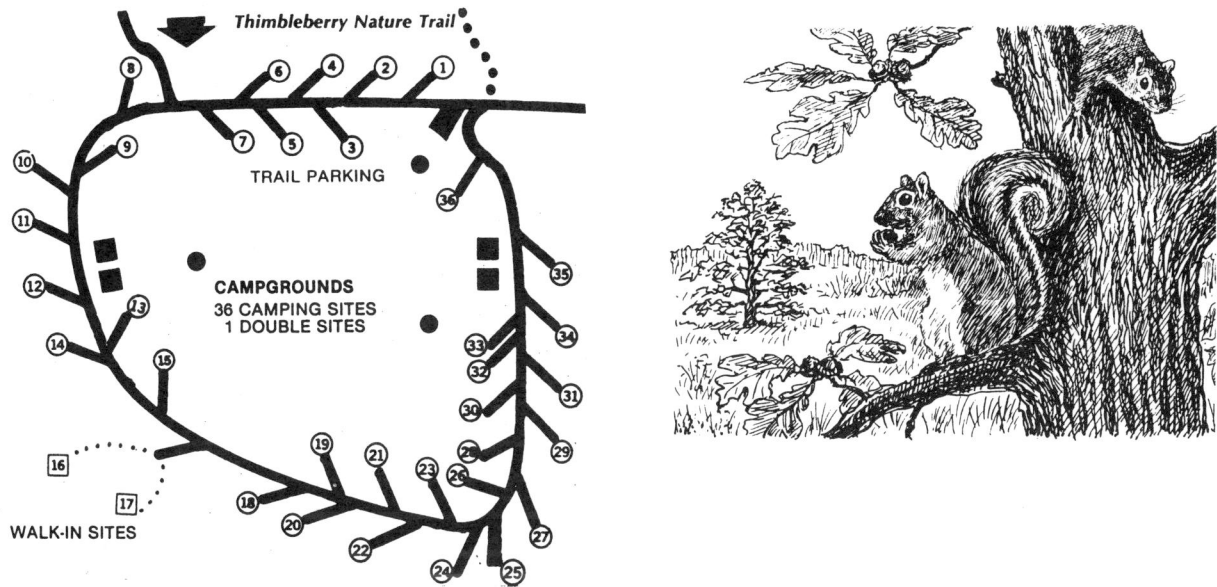

Pattison State Park: located south of Superior on Hwy 35; campsites, picnic area on Interstate Lake, toilets, drinking water, bathhouse, trails and swimming: Hwy 35 S, R 2 Box 435, Superior, WI 54880, (715) 399-2115 park; (715) 399-2115, ranger station.
Big Bay State Park: located on Madeline Island, off Cty H; 55 unit campsites; 1.5 mile beach, picnic area, hiking trail, handicapped campsite, water, toilets, boat landing; on Lake Superior. PO Box 589, Bayfield, WI 54814, (715) 779-3346.
Bois-Brule Campground Recreation Area, Brule River State Forest: located just south of Hwy 2 on Hwy 27; 23 sites; picnic area, boat landing, toilets, drinking water and hiking trails; Brule River; Brule River State Forest, Box 125, Brule, WI 54820, (715) 372-4866.
Copper Range Campgrounds, Brule River State Forest: located north of Hwy 2 at Brule on Cty H, then west of High Landing Rd; 17 sites; boat landing, toilets, drinking water; Brule River; Brule River State Forest, Box 125, Brule, WI 54820, (715) 372-4866.
Copper Falls State Park: located north of Mellen on Hwy 13, then about 2 miles east Hwy 169, then north on town road; picnic area, shelter, swimming and hiking; 56 sites: Box 438, Mellon, WI 54546, (715) 274-5123

Federal:

Chequamegon National Forest:

Hayward Ranger District: P.O. Box 232, Hayward, WI 54843; (715) 634-4821.
Black Lake Campground: 22 miles east of Hayward on Hwy 77, then south on Cty S and east on FR 164, then south on FR 173 and north on FR 1666; 29 units, boat access, swimming beach, interpretive trail, hiking trail, walk-in sites, handicap sites, picnic tables, fire rings, drinking water, pit toilets.
Moose Lake Campground: 22 miles east of Hayward on Hwy 77, then south on Cty S and east on FR 164 and west on FR 1643; 15 units, boat access, swimming beach, picnic tables, fire rings, drinking water, pit toilets.
Namekagon Lake Campground: east of Cable on Cty M, then north on Cty D to the end of the lake, and west on FR 209; 34 units, boat access, swimming beach, interpretive trail, play area, handicap sites, picnic tables, water, pit toilets.

Day Lake Recreation Area:

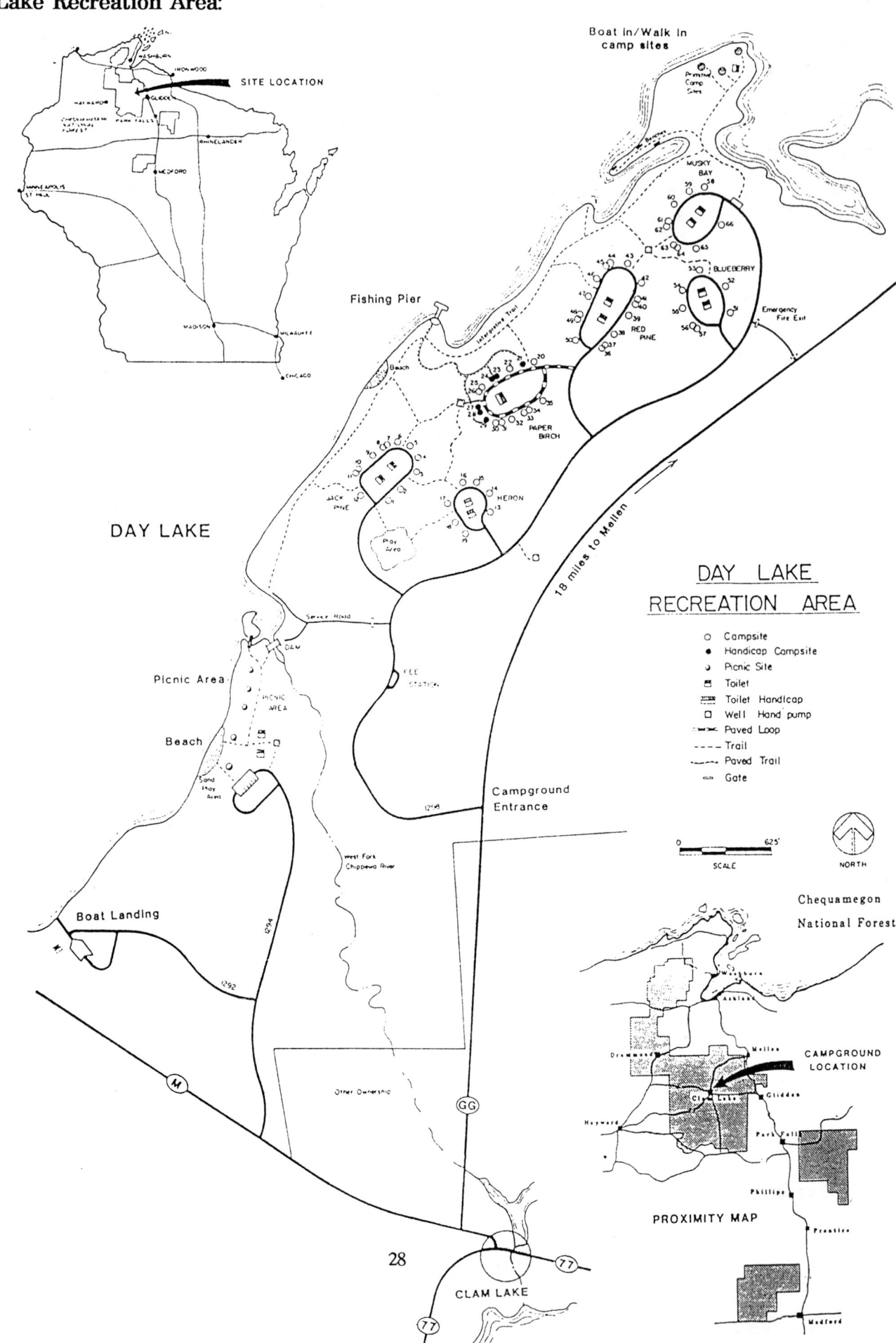

Glidden Ranger District: P.O. Box 126, Glidden, WI 54527; (715) 264-2511.

Beaver Lake Campground: west of Glidden on Cty GG, then north and west on FR 187, continue west on FR 198; 10 units, boat access, hiking trail, picnic table, fire ring, drinking water, pit toilets.
Day Lake Campground: from Clam Lake, take Cty Hwy M west to Hwy GG, turn right; 66 camping units; water, toilets, swimming, boat access, picnic tables, fire ring, drinking water, interpretive trail, walk-in sites, play area, handicap sites.
East Twin Lake Campground: from Clam Lake, take Cty Hwy M west, then Hwy GG north and just east on FR 193; 12 units, boat access, walk-in sites, picnic tables, fire rings, drinking water, pit toilets.
Lake Three Campground: west of Glidden on Cty GG, then north and west on FR 187; 8 units, boat access, hiking trail, picnic tables, fire rings, drinking water, pit toilets.
Mineral Lake Campground: about 7 miles west of Glidden on Cty GG; 11 units, boat access, picnic tables, fire rings, drinking water, pit toilets.
Stockbridge Farm Recreation Area: located 11 miles from Glidden off FR 164; 7 camping units with water and toilets, picnic area, fishing, boat ramp; on East Fork of the Chippewa River.

Washburn Ranger District: P.O. Box 578, Washburn, WI 54891; (715) 373-2667.

Birch Grove Campground: located on FR 435; 16 units, boat access, hiking trail, interpretive trail, fishing, picnic tables, fire rings, drinking water, pit toilets; on West Twin Lake, 16 acres, and East Twin Lake, 22 acres.
Perch Lake Campground: located on FR 223; 16 units, boat access, fishing, picnic tables, fire rings, drinking water, pit toilets, group camping by reservation; on Perch Lake, 72 acres.
Two Lakes Campground: from Cable, take Cty Hwy M to Lake Owen Dr, watch for signs; 91 sites on 65 acres; boat access, swimming beach, interpretive trail, hiking trail, walk-in sites, handicap sites, picnic tables, fire rings, drinking water, pit toilets; on Lake Owen, 1,323 acres, and Bass Lake, 59 acres.
Wanoka Lake Campground: located about 6 miles east of Iron River on Hwy 2, then just south on FR 234; 20 units, picnic tables, fire rings, drinking water, pit toilets, fishing; on Wanoka Lake, 15 acres.

Campground Name	Dates Open 1989	Camp-Site Fees	Camp Units Open	Boat Access	Swim. Beach	Interp. Trail	Hiking Trail	Walk-In Sites	Play Area	Handicap Sites
Beaver Lake	5/25-9/5	$4	10	●			●			
Lake Three	5/25-12/4	$4	8	●			●			
Mineral Lake	5/25-9/5	$4	11	●						
Day Lake 5	5/25-12/4	$4/5	66	●	●	●		●	●	●
East Twin Lake	5/25-9/5	$5	12	●				●		
Namekagon Lake 5	5/1-11/30	$5	34	●	●	●		●		●
Moose Lake 5	5/1-11/30	$4	15	●	●					
Black Lake 5	5/1-11/30	$5	29	●	●		●	●		●
Chippewa 1,5	5/15-9/18	$4/5/7/10	90	●	●				●	●
Birch Grove	5/1-11/1	$5	16	●		●	●			
Wanoka Lake	5/1-11/1	$5	20							
Perch Lake	5/1-11/1	$5	16	●						
Two Lakes	5/1-10/1	$5/6/7	91	●	●	●	●	●		●

AREA ACTIVITIES

Attractions:
Big Top Chautauqua: the old canvas tent-show stage, offering a variety of quality entertainment: theatre, comedy, music, magic and historical narratives. Box 455, Washburn, WI 54891; (715) 373-5851.
Blue Water Maritime Center: displays on small craft tradition in the Apostles, commercial fishing, lighthouse tending, boat building demonstrations; 2nd St & Maypenny Ave, Bayfield, WI 54814.
National Park Service Visitor Center: lighthouse & lakeshore exhibits, park information, film/slide show; Washington Ave & 4th St, Bayfield, WI 54814; (715) 779-3397.
National Park Service Contact Station, Little Sand Bay: lakeshore exhibits, park information; (715) 779-3397.
National Park Service Contact Station, Stockton Island: naturalist guided/self guided activities, natural and cultural history exhibits; (715) 779-3397.
Ojibwa Memorial Park: the site of festivals and religious celebrations of the Chippewa tribes of northern Wisconsin. Nearby the Indian burial ground has grave markers that date back over 200 years with members of the first Catholic church buried there.

Bike Rentals:
Bay City Cycles: mountain bike rentals. 412 2nd St. West, Ashland, WI 54806; (715) 682-2091.
Bodin's On The Lake: bike and sailboard rental; 121 Rittenhouse Ave, Bayfield, WI 54814; (715) 779-3400, and Lakeshore Dr, Ashland, WI 54806; (715) 682-6441.

Boat Rentals:
Bear Country: sporting goods, boat, motor, pontoon rental; Drummond, WI; (715) 739-6645.
Cable Service Center: pontoon boat sales & rentals; Cable, WI 54821; (715) 798-3444.
Club Chinook: sport-craft power boat rentals; 118 South 3rd St, Bayfield, WI 54814; (715) 779-5714.
The New Telemark Resort: boat rentals; P.O. Box 277, Cable, WI 54821; (715) 798-3811 or (800) 472-3001.
Wagner's Port Sand Resort & Campground: rental of boats, pontoon, motors, and kayaks; Rt 2 , Box 453, Webster, WI 54893; (715) 349-2395.

Canoe Sea Kayak Rentals:
The Big Bobber: canoe & tube rental; Box 209, Cty Hwy Y, Gordon, WI 54838; (715) 376-2696.
Brule Country: canoe & kayak rentals, group rates, shuttle service; located on Hwy 2 in Brule; (715)372-8588.
Trek 'N Trail: sea kayak rentals, instructions and excursions; Rittenhouse Ave, Bayfield, WI 54814; (715) 779-3320.
Wagner's Port Sand Resort & Campground: See listing under boat rentals.

Museum & Historical Sites:
Barkers Island: a manmade island in Superior, WI. There is the SS Meteor, here-wharf shops, playground and fish pond.
Bayfield Heritage Museum: located at 100 Rittenhouse Ave in Bayfield; exhibits illustrate the settlement, growth of industry and agriculture of Bayfield; (715) 779-3272 or 779-5060.
Bong Memorial: memorial, aircraft & museum in honor of Richard I. Bong, who served in WWII and shoot down 40 enemy aircraft; awarded the Congressional Medal of Honor. The memorial is located in the Tn of Poplar on Hwy 2
Buffalo Art Center: A museum and gift shop of the Lake Superior Chippewa Indians. Festivals, workshops and craft demonstrations throughout season. Red Cliff Reservation, P.O. Box 529, Bayfield, WI 54814; (715) 779-5858.
The Cooperage Museum & Gift Shop: watch a local cooper at work, assembling barrels around the huge open hearth, guided tours daily; P.O. Box 687, Bayfield, WI 54814; (715) 779-3400.
Drummond Mill Reservoir: located just outside of Drummond, west and adjacent to FR 223, 1/4 mile north of its intersection with Hwy 63; one of the last remnants of a sawmill constructed in 1883, provides a scenic view of the area.
Drummond Museum: logging & lumbering industry artifacts, wildlife artifacts; (715) 739-6669, 739-6256 or 739-6260.
Fairlawn Mansion-Museum: located on Hwys 2 & 53, Barker's Island, on the shore overlooking the bay in Superior; built by lumber baron Martin Pattison, the 42 room mansion houses the exhibits of the Douglas County Historical Society. Offers exhibits of railroad memorabilia, the Mary Branch Doll Collection and photographs of the Plains Indians; 906 East 2nd St, Superior, WI 54880; (715) 394-5712.
Madeline Island Historical Museum: visit the museum building, the history wall, the old jail, the pioneer barn, the pioneer home and the old sailor's home. La Pointe, WI 54850; (715) 747-2415.
Old Firehouse and Police Museum: located just off Hwy 2 on 23rd Ave East and 4th St in Superior; antique fire engines and equipment, group tours available; The Old Fire House, Box 775, Superior, WI 54880; (715) 398-7558.
S.S. Meteor Marine Museum & Marina: Follow US 2-13-53 to Barkers Island, Superior, WI; the last of the famous "whalebacks" that were built here in 1890's, guided tours, Seamen's Memorial Statue, the Dipper Dredge Col. D.D. Gaillard, Pilot House, Galley Display; SS Meteor, Box 775, Superior, WI 54880; (715) 392-5742.

Washburn Area Historical Society Museum: located in the lower level of the Washburn Public Library, at 307 Washington Ave; artifacts from Washburn's past; (715) 373-5345 or 373-2289.
Western Bayfield County Museum: located 1 block south of Main St and US Hwy 2, across from the post office; display of logging tools and markers, 300 other artifacts; (715) 372-4359 or 372-4456.

Ski Hills:
Mt Ashwabay Ski Hill: 11 downhill runs from beginner to expert, 30 km of x-country ski trails, instruction available, night skiing, rentals; P.O. Box 928, Bayfield, WI 54814; (715) 779-3227.
The New Telemark Resort: 11 downhill runs, 100 km of groomed & tracked x-country ski trails, lodge, tennis, horseback riding, sleigh rides, more; Box 277B, Cable, WI 54821; (715) 798-3811.

Scenic Tours & Sites:
Apostle Islands Cruise Service: scenic tours of Apostle Island; P.O. Box 691, Bayfield, WI 54814; (715) 779-3925.
Apostle Islands Water Taxi: water taxi service to the islands; P.O. Box 691, Bayfield, WI 54814; (715) 779-5153.
Apostle Islands Yacht Charter, Inc: charter sailboats; bareboat or captained, instruction; P.O. Box 188, La Pointe, WI 54850; (715) 747-2983 or 747-5353 or (800) 821-3480.
Catchun-Sun Charter Co.: sailboat rides, captained, lunch & dinner, sleeping on board, evening cruises provided; P.O. Box 955, Bayfield, WI 54814; (715) 779-3243 or (612) 825-5003.
Dave's Charter Service: scenic cruises; 414 West 7th St, Ashland, WI 54806; (715) 682-3379.
Hokenson Brothers Fishery Tour: hourly tours of a family owned commercial fishery by park interpreter; Little Sand Bay; (715) 779-3397.
Irie Vibes Yacht Charters: sailboat charters, bareboat or captained, lunch & dinner cruises, weekend or longer cruises; 410 Eichenwald, St. Paul MN 55814; (715) 747-2983 or (800) 821-3480.
Jacqueline Charters: captained sailboat charters of 1 day, weekends or longer aboard the 37 ft yacht "Jacqueline", instruction provided by licensed USCG captain; Box 188, Washburn, WI 54891; (715) 373-5021.
Madeline Island Ferry Line: ferry service, passengers & vehicles; P.O. Box 66S, La Pointe, WI 54850; (715) 747-2051.
Madeline Island Tours: narrated Madeline Island tours; P.O. Box 66S, La Pointe, WI 54850; (715) 747-2051.
Manitou Fish Camp Tour: hourly tours by park interpreter of historic fish camp; Manitou Island; (715) 779-3397.
Pier Trolling Headquarters: sailboat charters; City Dock, Bayfield, WI 54814; (715) 779-3330.
Raspberry Island Lighthouse Tour: hourly tours by park interpreter around lighthouse complex and through gardens reminiscent of lightkeeper's days; Raspberry Island; (715) 779-3397.
Sailboats,Inc: charters and instruction; 19 Front St, Box 840, Bayfield, WI 54814; (715) 779-3269.
Sno-Cation Tours: scenic snowmobile tours covering northwest Wisconsin. Guided tours for novice or expert. 1800 3rd St. W, Ashland, WI 54806; (715) 682-6196.
Trek 'N Trail: captained sailboat rides, kayak trips & lessons; Rittenhouse Ave, Bayfield, WI 54814; (715) 779-3320.
Vista Queen and King Harbor Cruises: located on Harbor Drive at the waterfront side of the Duluth Entertainment & Convention Center, at a dock next to the SS Meteor. Two hour, narrated cruises take you to the grain elevators, ore docks and the ships that frequent the harbor; Barkers Island, Superior, WI 54880; (715) 394-6846.
Vista Star Harbor Cruise: the newest ship, offers lunch and dinner cruises, live entertainment, private parties, charters up to 350; Barkers Island, Superior, WI 54880; (715) 394-6846.
Washburn Marine: sailboat charter fleet, with or without captain; P.O. Box 506, Washburn, WI 54891; (715) 373-5545.

EMERGENCY NUMBERS

Should you need help, listed below are the phone numbers for the sheriff and local hospitals.

Sheriff:

Ashland County: (715) 682-7023
Bayfield County: (715) 373-5607
Douglas County: (715) 394-0371

Hospitals:

Memorial Medical Center, 1615 Maple Lane, Ashland, WI 54806, (715) 682-4563
Superior Memorial Hospital, 3500 Tower Ave, Superior, WI 54880, (715) 392-8281
Bayfield CO. Memorial Hospital, 320 Superior St, Washburn WI 54891, (715) 373-2621

INFORMATION SOURCES

Snow & Fishing Hot Line: in the Washburn Area; (715) 373-5017.
Weather Report: 24 hrs/day in Apostle Island Area; (715) 682-8822.
Wisconsin Road Condition Report: (800) 762-3947

County:

Ashland County Forestry Office, Box 165, Glidden, WI 54527, (715) 264-3000
Bayfield County Forestry Dept, Courthouse, PO Box 445 Washburn, WI 54891, (715) 373-2191
Douglas County Forestry Dept, Box 211, Solon Springs, WI 54873, (715) 378-2219

State: WI Department of Natural Resources:

WI DNR, Brule Area Headquarters, Hwy 2, Box 125, Brule, WI 54820, (715) 372-4866. Covers Ashland, Bayfield and Douglas Counties.
WI DNR Ranger Station, Hwy 35 S, R 2 Box 435 Superior, WI 54880, (715) 399-8073.
WI DNR Ranger Station, Box 438, Mellen, WI 54546, (715) 274-5123.

Federal: U.S. Forest Service:

Chequamegon National Forest, Forest Supervisor 1170 4th Ave, Hwy 13 South, Park Falls, WI 54552, (715) 762-2461. Forest Headquarters plus Park Falls Ranger District.

Glidden Ranger District, Forest Service, Glidden, WI 54527 (715) 264-2511.
Hayward Ranger District, Forest Service, PO Box 232, 604 Hwy 27 North, Hayward, WI 54843, (715) 634-4821.
Washburn Ranger District, Forest Service, PO Box 578, 113 E. Bayfield St, Washburn, WI 54891, (715) 373-2667.

Chambers of Commerce:

Ashland County Clerk's Office, Courthouse, Ashland, WI 54806
Ashland Chamber of Commerce, 320 4th Ave, West, PO Box 746, Ashland, WI 54806, (715) 682-2500
Bayfield Chamber of Commerce, 42 Broad St, PO Box 138, Bayfield, WI 54814, (715) 779-3335
Bayfield Co. Tourism & Rec Assoc. Washburn, WI 54891 (800) 223-2774, ext 229
Cable Area Chamber of Commerce, PO Box 217, Cable, WI 54821, (715)(800) 533-7454
Douglas County Clerk's Office, Courthouse, Superior, WI 54880
Douglas County Recreation Ass'n, Rt 1, Box 67, Gordon, WI 54838
Four Seasons Vacationland, Hwy 53 & Y, Box 38, Gordon, WI 54838, (715) 376-2699
Glidden Area Chamber of Commerce, Glidden, WI 54527, (715) 264-4101
Iron River Business Ass'n, PO Box 64, Iron River, WI 54847 (715) 372-8558
Madeline Is Chamber of Commerce, PO Box 274, La Pointe, WI 54840
Mellen Chamber of Commerce, PO Box 793, Mellen, WI 54546, (715) 274-3131
Redcliff Chamber of Commerce, PO Box 529, Bayfield, WI 54814, (715) 779-5805
Superior/Douglas Co. Chamber of Commerce, 305 E. 2nd St., Superior, WI 54880 (715)394-7716, (800) 942-5313
Washburn Chamber of Commerce, 119 Washington Ave, Washburn, WI 54891, (715) 373-5017

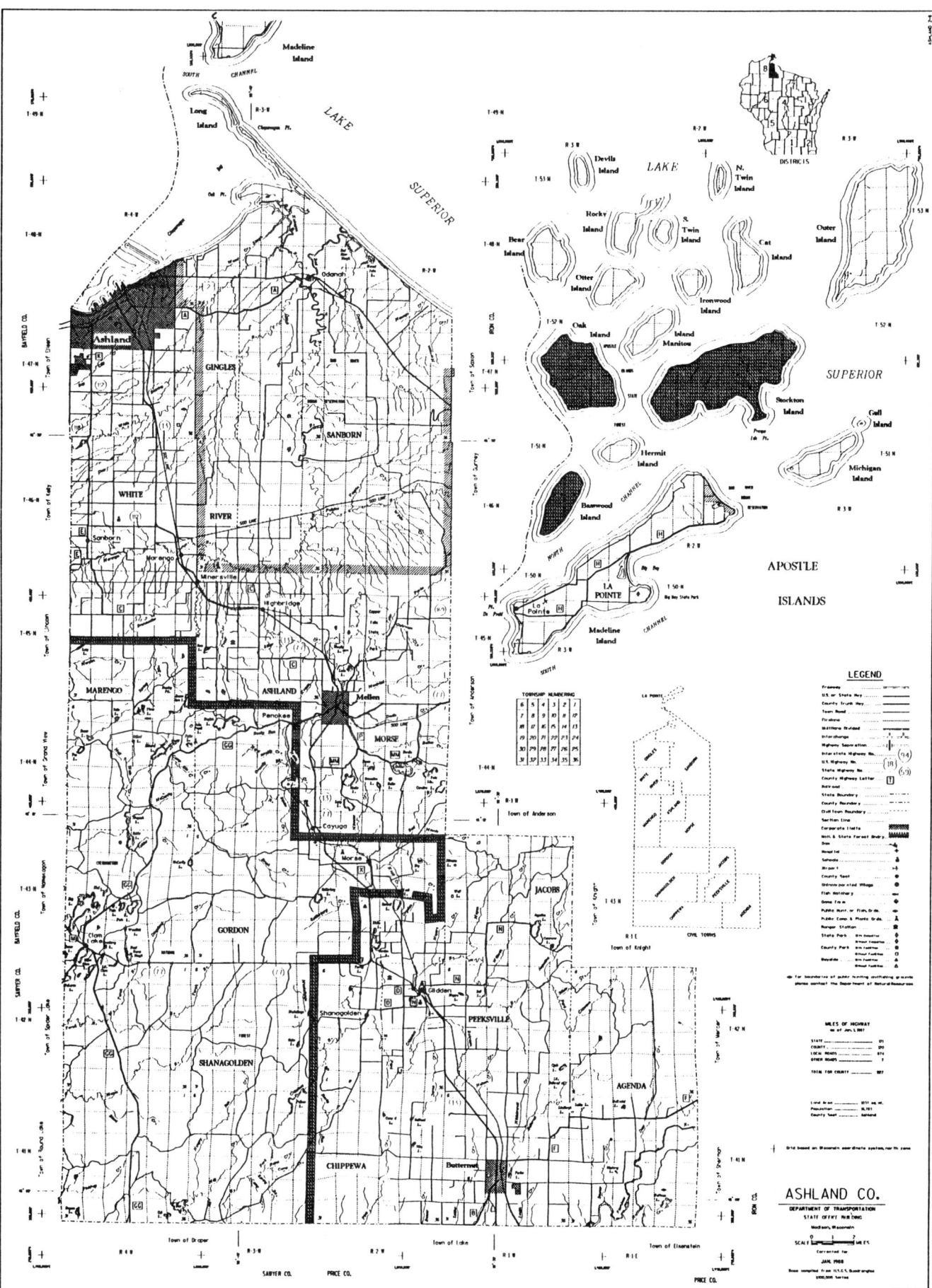

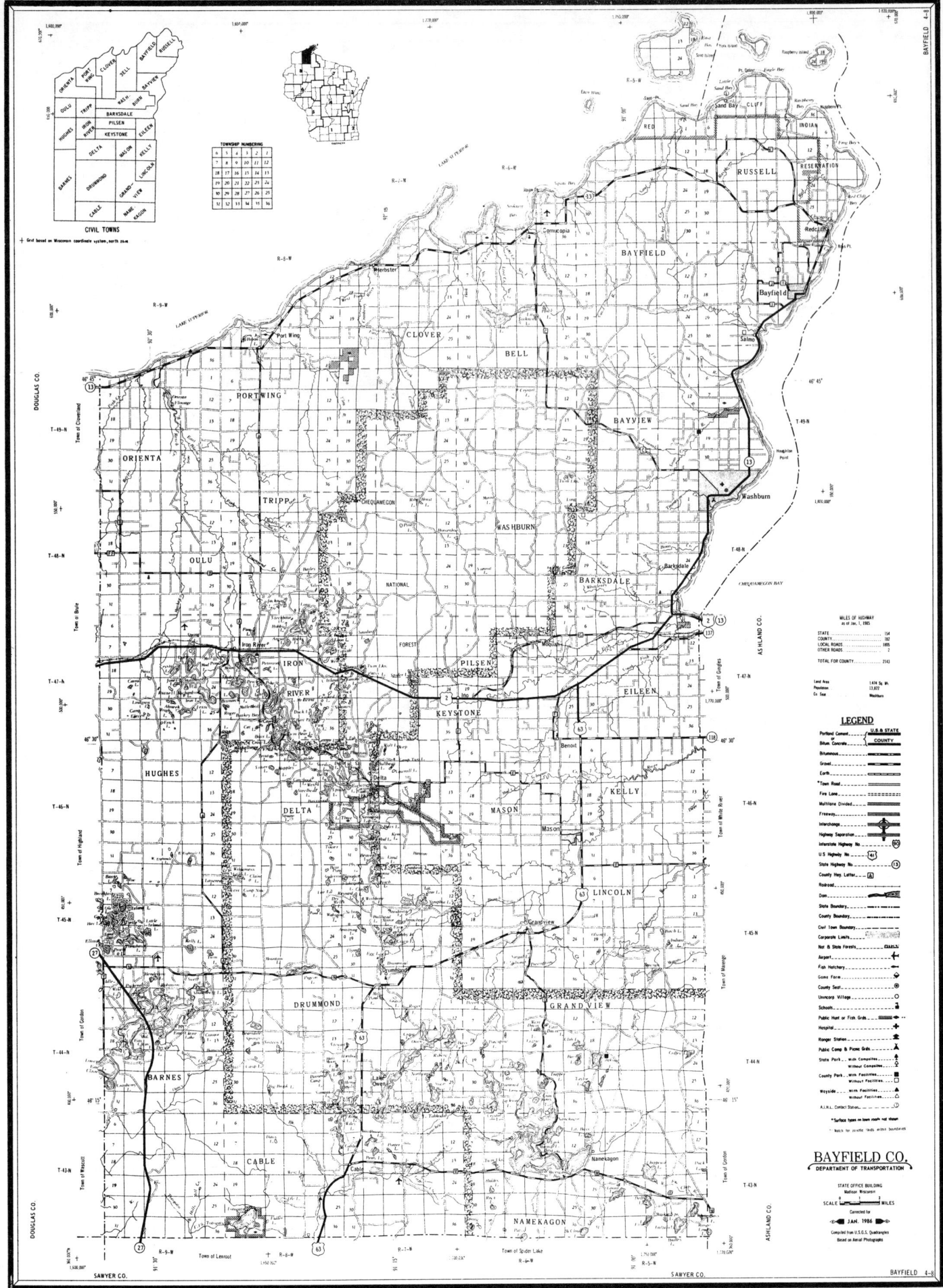

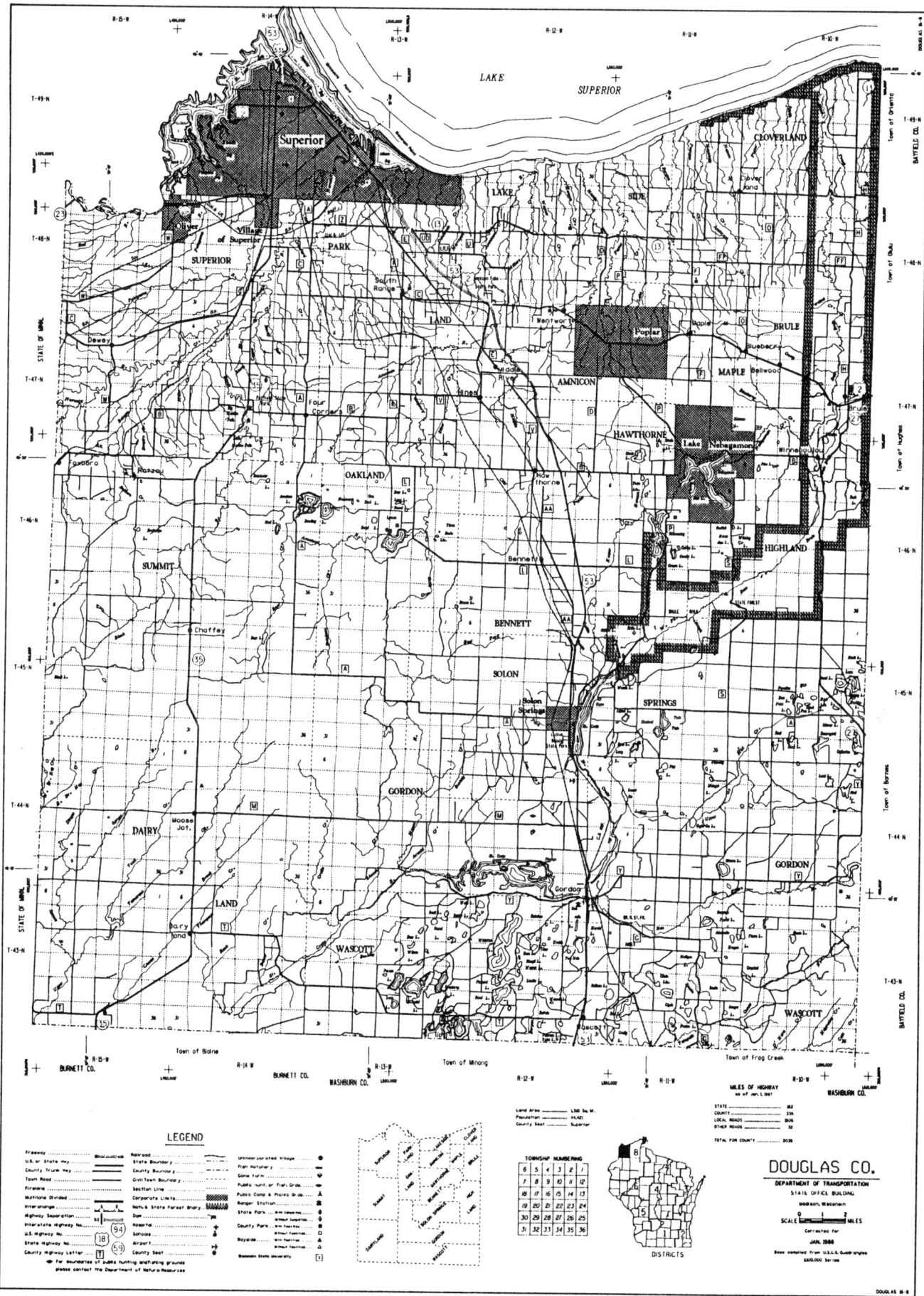

AREA 2
River Area
Burnett, Sawyer and Washburn Counties

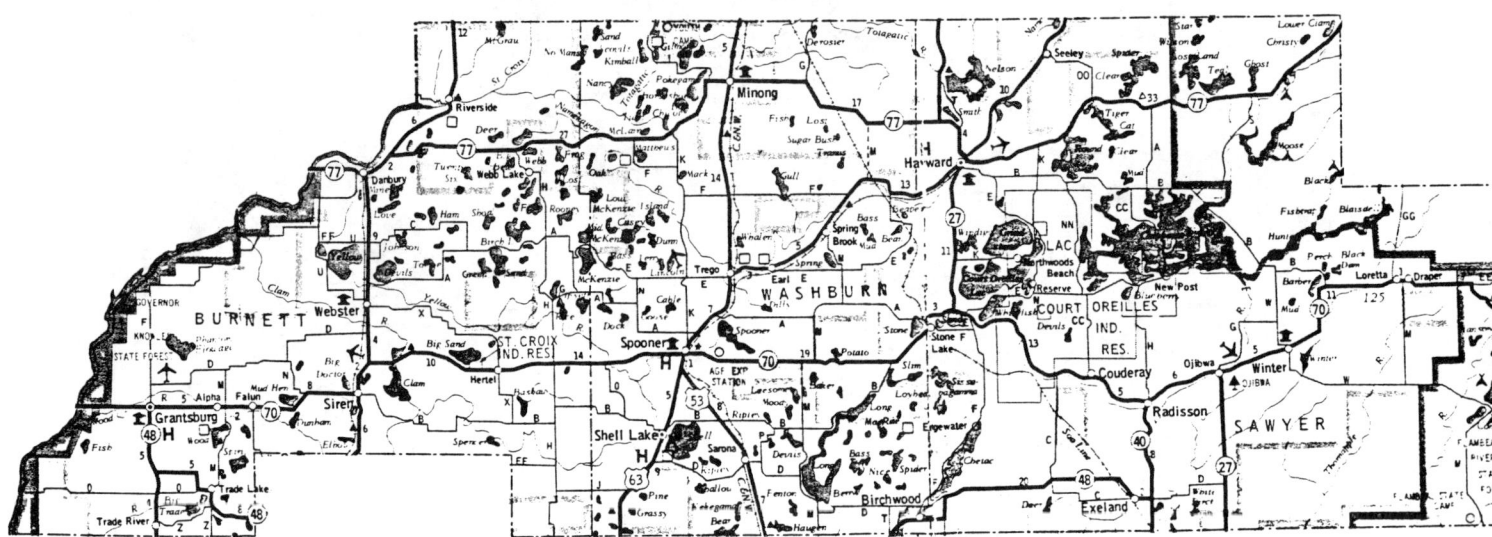

Tens of thousands of years ago the entire surface of Burnett, Sawyer and Washburn Counties were covered by the great ice sheets of the Wisconsin Glacier. As the glacier receded, its melt water created numerous lakes of various sizes and shapes, and carved out a number of rivers and streams. The southern portion of these counties were transformed into outwash plains, consisting of small lakes, bogs and swamps.

The headwaters of many rivers are found in the northern most portions of these counties. Two great rivers flank the area--the St. Croix on the west and the Flambeau on the east. Many other rivers, such as the Yellow, the Clam, the Namekagon and the Totagatic, are in between. These river systems were very instrumental in the early settling of the area. They served as major highways for the explorers, missionaries and fur traders, who traveled down from Lake Superior to the Mississippi. Later, in the 1800's, logging camps and sawmills found a booming industry here. Agriculture began with farms that supplied food to the lumber camps. With farming well on its way, the immigrants soon followed.

Today, may recreational opportunities can be found in the many state, county and federal projects in the area. The St. Croix National Scenic Riverway and the Governor Knowles State Forest are located along the Wisconsin/Minnesota border. To the east two more forests, the Chequamegon National Forest and the Flambeau State Forest, provide an unspoiled beauty for recreational enjoyment, and the wild North and South Branches of the Flambeau River offer a challenge to even the most experienced canoeist. In addition, there are many other rivers flowing south and west to the Mississippi River that provide recreation, establish habitat for fish and wildlife and produce electricity at the many hydroelectric dams throughout the region.

There are a number of cities plus a scattering of unincorporated settlements.
In **Burnett County**, Siren, the county seat, is located in the south central end of the county. Grantsburg is to the west on Hwy 70, Webster, Danbury and Riverside are to the north on Hwy 35, and Hertel to the east on Hwy 70.
In **Sawyer County**, Shell Lake, the county seat, is located on Hwy 63 in the southwestern corner of the county. Spooner, Trego and Minong are to the north on Hwy 53; Earl and Spring Brook to the northeast on Hwy 63; Sarona is to the east on Cty D/Hwy 53, and Birchwood is in the extreme southeast corner on Hwy 48.
In **Washburn County**, Hayward, the county seat, is located in the northwest corner of the county on Hwy 27 & 63. Stone Lake, Couderay, Radisson and Winter are on Hwy 70 across the central portion of the county. Exeland is on the southern county line on Hwy 48, east of Hwy 40.

RECREATIONAL WATERS

Lakes and Flowages:

There are 720 named, (111,027 acres) and 1,121 unnamed, (7,139 acres) lakes in the region, including several man-made flowages. This accounts for 12.3 % of the total number of Wisconsin lakes covering 11.6 % of the state's total inland surface water. This area is relatively close to Minneapolis/St Paul. Therefore, most lakes surrounded by private lands are well developed with cottages.

Burnett County has 218 named, (30,039 acres) and 213 unnamed, (1,605 acres), lakes. Once you get east of the St Croix Valley, the county is peppered with small to medium sized lakes. Many of them provide good recreation and fishing including;

Upper and Lower Clam Lake, 1,207 & 337 acres, located just east of Siren on Hwy 70. Upper Clam Lake is to the south. There is a wayside at the junction of the two lakes and the highway. Fisheries include bass, panfish, muskies and northern pike.
Yellow Lake, 2,287 acres, is located just northwest of Webster & Hwy 35, on Cty U. The lake is big enough to support a good fishery plus other water related activities. There are three access points including a county park on the east shore.
McKenzie Lake, 530 acres, is located 10 miles west of Trego on Cty E, on the county line. Landings are on the north and west shores. This clear water lake's shoreline is fairly well developed. Fisheries include panfish, walleye and northern pike.

Sawyer County has 244 named, (54,771 acres) and 253 unnamed, (1,421 acres) lakes. Most lakes can be found in the western half of the county. Some of good lakes include:

Chippewa Flowage, 15,273 acres, located southeast of Hayward on Cty CC, which passes through the middle of the flowage. This great expanse of water is the result of the damming the Chippewa River and flooding the ten original lakes. The shoreline, recently acquired by the state, is irregular with wooded hills, valleys and bogs. It has maintained most of its wilderness state; however, there is some development. A hundred and forty islands are scattered about. Landings can be found at the dam on Dam Rd, Cty CC and B. Water levels fluctuate, resulting in an average depth of 15 to 25 ft. Fishery is a good mix of game and panfish. With all the islands and bays the flowage is a great place to explore and enjoy.
Nelson Lake, 2,503 acres, is located 4 miles north of Hayward and can be reached by Hwy 27 and Hwy 63. The Totagatic River flows from the dam on the west end. Access points can be found on the east and west ends. The shoreline is irregular with several islands scattered throughout the lake. Fishery includes muskie, walleye and bluegills.
Grinding Stone Lake, 3,111 acres, is located south of Hayward on Hwy 27, then 3 miles east on Cty K or south of Hayward on Cty E. The lake is noted for its musky fishing.

Washburn County has 258 named, (26,217 acres) and 655 unnamed, (4,113 acres) lakes. Two flowages make up over half the surface water acreage.

Minong Flowage, 1,564 acres, is located on the northwest county line and half in Douglas County. From Minong, Hwy 53, take Hwy 70 west 1 .5 miles, then north about 7 miles on Cty I. The flowage will be to the east. The shoreline is irregular but has the general appearance of a comma shape. There is some development. However with over 5 miles of shoreline in public ownership, the area has maintained some of its natural look. Access is available at a county park and campgrounds. Fishery is a nice mix of walleye, northern pike and panfish.
Long Lake, 3,290 acres, is located southeast of Spooner on Hwy 53, then east on Cty D, then north or south on Cty M. The lake can also be reached by Cty B on the north end. As the name implies, this is a long, narrow lake with several islands and long, narrow bays. Undeveloped areas exist, adding to the scenic nature of the lake. Access can be found on the west shore and on East Side Rd. There is a nice mix of fish species, but no muskies.
Shell lake, 2,580 acres, is located on the east side of town. This is a shallow, 22 ft deep, clear water lake. There is a park and campground with a boat landing in town. Fishery includes muskie, walleye and panfish.

Rivers:

Chippewa River, flows south after leaving the Winter Dam, which forms the Chippewa Flowage. The river is mostly shallow and meandering with a few riffle areas. Radisson Flowage is the only impoundment in Sawyer County. State and county roads parallel much of the river. This plus the agricultural and residential development has diminished the wild look of the river. The river continues its flow south into Rusk County.

Flambeau River, considered one of the best canoeing rivers in Wisconsin, enters northeastern Sawyer County. The river has its start at the Turtle-Flambeau Flowage in Iron County and Round Lake in Price County. Both the North and South branches flow southwest to join in the Flambeau State Forest and continue south into Rusk County. The Flambeau River can be characterized as a fast flowing river with challenging rapids and a wild looking shoreline. The upper reaches of the North Branch can be challenging with several recommended portages. The South Branch can be dangerous and requires good skills. The lower North Branch provides enjoyable canoeing for most people. There are a number of access points throughout the forest.

St Croix and Namekagon River, please see park section below on the St Croix National Scenic Riverway.

Totagatic River, has its start in Sawyer County, then flows west to join the Namekagon just before they flow into the St Croix River. There are a number of flowages along the way. This river can be accessed from a number of bridge crossings. The river can be canoed but due to extreme water level fluctuations and size of the river you may walk a lot in low water and it can be dangerous in high water. Caution must be exercised.

Trout Streams:

The area has 125 streams classed as trout waters, covering 379 miles. There are 191 miles of Class I, 140 miles of Class II and 48 miles of Class III. Several of the noted streams include Sand Creek and Clam River in Burnett County; Namekagon River and Devil in Sawyer County and Sawyer Cr and Beam Brook in Washburn County.

Public Lands

County:

Burnett County, has 85,000 acres of county forest scattered throughout the northern three quarters of the county.

Anderson Township Area, is located in the extreme southwest corner of the county with Governor Knowles on the west, Fish Lake Wildlife Area on the north, the county line on the south and Hwy 87, 4 miles to the east.

Roosevelt Township, is located in the extreme southeast corner of the county. These two small parcels are 1 mile east and west of Cty H.

Sand Lake/Rusk Township, is located 6 miles east of Webster. This property is located a mile in from Cty A on the north, Cty H on the east and Cty X on the south.

Union/Lincoln Township, is located 5 miles west of Webster. Cty F is on the west border with Crex Meadows Wildlife on the south and west and Cty FF is on the east side.

Webb Lake Area, is in the northern 1/4 of the county. It is generally north of a line from Danbury through Webb Lake. Hwy 35 and 77 pass through the area.

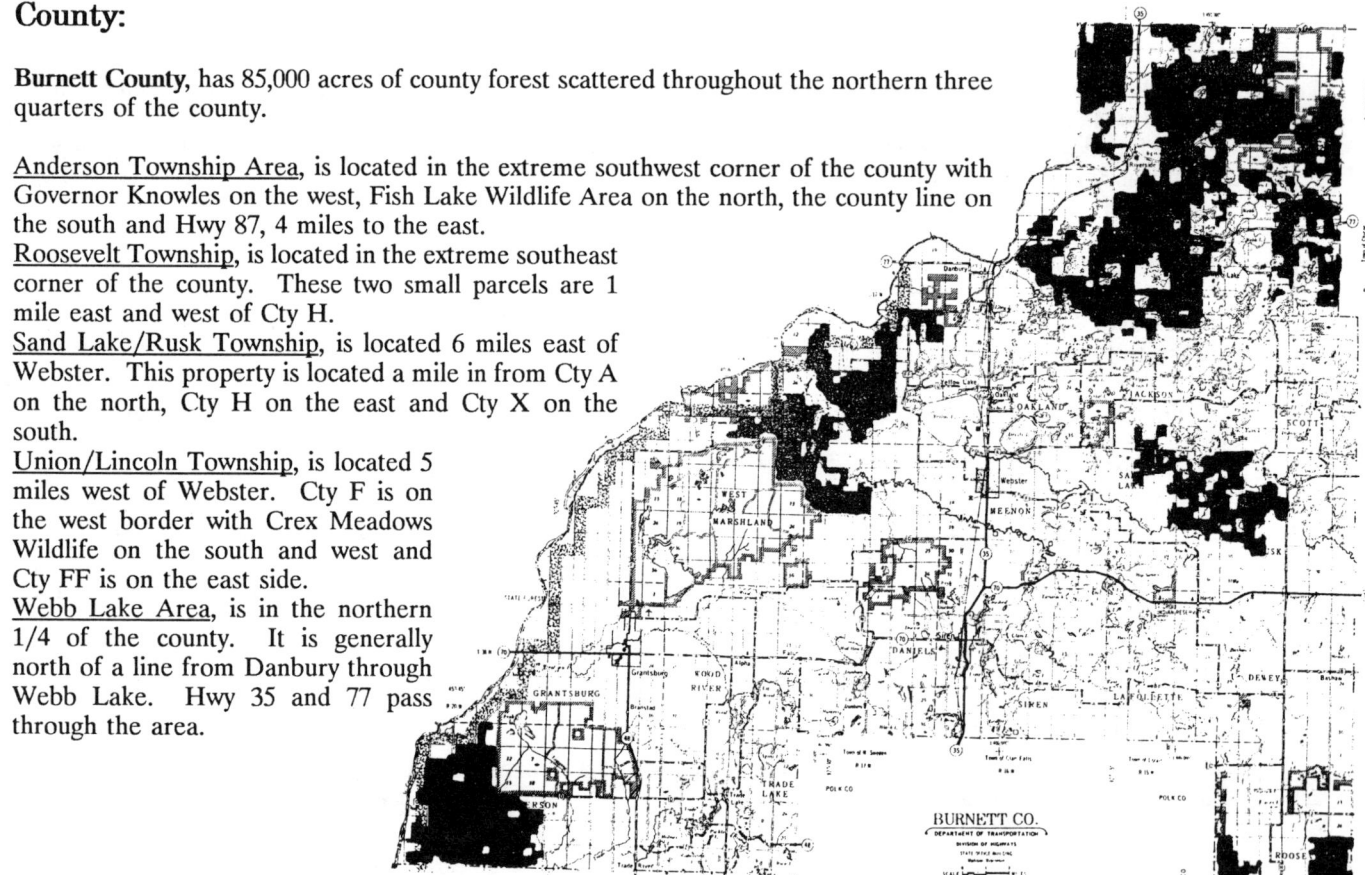

Sawyer County, has a large amount of lands in public ownership. The Chequamegon National Forest is in the northeast corner, Flambeau State Forest in the southeast corner, Lac Court Oreilles Indian Reservation in the west central and 96,000 acres of county land in 7 units. The county lands can be found;

1) In the southeast corner of the county with Hwy 27 on the west and Cty W to the north, state lands on the east and county line on the south. This the largest area.
2) Southeast of Loretta east of Cty M and south of Hwy 70 and east to state lands. This is a smaller area.
3) In the extreme southwest corner, with Hwy 48 on the west and north sides, county line to the south and Deer Lake on the east. This also in a small area.
4) In the southwest corner, south of Hwy 70 and Couderay, and east of Lemington on Cty C.
5) On the southwest county line, just northwest of Lake Chetac, with Cty F on the east and north sides. This is a long and narrow area.
6) Is northeast of Hayward in the northwest corner of the county. This area is a large wedge with Hwy 63 on the northeast side and Hwy 77 on the south side.
7) Is also north of Hayward. This area is in the extreme northwest corner of the county with the county lines on the north and west sides and Hwy 77 on the south and Hwy 63 to the east.

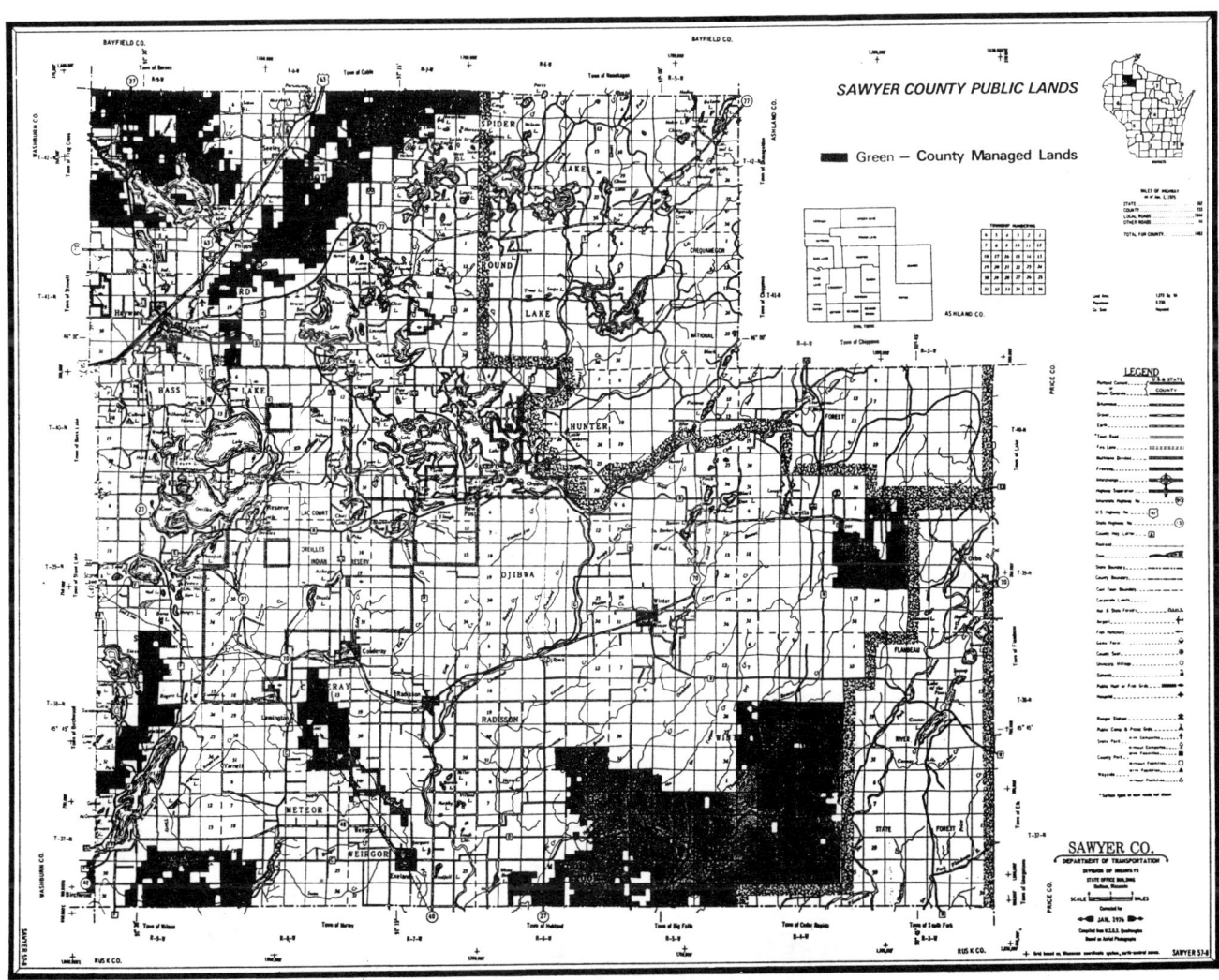

Washburn County, has 148,257 acres of the county forest in 12 units scattered throughout the county. A general location of each is listed below.

<u>Frog Creek, Gull Lake, Chippanazie, Brooklyn Units</u>, are in the northeast corner, east of Minong. These units contain the majority of lands in a 10 mile (north-south) by 15 mile (east-west) block of land.
<u>Spring Brook</u>, starts 2 miles east of Trego on the northern side of the Namekagon River.
<u>Namekagon/Sands, Unit</u>, is 7 miles west of Trego on Cty E. The unit extends north to the Namekagon River.
<u>Stone Lake Unit</u>, is located 7 miles east of Spooner on Hwy 70. This unit is a scattering of parcels located northeast and east of this point.
<u>Beaver Brook Unit</u>, is located 3 miles east of Spooner on Hwy 70 and is on the south side of the road. Hwy 53 is on the west side. This unit is roughly 3 miles square.
<u>Harmon Lake Unit</u>, is 10 miles east of Spooner on Hwy 70 and is on the south side of the road. This unit is 3 miles by 4 miles in dimension and has Long Lake on the south side.
<u>Birchwood Unit</u>, is east and south of Harmon Lake Unit. Cty T passes through the area. The village of Birchwood, on Hwy 48 is 3 miles south. This unit has the 5,000 acre primitive area.
<u>Welsh Lake Unit</u>, is located 1/2 mile south of Shell Lake, east of Hwy 63 and southwest of Cty D.

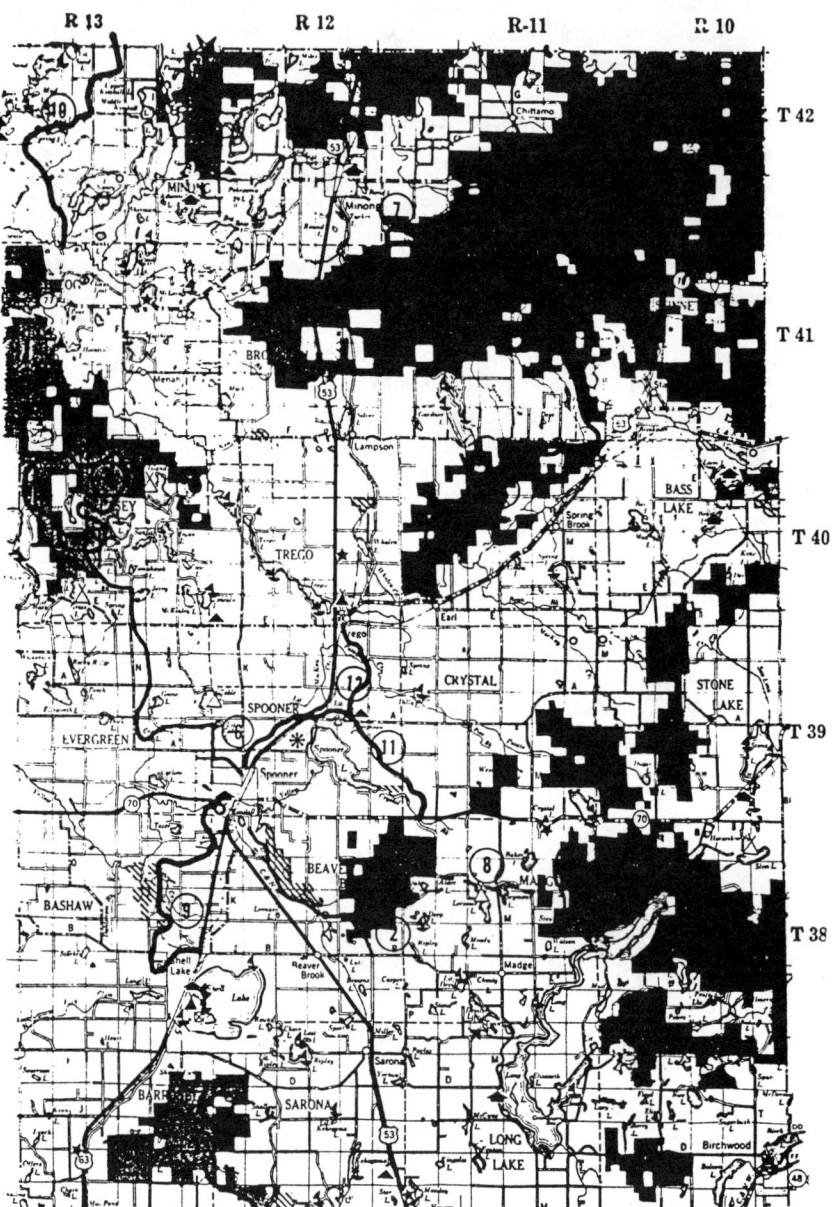

Limited Access Areas:

<u>Black Brook Area</u>, is located east of Minong on Hwy 77, then 2 miles north on Cty G. The area is bordered to the south by Wozny or East Frog Creek Firelane, Cty G on the west and the county line on the east and north sides. This area is a primitive, back country area with few roads. Development, roads and ATV use would be limited.
<u>Little Frog Creek Area</u>, starts 1 mile east of Minong on Hwy 77. It is bordered on the north by Hwy 77, Taylor Lake and Gull Lake Firelanes on the west, south and east sides. This area is a primitive, back country area with few roads. Development, roads and ATV use would be limited.

Special Use Areas:

Birchwood Primitive Area, is located about 5 miles north of Birchwood in the southeast corner of the county. The area can also be reached by taking Hwy 70 east of Spooner, then southwest on Cty B and south on Birchwood Firelane. This area, all the county forest lands east of Birchwood Firelane, is 5,000 acres with many small glacial lakes set aside to be maintained as a unique recreational resource. Development and use of motorized vehicles on the trails will be prohibited, however limited timbering would be permitted. Hiking and canoe routes including Sawmill Lake Canoe Route and the Loyhead Lake Canoe Route.

Harmon Lake Grouse Area (South of Hwy 70 & North of Cty B), Welsh Lake Management Unit, (south of Shell Lake) and Cedar Creek Recreation Area (Just south of Soo Line Railroad & north of Hwy 77) are managed as non-vehicle areas with forest activities limited to provide good habitat for wildlife.

State:

Clam River Wildlife Area, 1,451 acres, Burnette County, is located south of Shell Lake on Hwy 63, then east 5 miles on Cty J. Cty J is on the south border and Cty H on the west. This area is a mix of upland timber, wetlands and streams managed for grouse and deer and to provide access to the river.

Sand Creek Wildlife Area, 1,326 acres, Burnett County, is located 4 miles south of Siren on Hwy 35, then east 10 miles on Cty E, then 1/2 mile after the road turns south. There will be several town roads (a mile apart) that run east into the project. The area is a mix of timber and stream managed for deer and grouse.

Crex Meadow Wildlife Area, 30,098 acres, Burnett County, is located just north of Grantsburg on Cty F. This large wildlife area is managed to restore prairie waterfowl and grouse habitat. Today there are 18 miles of dikes to flood 11,000 acres of marsh. Islands and marsh edges are cleared by burning to provide good nesting habitat. There are a number of trails and observation points around the area to see the wildlife.

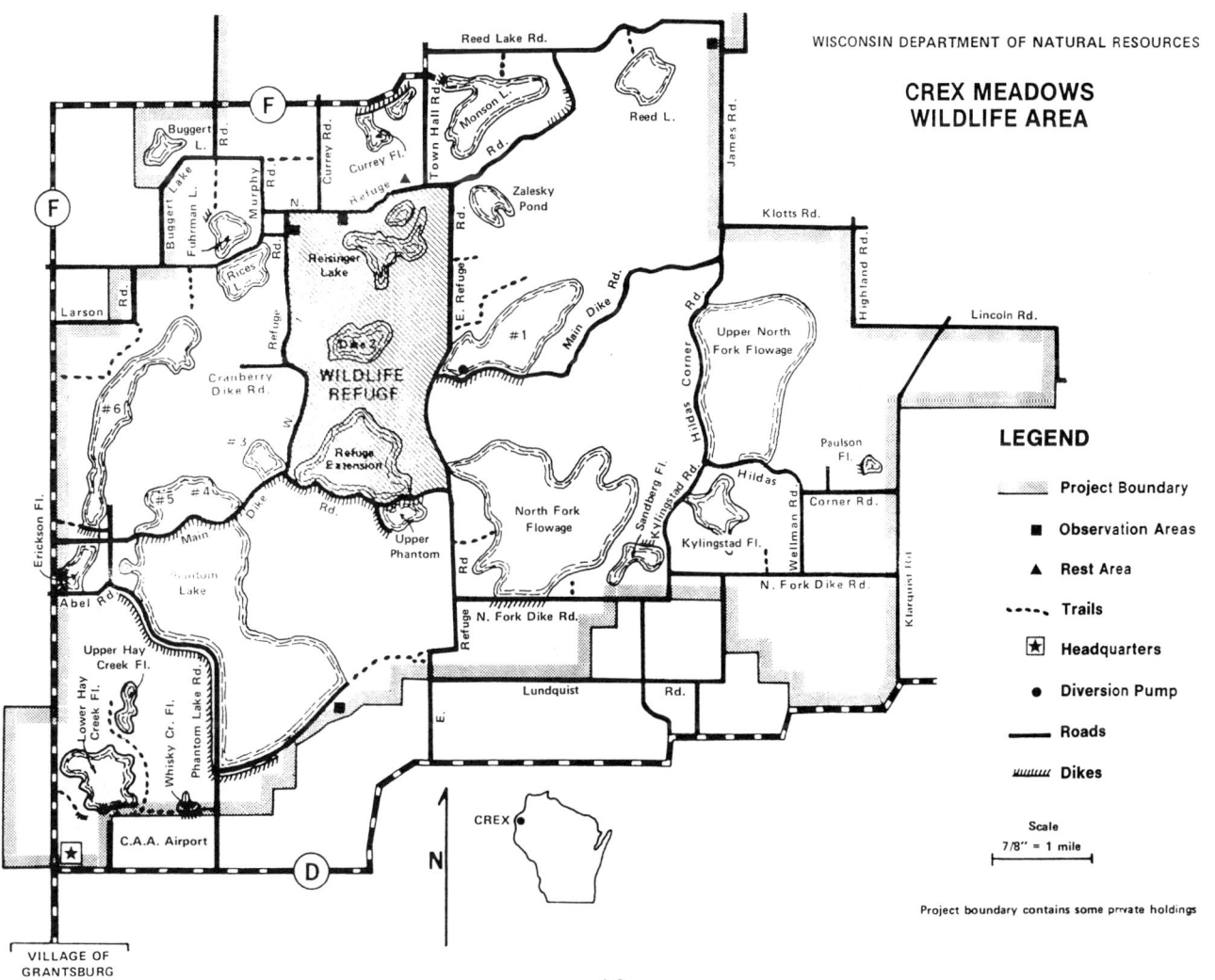

Amsterdam Sloughs Wildlife Area, 6,060 acres, Burnett County, is located 2 miles northwest of Siren. Take Hwy 70 west and Cty N north. Cty D & N are on the west side and Cty D is also on the north side. This project is very similar to Crex Meadow and Fish Lake. The area was acquired to restore the area's natural wetlands and prairies.

Kiezer Lake Wildlife Area, 1,352 acres, Burnett County, is located 1 mile north of Webster on Hwy 35, then east 4 miles on Cty A. This project is bordered by Cty A on the south and east, and Cty T on the west. Several lakes, marsh and upland timber are managed for grouse, waterfowl and deer.

Danbury Wildlife Area, 1,850 acres, Burnett County, is located 1 mile southwest of Danbury (Hwy 35 & 77). Take Cty F south and Broeffle Rd west 1/2 mile. This area is sand barrens with forested fringe. It is managed primarily for grouse.

Namekagon Barrens, 5,900 acres of leased lands, Burnett County, is located 2 miles west of Minong on Hwy 77, then about 5 miles north and west on Cty I and 8 miles west of St Croix Tr. At Dry Landing Road the project lands will extend a mile east and west, and 3 miles north of this point. This area is also sand barrens with timber fringe and is managed for sharp-tail grouse.

Fish Lake Wildlife Area, 13,157 acres, Burnett County, is located 2 miles south of Grantsburg, Hwy 70, on Hwy 48, then west on Fish Lake Rd. Cty O is the southern boundary of the property. There are 8 flowages and one natural lake plus a picnic area, observation points and several trails. Management activities are to restore the large expanse of wetlands and open areas for waterfowl and sharp-tail grouse. Several hundred acres of forest will remain.

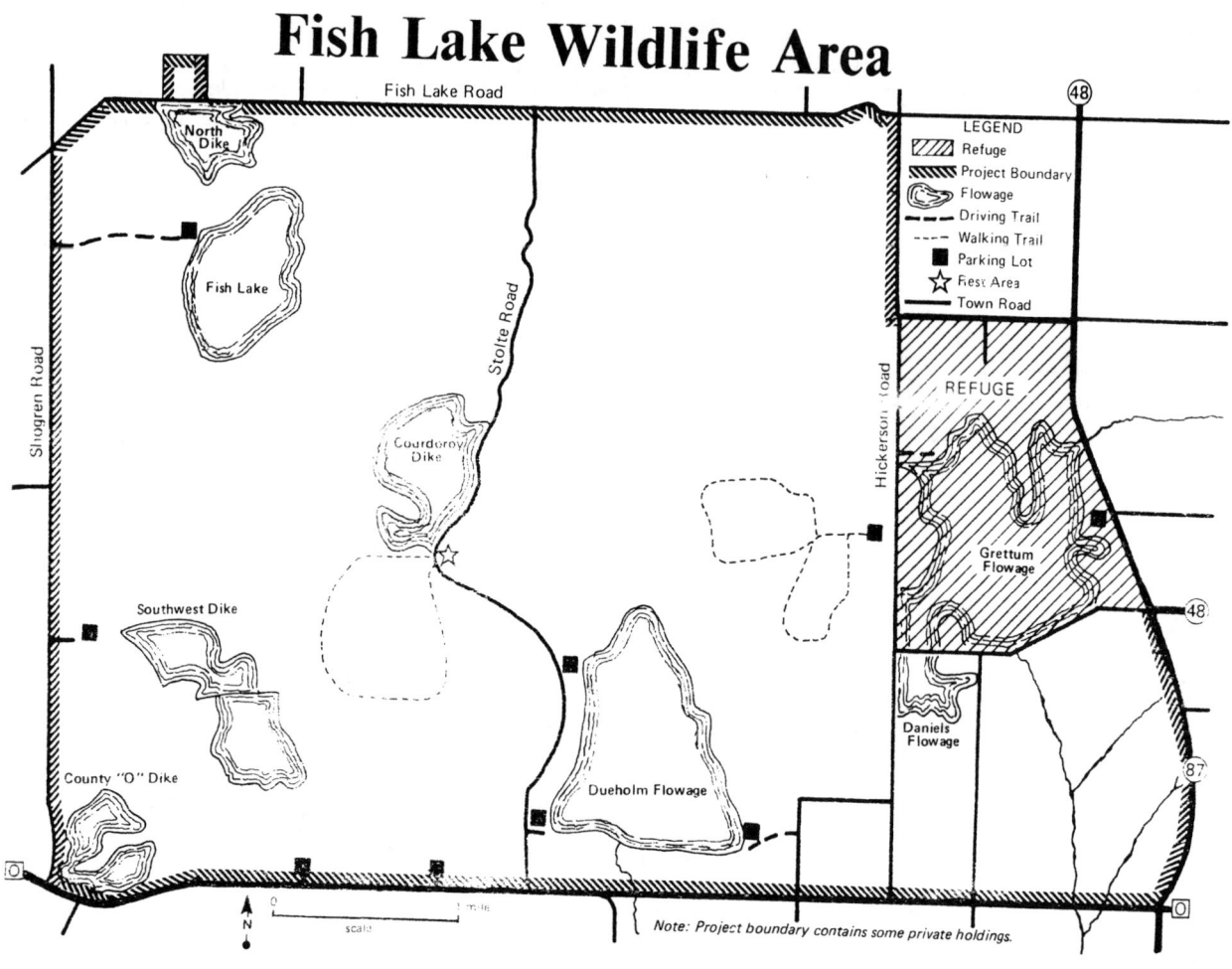

The following properties are smaller is size. They were acquired to provide access to area streams and provide hunting opportunities. The typical terrain is a mix of stream bottoms with timber and wetlands with upland forested fringe.

Mckenzie Cr, 80 acres, Washburn County, is located 1.5 miles west of Hwy 53 on Cty F, on the north side of the road.
Namekagon River, 160 acres, Washburn County, is located about 14 miles east of Trego on Hwy 63, then 1/2 mile south on Cty E, on the east side of the road.
Whalen Cr, 188 acres, Washburn County, 5 miles north of Trego on Hwy 53, then 1/2 mile east on Cty F, then south along the road next to the railroad tracks for 2 miles. The property is to the west.
Sawyer Cr, 744 acres, Washburn County, is located 1/2 mile west of Shell Lake on Cty B, then north 1 mile on town road. Project is to the north and west.
Bean Brook, 1,351 acres, Washburn County, is located east of Trego on Hwy 63, then 7 miles east on Cty E. From this point the project is to the north and east. Access is by town roads. The area is timber uplands with marsh areas along the stream. It is managed to provide access to the stream along with hunting for forest animals.
Beaver Brook Wildlife Area, 1,323 acres, Washburn County, is located just south of Spooner between Hwy 53 and 253. Access is by town road or Cranberry Rd. This area is timbered stream bottoms with surrounding hilly areas. The project provide access to the stream and is managed for waterfowl, grouse and deer.
Bear Lake Wildlife Area, 262 acres, Washburn County, is located south of Spooner on Hwy 53, then west 4 miles on Cty D and south about 4 miles on 13 3/4-16th St. The area is to the east at Boyer Cr. On the western end of Bear Lake the property is open water, marsh and streams managed for waterfowl and furbearers.

Chief River Wildlife Area, 1,180 acres, Sawyer County, is located 14 miles east of Hayward on Cty B, then 2.5 miles north on Cty A and east 1 mile through the project on Chief River Rd. This area is forested uplands and conifer swamps with three hunter walking trails plus a portion of the North Fork of the Chief River on the west side.
Kissick Swamp Wildlife Area, 941 acres, Sawyer County, is located 1 mile west of Hayward. The northern end of the project can be reached on Dear Farm Rd south of Hwy 77. The area is swamp with a timber fringe. There is a small lake on the southern end along with hunter walking trails.
Totagatic River Wildlife Area, 2,719 acres, Sawyer County, is located 6 miles north of Hayward on Hwy 27. It is to the west of Nelson Lake. The property is a 1,000 acre flowage with marsh and bog fringe, and wooded uplands of aspen and hardwood. Management is for waterfowl and furbearers.

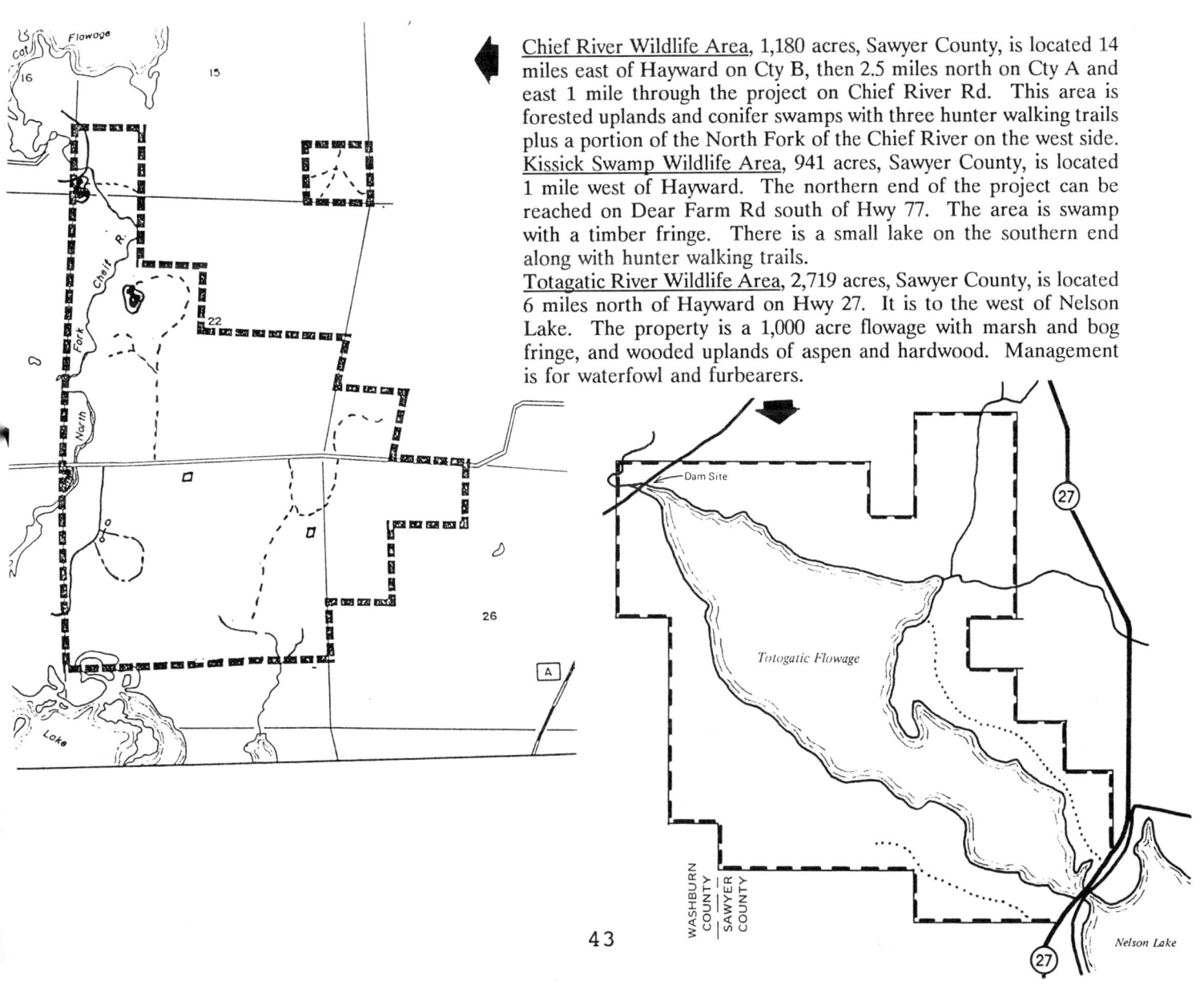

Weirgor Springs Wildlife Area, 2,050 acres, Sawyer County, extends northwest and southeast of Exeland (Cty C just west of Hwy 48) The upper end of the project is aspen forest with brush fringe along Weirgor Creek. The lower 2/3 are brush areas with grasses and muskeg. The project provides access to the creek plus habitat for wildlife.

Flambeau State Forest:

This 88,000 acre forest is located between Park Falls and Winter on Hwy 70. Cty M and W pass through the forest. The main feature is the 60 miles of river. The North and South Branch of the Flambeau combine within the forest, providing a great recreational resource. Recreational opportunities include 2 hiking and ski trail systems; campgrounds on Connor Lake and Lake of the Pines; canoe camping along the river; a picnic area on Connor Lake, and scenic areas.

Connor Lake Picnic Area, is located on Cty W about 1.5 miles east of the river and on the north shore of Connor Lake. There is a sandy beach and picnic pavilion.

Little Falls/Grundy Slough Scenic Area, is located on Cty M about 7 miles south of Cty W. A great spot to picnic or just view the splendor of the river.

Big White Pine, is a 300 year old pine 130 ft tall. Take Cty M 2 miles south of Cty W, then east a mile on Gill Lane/Price Creek Rd. It is a short walk from Gill Lane.

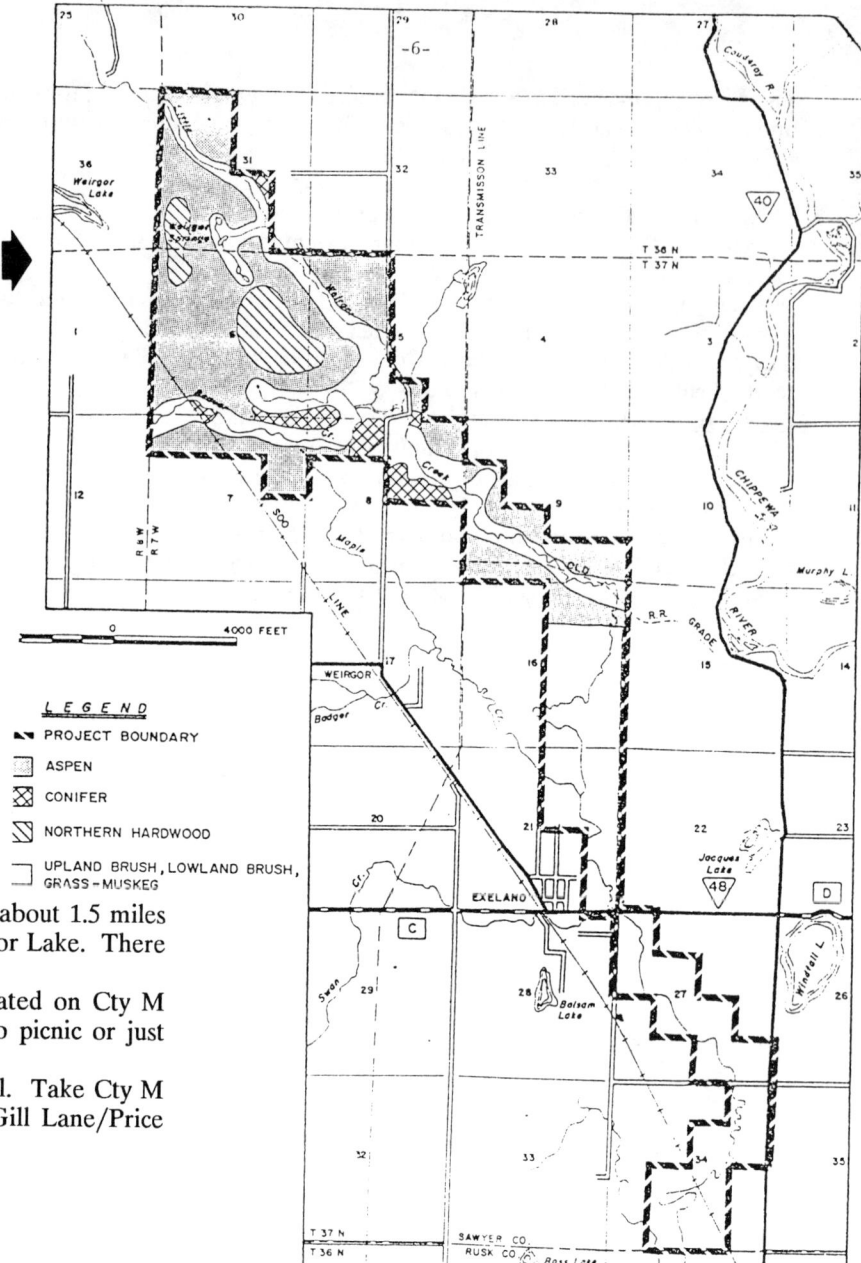

Governor Knowles State Forest:

This 32,000 acre forest is located on the state's western border just west of Grantsburg. Access is by Hwy 77 and 70 and Cty G, O and F. The forest is 55 miles long, but only up to 2 miles wide. This is due to the main feature of the forest, the St Croix River and its forested shoreline. The recreational opportunities include horse and hiking trails along the bluff. These trails cover over 45 miles. There is also a ski trail. A picnic area can be found on the south side of Hwy 70 at the river. There is only a youth group campground on the forest. Backpack camping is permitted; however a free permit is required.

PARKS, LANDINGS AND OTHER THINGS:

Burnett County:

Parks:

Devil's Lake Beach, is located 3.5 miles north of the jct of Cty X and Hwy 35 in Webster, then 2 miles east on Devils Lake Rd. The park is between the road and lake. There is a boat landing with a swimming beach.
26 Lake Park, is located about 7 miles east of Danbury on 26 Lake Rd, then take a town road south on the east side of the lake. Facilities include a swimming beach, bathhouse, picnic area and toilets.
Minerva Dam Park, is located east of Danbury on Hwy 77, south about 1/4 mile on Hwy 35. After crossing the Yellow River turn east on Minerva Rd, after about a mile go east on Flowage Rd. This is a small picnic area, well & toilets.
Jefferies Landing, is located 2 3/4 miles north of the jct of Cty X & Hwy 35 in Webster. Take the road to the west for 1/4 mile, then north along the road next to the railroad tracks. The landing is on the east side of the Yellow River. This is a landing with a small picnic area, well and toilet.
Lindberg Park, is located 5 miles west of Siren on Hwy 70 at the east side of Mud Hen Lake. There is a picnic area, boat landing, beach, toilets and open area.
Meenon Park, is located east of Hwy 35 on the south side of Clam River, 1 mile south of Webster. There is a picnic area on the river plus toilets.
Clam Dam, is located 1 mile east of Hwy 35 on Hwy 70, then 1.5 mile north on Kruger Rd and 1.5 mile east on Pike Bend Rd. There is access to both sides of Clam Lake Dam plus a picnic area and toilets.
Thoreson American Legion Park, Wood Lake, is located 2 miles south of Grantsburg on Hwy 48, then east 4.5 miles on Solness & Wood Lake Rd. At the lake go north on N Shore Drive. There is a beach, bathhouse and restroom, picnic area and well.

Municipal Park:

Benoit Lake, Tn of Rusk, is located about 14 miles east of Hwy 35 on Hwy 70, then 4.5 miles north on Cty H and then east a mile on Cty G. The lake is to the north with a beach, toilets and boat landing.
Clear Lake, Siren, is located 1 mile south of Hwy 70 on Hwy 35. There is a beach and boat landing west of the highway.
Crooked Lake Park, Siren, located on the north end of Siren and east of Hwy 35/70, has a beach and boat landing.
Memory Lake, Grantsburg, is located on Olson Dr, west of Oak St. in Grantsburg. The park, on the south shore of the lake, has a campground, picnic area, showers, playground and restrooms, (715) 463-2405.

State Waysides:

Hwy 70, 2 miles east of Hwy 35 (Lower Clam Lake), has a boat landing, picnic area, well and toilets.
Hwy 70, 5 miles east of Hwy 35 (Viola Lake), has a scenic overlook.
Hwy 35, at Riverside (St Croix River), has a boat landing, picnic area, well and toilets.
Hwy 35, 2.5 miles south of Siren, has a picnic area, well and toilets.

Sawyer County:

Parks:

There are no county operated parks, campgrounds or picnic areas.

Municipal Parks:

Hayward City Park/Beach, is located just east of Hwy 63 on Hwy 27, after crossing the bridge on the Namekagon River, go to the north. Facilities include beach, dock, picnic area, bathhouse, and restroom.
Fire Hall Park, Radisson, located at the corner of Hwy 40 and Hwy 70 in Radisson has a picnic area.
Grimh Dam, Radisson, is south of Hwy 70 on Hwy 40, to the west side just after crossing the Couderay River.
Silverhome Lake, Tn of Lenroot, is located 1 mile north of Seely, on west side of Hwy 63. The park is on the north end of the lake. Facilities include a beach, shelter, change rooms, restroom and playground.
Etytcheson Park, Tn Lenroot, is located north of Hayward on Hwy 27/77, then 1/2 mile east on Cty T, on the south end of Smith Lake. Facilities include beach, restrooms and boat landing.

Ojibaw State Park, is located 1 mile east of Ojibwa on Hwy 70. This state park is operated by the local Lions Club with a possible change in ownership. The park is located between the Chippewa River and the Tuscobia State Trail and has a picnic area, camping and shelter. Winter Lions Club, Winter, WI 54896, (715) 266-2752.

Stone Lake Lions Club Park, is located on Hwy 70, Stone Lake, at the Washburn County line. Facilities include organized sports, picnic area, shelter and restrooms.

Summit Lake Park, Tn of Stone Lake, is located north on Hwy F from Hwy 48 east of Birchwood, 1 mile north of Edgewater go east 1 mile on Summit Lake Rd. The park is to the west. Facilities include swimming beach, picnic area and boat landing.

Round Lake Peninsula Beach, Tn of Hayward, is located east of Hayward on Hwy 77, south on Cty K and east 1 1/4 mile on Linden Rd. The park is to the east, on the west side of Round Lake. Facilities include beach, change house, restrooms and boat landing.

State Waysides:

Hwy 27, 4.2 miles south of county line (Totagatic River), has a boat landing, picnic area with well and toilets.
Hwy 77, 0.7 miles west of Cty A (Dead Cr.), has a picnic area.
Hwy 70, west of Oxbow Bridge on Flambeau River, has a picnic area.

Washburn County:

Parks:

Sawmill Lake Camp, is located east of Spooner on Hwy 70, then southeast on Cty B, then south on Birchwood Firelane. Facilities include campground, small beach, boat landing, picnic area and toilets on Sawmill Lake.

Totogatic Park, is located 8 miles west of Minong, first on Hwy 77, then Cty I to Minong Flowage. Facilities include campgrounds, swimming, boat landing, picnic area, shelter, toilets and water.

Slim Creek Flowage, is located about 13 miles east of Spooner on Hwy 70, then south 1 mile on Cty B. The park is to the east. This is a secluded picnic area with boat landing.

Harmon Lake, is located about 10 miles east of Spooner on Hwy 70, then 2 miles south on town road. This road is 1 mile west of fire tower, the park is just to the east. There is a picnic area with toilets and boat landing.

Leisure Lake, is located 3 miles west of Trego on Cty E, then 3 miles north on Cty K, then 2 miles west on Spring Lake Rd, then about 1.5 miles north on Island Lake Rd, camp is to the east. This is the site of the 4-H Camp. When not in use, the beach, picnic area and landing are open to the public.

County Boat Landings:

These are landings not listed with other county properties. Spider Lake, Loyhead Lake, Wolf Lake, Chippanazie Flowage, Chippanazie Lake, McKenzie Lake, Birchwood Dam and Elbow Lake.

Municipal Parks:

Bass Lake Park, is located 2 miles southwest of Minong on Hwy 77, then 2 miles west on Bass Lake Rd. Facilities include beach, boat landing, picnic area, change house and toilets.

Birchwood Park, is located on Birch Lake on the north side of town. From the west, when Hwy 48 turns sharply south, go north on town road. Facilities include picnic area and campgrounds.

Shell Lake Park, is located just east of Hwy 63 in downtown Shell Lake. Facilities include picnic area, beach and campgrounds.

Stinnett Park, Stanberry, is located 1/2 mile north of Hwy 63 on Cty M. The park is to the east. There is a restroom, shelter and well.

Trego Park, is located on the north end of Trego. Take Hwy 53 1/2 mile north on Hwy 63. The park is to the east, just past the Namekagon River. Facilities include camping, picnic area, swimming and boat landing.

State Waysides:

Hwy 63, 2.2 miles north of Cty M, has a picnic area with well and toilets.
Hwy 63, 2.8 miles north of county line, has a picnic area with well and toilets.
Hwy 53, 3.5 miles south of Hwy 77 at Minong, has a picnic area with well and toilets.

Federal:

Chequamegon National Forest:

This is one of two national forests in Wisconsin. For more information on this national forest please see Area 1, page 10. Trail information can be found on page 19 and campground information on page 27.

Hayward Ranger District Headquarters is located on Hwy 27/77 N, Hayward, WI 54843, (715) 634-4821.

St Croix National Scenic Riverway:

Wisconsin has many majestic rivers which have been important to the exploration and settling of the state. However few retain their natural undisturbed beauty. Congress and the Department of the Interior endorsed efforts to preserve rivers due to their unique natural value. The Upper St Croix River and its tributary, the Namekagon, are to be preserved as relatively free-flowing rivers in a near primitive condition, and to protect and make it accessible for outdoor use by the public. The Park Service is also developing an interpretive program about the river and its environment, with emphasis on its prehistory and history.

The riverway covers the 164 mile length of the St Croix and the 98 mile length of the Namekagon Rivers. The riverway is broken into two sections which include the upper St Croix and the Namekagon Rivers and the Lower St Croix.

The riverway is also classified as scenic river area, free of impoundments and largely undeveloped shoreline as seen from the river, and as a recreational river area, where there is some impoundments, lightly developed and/or easily accessible.

On the upper St Croix there are 89.5 miles of scenic riverway with only the last 12.5 miles above St Croix Falls classed as recreational. On the Lower St Croix the first 10.5 miles below St Croix Falls is classified as scenic. The rest of the river, 41.5 miles is recreational. On the Namekagon all but 6.5 miles at Trego is classed as scenic with the Trego section classed as recreational. This means that much of this river system can be enjoyed in a natural state with the majority of use being on the lower sections by the Twin Cities.

River Facts:

St Croix River System is a major tributary to the Mississippi River. It starts at Solon Springs and flows southwesterly then south for 164 miles to Prescott where it joins the Mississippi River. Along this route the river drops 341 ft; most of the drop in the upper reaches. The river width changes from 40 ft at the up stream end to 1,200 ft. Both rivers tend to be shallow with sand, gravel and boulder strewn bottoms. There are over 250 islands in the river system.

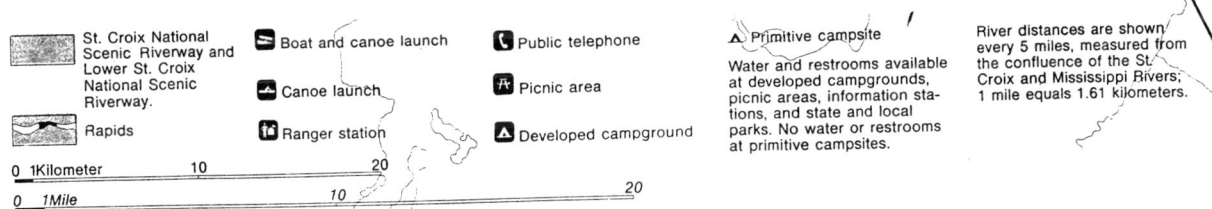

Upper St Croix:

At Solon Springs the river has its start. It flows through wooded and swampy areas with occasional high sandy banks and rolling terrain. There are several stretches of rapids, but are considered not difficult. At St Croix State Park, MN, there are the Kettle Rapids, a 7 mile stretch of medium difficult. Below the rapids the river widens and becomes straight and well defined. The swamps disappear to a forest cover of hardwoods. Towards the lower end of this section one passes through the site of Nevers Dam, which was removed in 1955. Within several miles the river widens into the St Croix Falls Flowage which is 10 mile long and partially fills the 1/2 mile wide valley.

Namekagon River:

This river has its start at Namekagon Lake and flows south and west 98 miles, where it joins the St Croix River three miles east of Hwy 35. The upper section of the river, above Trego, varies from an intimate, cold water trout stream closed in by forest to a slow moving, wider stream flowing through marshy areas. The river flows through Hayward and Trego. In the lower section, the valley becomes more prominent. Banks are higher, up to 80 ft. The river also meanders more. River bottom, timber lands and marshy areas increase near the junction with the St Croix. In the last few miles the Namekagon is joined by the Totagatic River, also noted for its wilderness appearance.

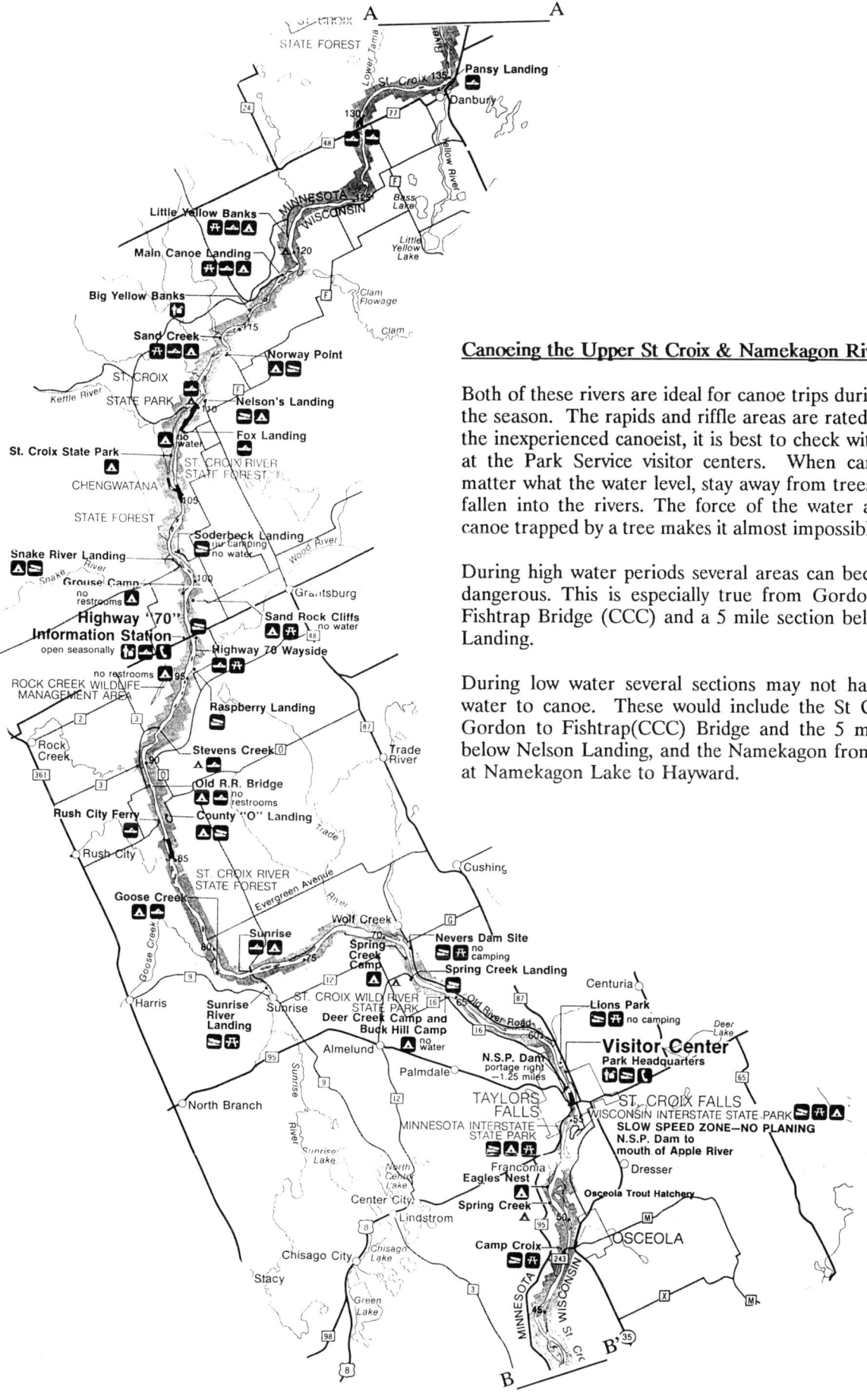

Canoeing the Upper St Croix & Namekagon River:

Both of these rivers are ideal for canoe trips during most of the season. The rapids and riffle areas are rated easy. For the inexperienced canoeist, it is best to check with the staff at the Park Service visitor centers. When canoeing, no matter what the water level, stay away from trees that have fallen into the rivers. The force of the water against the canoe trapped by a tree makes it almost impossible to move.

During high water periods several areas can become quite dangerous. This is especially true from Gordon Dam to Fishtrap Bridge (CCC) and a 5 mile section below Nelson Landing.

During low water several sections may not have enough water to canoe. These would include the St Croix from Gordon to Fishtrap(CCC) Bridge and the 5 mile stretch below Nelson Landing, and the Namekagon from the Dam at Namekagon Lake to Hayward.

Lower St Croix River:

At St Croix Falls, the river flows over the hydro dam and through a narrow, metamorphic rock gorge, the Dales. This area is well known for its stratified and precipitous rock formations. The walls of the gorge reach up to 200 ft above the river. From below the Dales to the Soo Line Railroad Swing Bridge, the river flows through a heavily wooded, steep valley with occasional sandstone and limestone bluffs. From the Soo Line Swing Bridge to the high bridge the river character changes little. However there is an increase in development on the Minnesota side. There are several unincorporated villages and Williams O'Brien State Park, MN. High Bridge you will find a 60 year(+) old Soo Line Bridge, a unique steel arch bridge 150 ft above the river.

South of the bridge, the river character changes, becomes wider and gradually loses the small islands and slough environment. From Stillwater to Prescott the river is wide and deep, much like a reservoir. In this section there are three major constrictions in Lake St Croix. These include the narrow at Hudson, the delta at the Kinnickinnic River and at Prescott where it enters the Mississippi River.

Boat Rules on the Lower St Croix:

Due to the high use of the Lower St Croix, special boating rules have been implemented. From St Croix Falls to the Arcola Sandbar to the mouth of the Apple River there is a Slow Speed Zone. This means boats are operated at a leisurely speed, less than planning speed, whereby the wake or wash created by the boat is minimal.

From Arcola Sandbar to the Mississippi River there are seven Slow No Wake Zones plus there is a special Slow No Wake Rule. This rule is in effect within 100 ft of any shore, including islands and any swimmer.

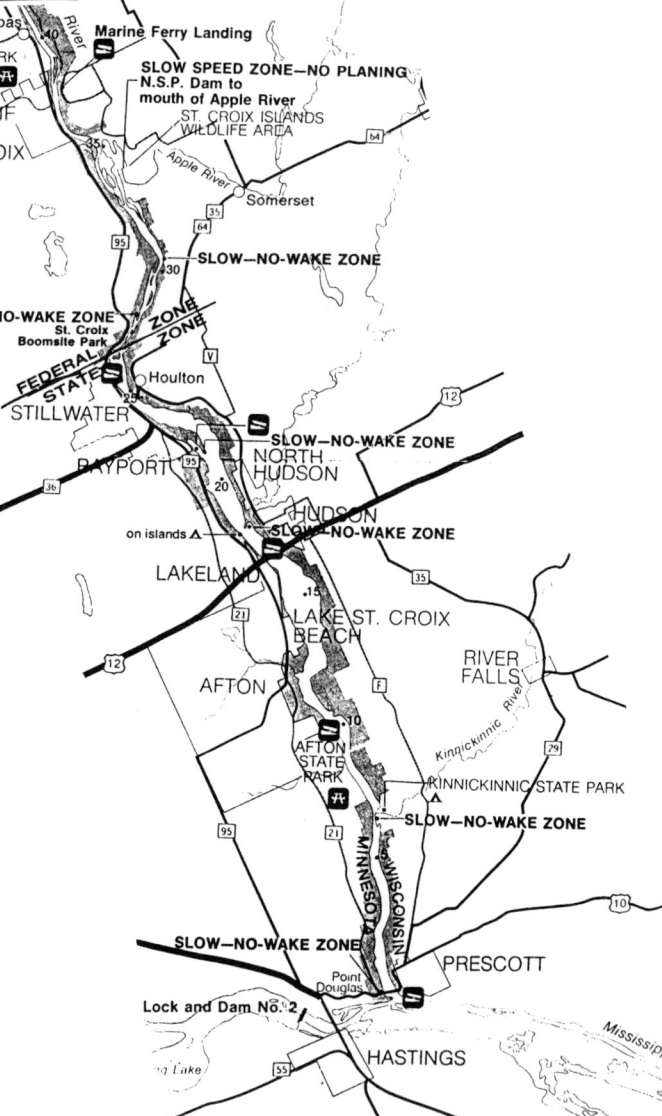

Recreation Restrictions:

Camping is permitted only in sites designated by the NPS which includes primitive sites along the riverway.
The use of all terrain vehicles, mountain bikes and horses is not permitted on National Park Service Property.

Visitor Centers:

There are a number of visitor centers open either year round or seasonal along the entire riverway. These include:
Trego Information Station, PO Box 100, Trego, WI 54888, (715) 635-8346, east of Trego on Hwy 63, open seasonally.
Hwy 70 Information Station, Rt 1, Box 134, Pine City, MN 55063, (612) 629-2148, on Hwy 70 at St Croix River, seasonally.
St Croix National Scenic Riverway HQ, PO Box 708, St Croix Falls, WI 54024, (715) 483-3284, Hwy 87 N, St Croix Falls.

State Parks and Forest:
There are a number of Wisconsin and Minnesota State Parks and Forests along this riverway. These include:
In **Wisconsin** there is Interstate Park at St Croix Falls and Kinnickinnic State Park south of Hudson. Governor Knowles State Forest extends from north of St Croix Falls to Danbury. St Croix Island Wildlife Area is between Oceola and Hudson.
In **Minnesota** there is St Croix State Park north of Hwy 70, St Croix Wild River State Park north of Taylor Falls, Minnesota Interstate Park at Taylor Falls and William O'Brien State Park just north of Marine on St Croix. There is the St Croix State Forest at Riverside & Chengwatana State Forest at Hwy 70.

TRAILS

Mountain Bikes:

Burnett County, permits the use of bikes on county's trails.
Sawyer County, permits the use of bikes on trails.
Washburn County, permits the use of mountain bikes on county trails, except on ski and snowmobile trails when there is snow.
Chequamegon National Forest, permits the use of bikes on all trails, with the exception of trails within Rainbow Lake & Porcupine Lake Wilderness.
St Croix National Scenic Riverway, does not permit bikes on their properties.
Wisconsin DNR, permits the use of these bikes on selected trails managed by the Department. It is best to contact the property manager to get the latest information.

All Terrain Vehicles:

Burnett County, permits ATVs on county property, except where posted.
Sawyer County, are not prohibited except where gated or signed. There are two approved county trails, 23 miles near Seely and 8 miles near Drapper.
Washburn County, limits ATV use. They may not be used in limited access areas, gated and/or signed trails, Harom Lake Area, Walsh Lake Area, Birchwood Canoe area and special use areas. There is also a weight limit of 500 lbs on selected trails.
Chequamegon National Forest, permits the use of ATVs and motorcycles on trails controlled by the Forest Service, except where the trails are posted closed or in the wilderness areas.
St Croix National Scenic Riverway, does not permit ATVs on their properties.
Wisconsin DNR, does not permit the use of these vehicles on any of the trails managed by the Department.

Horses:

Burnett County, permits the use of horses on county trails, except where posted.
Sawyer County, permits the use of horses on trails unless signed. The use of the Birki Trail is discouraged.
Washburn County, permits horses on county trails but not on ski and snowmobile trails when there is snow.
Chequamegon National Forest, permits horses on trails.
St Croix National Scenic Riverway, does not permit horses on their properties.
Wisconsin DNR, policies vary with the properties, therefore it is best to contact the property manager to get the latest information.

Hiking, Hunting and Cross Country Ski Trails

Sawyer County ATV Trail, operated by the county, is located 2 miles east of Hayward on Cty B. The trail travels northeast about 2 miles east of Hwy 63. One mile north of Cty OO, the trail makes a 8 mile loop to the east.
Sawyer County Hunter Hiking Trails, are located throughout the county forest. Presently there are 30 trails. Individual maps are available from the County Foresters office.
Nordic Woods Ski Trail, is located 21 miles east of Spooner on Hwy 70. The northern parking lot is at Hwy 70 and Dugan Lake Rd and the southern parking lot is on Cty B. There are 15 miles of trail in three main loops which pass around a number of small lakes. It is rated for beginners to intermediate. (715) 865-2801.
Webb Lake Ski Trail, is located 1 mile north of Webb Lake on Cty H, then west on Bear Lake Dr. A second trail head can be found on Bear Lake Rd to the south. Loop 1 is 2 km long, loop 2 is 2.5 km long and loop 3 is 4.2 km long, (715) 259-3329 for trail information.
HASTA Ski Trail, is located at the Hayward Memorial Hospital on Hwy 27/77. There is a 3 km beginner loop and a 2 km intermediate loop through rolling and wooded terrain. For more information on this and area trails call New Moon Ski Shop at, (715) 634-8656.
Uhrenholdt Forest, is a parcel of land donated to WI DNR. It is located just east of Seely and split by Cty OO. The area north of road has been left in a natural state while the southern area has been managed using sound forest management practices. There are nature trails throughout the area.

Timberland Hills Cross Country Ski Trail, is located in the southeastern corner of Burnett County. From Spooner, go south on Hwy 63 to Cumberland, then north on Cty H, then east on Boyd Road to the trail head. There are 19.5 km of trails in 7 different loops. The trails, rated beginner and intermediate have over 250 ft of elevation change. During the non-ski season the trails are mowed for hiking and mountain bike use.

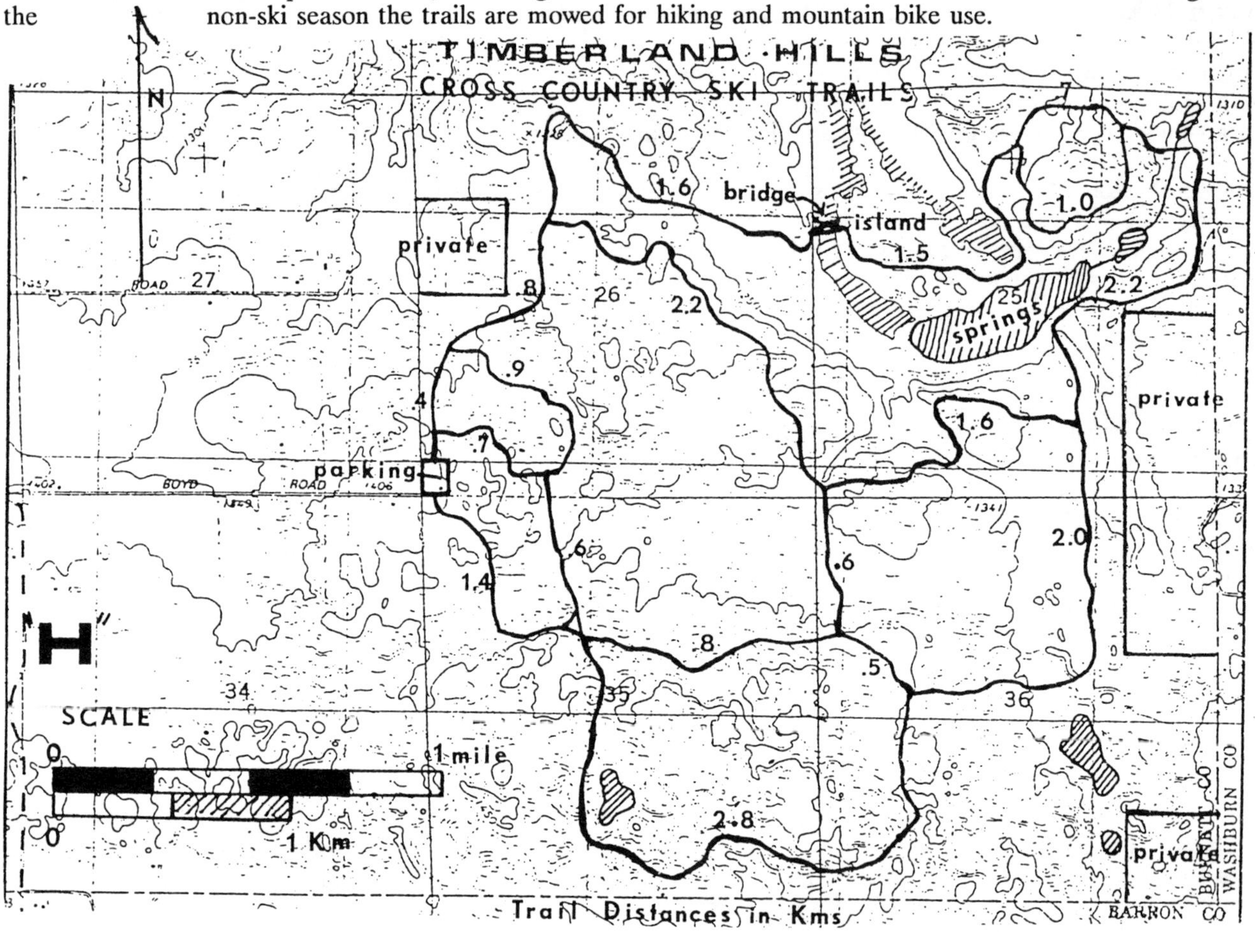

Beaver Brook Ski Trail, is located east on Hwy 70, then south on Hwy 53, then east and south on Cranberry Marsh Rd. The parking lot is on the west side. The trail, 4.9 miles long, extends west and north following Beaver Brook. There are three loops off the main trail. The trail is rated beginner to intermediate and travels through gentle, rolling terrain covered with hardwoods, except for the ridge lands on the C loop.

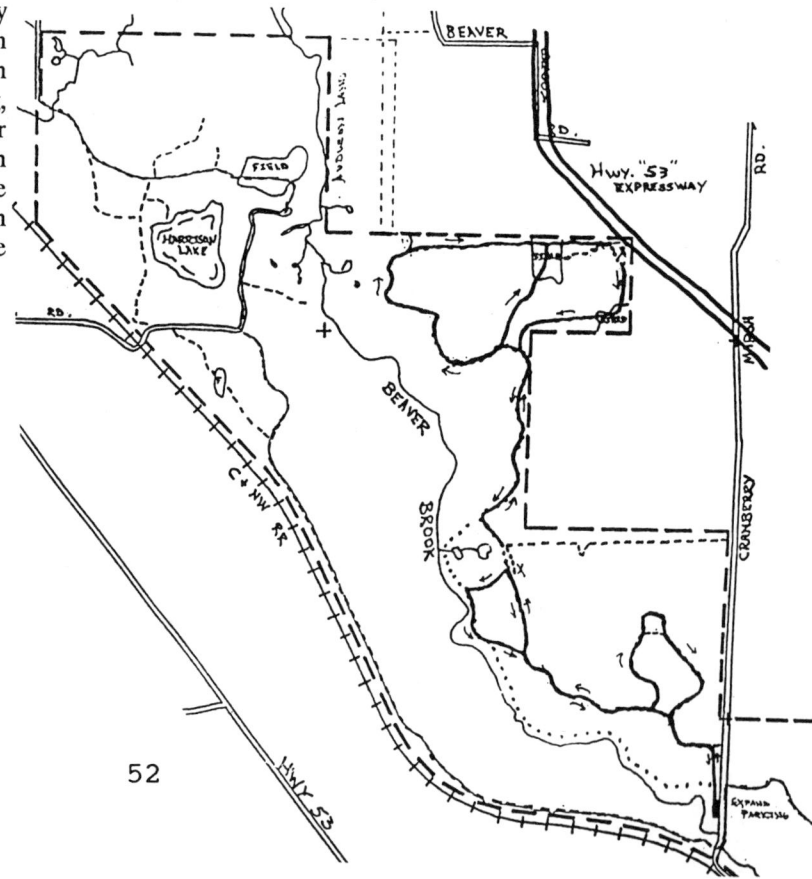

Birkebeiner Ski Trail, is a 30 mile long trail from Hayward to Telemark Lodge, east of Cable. Each year the world famous American Birkebeiner Ski Race is held on this trail. The trail starts in Hayward, roughly parallels Hwy 63 to Cable and can be accessed at Hayward, Mosquito Brook Rd, Cty OO and Telemark Lodge. Rating is intermediate to advanced. Preparedness is advised because of the trail length, the wilderness setting and rating, (715) 634-4839.

North Lost Land Lake Ski Trail, is located 15 miles east of on Hwy 77, then at Dow's Corner go 5 miles north and east on Upper "A" Rd. The trail head starts at Empire Lodge or Deer Path Lodge. There are 5 loops covering over 10.4 km of trails through a gentle, rolling and wooded setting. Rating is for beginner to intermediate, (715) 462-3772.

Totagatic Ski Trail, is located 1 1/2 miles north of Mining on Hwy 53. The parking lot is on the west side just across from Greenwood Rd. There are two loops; a beginner loop covering 1.5 miles and a advanced loop of 2.8 miles.

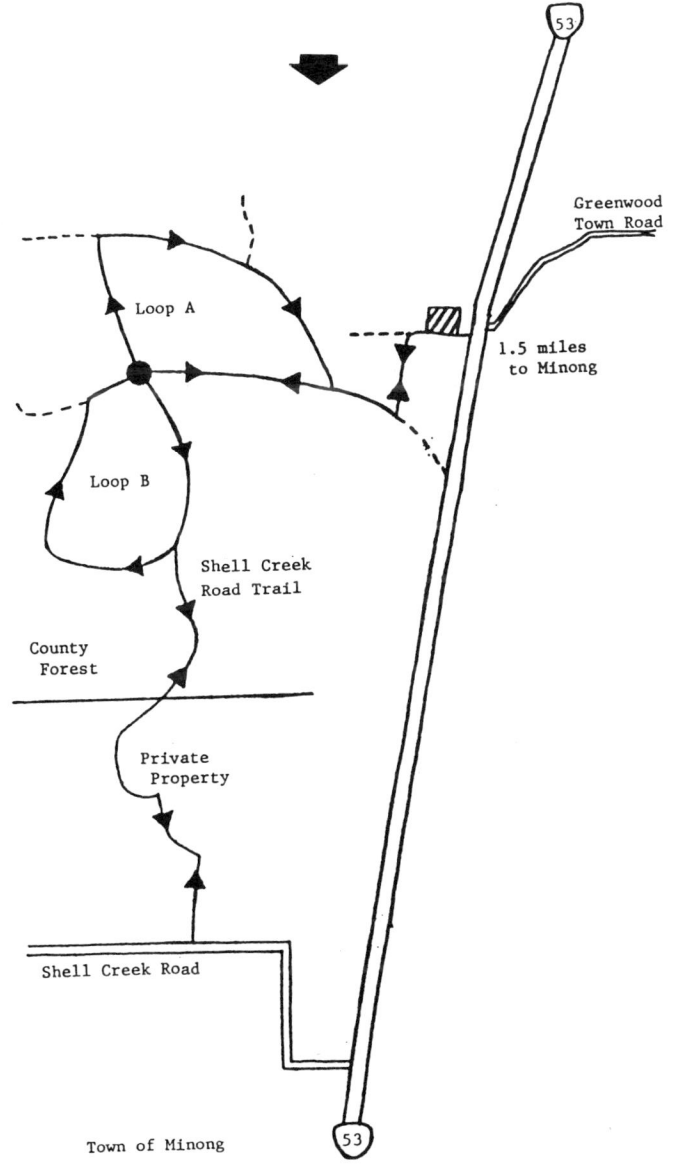

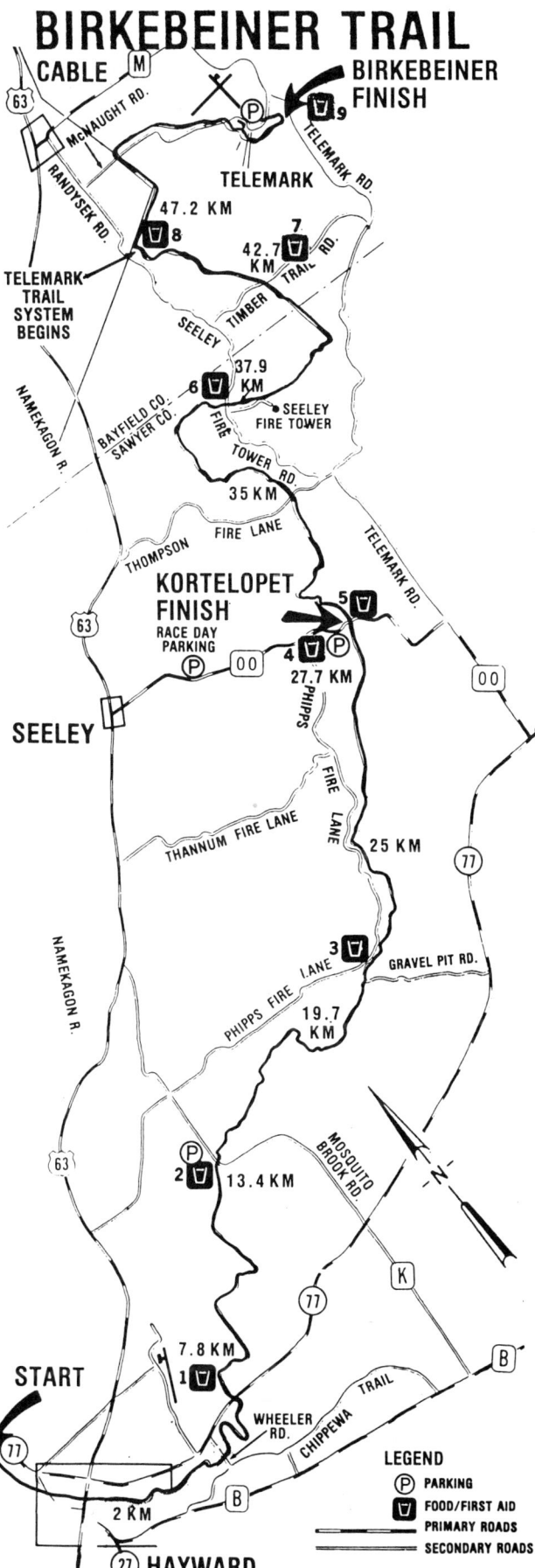

Gull Lake Ski Area & Trail, Washburn County Forest, is located north of Trego on Hwy 53, then east on Cty F to Lampson, then north 1 mile on Old 53, east on East Road and north on Hays Rd. The trail runs north a mile then branches out into 4 loops. There are plans to expand the trail north and west. The terrain is hilly.

Welsh Lake Ski Trail, Washburn County Forest, is located east of Hwy 63 in Shell Lake. Take Cty D east, when the road makes a sharp turn east, continue south 1/2 mile to the parking lot. This is a single loop trail about 3 miles long which passes Little Grassy and Welsh Lakes.

Grantsburg Nordic Ski Trail, is located on Olson Dr west of Oak St in Grantsburg. This is a 11.5 km trail with 3 long loops which run along both Wood River and Hay Creek through a variety of terrain. For trail conditions call (715) 463-2345 or trail information (715) 463-2405.

Wilbur Nelson Nature Trail, is located on Olson Dr west of Oak St in Grantsburg. This is a 1 mile nature trail through an environment of natural springs, prairie and marsh areas and is on the north side of Wood River.

Grettum Ski Trail, at Fish Lake Wildlife Area, is located south of Grantsburg Hwy 48, then west on Fish Lake Rd and south on Hickerson Rd. The trail, a 2.2 mile figure eight, is to the west. The terrain is gently rolling with no steep hills.

Fish Lake Wildlife Area, is located south of Grantsburg Hwy 48, then west on Fish Lake Rd. There are several walking trails in this project. They can be found on Stolte Road and Hickerson Road.

State Trails:

Tuscobia-Park Falls State Trail, is a 76 mile abandoned railroad grade open for hiking, biking, horseback riding. The western end of the trail is part of the Ice Age Trail. Any motorized vehicles are prohibited on that section. Many of the bridges and culverts which were removed by the railroad during abandonment have been replaced. Presently there is a short detour at Radisson. The surface of the trail is cinders making it difficult for use by most bikes. For more information contact, DNR Ranger Station, Winter WI 54896 (715) 266-3511.

Governor Knowles State Forest:

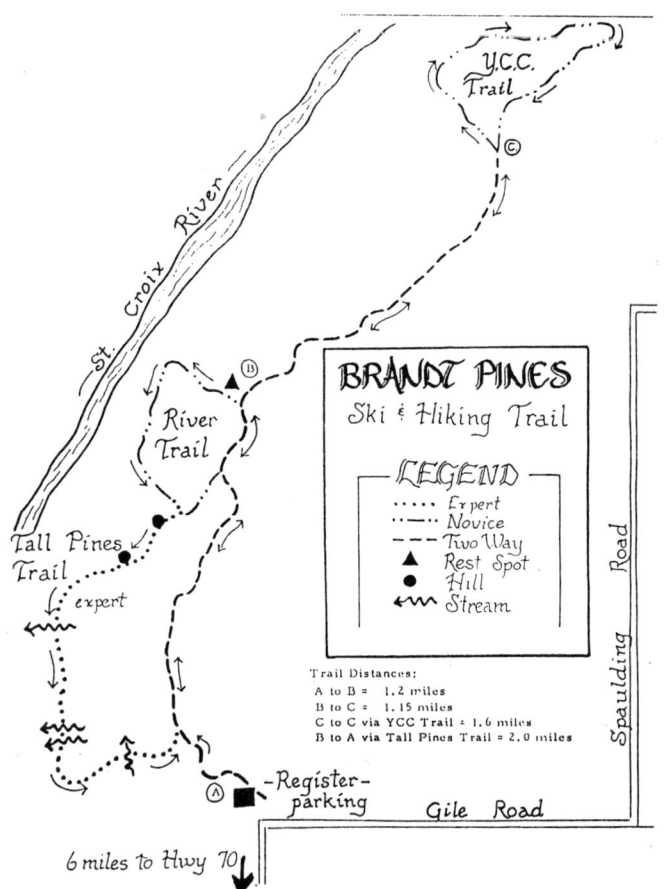

Brandt Pine Ski Trail, is located about 4.5 miles north of Grantsburg on Cty F, then 2 miles west on Bloom Rd and 3/4 mile north on Gile Rd. There are two loops with two trails which are 2.7 & 6.5 miles long. The trails are east of the St Croix River and run through tall pines and over hills. One of the loops is rated expert.

Horse Trail, is located in the southern half of the forest. This 26 mile trail starts north of St Croix Falls on Hwy 87, then west on Evergreen Ave and south on 300th St to the parking lot. The trail runs west and north to Fish Lake Rd which is west of Hwy 48 and south of Grantsburg.

South Hiking Trail, is about 22 miles long. The trail head is north of St Croix Falls on Hwy 87, then west on Evergreen Ave and south on 300th St. The trail runs west to the St Croix River, then turns north. About halfway the trail reaches Rush City Ferry Landing on Cty O. The trail continues north to Skog Rd, 3/4 of a mile north of Fish Lake Rd.

North Hiking Trail, is on the northern half of the forest. A starting point is the parking lot at Fox Landing. From Grantsburg go north on Cty F, then west on Landing Rd. From here the trail follows the river with access points at Nelson Landing, Norway Point and Cty F. The trail ends at Sioux Portage Group Campground west of Cty F on N River Rd.

Flambeau State Forest:

The forest has two hiking and ski trail systems and three hunter walking trails. Trail maps are available from the forest headquarters. Backpacking is permitted however a free permit is required, (715) 332-5271.

Flambeau Hills Hiking & Ski Trails, is located 16 miles east of Winter on Cty W. There are 10 miles of trail in 5 loops, runs and trails, rated beginner to advanced. Snuss Trail, 4 miles long, connects the two ski/hiking areas.

Oxbow Ski & Hiking Trail, is located about 20 miles east of Winter on Hwy 70. The trail head is opposite Snuss Blvd. This are 8 miles of trails in 5 loops in an oxbow bend of the river. For skiing, the trails are rated beginner to advanced.

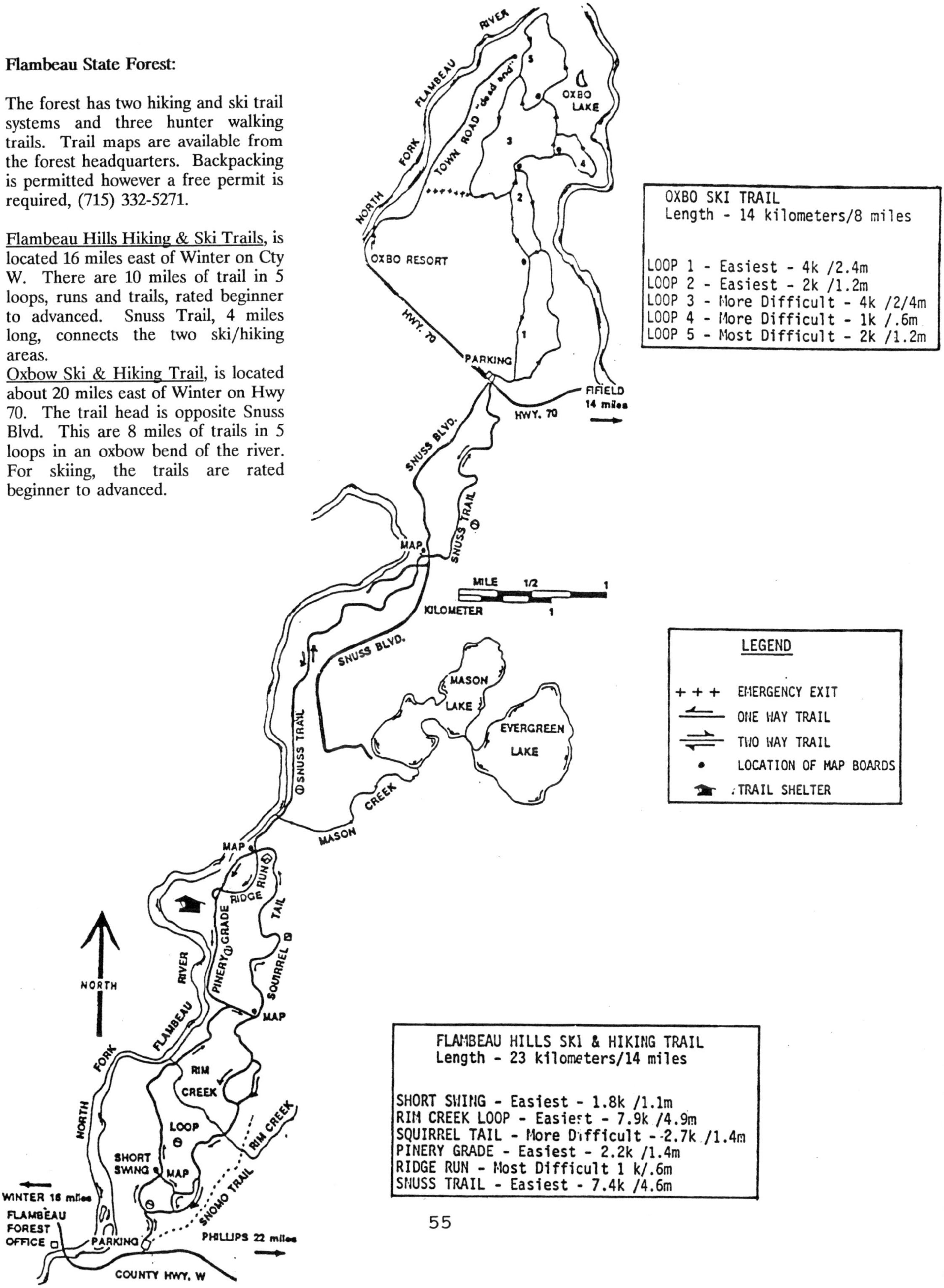

```
OXBO SKI TRAIL
Length - 14 kilometers/8 miles

LOOP 1 - Easiest - 4k /2.4m
LOOP 2 - Easiest - 2k /1.2m
LOOP 3 - More Difficult - 4k /2/4m
LOOP 4 - More Difficult - 1k /.6m
LOOP 5 - Most Difficult - 2k /1.2m
```

LEGEND

- +++ EMERGENCY EXIT
- ⇐ ONE WAY TRAIL
- ⇌ TWO WAY TRAIL
- • LOCATION OF MAP BOARDS
- TRAIL SHELTER

```
FLAMBEAU HILLS SKI & HIKING TRAIL
Length - 23 kilometers/14 miles

SHORT SWING - Easiest - 1.8k /1.1m
RIM CREEK LOOP - Easiest - 7.9k /4.9m
SQUIRREL TAIL - More Difficult - 2.7k /1.4m
PINERY GRADE - Easiest - 2.2k /1.4m
RIDGE RUN - Most Difficult 1 k/.6m
SNUSS TRAIL - Easiest - 7.4k /4.6m
```

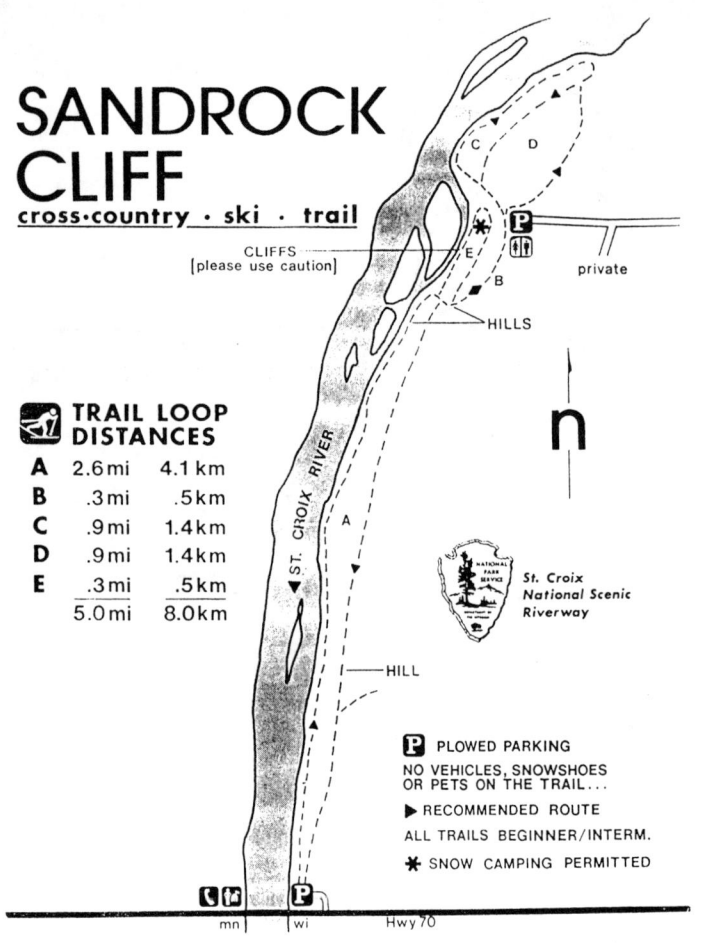

Chequamegon National Forest:

Please see Area 1, page 19, trail information.

St Croix National Scenic Riverway:

<u>Sandrock Cliff Ski and Hiking Trail</u>, operated by National Park Service, is located west of Grantsburg on Hwy 70. The trail starts at the river and extends north to Tennessee Rd. The terrain is gently rolling "through a corridor of wilderness". The trail is suited for most skill levels.

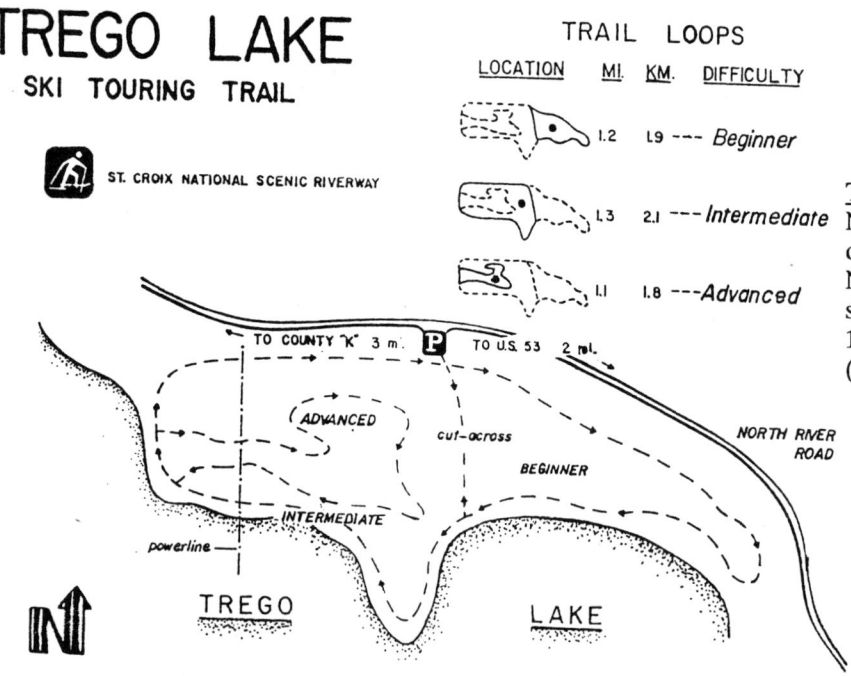

<u>Trego Lake Ski Touring Trail</u>, operated by National Park Service, is located 1 mile north of Trego on Hwy 63, then west 2 miles on North River Road. Parking lot is on the south side. There are three loops; 1.2 mile beginner, 1.3 mile intermediate and 1.1 mile advanced, (715) 635-8850.

Canoe Trails:

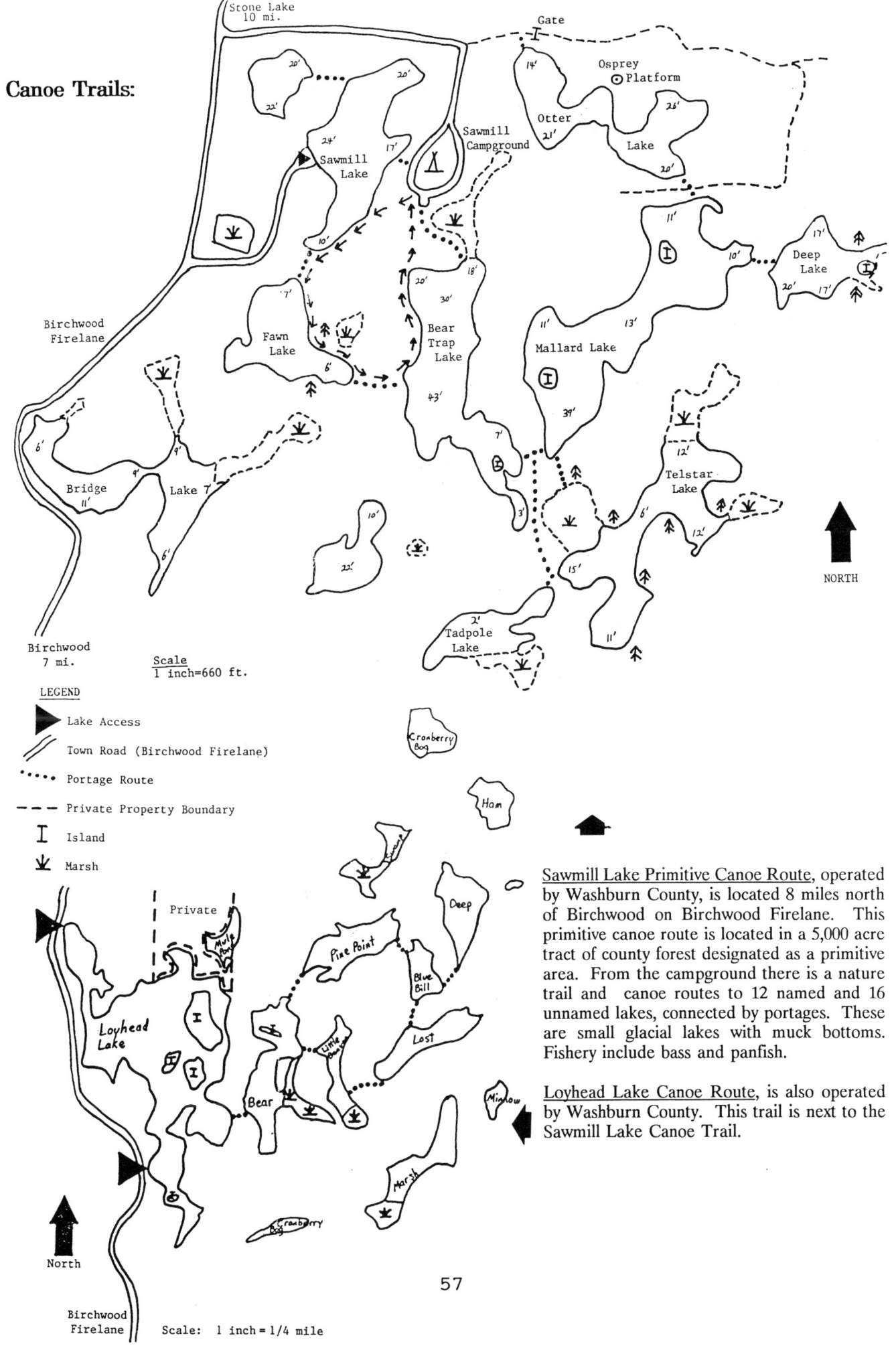

Sawmill Lake Primitive Canoe Route, operated by Washburn County, is located 8 miles north of Birchwood on Birchwood Firelane. This primitive canoe route is located in a 5,000 acre tract of county forest designated as a primitive area. From the campground there is a nature trail and canoe routes to 12 named and 16 unnamed lakes, connected by portages. These are small glacial lakes with muck bottoms. Fishery include bass and panfish.

Loyhead Lake Canoe Route, is also operated by Washburn County. This trail is next to the Sawmill Lake Canoe Trail.

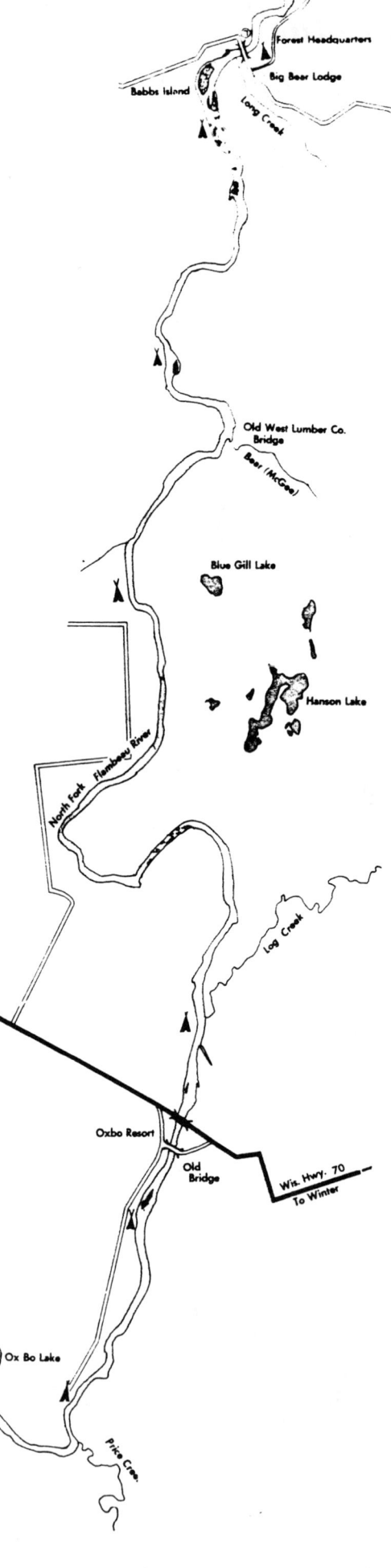

Chippewa River, flows south after leaving the Winter Dam, which forms the Chippewa Flowage. The river is mostly shallow and meandering with only riffle areas. Radisson Flowage is the only impoundment in Sawyer County. State and county roads and the agricultural and residential development have diminished the wild look of the river.

St Croix and Namekagon River, please see section on the St Croix National Scenic Riverway.

Totagatic River, has its start in Sawyer County then flows west to join the Namekagon just before it flows into the St Croix River. The river is canoed but due to extreme water level fluctuations, rapids and falls, it can be dangerous in high water. Caution must be exercised.

Flambeau River, considered one of the best canoeing rivers in Wisconsin, enters northeastern Sawyer County. The Flambeau River can be characterized as a fast flowing river with challenging rapids and a wild looking shoreline. The upper reaches of the North Branch can be challenging with several recommended portages. The South Branch can be dangerous and requires good skills. The lower North Branch provide enjoyable canoeing for most people. There are a number of access points throughout the forest.

Flambeau River Map:

Maps on three sections of the Flambeau River are presented here. It starts at the Oxbow (section 1) west of Park Falls to Cty W, extends from Hwy W to the joining of the North & South Branches (section 2) and ends with the section from the two branch to the flowage just above Ladysmith (section 3). These maps are opposite of many other maps. Here, north is down, the rivers flow south or up the page.

Section I

58

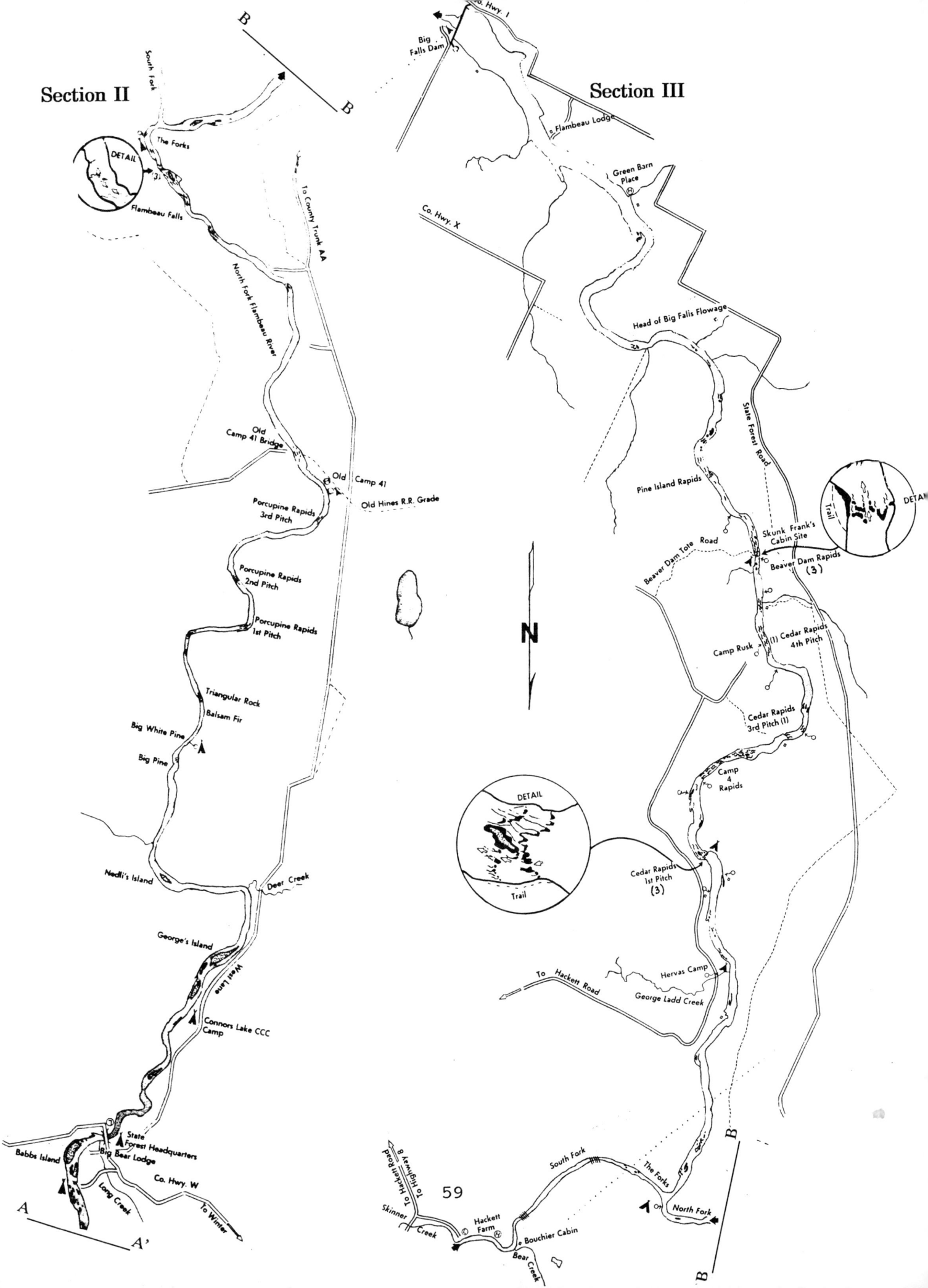

GUIDES AND BAIT SHOPS

Area Bait Shops:

DELS BAIT	RT 2	BIRCHWOOD	WI 54817
JOE'S BAIT & TACKLE	RT 2	BIRCHWOOD	WI 54817
JOHN'S BOW BARREL & BAIT	RT 1	BIRCHWOOD	WI 54817
SPORTSMANS LODGE	RT 1	BIRCHWOOD	WI 54817
THE SPORTS HUT	MAIN ST	BIRCHWOOD	WI 54817
CHIPPEWA PINES RESORT	BOX 68D	COUDERAY	WI 54828
INDIAN TRAIL RESORT	RT 1	COUDERAY	WI 54828
KEN'S STORE	RT 1	COUDERAY	WI 54828
NORWOOD STORE	RT 1	COUDERAY	WI 54828
SHADY NOOK RESORT	RT 1	COUDERAY	WI 54828
TIGER MUSKY RESORT INC	RT 1	COUDERAY	WI 54828
TIMBERLAKE LODGE	RT 1 BOX 50	COUDERAY	WI 54828
HAPS BAR	RT 2 BOX 100	DANBURY	WI 54830
\HOUMAN'S RESORT	29460 CCC RD	DANBURY	WI 54830
IKEWALTON LODGE	STAR RT 2 BOX 214	DANBURY	WI 54830
LOG CABIN STORE	30217 HWY 35 & 77	DANBURY	WI 54830
ROBERTSON'S	RT 3 BOX 142	DANBURY	WI 54830
WEBB LAKE BAIT	36869 NAMEKAGON TRL	DANBURY	WI 54830
EDGEWATER STORE	HWY F	EDGEWATER	WI 54834
FRP LTD	BOX 66	EXELAND	WI 54835
METEOR BAIT	RT 1 BOX 64	EXELAND	WI 54835
WINDFALL LAKE STORE	RT 1	EXELAND	WI 54835
HWY 70 SPORTS-BAIT	RT 1 BOX 45	GRANTSBURG	WI 54840
J & J BAIT SUPPLY	RT 2 BOX 1275	GRANTSBURG	WI 54840
TRADE LAKE VALLEY STORE	RT 1 BOX 510A	GRANTSBURG	WI 54840
WILD RIVER'S OUTFITTERS	RT 2 BOX 1138	GRANTSBURG	WI 54840
WILLIAMS CEDAR POINT RESOR	RT 2 BOX 530	GRANTSBURG	WI 54840
AL'S MINNOW FARM	RT 4 BOX 4348	HAYWARD	WI 54843
BIG MUSKY RESORT	RT 9 BOX 9355	HAYWARD	WI 54843
BLACK BEAR LODGE	RT 5 BOX 5393	HAYWARD	WI 54843
CHIEF LAKE LODGE	RT 5 BOX 5374	HAYWARD	WI 54843
CLEMENTS RESORT	RT 4	HAYWARD	WI 54843
D & B BAIT	RT 4	HAYWARD	WI 54843
DAN-BAR'S RESORT	RT 9	HAYWARD	WI 54843
DEER RUN RESORT	RT 4 BOX 4222	HAYWARD	WI 54843
DOW'S CORNER STORE	RT 7 BOX 7336	HAYWARD	WI 54843
EARL'S MARINE INC	RT 2	HAYWARD	WI 54843
EMPIRE LODGE	RT 7 BOX 7574	HAYWARD	WI 54843
GOETSCH'S RESORT	RT 5 BOX 5383	HAYWARD	WI 54843
GOLDEN FAWN LODGE INC	RT 9	HAYWARD	WI 54843
GREGORYS KNOTTY PINE BAIT	RT 2 BOX 2315	HAYWARD	WI 54843
HAHNS RESORT	RT 7 BOX 7592	HAYWARD	WI 54843
HALEY'S BAIT & TACKLE	RT 3 BOX 3284	HAYWARD	WI 54843
HAPPY HOOKER BAIT & TACKLE	RT 7 BOX 7342	HAYWARD	WI 54843
HAYWARD BAIT & TACKLE INC	RT 10 BOX 126	HAYWARD	WI 54843
HERMAN'S LANDING INC	RT 9	HAYWARD	WI 54843
INDIANHEAD RESORT	RT 1	HAYWARD	WI 54843
JENK'S BAIT & TACKLE	RT 4 BOX 4347	HAYWARD	WI 54843
JERRY'S BAIT & CRAFT	RT 4 BOX 4211	HAYWARD	WI 54843
JOHNSONS RESORT	RT 4 BOX 4257	HAYWARD	WI 54843
MILL INN RESORT	RT 4 BOX 4231	HAYWARD	WI 54843
MITTLESTADT'S SPORTSMAN'S	RT 4	HAYWARD	WI 54843
MUSKY RUN RESORT	RT 7 BOX 7262	HAYWARD	WI 54843
MUSKY TALE INC	RT 4 BOX 4259	HAYWARD	WI 54843
MUSKY TALE LODGE	RT 7 BOX 7420	HAYWARD	WI 54843
NASH'S BAIT BOX	RT 9 BIG MUSKY RESORT	HAYWARD	WI 54843
PARADISE RESORT & BAIT SHOP	RT 3 BOX 3116	HAYWARD	WI 54843
PARK ISLAND RESORT	RT 3 BOX 3111	HAYWARD	WI 54843
PASTIKA'S	217 S DAKOTA AVE	HAYWARD	WI 54843
PAT'S LANDING RESORT	RT 5 BOX 5377	HAYWARD	WI 54843
PYPER'S PUB	RT 4 BOX 4037	HAYWARD	WI 54843
RED FOX RUN	RT 1	HAYWARD	WI 54843
REEL LIVIN RESORT	RT 7 BOX 7395	HAYWARD	WI 54843

Area Bait Shops:

REST HAVEN RESORT INC	RT 5 BOX 5373	HAYWARD	WI 54843
REVELLE'S RESORT & CAMPGRO	RT 3 NELSON LAKE	HAYWARD	WI 54843
ROSS' TEAL LAKE LODGE	RT 7	HAYWARD	WI 54843
ROUND LAKE MARINA	RT 5 BOX 5156	HAYWARD	WI 54843
ROUND LAKE STORE	RT 1 BOX 1233	HAYWARD	WI 54843
S S PINE POINT RESORT	RT 9 BOX 9338	HAYWARD	WI 54843
SPORTSMART	RT 10 BOX 372	HAYWARD	WI 54843
SQUAW BAY LODGE	RT 5 BOX 5397	HAYWARD	WI 54843
TREELAND COTTAGES INC	RT 4 BOX 4288	HAYWARD	WI 54843
VALHALLA BOMIJA INC	RT 2 BOX 2067	HAYWARD	WI 54843
VIRGIN TIMBER RESORT	MOOSE LAKE RT 4 BOX 4184	HAYWARD	WI 54843
COUNTRY SIDE SPORT SALES	RT 1 BOX 224	HERTEL	WI 54845
MISTY PINES INN LTD	BOX 77 CO X & HWY 70	HERTEL	WI 54845
HAUSER'S LIVE BAIT	RT 1 BOX 153	LORETTA	WI 54896
HOEFT'S LIVE BAIT	BOX 73C	LORETTA	WI 54852
GREENWOOD'S BAR 'N' BAIT	RT 1 BOX 245	MINONG	WI 54859
SPORTSMANS HDQTS	BOX 530	MINONG	WI 54859
DAHLE'S BAIT SHOP	STAR RT 1 BOX 119	SARONA	WI 54870
FRED'S LIVE BAIT	RT 1 BOX 200	SARONA	WI 54870
LUCY'S LIVE BAIT	STAR RT BOX 182	SARONA	WI 54870
THE BAIT SHOP	RT 1 BOX 192	SARONA	WI 54870
WALTERS LONGLAKE SPORT & B	RT 1 BOX 111	SARONA	WI 54870
CIRCLE C FOODS	BOX 303	SHELL LAKE	WI 54871
DOLLY'S BAIT	RT 1 BOX 38A	SHELL LAKE	WI 54871
STEVE'S BAIT	RT 1 BOX 113	SHELL LAKE	WI 54871
ANDY'S BAIT SHOP	RT 1 BOX 714	SIREN	WI 54872
BAIT & BOTTLE	BOX 511	SIREN	WI 54872
CLAM LAKE TACKEL	6700 CTH HWY 70	SIREN	WI 54872
MOE'S BAIT - TACKLE	24107 HWY 35 N	SIREN	WI 54872
SUNFISH BAY RESORT	RT 2 BOX 522	SIREN	WI 54872
WINBERG'S INC	RT 2 BOX 560	SIREN	WI 54872
YOURCHUCK VIDEO	BOX 342	SIREN	WI 54872
ANDREE'S RESORT	STAR RT BOX 107	SPOONER	WI 54801
BREDES BAIT	STAR RT BOX 470	SPOONER	WI 54801
HARRIET'S STORE	RT 3 BOX 3099	SPOONER	WI 54801
MIKE'S SPT SHOP	110 S RIVER ST	SPOONER	WI 54801
SUPERAMERICA	730 S RIVER ST	SPOONER	WI 54801
TRIPLE V BAIT	STAR RT BOX 419	SPOONER	WI 54801
BLAIR'S FUR LIVE BAIT	RT 1 BOX 1132	SPRINGBROOK	WI 54875
HAUER BAIT & TACKLE	RT 2	STONE LAKE	WI 54876
HOOK LINE & SINKER	N2182 HWY 70	STONE LAKE	WI 54876
MIDWAY BAIT &. TACKLE	RT 2 BOX 63	STONE LAKE	WI 54876
STONE LAKE BAIT & TACKLE	BOX 146	STONE LAKE	WI 54876
DALE'S BAIT	RT 1 BOX 1249	TREGO	WI 54888
DICK'S 24 HOUR LIVE BAIT	BOX 82	TREGO	WI 54888
THE MAIN STORE	STAR RT 1 BOX 330	WEBB LAKE	WI 54830
A & H OUTPOST	HC RT 70 BOX 281	WEBSTER	WI 54893
LEE'S SPORT SHOP	RT 1	WEBSTER	WI 54893
SHAWTY BAIT	25597 HWY 35	WEBSTER	WI 54893
SOUTH SHORE RESORT	RT 3 BOX 62	WEBSTER	WI 54893
WEBSTER SPORTING GOODS	26798 LAKELAND AVE N	WEBSTER	WI 54893
ALLEN'S NORTHWOODS	HC RT BOX 67B	WINTER	WI 54896
ANDREWS' FIN&FUR SPT&BAIT	HWY 70 BOX 237	WINTER	WI 54896
BEBAK'S FOREST LODGE	HC RT BOX 64	WINTER	WI 54896
EAST FORK RESORT	RT 1 BOX 292	WINTER	WI 54896
TW SPORT & BAIT	MAIN ST	WINTER	WI 54896
WANNIGAN RESORT	RT 2 BOX 39	WINTER	WI 54896

Area Guides:

GRYZIK	WILLIAM	HCR 01 BOX 63	CLAM LAKE	WI 54517
BERRY	DARWIN	RT 1 BOX 55H	COUDERAY	WI 54828
BLANK	PETER	RT 1 BOX 38	COUDERAY	WI 54828
DETTLOFF	JOHN	RT 1	COUDERAY	WI 54828
HAACK	GARY	RT 1 BOX 73	COUDERAY	WI 54828

Area Guides: continued

JASEK	JOSEPH	RT 1 BOX 55C	COUDERAY	WI 54828
RASINE	SUSAN	RT 1 BOX 94AA	COUDERAY	WI 54828
SEIBERT	DANIEL	RT 1 BOX 94B	COUDERAY	WI 54828
SMITH	HARRY	RT 1	COUDERAY	WI 54828
SPEROS	JEFF	RT 1	COUDERAY	WI 54828
SPEROS	RICHARD	RT 1	COUDERAY	WI 54828
JEWELL	BENJAMIN	29708 ARBUTUS RD	DANBURY	WI 54830
LUDDEN	MITCHELL	8598 W BASS LK RD	DANBURY	WI 54830
MAHLEN	MICHAEL	30374 TOWER RD	DANBURY	WI 54830
BURTON	JERRY	RT 2 BOX 791	GRANTSBURG	WI 54840
PAQUETTE	THOMAS	RT 3 BOX 170	GRANTSBURG	WI 54840
SUNDQUIST	DOUGLAS	RT 3 BOX 770	GRANTSBURG	WI 54840
BANGS	JAMES	RT 5 BOX 5374	HAYWARD	WI 54843
BARON	DANIEL	RT 9	HAYWARD	WI 54843
BLOOM	JOHN	BOX 227	HAYWARD	WI 54843
BOCHMANN	EDWIN	RT 1 BOX 1273	HAYWARD	WI 54843
BRALICK	TONY	BOX 565	HAYWARD	WI 54843
BROKAW	TOM	RT 7 BOX 7210	HAYWARD	WI 54843
CAMMACK	ROBERT	RT 2 BOX 2441	HAYWARD	WI 54843
CAMPBELL	JEFFREY	RT 8 BOX 8414	HAYWARD	WI 54842
CAMPBELL	K	RT 6 BOX 6931 M	HAYWARD	WI 54843
CONE	DAVID	BOX 692	HAYWARD	WI 54843
DANIELSON	BRETT	RT 3 BOX 3275	HAYWARD	WI 54843
DETTLOFF	RONALD	RT 9 BOX 9412A	HAYWARD	WI 54843
DIECKMAN	MILTON	RT 10 BOX 479	HAYWARD	WI 54843
DONNELLAN	JOE	BOX 111	HAYWARD	WI 54843
DORAZIO	DAVID	RT 9	HAYWARD	WI 54843
DUDLAY	RICHARD	RT 3 BOX 3219	HAYWARD	WI 54843
FETZNER	WILLIAM	RT 4 BOX 4259	HAYWARD	WI 54843
GERICH	MARTIN	RT 4 BOX 4309	HAYWARD	WI 54843
GROAT	LYMAN	RT 8 BOX 8318	HAYWARD	WI 54843
GUTSCH	RANDY	RT 4 BOX 4310	HAYWARD	WI 54843
GUTSCH	WAYNE	BOX 292	HAYWARD	WI 54843
GUYER	ROBERT	RT 7 BOX 7340	HAYWARD	WI 54843
HANSON	WILLIAM	RT 4 BOX 4326	HAYWARD	WI 54843
HARTNETT	ROGER	RT 10 BOX 151	HAYWARD	WI 54843
HEDRICK	GERALD	RT 9 BOX 9051	HAYWARD	WI 54843
HOCHSTEIN	GARY	BOX 802	HAYWARD	WI 54843
JUUL	ARNE	RT 7 BOX 7432	HAYWARD	WI 54843
KISER	ANGUS	RT 6	HAYWARD	WI 54843
KOCKA	MARK	RT 4 BOX 4306	HAYWARD	WI 54843
KORN	CLIFTON	RT 6 BOX 6776	HAYWARD	WI 54843
LEIGHTY	THOMAS	RT 9 BOX 9175	HAYWARD	WI 54843
LESNIAK	EDWARD	RT 9 BOX 9355	HAYWARD	WI 54843
LINDGREN	BRUCE	BOX 1247 RT 1	HAYWARD	WI 54843
LUGNER	ANDREW	RT 1 BOX 1428	HAYWARD	WI 54843
LYLE	JAMES	RT 9 BOX 9378	HAYWARD	WI 54843
MAINA	PETER	RT 7	HAYWARD	WI 54843
MAINA	RICHARD	RT 7	HAYWARD	WI 54843
MARIENFELD	KEN	RT 6 BOX 715	HAYWARD	WI 54843
MCCARTHY	EUGENE	RT 3 BOX 3286	HAYWARD	WI 54843
MCKENZIE	ROBERT	RT 9 BOX 9414	HAYWARD	WI 54843
MCMAHON JR	WILLIAM	RT 9 BOX 9396	HAYWARD	WI 54843
MYHRE	JOHN	RT 4 BOX 4162	HAYWARD	WI 54843
NEHRING	ROBERT	438 MAIN ST BOX 142	HAYWARD	WI 54843
NELSON	LEONARD	RT 9 BOX 9024	HAYWARD	WI 54843
OLSON	ROBERT	RT 4 BOX 4263	HAYWARD	WI 54843
OLSON	TRAVIS	RT 4	HAYWARD	WI 54843
PARNUM	ROBERT	BOX 651	HAYWARD	WI 54843
PAULLIN	DANIEL	RT 3 BOX 3441	HAYWARD	WI 54843
PERSSON	MICHAEL	RT 2 BOX 2005	HAYWARD	WI 54843
PETERS	RODNEY	RT 7 BOX 7189	HAYWARD	WI 54843
PETERSON	TERRANCE	RT 7 BOX 7420	HAYWARD	WI 54843
PRICE	TIMOTHY	RT 9 BOX 9235 SANDY BEACH	HAYWARD	WI 54843
PRIMLEY	DONALD	RT 4	HAYWARD	WI 54843
RINDAHL	JEFF	RT 3 BOX 3489	HAYWARD	WI 54843
ROBB	WALTER	RT 4 BOX 4223	HAYWARD	WI 54843

Area Guides: continued

ROSS	JERRY	RT 4 BOX 4007	HAYWARD	WI 54843
SHUMATE	NELSON	RT 5 BOX 5374	HAYWARD	WI 54843
SHUMWAY	WILLIAM	RT 3 BOX 3384A	HAYWARD	WI 54843
SISKO	STEVEN	RT 9 BOX 9338	HAYWARD	WI 54843
SOVA	LAWRENCE	RT 2 BOX 2437A	HAYWARD	WI 54843
SPEROS	JASON	RT 8 BOX 8151	HAYWARD	WI 54843
TON	ERIK	RT 2 BOX 2186	HAYWARD	WI 54843
TORGRIMSON	THOMAS	RT 4 BOX 4317	HAYWARD	WI 54843
TURNBULL JR	EMERY	RT 7 BOX 7761	HAYWARD	WI 54843
UNOLD	KENNETH	RT 7 BOX 7338	HAYWARD	WI 54843
VABALAITIS	BRUNO	RT 8 BOX 8211	HAYWARD	WI 54843
VAGHY	JAMES	RT 4 BOX 4222	HAYWARD	WI 54843
VILLA	JOHN	RT 5 BOX 5082C	HAYWARD	WI 54843
WATRAL	HARRY	620 S MINN AVE RT 6	HAYWARD	WI 54843
NELSON	EDWARD	BOX 305	MINONG	WI 54859
FEATHERLY	KENN	BOX 53	OJIBWA	WI 54862
WILLIAMS	EARL	BOX 28	OJIBWA	WI 54862
BART	FRANK	RT 1 BOX 189-2	RADISSON	WI 54867
HEATH	MARK	BOX 52	RADISSON	WI 54867
OLSON	WILLIAM	STAR RT BOX 126	SARONA	WI 54870
SCHULTZ	ANSEL	RT 1 BOX 177	SARONA	WI 54870
SLIZ	FRANK	RT 1, BOX 208	SARONA	WI 54870
SMITH	DOUGLAS	STAR RT	SARONA	WI 54870
WEIDEMAN	WAYNE	STAR RT BOX 182	SARONA	WI 54870
SCHULTZ	JOHN	RT 2 BOX 111	SHELL LAKE	WI 54871
MAURER JR	ROBERT	RT 2 BOX 628	SIREN	WI 54872
BLAIR	EDWARD	RT 2 BOX 2303	SPOONER	WI 54801
BOWN	LORN	RT 1 BOX 1150	SPOONER	WI 54801
HALVORSON	ARLEN	421 OAK ST	SPOONER	WI 54801
MURPHY	THOMAS	806 ELM	SPOONER	WI 54801
BLAIR JR	CHARLES	RT 1 BOX 1132	SPRINGBROOK	WI 54875
CZUB	TIMOTHY	RT 2 BOX 68D	STONE LAKE	WI 54876
KELLEY	JOE	RT 1 BOX 23	STONE LAKE	WI 54876
LAMBERT	GEORGE	RT 2 BOX 202	STONE LAKE	WI 54876
SMIALEK	MICHAEL	RT 2 BOX 241	STONE LAKE	WI 54876
SMIALEK	WILLIAM	RT 2 BOX 241	STONE LAKE	WI 54876
STRAND	RAYMOND	RT 2	STONE LAKE	WI 54876
BLANCLETTE	DALE	RT 1 BOX 1249	TREGO	WI 54888
FLUGER	FRED	RT 2 BOX 2064	TREGO	WI 54888
SHEPHERD	STUART	RT 2 BOX 2143	TREGO	WI 54888
ZARR	WILBUR	RT 1 BOX 1041	TREGO	WI 54888
CARLSON	LYLE	25597 HWY 35	WEBSTER	WI 54893
JOHNSON	JEFFREY	RT 2 BOX 284 STARR RD	WEBSTER	WI 54893
MCGARRY	TIMOTHY	7530 ASH ST W	WEBSTER	WI 54893
ECK	KENNETH	RT 2 BOX 8E	WINTER	WI 54896
FOLEY	RONALD	HC RT BOX 43	WINTER	WI 54896
NOFFKE	GARY	HC RT BOX 72	WINTER	WI 54896
SCHMITT	ROGER	HC RT BOX 21	WINTER	WI 54896
SEEFELDT	GENE	RT 1 BOX 236	WINTER	WI 54896
SHOTLIFF	DAVE	RT 2 BOX 36	WINTER	WI 54896
WITTBROT	THOMAS	BOX 298	WINTER	WI 54896
WRIGHT	WILLIAM	RT 1 BOX 253	WINTER	WI 54896

CAMPGROUNDS

Dispersed Camping:

Burnett County, permits dispersed camping.
Sawyer County, does not permit dispersed camping.
Washburn County, permits dispersed camping with a tent for less then 9 days. There are specific area and time restrictions. Check with the county forester.
Chequamegon National Forest, permits dispersed camping, except in posted areas.
St Croix National Scenic Riverway, does not permit dispersed camping. All camping must be at designated sites, including primative sites along the river.
WI DNR, does not permit dispersed camping on its properties.

Private Campgrounds:

Hayward Area:

Angler's Shady Bay Resort & Campground: water, elec, flush toilets, showers, firewood, picnic tables, boat launch, boats, swimming beach; Angler's Shady Bay Resort & Campground, Rt 3, Box 3242, Hayward, WI 54843; (715) 634-2097.

Arrowhead Resort & Lakeside Trailer Park: located 5 miles north of Hayward on Hwy 63, then turn left at the Nelson Lake Rd intersection, follow the signs; water & elec, toilets, showers, picnic tables, boat launch, beach, playground; on Nelson Lake; Arrowhead Resort & Lakeside Trailer Park, Rt 3, Box 3224, Hayward, WI 54843; (715) 634-2985.

Black Bear Lodge Resort & Campground: 25 campsites; water, elec, toilets, showers, picnic tables, dump station, boat launch, playground, beach; on Chippewa Flowage; Rt 5, Box 5393, Hayward, WI 54843; (715) 945-2676.

KOA Campground-Hayward: located 3 miles from Hayward on Hwy 63; water, elec, pull-through shaded sites, flush toilets, showers, firewood, picnic tables, dump station, laundry, boats, heated swimming pool, playground, camp store; Hayward KOA, Rt 3, Hayward, WI 54843; (715) 634-2331.

Lake Chippewa Campground: 100 campsites, some with full hook-ups, flush toilets, showers, firewood, picnic tables, dump station, boat launch, beach, playground; on the Chippewa Flowage; Lake Chippewa Campground, Rt 9, Box 9345, Hayward, WI 54843; (715) 462-3672.

Boulder Lodge Campground & Resort: located 22 miles east of Hayward on Hwy 77 East; grassy RV & tent sites, water & elec, flush toilets, hot showers, firewood, picnic tables, boats and motors, boat launch; on Ghost Lake in the Chequamegon National Forest; Boulder Lodge Campground & Resort, Rt 7, Hayward, WI 54843; (715) 462-3002.

Callahan Lake Resort & Campgrounds: wooded lakeside campsites, electricity, flush toilets, showers, picnic tables, dump station, playground, beach, boat launch; on Callahan Lake; Callahan Lake Resort & Campground, Rt 4, Box 4337, Callahan Rd, Hayward, WI 54843; (715) 462-3244 or (715) 462-3371.

Damcamp: located 8 miles north of Hayward on Hwy 27; a Good Sampark; RV & tent sites, some hook-ups, toilets, showers, picnic tables, dump station, boat launch, beach; on Nelson Lake; Rt 3, Hayward, WI 54843; (715) 634-2213.

East Fork Resort & Campground: some sites with water & elec, pit toilets only, firewood, picnic tables, boat launch, boats, swimming beach; East Fork Resort & Campground, Rt 1, Box 292, Winter, WI; (715) 266-5723.

Everson's Nelson Lake Lodge: RV park, full hook-ups, flush toilets, showers, picnic tables, dump station, playground, laundry, boat launch, beach; on Nelson Lake, Everson's Nelson Lake Lodge, Rt 3, Hayward, WI 54843; (715) 634-3750.

Musky Blvd. Resort & Campground: 35 wooded campsites, shoers, elec, dump station, firewood, sandy beach, playground; on Big Sissabagama Lake; Musky Blvd Resort & Campground, Rt 1, Stone Lake, WI; (715) 865-4545.

Musky Tale Resort: water, elec, boat launch, boats, motors, swimming beach, playground, liquor bar, snack bar; on the west fork of the Chippewa Flowage; Musky Tale Resort, Rt 4, Box 4259, Hayward, WI 54843; (715) 462-3838.

Nelson Lake Landing & RV Park: located 7 miles north of Hayward on Hwy 27; campground with 20 full hook-ups, restrooms, showers, liquor bar & grill, sandy beach, boat & motor rentals, boat ramp; Nelson Lake Landing & RV Park, Rt 3, Box 3104, Hayward, WI 54843; (715) 462-3807.

Reel Livin' Resort: wooded tent and trailer sites, water, elec, flush toilets, showers, picnic tables, playground, boat launch, boats, swimming beach; on Lost Land Lake; Reel Livin' Resort, Rt 7, Box 7395, Hayward, WI 54843; (715) 462-3822.

Revelle's Campground & Resort: lakeside camping, full hook-up trailer court, water & elec, toilets, showers, picnic tables, dump station, playgrounds, beach, boat launch; on Nelson Lake; Rt 3, Hayward, WI 54843; (715) 634-4216.

Sand Lake Pines Resort & Campground: located 11 miles south of Hayward on Hwy 27 & 70; full hook-ups, hot showers, playground, swimming; on Sand Lake; Rt 2, Box 36, Stone Lake, WI 54876; (715) 865-2309.

Trails End Resort & Campground: 50 sites, 12 with full hook-ups, toilets, showers, firewood, picnic tables, dump station, laundry, boat launch, beach; on Lac Court O'Reilles; Rt 2, Box 2339, Hayward, WI 54843; (715) 634-2423.

Wi-Do-To Campground: shaded lakeside campsites, full RV hook-ups, tent area, showers, beach, fishing, boat launch, motors, laundry, playground; Wi-Do-To Campground, Rt 7, Box 7820, Hayward, WI 54843; (715) 462-3807.

Spooner/Shell Lake Area:

Bashaw Lake Resort: located 3 miles SE of Hertel off Hwy 70; wooded sites, water & elec, dump station, fishing, boats, motors; on Bashaw Lake; Bashaw Lake Resort, Rt 2, Box 195, Shell Lake, WI 54871; (715) 468-2310.
Benoit Lake Campground: located 16 miles northwest of Spooner on Hwy G; 65 shaded sites, full hook-ups, sandy beach, playground, game room, camp store, laundry, fishing, boat, motor and canoe rental; on Benoit Lake; Benoit Lake Campground, Star Rt, Box 423, Spooner, WI 54801; (715) 635-2421.
Bulik's Wheel-in Campground: located just north of Spooner on Hwy 63; campground with mini golf, go kart track, drive-in restaurant; (715) 635-3801.
Highland Park Campgrounds: located 2 1/2 miles west of Spooner on Hwy 70, turn at Club 70, follow signs; on Cyclone Lake; Highland Park Campgrounds, Rt 1, Box 1065, Spooner, WI 54801; (715) 635-2462.
Northwinds Resort: located 17 miles northwest of Spooner on Cty Hwy G; campsites available, boat rental, liquor bar, food; on Rice Lake; Northwinds Resort, Star Rt, Box 438, Spooner, WI 54801; (715) 635-8089.
Red Barn Campground: located 2 miles east of Shell Lake on Cty Trunk B; full hookups, showers, playground, horse rides for children, nature trails, hayrides; (715) 468-2575.
Scenic View Campground: located 9 miles west of Spooner on Hwy 70; 32 sites, restrooms, hot showers, dump station, playground, beach; on Poquette Lake; Scenic View Campground, Rt 1, Box 1188, Spooner, WI 54801; (715) 468-2510.
Blueberry Hill Resort & Campground: lakefront sites, full hook-ups, showers, flush toilets, laundry, bar, cafe, boats, motors; Blueberry Hill Resort & Campground, Rt 1, Box 63, Couderay, WI 54828; (715) 945-2686.

Birchwood Area:

Big Chetac Resort & Campground: located 7 miles north of Birchwood; shaded sites, water & elec, flush toilets, showers, firewood, picnic tables, boat launch, boat, motor, canoe and paddleboat rental, swimming beach, playground; on Big Chetac Lake; Big Chetac Resort & Campground, Rt 1, Birchwood, WI; (715) 354-3865.
Birch Lakes Resort & Campground: located 2 miles north of Birchwood on Cty Hwy FF; water, elec, some primative campsites, picnic tables, showers, flush toilets, dump station, heated pool, playground; on Big Birch & Chetac Lakes; Birch Lake Resort & Campground, Rt 1, Birchwood, WI 54817; (715) 354-3880.
The Kamping Place on Devil's Lake (KOA Campground): located north of Rice Lake off of Hwy 53; campground with full hook-ups, dump station, showers, restrooms, playground, swimming pool, beach, laundry; The Kamping Place on Devil's Lake, P.O. Box 3, Haugen, WI 54841; (715) 234-2360.
Lincolnwood Resort: located 5 1/2 miles west of Birchwood on Hwy D; water, elec, picnic area, playground, horseshoes, volleyball, swimming raft, fishing; on Long Lake; Lincolnwood Resort, Rt 2, Birchwood, WI 54817; (715) 354-3533.
River's Edge Campground: located 1 mile south of Long Lake Dam on Gravel Pit Rd, follow signs; 15 campsites, water and elec, restrooms, handicap facilities; on the Brill River; Rt 2, Box 231, Birchwood, WI 54817; (715) 354-3798.
Spider Lake Resort: located 6 miles north of Birchwood on Cty Hwy T; 25 campsites, water, elec, paddleboat, boats and motor rental, cabins; on Spider Lake; Spider Lake Resort, Rt 2W, Birchwood, WI 54817; (715) 354-3723.
T.P. Resort & Campground: 34 wooded sites, 17 full hook-ups, 17 with elec, showers, dump station, firewood, laundry, playground, boat launch; on Big Chetac Lake; T.P. Resort & Campground, Rt 1, Birchwood, WI 54817; (715) 354-3538.

Trego Area:

Canfields Campgrounds: located at Jack's Canoe & Tube Rental, east on Hwy 63 towards Hayward, 2nd drive on the left; water & elec, swimming; Rt 2, Box 2018, Trego, WI 54888; (715) 635-3300 or (715) 635-3211.
Cardarelli's Resort & Campground: located 6 miles north of Spooner at Trego (53 & 63), turn right toward Hayward on 63, 1st driveway on left; water, elec, playground, camp store, beach, canoe & river trips available; on the Namekagon River; Cardarelli's Resort & Campground, Rt 2, Box 2019, Trego, WI 54888; (715) 386-2149.
Fluger's Campground: located 1/2 mile west of Trego on Cty E; water & elec, canoe rentals, shuttle service; on the Namekagon River; Fluger's Campground, Rt 2, Box 2064, Trego, WI 54888; (715) 635-2015.
Shangri-La Lodge, Inc. Campground & Resort: located 10 miles west of Minong on Hwy 77; showers, camp store, rec room, dump station, laundry; on Twin Lake; Shangri-La Lodge, Rt 1, Box 1253, Trego, WI 54888; (715) 466-2728.
Trego Park Campground: located on Hwy 53 north at Trego; 50 campsites with water, elec; on the Namekagon River; Trego Park Campground, Rt 2, Box 2037A, Trego, WI 54888; (715) 635-2091.
Whispering Pines Lodge: located 17 miles north of Spooner on Cty Trunk F; wooded sites, water, elec, restrooms, sandy beach, cabins; on Mathew Lake; Whispering Pines Lodge, Rt 1, Trego, WI 54888; (715) 466-2845.

Danbury Area/Webster/Webb Lake Area:

Birchwood Beach Campground & Resort: located on Spirit Lake in Frederick; quiet, scenic campsites, cabins, fishing, beach, playground, horseshoes; on Spirit Lake, 500+ acres; Rt 1, Box 168, Frederic, WI 54837; (715) 327-8965.
Bosley's Upper Webb Lake: located in northern Burnett Cty off of Hwy 77; water & elec, showers, dump station; on Webb Lake; Bosley's Upper Webb Lake, Box 537, Webb Lake, WI 54830; (715) 259-3363.
Devil's Lake Park Resort & Campground: located north of Webster off of Hwy 35; RV hook-ups, showers, boats, refreshments; Devil's Lake Park Resort & Campground, Rt 1, Box 257, Webster, WI 54893; (715) 866-7268.
DuFour's Pine Tree Campground: located 6 miles north of Webster on 35, 1/2 mile west on Hayden Lake Rd; 62 shady campsites, water & elec, sewer, pool, canoe rental, boat launch; on the Yellow River; DuFour's Pine Tree Campground, Box 335, Webster, WI 54893; (715) 645-7844.
Cedar Point Resort & Campgrounds: located south of Grantsburg off of Hwy 48; campsites, water & elec, swimming; on Big Trade Lake; Cedar Point Resort & Campgrounds, Rt 2, Box 530, Grantsburg, WI 54840; (715) 488-2224.
Gulden's Yellow River Campground: located east of the Danbury Wildlife Area; 45 campsites, full hook-ups, canoe rental; on the Yellow River; Gulden's Yellow River Campground, Box 67, Danbury, WI 54830; (715) 656-4402.
Hap's Camping: located near the north end of Gov. Knowles State Forest on the Clam Flowage; wilderness camping, water & elec, showers, hiking, fishing, boat rental; Hap's Camping, Rt 2, Danbury, WI 54830; (715) 656-3123.
Hi-Haven Resort: year round trailer sites, RV hook-ups; Hi-Haven Resort, Star Rt 2, Box 252, Danbury, WI 54830; (715) 866-7295.
Howe's Resort & Campgrounds: located off of Hwy 70 on Big Clam Lake; level, shady lakeside campsites, water & elec, sewer; Howe's Resort & Campgrounds, Rt 2, Box 607, Siren, WI 54872; (715) 349-5185.
Wagner's Port Sand Resort & Campground: located on Hwy 70, 16 miles west of Spooner; lakeshore sites, water/elec, dump station, laundry, picnic tables, beach; on Big Sand Lake; Rt 2, Box 453, Webster, WI 54893; (715) 349-2395.
Williams Cedar Point Resort: wooded lakefront campsites with water & elec, showers, picnic tables, playground, beach, boat launch; on Big Trade Lake; Williams Cedar Point Resort, Rt 2, Box 530, Grantsburg, WI 54840; (715) 488-2224.
Winberg's Resort & Campgrounds: located off Hwy 70 on Lower Clam Lake; level, shady campsites, water & elec, dump station, sewer, sandy beach; Winber's Resort & Campgrounds, Rt 2, Box 560, Siren, WI 54872; (715) 349-5160.

Municipal Campgrounds:

Doolittle Village Park, Birchwood: located 1 mile north of Birchwood on Cty Trunk D, turn right on Hinman Dr; 40 campsites, 30 with elec, flush toilets, dump station, picnic area, sandy beach, boat launch, fishing; on Birch Lake; Doolittle Village Park, Birchwood, WI 54817; days (715) 354-3300, nights (715) 354-3863.
Shell Lake Campground, Shell Lake: located next to the Shell Lake public beach; 45 sites, most with water & elec, showers, dump station, firewood, swimming beach with lifeguard, basketball, volleyball, horseshoes, playground; during the summer-(715) 468-7846, off season-(715) 468-7679.
Ojibaw Park: 1 mile east of Ojibwa on Hwy 70; 6 units; elec, toilets, picnic area; Operated by the Winter Lions Club, Winter, WI 54896, (715) 266-2752.

County Campgrounds:

Totogatic Park Campground: located on the west side of the Minong Flowage; 75 campsites, 25 with elec, flush toilets, docking facilities, fishing, picnic area; owned and operated by Washburn County.

AREA ACTIVITIES

Attractions:

Chippewa Queen: located on the Chippewa Flowage; 1 1/2 hour cruises daily through Aug 31, dinner, cocktail and fall color cruises; (715) 462-3874.
M & M Sport: located on Hwy B outside of Hayward; parasailing; (715) 634-3146.
Raging Rapids Waterslide: located 3 miles north of Hayward on Hwy 63, next to KOA Campground; Hayward, WI; (715) 634-2472.
Scheer's Lumberjack Shows: located 1 mile south of Hayward on Hwy B at the Lumberjack Bowl Pancake House; world class lumberjacks compete in a variety of events, refreshments, dinner shows; Hayward, WI.

Boat Rentals:

Big Bear Enterprises: located in the Flambeau River State Forest, HC Rte, Box 50, Winter, WI 54896; (715) 332-5261.
Chippewa Flowage Boat Rentals: Box 4288, Hayward, WI 54843; (715) 462-3874.
Dave's Outboard: pontoon and speedboat rentals; Sarona, WI 54870; (715) 354-3430.
Fluger's Canoe Rental: located west of Trego, off Cty Hwy E on South River Rd; Rt 2, Box 2064, Trego, WI 54888; (715) 635-2015.
Jack's Canoe & Tube Rental: located east on Hwy 63 towards Hayward, 2nd drive on the left; Rt 2, Box 2018, Trego, WI 54888; (715) 635-3300.
Namekagon Canoe Rental: located at Mack Lake Tavern, Rt 1, Trego, WI 54888; (715) 466-5181.
Pappy's Bar, Canoe Rental & Shuttle: Rt 1. Box 1302, Trego, WI 54888; (715) 466-2568.
Sliz' Reel-Em Inn: boat and motor rental; Rt 1, Box 208, Sarona, WI 54870; (715) 354-3700.
Skorseth's Wild River Inn Canoe & Tube Rental: located on Hwy 27 South, Hayward; (715) 634-2631.
Wild River Outfitters: canoe rental; Rt 2, Box 1138, Hwy 70, Grantsburg, WI 54840; (715) 463-2254.

Horseback Riding:

Hay Lake Ranch: from Hwy 63, turn left on Hwy F; 1-2 hour trail rides, 5-6 hour trail rides, overnight pack trips; Rt 1, Box 1490, Springbrook, WI 54875; (715) 766-2305.
Lakeside Trails: located at Birchwood Beach Campground & Resort on Spirit Lake; guided horseback; (715) 327-8965.
Mrotek's Stables: located 10 miles east of Hayward on Hwy 77; guided trail rides; (715) 462-3674.
Timberland Trails: located west of Hayward on Hwy B, 1/4 mile east of the junction of Hwys B and A; riding stable; (715) 462-3499.

Museums:

Al Capone's Hideout Museum: located 6 miles north of Couderay on Hwy CC; includes main lodge, garage, guntower, bunk house, jail cell, gift shop, bar, restaurant, guided tours; (715) 945-2746.
Burnett County Historical and Natural Society Museum: located at the Webster Fair Grounds; Webster, WI.
Clam Lake Wood Carvers Museum: located on Hwy 77 in Clam Lake; Clam Lake, WI.
Fishing Hall of Fame: located 3 blocks south on Hwy 27 in Hayward; museum in the shape of a 500 ton musky; antique outboard motors, fishing equipment, 400 fish mounts of fresh water fish, refreshments, gift shop; Box 33, Hall of Fame Drive, Hayward, WI 54843; (715) 634-4440.
Forts Folle Avoine: located 4 miles north of Webster on Hwy 35 to Hwy U, go west on U for 2.6 miles, follow signs; reconstruction of an 1802 fur trading post, filled with artifacts of the original structure being unearthed by archeologists, guided tours provided; Burnett County Historical Society, P.O. Box 31, Siren, WI 54872; (715) 349-2219.
Grantsburg Area Museum: displays of local history, free admission; 133 W. Wisconsin Ave, Grantsburg, WI
Historyland: located 1 mile east of Hayward on Cty Trunk B; Chippewa Indian village and logging camp, cook shanty restaurant, guided tours, boat trips; Hayward, WI 54843; (715) 634-2579 or (800) 255-5937.
Pioneer Village Museum: located 1 1/2 miles westof Cameron on Museum Rd or Cty Hwy W; 21 pioneer buildings.
Sawyer County Historical Museum: located on 4th & Wisconsin in Hayward.
St Francis Mission: located 15 miles SE of Hayward on Cty Hwy E in Reserve; mission built in 1880 by the Franciscan Order, features handcrafted Chippewa items; Reserve, WI.
Washburn County Historical Museum: located in downtown Shell Lake, off Hwy 63; logging and railroad artifacts; 200 West 2nd St, Shell Lake, WI 54871; (715) 635-8698.

Scenic Areas:

Artesian Wells: located 3 miles south of Hauer on Cty Trunk F.
Brunet Falls: located 4 miles south of Winter on J, across bridge, take trail to west.
Ghost Hill: located 22 miles east of Hayward on Hwy 77, north on FR 175; scenic overlook, wilderness picnic area.
Largest White Pine in Wisconsin: located south of Winter on Cty Hwy W, south on Cty M in the Flambeau State Forest.
Pipestone Falls: located 6 miles north of Radisson on Cty Hwy H.
White Pine Nature Center: located off Cty Hwy B on Hwy A, look for sign.

Zoos & Wildlife Displays:

Wilderness Walk: located 3 miles south of Hayward on Hwy 27; recreational park, wild and domestic animals, petting zoo, western town, gift shop, refreshments; Rt 2, Box 2005, Hayward, WI 54843; (715) 634-2893.

EMERGENCY NUMBERS

Should you need help, listed below are the phone numbers for the sheriff and local hospitals.

Sheriff:

Burnett County: (715)-349-2121; emergency 1-800-472-6730.
Sawyer County: (715) 634-4858
Washburn County: (715) 468-2721.

Wisconsin State Road Condition Report: (800) 762-3947

Hospitals:

<u>Burnett General Hospital</u>, 257 W. St. George Ave, Grantsburg, WI 54840, (715) 463-5353
<u>Hayward Area Memorial Hospital</u>, Hwy 27/77, Rt 3, Box 3999, Hayward, WI 54843, (715) 634-8911
<u>Indian Head Medical Center</u>, 215 4th St West, Shell Lake, WI 54871, (715) 468-7833.
<u>Spooner Community Memorial Hospital</u>: 707 Ash St, Spooner, WI 54801, (715) 635-2111.

OTHER INFORMATION SOURCES

County:

Burnett County Forestry Office, Rt 1, Box 300-106, Siren, WI, 54872-9786, (715) 349-2157.
Sawyer County Forestry Dept, Courthouse, PO Box 351, Hayward, WI 54843, (715) 634-4839.
Washburn County, Forester, 342 Walnut St, Spooner, WI 54801, (715) 635-2886

State: WI Department of Natural Resources:

WI DNR, Park Falls Area Headquarters, Case Ave., PO Box 220 Park Falls, WI 54552, (715) 762-3204. Covers Price, Taylor, Rusk and Sawyer Counties.
WI DNR, Cumberland Area Headquarters, 1341 2nd Ave, Box 397, Cumberland, WI 54829, (715) 822-3590. Covers Burnett, Barron, Polk and Washburn Counties.
WI DNR Ranger Station, Hwy 70, Box 367, Grantsburg, WI 54840, (715) 463-2897.
WI DNR Ranger Station, Hwy 27 S, Rt 2, Box 2003, Hayward, WI 54843, (715) 634-2688
WI DNR Ranger Station, Box 187, Winter, WI 54896, (715) 266-3511.
WI DNR Flambeau State Forest, HCR Box 51, WInter, WI 54896, (715) 332-5271.
WI DNR Governor Knowles State Forest, Hwy 70, Box 367, Grantsburg, WI 54840, (715) 463-2898.

Federal:

U.S. Forest Service

Chequamegon National Forest, Forest Headquarters, 1170 4th Ave South, Park Falls, WI 54552, (715) 762-2461.
Hayward Ranger District Headquarters, is located on Hwy 27/77 N, Hayward, WI 54843, (715) 634-4821.

National Park Service:

St Croix National Scenic Riverway Information Center, Trego, PO Box 100, Trego, WI 54888, (715) 635-8346.
St Croix National Scenic Riverway Headquarters, St Croix Falls, PO Box 708, St Croix, WI 54024, (715) 483-3287.

Chambers of Commerce:

Birchwood Area Lakes Ass'n, PO Box 100, Birchwood, WI 54817, (715) 354-7846
Burnett County Dept of Tourism & Infor., Rt 1, Box 300-112, Siren, WI 54872, (715) 349-2979
Burnett County Resort/Campground Owners Assoc., PO Box 48, Siren, WI 54872, (715) 349-2000
Grantsburg Chamber of Commerce, 416 South Pine St, Box 451, Grantsburg, WI 54840, (715) 463-2405
Hayward Chamber of Commerce, Box 726, Hayward, WI 54843, (800) 472-3474
Musky & Snow Country, Box 404, Hayward, WI 54843
Sarona, Long Lake Chamber of Commerce, Rt 1, Box 327, Sarona, WI 54870, (715) 635-3976
Sawyer County, Recreation Assoc., Box 351, Hayward, WI 54843, (715) 634-4839
Shell Lake, Chamber of Commerce, Box 121, Shell Lake, WI 54871, (715) 468-2256
Siren Area, Chamber of Commerce, President, Siren, WI 54234, (715) 349-2440
Spooner Chamber of Commerce, PO Box 406, Spooner, WI 54801, (715) 635-2168
Stone Lake, Chamber of Commerce, Rt 1, Stone Lake, WI 54876, (715) 865-4545
Trego Chamber of Commerce, Rt 2, Trego, WI 54888, (715) 635-9168
Washburn County, Tourism Assoc., Rt 1, Box 327, Sarona, WI 54870, (800) 367-3306
Webster, Chamber of Commerce, PO Box 48, Webster, WI 54893, (715) 866-4251
Winter Tourism Information Center, Rt 1, Box 255, Winter, WI 54896, (715) 266-2200

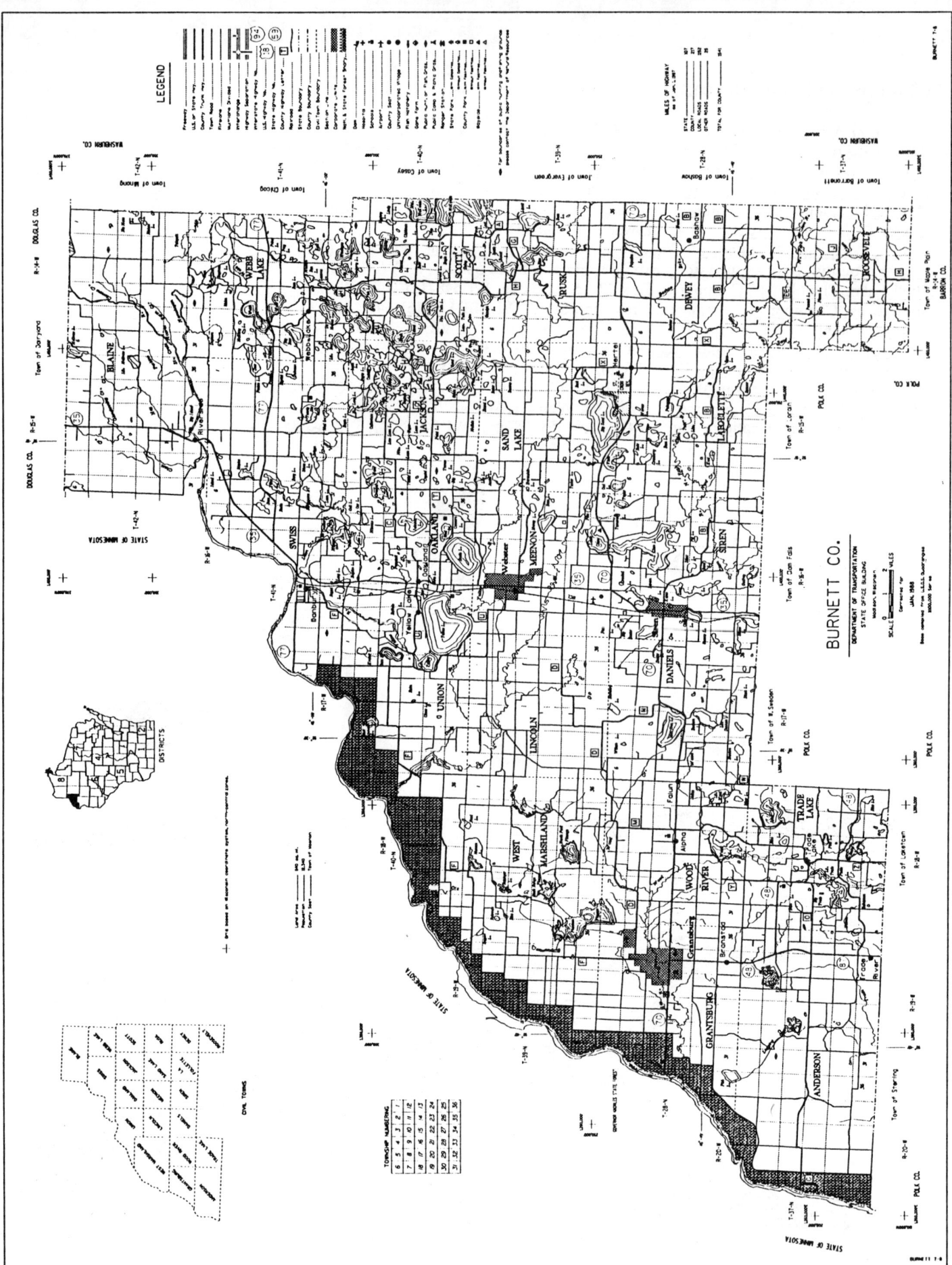

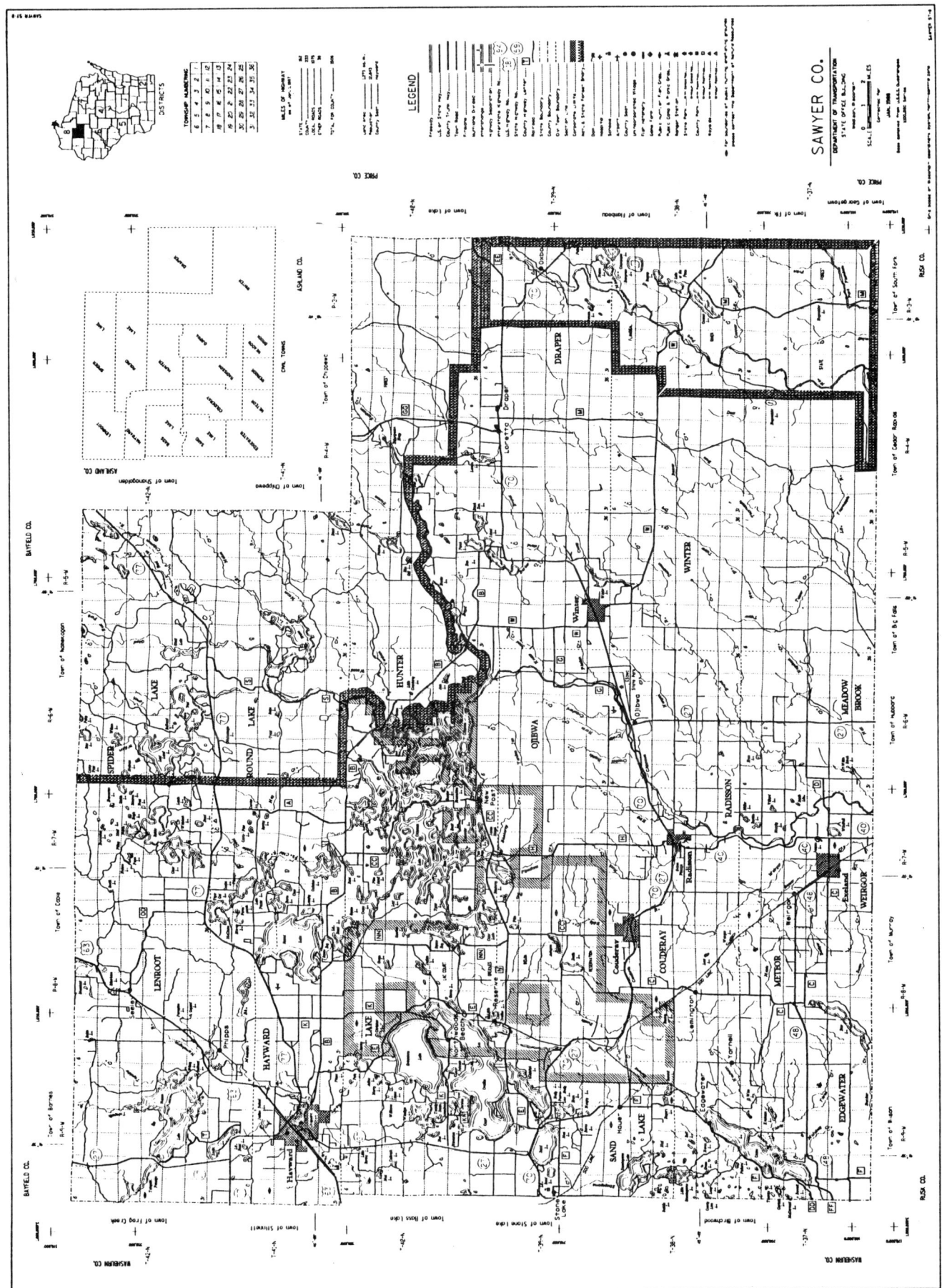

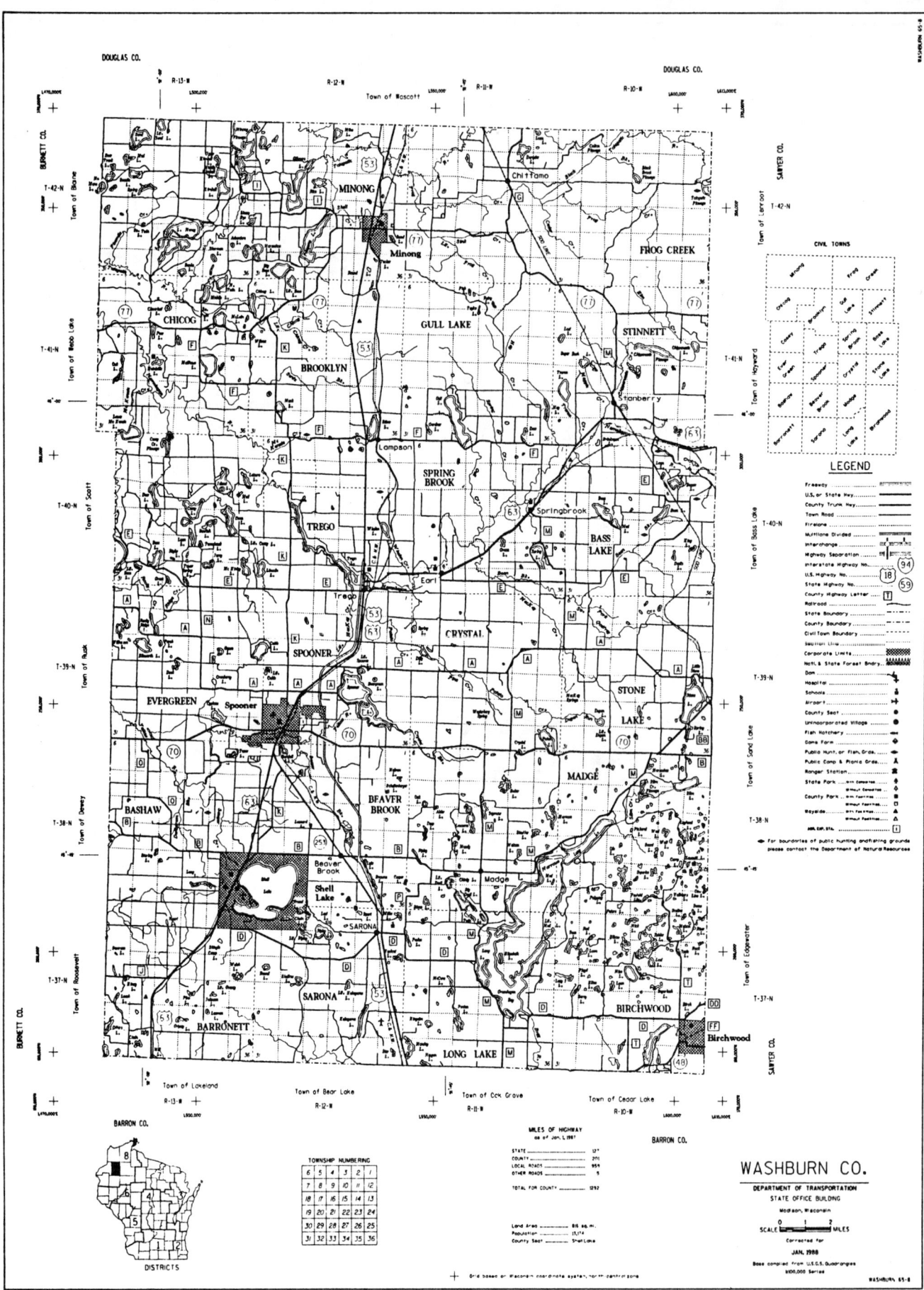

HOW WISCONSIN'S LANDSCAPE WAS SHAPED BY THE GLACIERS

"Nowhere is the evidence of the glaciers better preserved than across Wisconsin. As you drive around the State you can see many lakes and ponds, forested hills and ridges, and gently rolling farmlands that remind us of the glacier's visit. Moving slowly, glaciers attacked the land, grinding bedrock into fine powder. Then, once released the staggering torrents of meltwater tore across the landscape, carving the gorge known as the Dalles of the St. Croix River. The waters' sustained force is evident in potholes abraded into bedrock. But most apparent on the Wisconsin landscape are features resulting from stagnant ice conditions and from deposition. When the forward movement of glaciers reached equilibrium with meltback, stagnant ice resulted. Conical hills, called **kames**, grew as debris washed through holes in the ice. As stream tunnels beneath glaciers filled up with debris, **eskers** formed. Eskers look like inverted streams winding across the landscape. Depressions in the ground, known as **kettles**, formed as stranded ice blocks melted and the debris covering them subsided. Some kettles are simple bowl-shaped depressions, but others are now bogs, marshes, or lakes. Features deposited by the ice itself, not by meltwater, include ground and end moraines, drumlins and erratics. **Ground moraines** were deposited under moving ice, or were just let down like a carpet as stagnant ice melted. **End moraines** represent glacial dumps at the edge of moving ice. **Erratics** are rocks carried from a distance in or on the ice. **Drumlins** look like the upside-down bowls of teaspoons, or halves of teardrops. They were built up in layers beneath moving glaciers and usually occur in groups behind the end moraines."

Quote and pictures from WI DNR & National Park Service

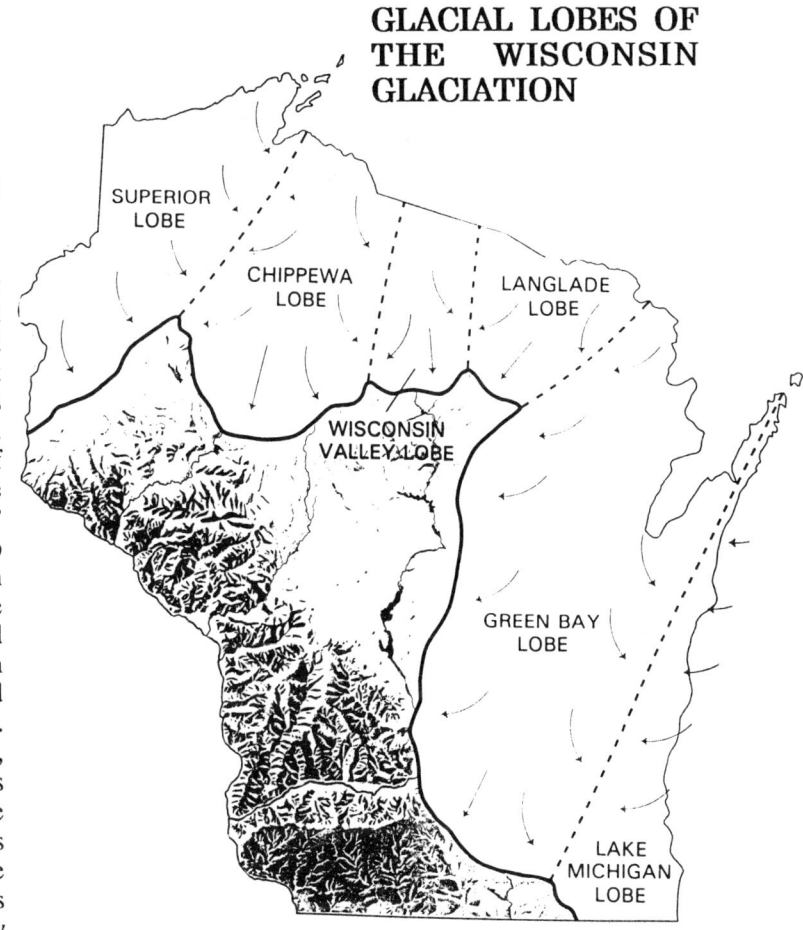

GLACIAL LOBES OF THE WISCONSIN GLACIATION

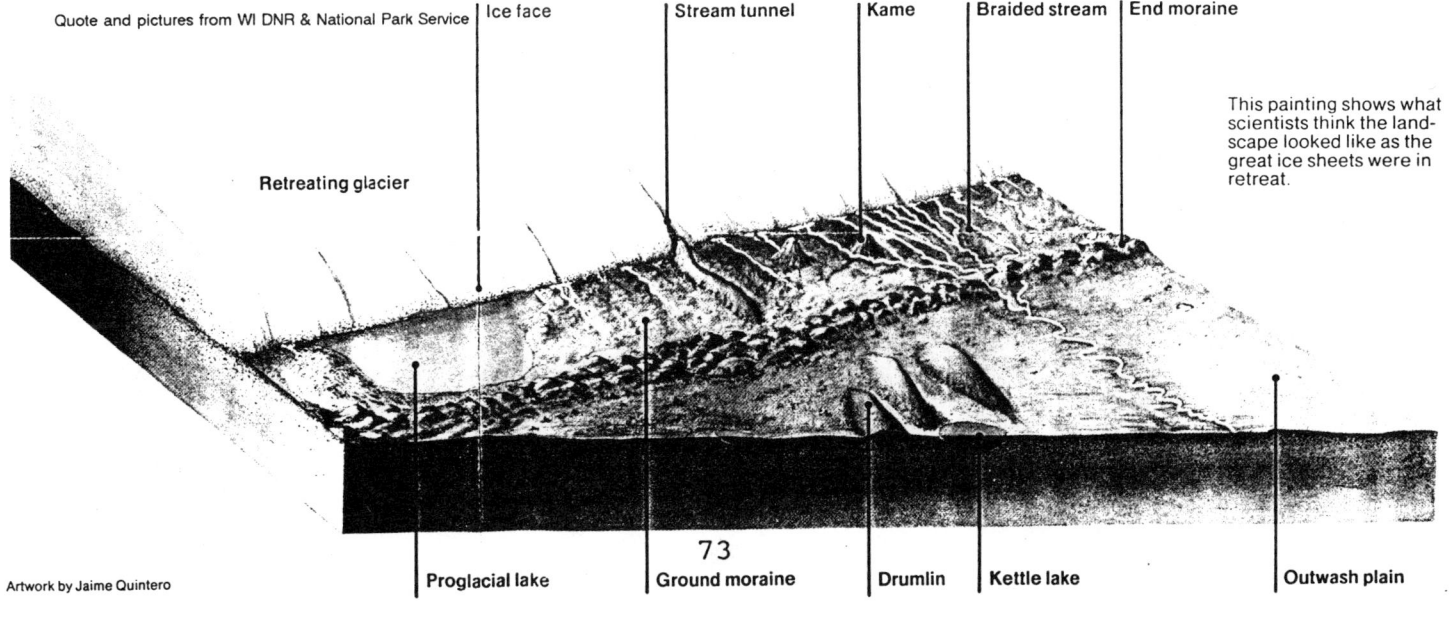

This painting shows what scientists think the landscape looked like as the great ice sheets were in retreat.

Artwork by Jaime Quintero

AREA 3
Blue Hills Area
Barron, Polk and Rusk Counties

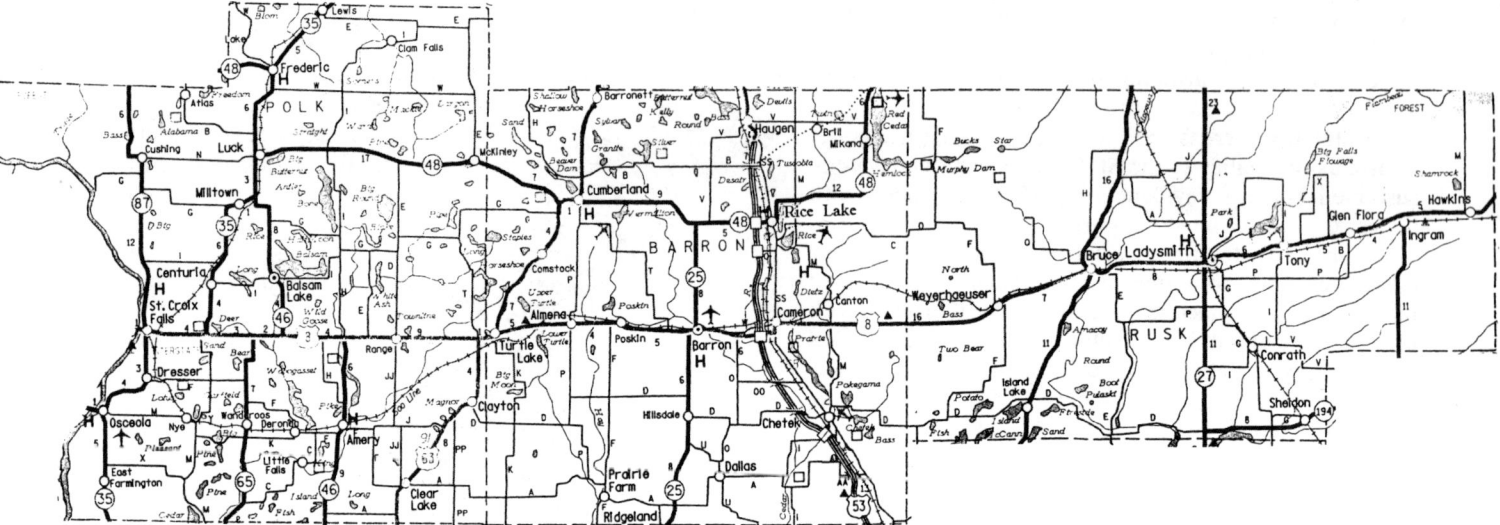

The Blue Hills of Barron and Rusk Counties is an area of quartzite ridges and glacial end moraines created by the receding Wisconsin Glacier. These hills rise 300-600 feet above the surrounding countryside and are 25 miles long and nearly 10 miles wide. It is estimated that these hills were once part of an ancient, massive mountain range, equal in size to the Rocky Mountains. Overlying glacial till is thin, so consequently, the water storage capacity of this region is small and there are no natural lakes. South of the Blue Hills the young drift area of the terminal moraine is hilly and contains a large number of kettle holes, bogs, irregularly shaped lakes and swamps, characteristic of glacial landscape.

West of the Blue Hills, in Polk County, the geography of the land is considerably different. Ten thousand years ago glacial melt water from the receding Wisconsin Glacier filled the Lake Superior water basin and overflowed to the southwest. The escaping water ran with such volume and force that it created a new route for the St Croix River, forming the large gorge now known as the Dalles of the St. Croix. Rocks, carried by the torrent of water, carved potholes and magnificent formations out of the lava rock of the gorge on both sides of the river, much of which can still be seen today.

In between the St. Croix River and the Blue Hills are the outwash plains of Polk and Barron Counties. The landscape is dotted with a large number of lakes and streams which provides for great fishing and canoeing.

There are a number of cities plus a scattering of unincorporated settlements.
In **Barron County**, Barron, the county seat, is located in the center of the county at the junction of Hwy 8 and 25. To the east on Hwy 8 is Cameron and to the west is Almena and Turtle Lake. To the northeast on Hwy 53 is Rice Lake and to the southeast is Chetek. Cumberland is to the northwest on Hwy 48 & 63. To the south on Hwy 25 and east on Cty A is Dallas and west on Cty A is Prairie Farm.
In **Polk County**, Balsam Lake, the county seat, is located on Hwy 46 in the middle of the county. Along Hwy 35 which runs from the southwest corner to the north central end of the county is Osceola, Dresser, St Croix Falls, Centuria, Milltown, Luck and Frederic. In the southeast corner along Hwy 63 is Clear Lake and Clayton.
In **Rusk County**, Ladysmith, the county seat is located in the central of the county on Hwy 8. To the east is Tony, Glen Flora, Ingram and Hawkins. To the west is Bruce and Weyerhauser. To the south on Cty G is Conrath and Sheldon.

RECREATIONAL WATERS

Lakes and Flowages:

There are 737 named, (43,524 acres) and 693 unnamed, (3,128 acres) lakes in the region, including several man-made flowages. This accounts for 9.6 % of the total number of Wisconsin lakes covering 4.9 % of the state's total inland surface water. Many of the lake closer to Minnesota have been developed with homes and cottages.

Barron County has 110 named, (15,958 acres) and 257 unnamed, (1,324 acres), lakes. Several noted lakes include:

Chetek Chain of Lakes, is located in the southeast corner of the county at Chetek, 6 miles south of Hwy 8 on Hwy 53. There are 6 interconnected lakes including Lake Chetek, 770 acres; Ten Mile, 376 acres; Pokegama Lake, 509 acres; Prairie Lake, 1,534 acres; Moose Ear, 34 acres; and Ojaski Lake, 578 acres. These lakes are shallow with depth of 20 ft. The shoreline is a combination of forested uplands and wetland areas with development on all the lakes. Access is available in Chetek and throughout the chain. Fishery is a good mix of panfish and game fish without any muskies.
Red Cedar Lake Chain, (Red Cedar Lake, 1,841 acres, Hemlock Lake, 357 acres & Balsam Lake, 295 acres) is located in the extreme northeastern corner of the county with Hwy 48 along the west shore. Access can be found on the west shore of each lake and at a county park on Red Cedar. The shorelines have been developed. The fishery is good with no muskies present.

Polk County has 172 named, (20,525 acres) and 259 unnamed, (1,032 acres) lakes. The more noted ones include:

Balsam Lake, 2,054 acres, is located just north of Balsam Lake with Hwy 46 on the west shore and Cty I on the south shore. It has an irregular shoreline with several long, narrow bays and islands. Access can be found in town and on each end of the lake. Fisheries include walleyes, northern pike and panfish; there are no muskies.
Bone Lake, 1,781 acres, is located 4 miles north of Balsam Lake on Hwy 46, then 3 miles east on Cty G and north on Cty GG. Town roads for the next 4 miles to the east will take you to the lake. The lake is considered excellent for muskie with bass and panfish but no walleye.
Wapogasset Lake, 1,186 acres is located 2 miles west of Amery, Hwy 46, on Cty F, then Cty C north along the east shore or Cty F to the west shore. There are a number of bays and islands with the fishery having a little bit of everything.

Rusk County has 73 named, (7,041 acres) and 177 unnamed, (772 acres) lakes. Two flowages make up over half the surface water acreage.

Dairyland Flowage, 1,747 acres, is located 2.5 miles northeast of Ladysmith. Cty J is off the west shore and Cty I cuts across it. This "S" shaped flowage on the Flambeau River is narrow and meandering. Access can be found near the dam or at Josie Cr County Park. Fishery is a mix of game and panfish.
Island Lake Chain, is located in the southwest corner of the county. From Bruce and Hwy 8 head south on Hwy 40. The lakes start 1 mile south of Cty D. Either take Cty D to the west and south on Plummer Rd or stay on Hwy 40 and west on 44 Rd. There are 4 lakes in a straight line that make up the chain. There is Island, 525 acres; McCann, 133; Clear, 19; and Chain, 469 acres. These lakes provide some deeper waters than many chains. Except for Clear, 19 ft deep, maximum depths are from 38 to 78 ft. Fisheries include northern pike, muskie, walleye, and bass plus panfish.

Rivers:

Red Cedar River, begins its flow 2 miles south of Hwy 8 and west of Hwy 53. The river provides a good float along its meander 25 miles, south to the Dunn County line. Cty A, OO, D and I cross the river. There is a excellent warm water fishery including smallmouth bass, walleye and muskies.
Flambeau River, enters the northeastern corner of the county in the Flambeau State Forest and flows 24 miles southwest through the county. After leaving the state forest you first encounter Big Falls Flowage Dam and then Dairyland Flowage. The river environment reflects this by its slow flow along a wide river. From Dairyland Flowage it is a short distance to Ladysmith and another dam. Below Ladysmith there is 1 other dam before the river joins the Chippewa. Shoreline is forested uplands and agriculture with the stream bed gravel and boulders. The river fishery includes most game fish, including catfish.
Chippewa River, flows freely 40 miles south through the western half of the county with no impoundment until it reaches Holcombe Flowage at the county line. The river is a meandering, shallow river with half of the shoreline in farmlands. State and county roads parallel much of the river. Access is available at road crossings. Fisheries include catfish, northern pike, walleye and muskies.

Trout Streams:

The area is known for its trout streams. There are 93 streams classed as trout waters, covering 324 miles . There are 117 miles of Class I, 118 Miles of Class II and 89 miles of Class III. Several of the noted streams include the McKenzie Cr in Polk; Yellow, Hingel, Barron; South Fork Main Cr in Rusk County.

Public Lands

County:

Barron County, has 14,000 acres of county forest with the larger blocks along the northern and eastern borders. There are several small parcels of forest lands, scattered throughout the county. The main blocks are:

Maple Plains, 2,584 acres, is located in the extreme northwestern corner of the county. There are six individuals parcels with a general boundary of Hwy 63 on the east with 26 1/2 Ave to Cty H, then 28 1/2 Ave to 26 1/2 Ave to the county line for the southern boundary.
Bear Lake, 4,121 acres, is located on the Washburn County line and west of Bear Lake. 16th St, northwest of Cty V, splits the parcel in half.
Milkana, 1,990 acres, is located just west of Milkana on Hwy 48. This forest block is split by Swamp Rd (26th) Ave) with Cty V to the north and the Red Cedar River to the south.
Cedar Lake, 2,360 acres, is located in the extreme northeast corner of the county, just east of Cedar Lake and north of Hemlock Lake and on the Burnett and Rusk County lines. Access is from Hwy 48, south on Cty F and west on either Valley Rd or Bolgers Rd.
Doyle, 1,720 acres, is located east of Rice Lake and near the Rusk County line. Rock Cr forms the south border and Cty C, 19 & 19 1/2 Ave form the north.
Silver Cr, 1,120 acres, is located in the southwest corner of the county on Silver Cr. The general boundary is Cty D on the north, Cty P on the northeast, 4 1/2 Ave on the south and 5th St on the west.

Polk County, maintains 15,000 acres in two forest units.

Sterling County Forest, the largest unit, is in the northwestern corner of the county. It is bordered by Governor Knowles State Forest on the west, south and east sides, and Burnett County on the north. Access to the forest are town roads and Cty G west of Hwy 87.
Loraine County Forest, is located in the northeast corner of the county. From McKinley on Hwy 48 travel north on Cty E 5 miles. The forest is to the east and extends north to state owned property.

Rusk County, has 90,000 acres in the of the county.

Blue Hills Unit, 65,000 acres, is in the northwestern corner of the county. A general boundary would include 3 miles north of Hwy 8 to Weyerhauser, north on Norwegian Rd, east on Cty O, east on Mansky Rd, north on Dearhamer Rd, east on Town Line Rd and north on Hwy H.
Lea Lake Unit, 7,700 acres, is on the Sawyer County line. The general boundary starts 6 1/2 miles north of Ladysmith on Hwy 27. Hwy 27 is on the west side and Cty J is on the south side.
Cedar Rapids Unit, 15,000 acres, is in the northeast area of the county and just south of the Flambeau River State Forest. The general boundary is 1 mile west of Cty M, 3 to 4 miles north of Hwy 8 and east of the Flambeau River.
Big Bend Unit, 1,200 acres, is located about 9 miles south of Bruce on Hwy 40, then east 2 1/2 miles on Cty D. The unit is to the south for 2 miles.

State:

Barron County:

Grassy Lake Wildlife Area, 360 acres, is located about 4 miles east of Cumberland on Cty B, then 1 mile north on 10th St. This area includes several small lakes and uplands with timber and marshes which are managed for ruffed grouse and deer.
Yellow River, 708 acres, is located 5 miles east of Cumberland on Hwy 48 and extends north 1 mile and south 2 miles. This project provides access to the Yellow River and habitat for small game and non-game animals. The terrain includes the streams with marsh areas and timbered uplands.

The following areas are managed primarily for waterfowl; however other game and non-game animals will be present. The habitat will normally be marsh, brush lowlands, creek bottoms and upland timber fringes.
Loon Lake, 2,392 acres, starts 3 miles north of Turtle Lake, Hwy 8, on Hwy 63. The project is to the west and north.
Lighting Creek, 329 acres, is located 1 mile northwest of Almena, Hwy 8, on 15 1/2 St.
Sweeny Pond Creek, 281 acres, is located 4 miles west of Barron on Hwy 8, then south 1 mile on 10th St.
Quaderer Cr, 350 acres, is located 1 mile west of Barron on Hwy 8, then 1 mile south on 13th St.
New Auburn, 1,219 acres, is located 4 miles southeast of Chetek on Cty S. Project is to the east.

Polk County:

McKenzie Creek Wildlife Area, 5,490 acres, is located eight miles east of Frederic on Cty W. The project extends 3 miles to the north with Cty O on the east side. A second parcel is 1 mile to the south with Cty O on the southern border. There are lakes, timbered uplands along with stream bottoms throughout the project. Habitat is managed for deer, waterfowl and small game animals.
Rice Beds Creek, 3,101 acres, is located 6 miles west of Turtle Lake (county line) on Hwy 8, then 4 miles north on Cty D to the southern border of the project. Cty V is on the southern border with Cty G on the north. The terrain includes stream bottoms with marsh lands and timbered uplands. Management is for waterfowl, deer and small game.
Joel Marsh Wildlife Area, 829 acres, starts 3 miles west of Turtle Lake (county line) on Hwy 8. The project is to the south and west. The area is a mix of wetlands, woodlot, brush and grass lands. It is managed for waterfowl, deer and small game animals.

These are smaller projects managed to provide access to area streams and habitat for waterfowl and other wildlife.
Balsam Branch, 180 acres, is located 7 miles east of St Croix Falls on Hwy 8, then 3 miles south on Hwy 65 and 2 miles east on Cty C. Project is to the north.
Snake Creek, 200 acres, is located 2 miles south of Amery on Hwy 46, then east on 35th and north 1/4 mile on 90th St. Project is to the east.
Parker Cr, 219 acres, is located 2 miles south of Amery on Hwy 46, then west 1 mile on 35th.
Behning Cr, 170 acres, is located 3.5 miles east of Hwy 35 at Dresser on Cty F and south 1.5 miles on 195th St.

Governor Knowles State Forest, has its start in Polk County along the St Croix River, but the majority of the property is in Burnett County. Please see page 44 for more information.

Rusk County:

Potato Creek Wildlife Area, is located in the southwest corner of the county. Take Cty D 1 1/2 miles west of Hwy 40, then west on town road to landing on the Potato River. This 984 acre wildlife area was established for waterfowl habitat. Besides the impoundment there are 25 potholes and numerous ponds up to 10 acres in size. The area along the creek is bog and sedges with the uplands of hardwoods and croplands.

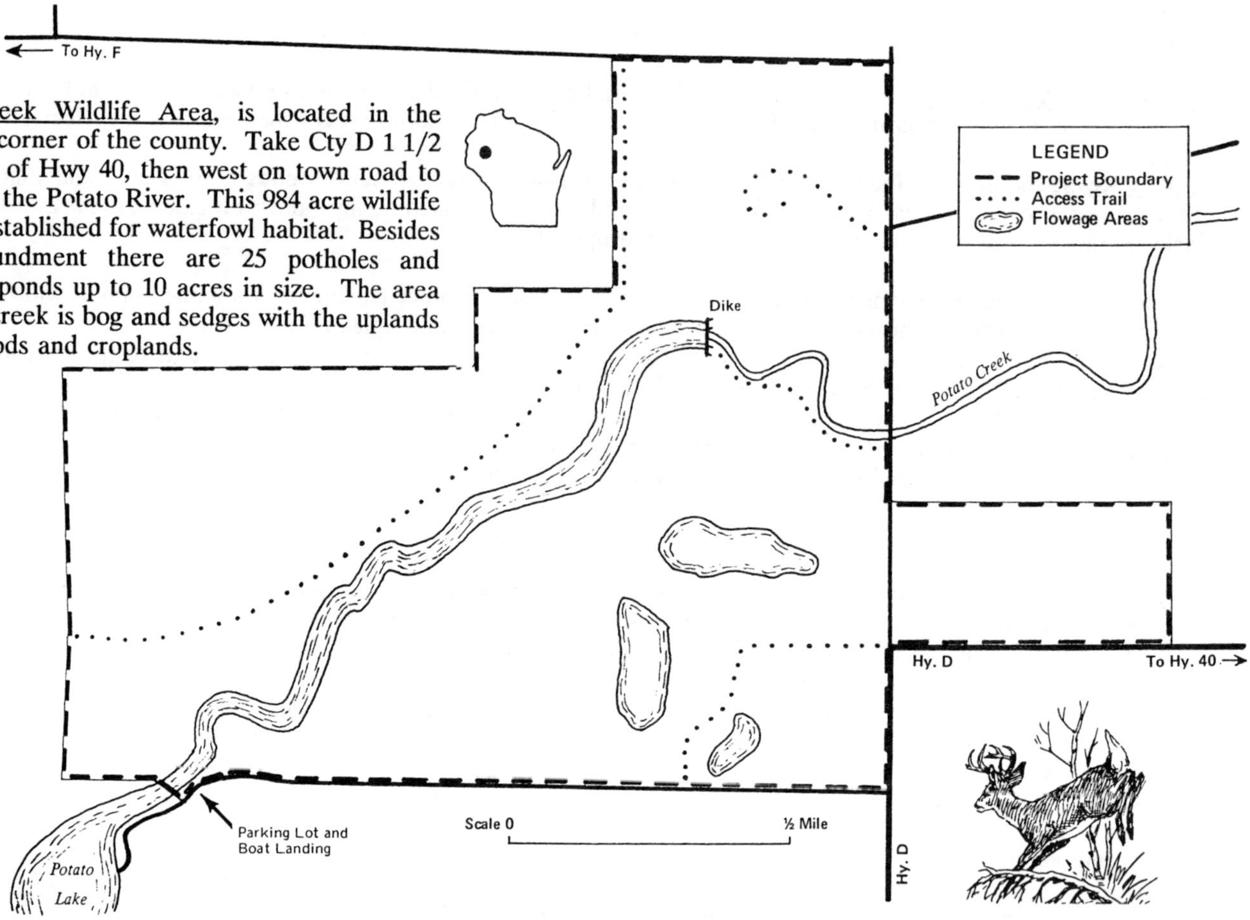

Washington Creek Wildlife Area, 516 acres, is located 9 miles south of Bruce, Hwy 8, on Cty E. This area was developed as waterfowl habitat. There is a 230 acre flowage fringed by bogs and sedge marsh. The highlands are a mix of oaks and aspens. Access to the flowage is by small boats off Cty E. The area supports waterfowl, fur bearers and upland game plus nongame species

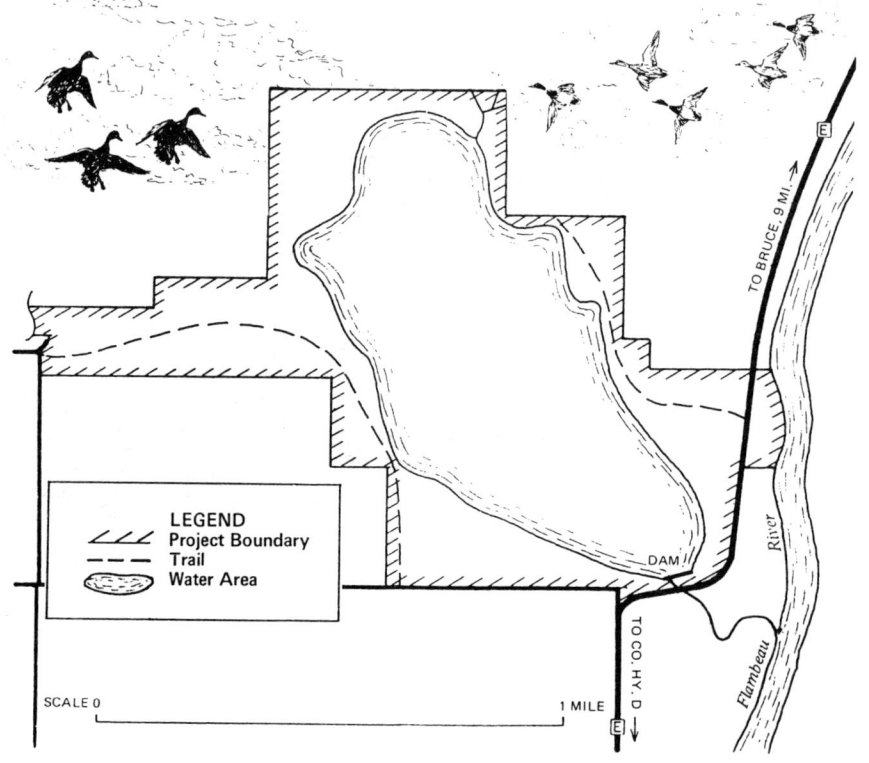

Tenmile Creek Wildlife Area, 213 acres, is located in the extreme southwest corner of Rusk County. From Bear Lake take Cty D west several miles. The property is on the north side between Rice Bed Rd and 30th St. The area is a marsh stream bottom with timber fringes on the east and croplands on the west. Animals include grouse, waterfowl, woodcock and furbearers.

Private Forest:

Consolidated Papers has scattered parcels of company forest that are open for hiking, hunting and other selected uses. The largest parcel in Rusk County is located 2 miles south of Hawking of Cty M. The property extends generally two miles on both sides of the road for about 5 miles. There are private parcels through the area. For more information contact: Public Affairs Dept. Consolidated Papers, PO Box 50, WIsconsin Rapids, WI 54494.

PARKS, LANDINGS AND OTHER THINGS:

Barron County:

Parks:

Southworth Memorial Park, (Ten Mile Park) is located south of Chetek on Cty SS, then east on 6th Ave (Partridge Ln). The park is on the west shore of Ten Mile Lake. Facilities include camping, picnic area, drinking water, toilets and boat landing.
Veterans Memorial Park, is located south of Cameron on Cty SS, then east on 12 1/2 Ave to the park which is located on the west shore of Prairie Lake. Facilities include camping, picnic area, drinking water, toilets, playground, hiking trails and boat landing.
Waldo Carlson Park, (Red Cedar Lake Park) is located north of Mikana on Hwy 48, then east on 29th Ave (Park Rd) to Red Cedar Lake. Facilities include camping, picnic area, drinking water, toilets, playground, swimming and boat landing.
Grant Park, is located east of Cumberland on Cty B. The park is on the south shore of Silver Lake just north of Cty B. Facilities include picnic area, toilets, sandy beach and boat landing.

Boat Landings:

The county maintains 22 boat landings throughout the county. These range from a ramp to a fully equipped picnic area. These include N Horseshoe, Kirby, North, Scotts, Horseshoe, Moon, Hemlock, Red Cedar, Bear, Granite, Little Dummy, Butternut, Spider, L. Vermillion, Prairie, Montanis and Ten Mile Lake. The County also has a series of landings on the Red Cedar River to provide access for canoeing. These points can be found where Cty A, D, OO and 16 1/2 Ave west of Cty SS cross the river.

Municipal Parks:

Rice Lake City Beach, is located on Lakeshore Dr on the west shore of Rice Lake. Facilities include a 200 ft sandy beach.
Chetek City Park, is located east of Cty SS and the dam, and north of the airport on Lake Chetek. Facilities include beach and picnic area.
Cumberland City Beach and Tourist Park, is located at the north end of town and west of Hwy 63 on Beaver Dam Lake. There is a city beach, picnic and recreation area.
Bandli Park, is located north of Hwy 8, east of Cameron on Cty M, then 1 1/2 miles north of Canton on Cty M. Located on Silver Cr, the park has a picnic area with toilets.
Guy Spears Park & Beach, is located south of Hwy 8 on west side of Cranberry Cr in Cameron. Facilities include sandy beach, picnic area, playground and shelter.
Pioneer Park, Prairie Farm is located in southwestern Barron County. From Hwy 25 take Cty A west to Prairie Farm, then north on Cty F through town and west on Cty A. Turn south on the first road to the park. Facilities include camping, picnic area, shelters, swimming and boat landing.
Turtle Lake Village Park, located near the jct of Hwy 8 and 63 offers camping, showers, pavilion, water and a playground.

State Waysides:

Hwy 8, 2.5 miles west of Rusk County line, has a picnic area with water and toilets.
Hwy 8, 2.0 miles east of Turtle Lake, has a picnic area with water and toilets.
Hwy 53, 2 miles north of New Auburn, has a picnic area with water and toilets.
Hwy 53, 1.6 miles south of Cty I at Chetek, has a picnic area with water and toilets.

Rusk County:

Community Park (Lake Flambeau Park), is located 2 miles east of town on Old Hwy 8 and adjacent to the dam. Facilities include boat landing and picnic area.
Josie Creek Campground and Park, is located just east of Tony on Hwy 8, then 2 miles north on Cty X. The park, on the north side of Cty X, is at the junction of Josie Cr and the Flambeau River. Facilities include a camping area, picnic area, swimming, a walking archery range, pistol and rifle range, boat landing,

Audie/Perch Lake Campground and Park, is located north from Hwy 8 at Bruce on Cty O, then continue 1 mile north on Blue Hills Trail and west on Perch Lake Rd. Facilities include picnic area, camping, nature trail, hunter walking trails, boat landing to both lakes.
Lea Lake Area, is located 9 miles north of Ladysmith on Hwy 27, then east 1 mile on Lea Lake Rd, continue east and south on Town road to park. Facilities include picnic area and boat landing.
Hawkins Millpond, located in Hawkins, provides a recreation area including a picnic area and camping.

Boat Landings:
Rusk County maintains 11 additional public boat landings which include; Hatch Landing (Chippewa River), D Bridge Landing (Holcombe Flowage, Fireside lake, Sand Lake, Clear Lake, Island Lake, McCann Lake, Potato Lake, Bucks Lake, Lea Lake and Amacoy Lake.

Other Points of Interest:
Blue Hills which are located in northwestern Rusk and northern Barron Counties, are the remnants of mountains older than the Rocky and Appalachian mountains. These mountains were estimated to be taller the 20,000 ft, but have been eroded over time by the advances of the glaciers and other forces of nature. Today it is one of the more scenic areas of the state.

Municipal Parks:
Haley Park, Sheldon, located in the southeast corner of the county, is on Cty G just south of Hwy 194. The park is on the Jump River and provides a camping area, canoe put in and swimming area.
Memorial Park, City of Ladysmith is located on Hwy 8 on the east side of the Flambeau River. Facilities include picnic area, swimming, boat landing and playground.

State Waysides:
Hwy 8, 1.6 miles east of Ingram has a picnic area with water and toilets.
Hwy 27, 1.0 mile south of Sawyer County has a picnic area with water and toilets.

Polk County:

Apple River County Park, is located about 5 miles north of Amery on Hwy 46, then west 3/4 mile on Main Crossing Rd to the Apple River. Facilities include primitive camping, playground, hiking, shelter, picnic area, well and toilets.
Atlas County Park, is located about 19 miles north of St Croix Falls on Hwy 87, then east about 3 1/2 miles of Cty B. The park is to the south on Long Trade Lake. Facilities include picnic area with playground and well.
Black Brook County Park, is located west of Amery 1 mile on Cty F, then south on Cty C and east 1/2 mile on Cty CC. There is a playground, picnic area, tubing and canoe access to river, well and toilets. There is a boat landing near by.
East Lake (Lotus Lake) County Park, is located about 1 mile east of Dresser, Hwy 35 on Cty F, then 1/2 mile east of 90th Ave, the park is to the south. Facilities include picnic area, boat landing, hiking, playground and restrooms.

Municipal Parks:
Coon Lake Park, Village Frederic, located east of Hwy 35 on the west shore of the lake, has a picnic area with shelter.
Big Butternut Beach, Village of Luck, is located east of Hwy 35 on Butternut Ave, then south and east on South Shore Drive. The beach and picnic area are on the north side of the road.
Bone Lake Beach, is located 2 miles east of Luck on Hwy 48, then 1 mile south on Cty GG, then east 1/2 mile on town road, then south to beach and boat landing.
Clear Lake Park, Clear Lake, is located in the northwest corner of town just west of Cty JJ and north of Hwy 63. There is a picnic area and beach.
Half Moon Lake Park, Milton, is located 3 miles east and south of town on Hwy 46, then east on 200th Ave. There is a beach, picnic area and boat landing.
Magnor Lake, Clayton, is located about 1 1/2 mile west on Hwy 63. The beach is on the north side of the road.
Sand Lake Town Park, is located several miles east of St Croix Falls on Hwy 8, then south about 2 miles on Cty Y. Access to the park is to the west. Facilities include beach, restrooms, and changing house.
Ace Park, Amery, is located on the east end of North Twin Lake on Hwy 46 and offers a picnic area.
Amery City Beach, is on the east end of South Twin Lake and west of Hwy 46. Facilities include a beach area.

State Waysides:
Hwy 46, 0.8 miles north of Cty I (Balsam Lake), there is a boat landing.
Hwy 35, at Hwy 8 has a picnic area with toilets and water.

State Parks:

<u>Interstate State Park</u>, DNR, Box 703, St Croix Falls, WI 54024, (715) 483-3747, is located on the south edge of St Croix on the St Croix River. This unique park has many features of glaciation including the Dales of the St Croix which were cut deep into the bedrock by glacial melt waters. Also being the western end of the Ice Age Trail, there is the Ice Age Interpretive Center at the park. The park has many recreational activities including swimming, seven picnic areas, hiking, wilderness areas, observation points, playgrounds, campgrounds and shelters. Across the river the State of Minnesota also has developed a park to help preserve this area.

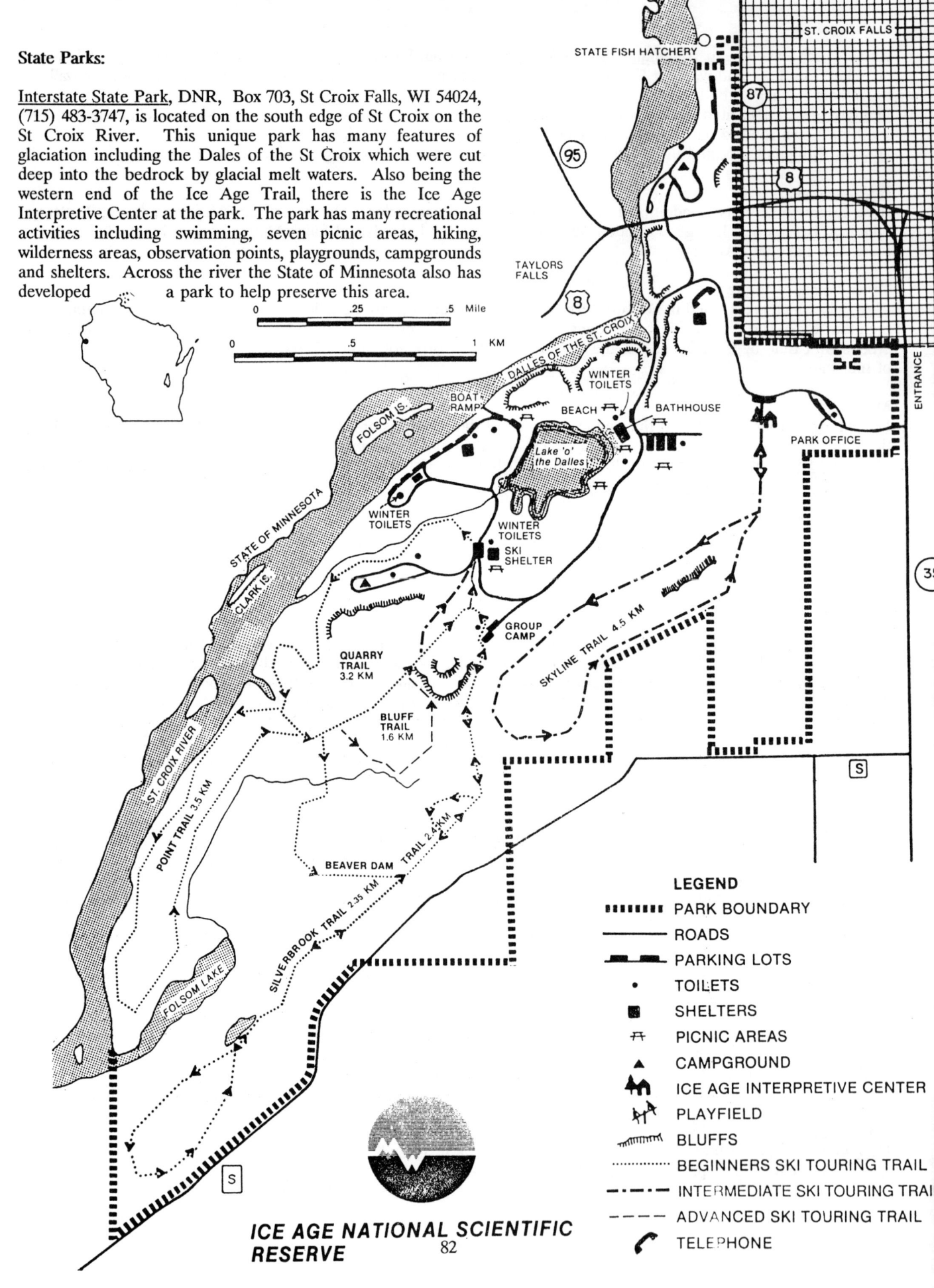

TRAILS

Mountain Bikes:

Barron County, does not permit bikes on gated trails and/or where posted.
Polk County, permits the use of mountain bikes on county trails.
Rusk County, permits the use of bike on trails throughout the county forest.
Wisconsin DNR, permits the use of these bikes on selected trails managed by the Department. It is best to contact the property manager to get the latest information.

All Terrain Vehicles:

Barron County, does not permit ATVs on gated trails and/or where posted.
Polk County, does not permit ATVs on county property.
Rusk County, does not permit ATVs on county property.
Wisconsin DNR, does not permit the use of these vehicles on any of the trails managed by the Department.

Horses:

Barron County, permits the use of horses on county trails.
Polk County, permits the use of horses in the Sterling Forest where there are over 25 miles of trails and logging roads.
Rusk County, permits horses on county trails except on designated ski trails and in parks.
Wisconsin DNR, policies vary with the properties; it's best to contact the property manager for the latest information.

Hiking, Hunting and Cross Country Ski Trails

Barron County:

Bear Lake Cross Country Ski & Hiking Trails, are located on the Washburn County Line and west of Bear Lake. 16th St (Narrow Gauge Rd) northwest of Cty V splits the parcel in half. Parking lots can be found on Narrow Gauge Rd and 29th Ave. The trails lead to a number of small lakes.

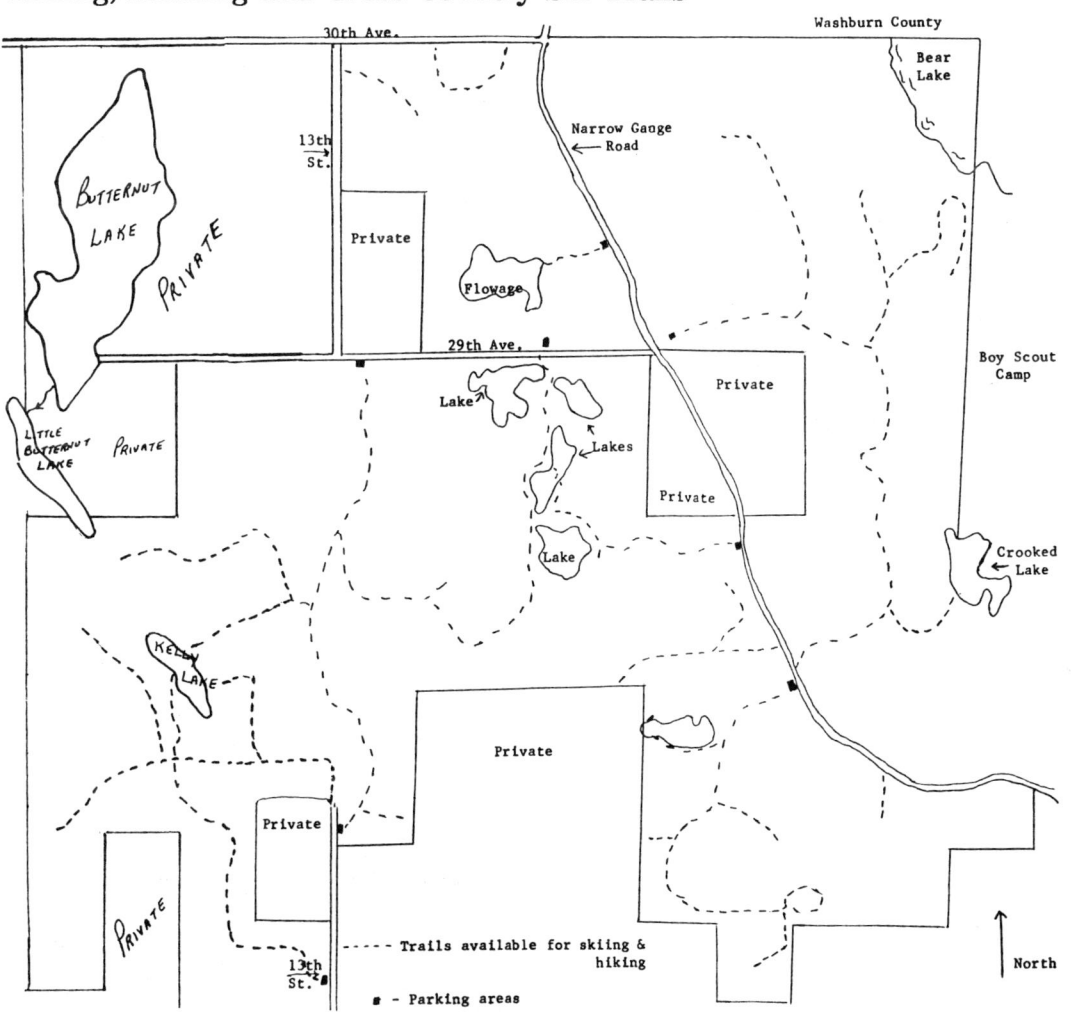

83

Cedar Lake Cross Country Ski & Hiking Trails, are located about 7 miles east of Mikana on Hwy 48, south on Cty F and west on either Valley Rd or Bolgers Rd. There are also two parking lots off roads on the east shore of the lake. The Ice Age Trail also passes through this area.

Pipestone Quarry Cross Country Ski & Hiking Trails, are located about 7 miles east of Rice Lake on Hwy 48, then 2 miles south on Cty NN, then about a 1 mile south on Cty C. Continue south on 27 1/2 St to the parking area. There are two loops, intermediate (3 1/4 mile) and advanced (2 miles). The trails, considered quite difficult due to the rough terrain, are not groomed.

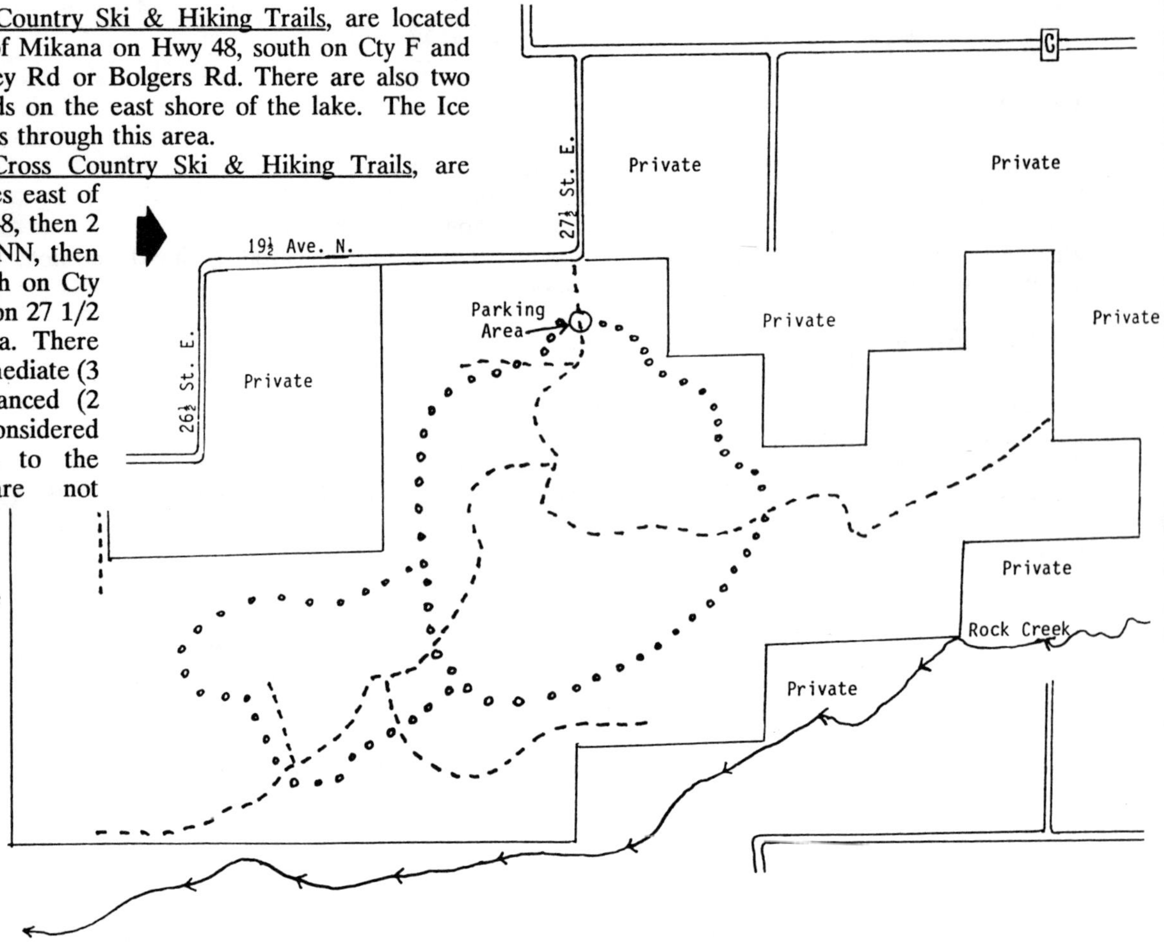

Mikana Cross Country Ski & Hiking Trails, are located about 2 miles west of Mikana (Hwy 48) on Swamp Rd. There is a parking lot on the north side of the road just west of Mirror Lake. There is a series of trails throughout the area which lead to a number of lakes and to Cty V, to the north.

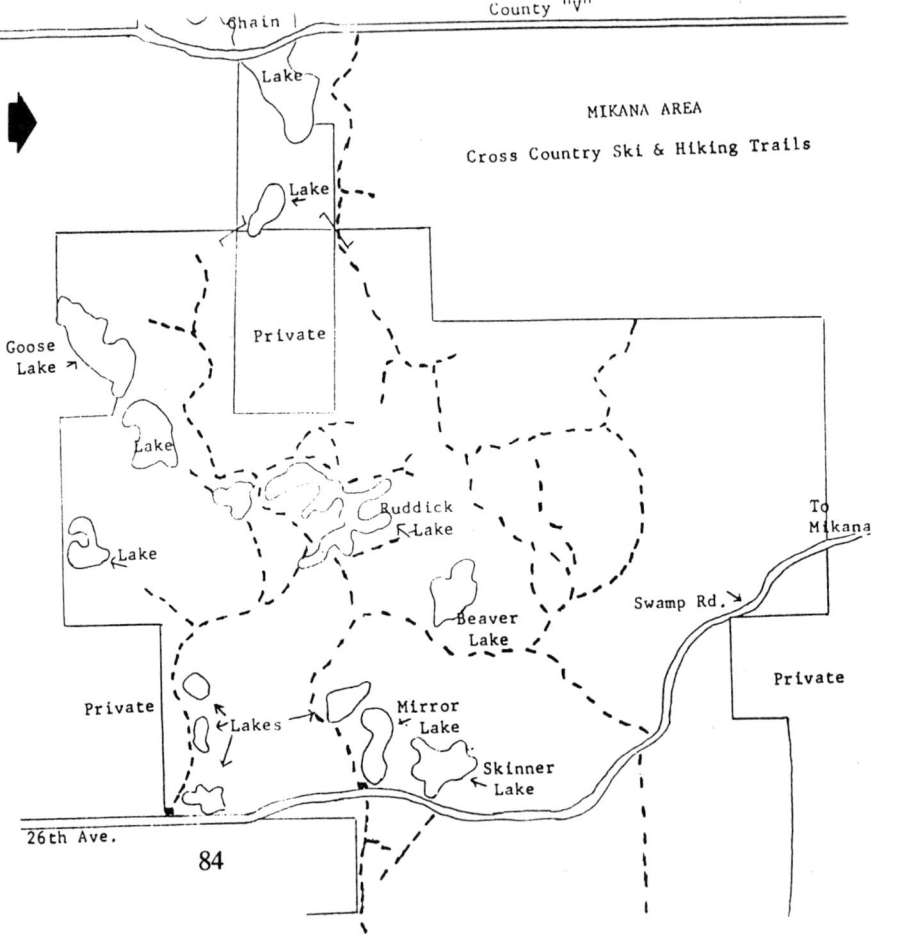

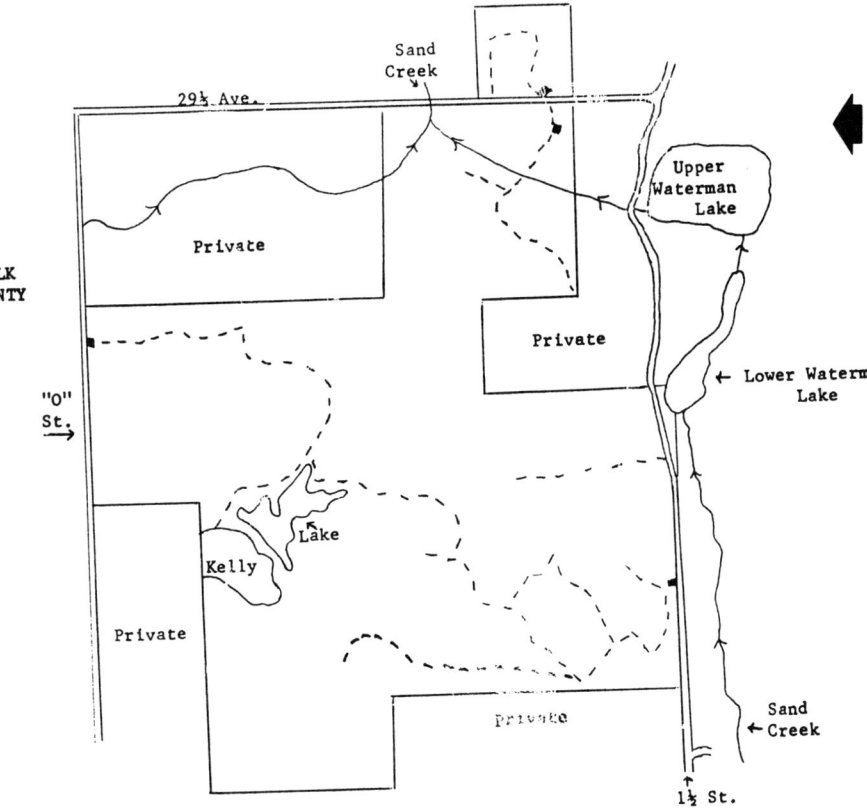

Maple Plain Cross Country Ski & Hiking Trails, are located on the Washburn County Line. From Cumberland take Hwy 48 west, then 1st St north, then 27 1/2 Ave east and 1 1/2 St north. Parking lots can be found on 1 1/2 St, 29 1/2 Ave and O St.

Mt Hardscrabble, PO Box 526, Rice Lake, WI 54868, (715) 234-3412, is located 5 miles east of Rice Lake on Cty C, then south on Hardscrabble Road. Facilities include a fully equipped down hill ski hill plus 15 miles of groomed cross country ski trails. There are many interconnecting trails for the beginner, intermediate and advanced skier.

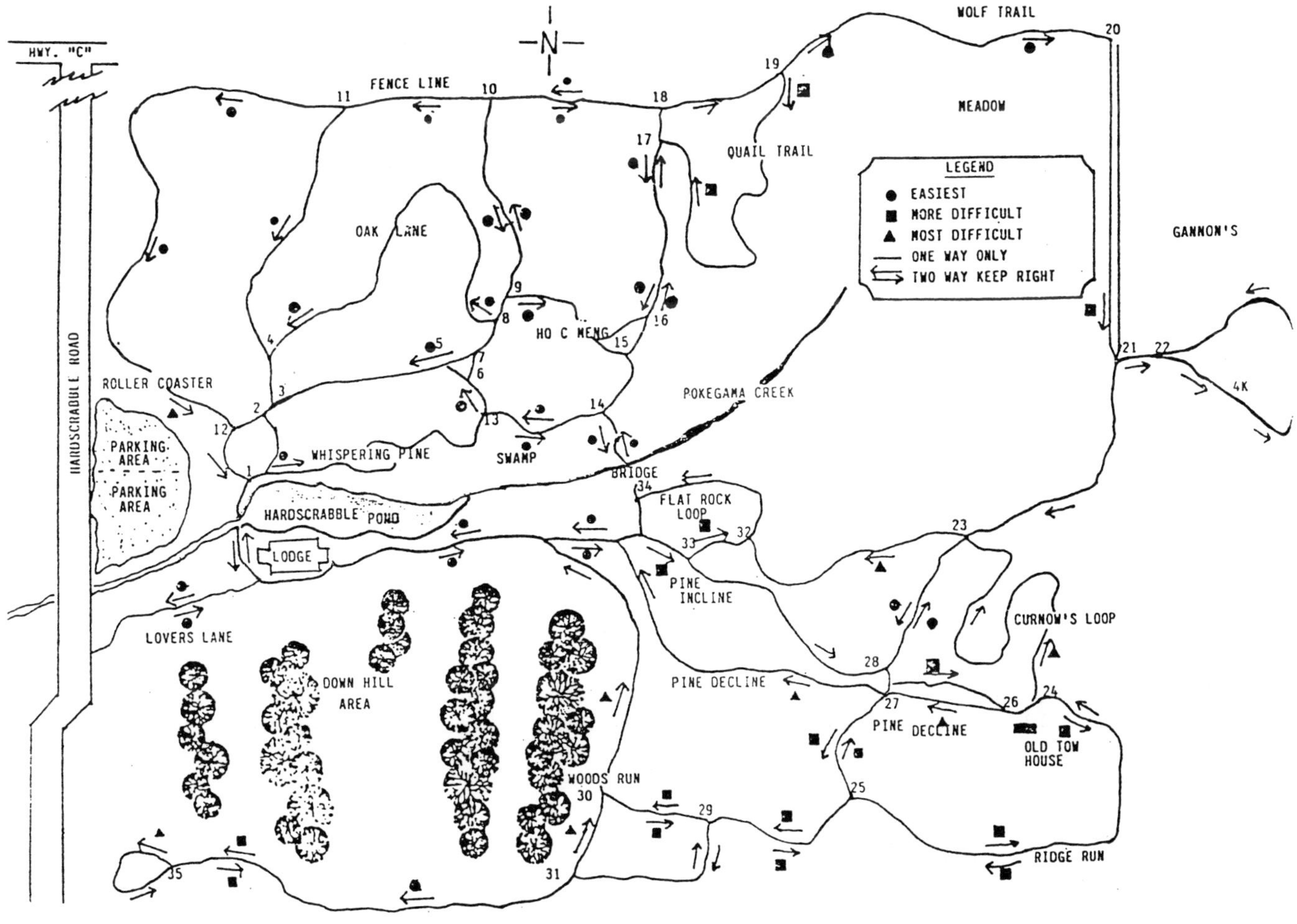

Polk County:

Somers Lake Recreation Area, is located 5 miles east of Hwy 35, Frederic on Cty W, then north about 2 1/2 miles on Cty I and east 1/4 mile on 320th Ave, then south to the area. The property has a series of multi use trails.

Apple River County Park, is located about 5 miles north of Amery on Hwy 46, then west 3/4 mile on Main Crossing Rd to the Apple River. There are hiking trails through the park.

East Lake (Lotus Lake) County Park, is located east of Dresser on Cty MM, then east on 90th Ave. There are hiking trails from the picnic area.

Interstate State Park, is located on the south side of St Croix Falls. There is an extensive trail system in the park which includes 8 1/2 miles of hiking and 10 miles of cross country ski trails.

Kennedy Environmental Area, is located about 8 miles east of St Croix Falls on Hwy 8, then 1 1/2 miles south on Hwy 65, then 1 1/2 east on Kennedy Mills Ave to the river. Presently there are 8 miles of cross country ski trails formally called Balsam Branch Ski Area. The trail heads will be moved to the Kennedy Environmental Area. Additional development will include more trails, handicap interpretive trail, restrooms and picnic area.

Sterling County Forest, the largest unit, is in the northwestern corner of the county. It is bordered by Governor Knowles State Forest on the west, south and east sides, and Burnett County on the north. Access to the forest are town roads and Cty G west of Hwy 87. There are over 25 miles of trails throughout the forest for multi use including hiking, horses, skiing and mountain biking.

Rusk County:

Blue Hills Cross Country Ski Trails, Rusk County Trail Association, W 13621 Cty O, Bruce, WI 54819, is located north from Hwy 8 at Bruce on Cty O, then continue 1 mile north on Blue Hills Trail. The trail heads can be found along the east side of the road and on Meadow Dam Rd. Presently 6 miles of trails have been developed with more in the future. The trails are open to hiking, skiing, horseback riding, and non-motorized uses. There are also 3 primitive camping spots around Hill Trail Flowage.

Old Blue Hills Auto Trail, is located north of Hwy 8 at Bruce on Cty O. The road parallels Devil's Creek to the north through the heart of the Blue Hills. There are several picnic areas on or near the road.

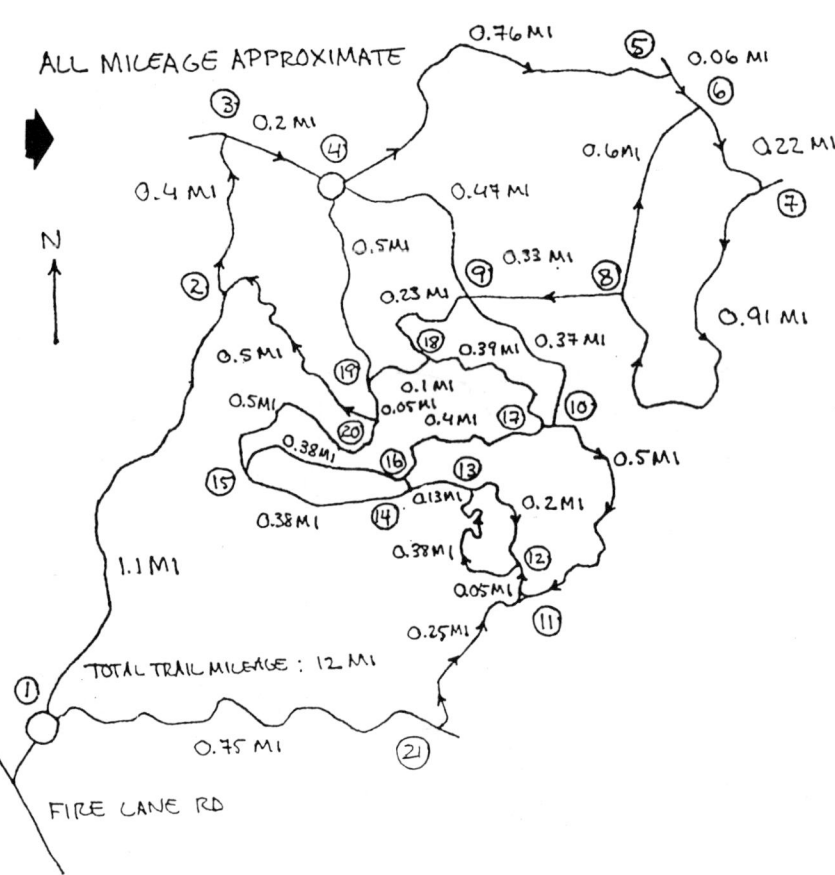

Blue Hills Nature Trail, is located by Perch Lake Campgrounds. From Hwy 8 at Bruce go north on Cty O, then continue north on Blue Hills Trail and west on Perch Lake Rd. This is a 1 1/2 mile trail with 23 information stations.

State Trails:

Tuscobia-Park Falls State Trail, is a 76 mile abandoned railroad grade open for hiking, biking and horseback riding; DNR Ranger Station, Winter WI 54896 (715) 266-3511.

Ice Age National Scenic Trail System:

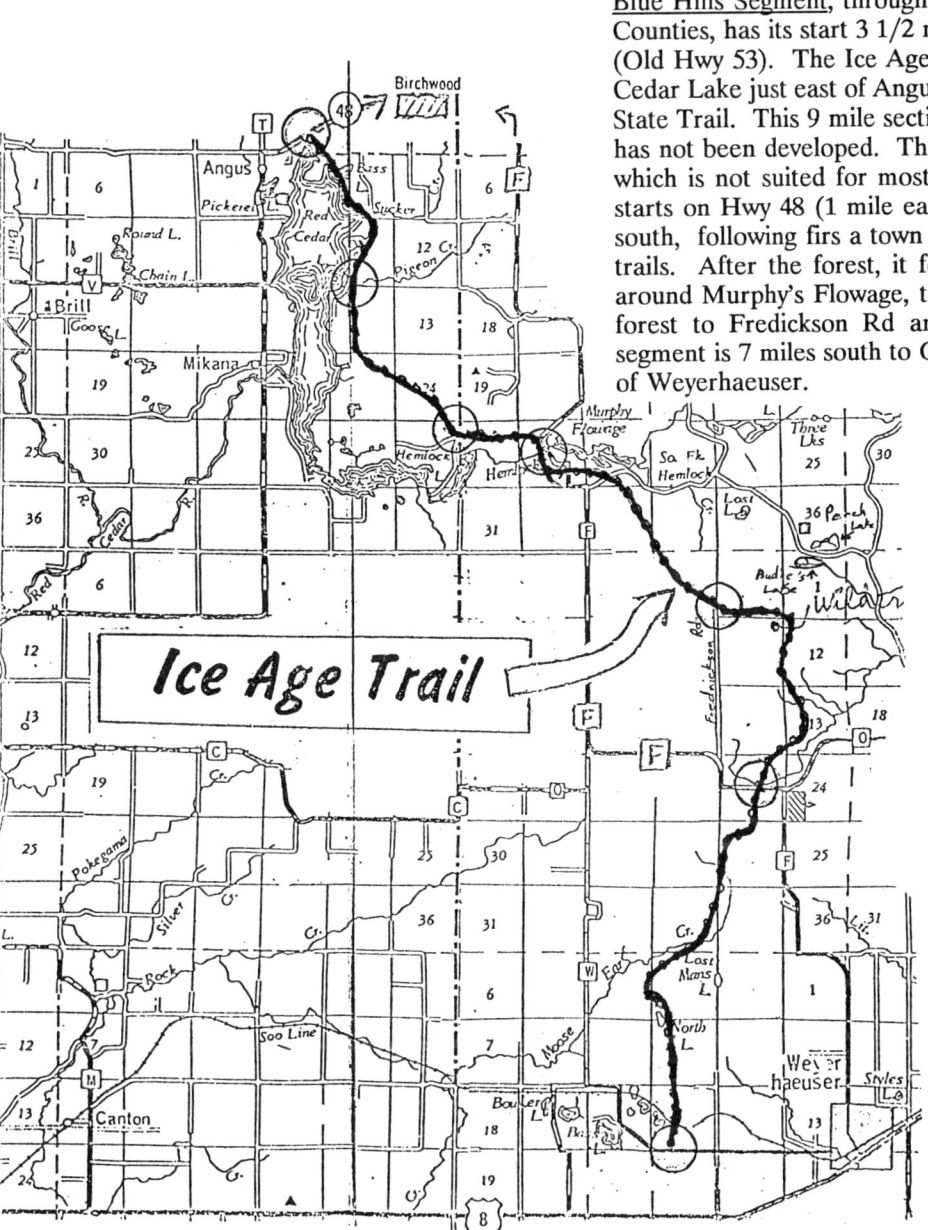

Blue Hills Segment, through eastern Barron and western Rusk Counties, has its start 3 1/2 miles north of Rice Lake on Cty SS (Old Hwy 53). The Ice Age Trail from here to the tip of Red Cedar Lake just east of Angus is part of the Tuscobia-Park Falls State Trail. This 9 mile section was an abandoned railroad and has not been developed. The surface is the original cinder bed which is not suited for most bikes. The next 15 miles section starts on Hwy 48 (1 mile east of Angus) where the trail heads south, following firs a town road and then county forest hiking trails. After the forest, it follows Bolgers Rd to Cty F south around Murphy's Flowage, then southeast again across country forest to Fredickson Rd and down to Cty O/F. The final segment is 7 miles south to Old 14th Rd about 2 1/2 miles east of Weyerhaeuser.

Canoe Trails:

Rivers to consider would include:

Flambeau River, upper reaches it contains rapids and wilderness and the lower portions contain flat water and flowages.
Chippewa River, throughout the county is flat, meandering and easy canoeing.
Red Cedar River, below Hwy 8 provides you with meandering, flat water floats with good fishing along the way.

GUIDES AND BAIT SHOPS

Area Bait Shops:

JAY'S SPORT SHOP	HWY 8 & GARFIELD ST	ALMENA	WI 54805
A & M SPORTS	RT 4 BOX 14L	AMERY	WI 54001
APPLE RIVER SPORTS	RT 1 BOX 213	AMERY	WI 54001
DERONDA BAIT & SMALL ENGINE INCRT 2		AMERY	WI 54001
MORT'S MARINA	RT 3	AMERY	WI 54001
RANDOM DRIVE BAIT	RT 2 BOX 263A	AMERY	WI 54001
RICK'S SPORT SHOP	RT 3 BOX 385	AMERY	WI 54001
ROGER'S BAIT AND SPORT SHOP	RT 3 BOX 385	AMERY	WI 54001
FARRELL'S RESORT	701 PARK DR	BALSAM LAKE	WI 54810
HIDDEN BAY RESORT	RT 1 BOX 438	BALSAM LAKE	WI 54810
JONZY MARKET	RT 1	BALSAM LAKE	WI 54810
PAP'S GENERAL STORE	RT 1	BALSAM LAKE	WI 54810
REED'S SUNNYSIDE MARINA	RT 1 BOX 225	BALSAM LAKE	WI 54810
BARRON TRUE VALUE	341 E LASALLE	BARRON	WI 54812
BARRONS BAIT & TACKLE	1760 E DIVISION	BARRON	WI 54812
AMACOY BAIT SHOP	N3145 HWY 40	BRUCE	WI 54819
CHUCK & EVIE MINNOW	W12174 MEADOW DAM RD	BRUCE	WI 54819
LEO HOEFT'S TRAPPERS SUPPLY	RT 1	BRUCE	WI 54819
S & S SPORT MART	305 S 1ST ST	CAMERON	WI 54822
TOLLY'S REST COVE RESORT	1296 21 3/4 ST	CAMERON	WI 54822
SUNRISE BAIT & TACKLE	BOX 159A	CENTURIA	WI 54824
"TRAPPER'S CROSSING"	2634 CO D	CHETEK	WI 54728
BILL'S TRADING POST	303 DALLAS ST	CHETEK	WI 54728
DONNY'S WINE & CHEESE	728 2ND ST	CHETEK	WI 54728
FAMILY AFFAIR BAIT & TACKL	844 BANKS LA	CHETEK	WI 54728
ROD & GUN SHOP	513 2ND ST	CHETEK	WI 54728
SHADY GROVE RESORT	1093 22 3/4 ST	CHETEK	WI 54728
T J'S TIMBERLINE	1189 N POTATO LAKE RD	CHETEK	WI 54728
TIMBER N TACKLE	W15165 CO HWY D	CHETEK	WI 54728
WELCOME INN RESORT	1211 N POTATO LK RD	CHETEK	WI 54728
WILDWOOD RESORT	865 8 1/4 AVE	CHETEK	WI 54728
LAKE MAGNOR STORE	RT 1	CLAYTON	WI 54004
MOON LAKE RESORT	RT 2	CLAYTON	WI 54004
KOSTICK'S RESORT	N197 WHISPERING PINES DR	CONRATH	WI 54731
FRIESSES MINNOW FARM	736 20TH AVE	CUMBERLAND	WI 54829
INDIANHEAD SPORT SHOP	HWYS 63 & 48 RT 3	CUMBERLAND	WI 54829
JOE'S SPORT SHOP INC	RT 3 BOX 1	CUMBERLAND	WI 54829
ROMAR LTD	RT 4	CUMBERLAND	WI 54829
ANDERSON'S CUSHING HARDWARE	CO RD N	CUSHING	WI 54006
CUSHING CORNER	RT 1 7B	CUSHING	WI 54006
DERONDA BAIT & SMALL ENGINE	RT 2	DERONDA	WI 54008
MINNOW MARKET	RT 2	DERONDA	WI 54008
AMUNDSON SPTG GOODS	503 WISCONSIN AVE	FREDERIC	WI 54837
C J'S LAKEVIEW RESORT	BOX 186 1748 28 3/4 AVE	HAUGEN	WI 54841
MOUSE'S BAIT		HAWKINS	WI 54530
JAMES SPORT SHOP	206 W 2ND ST N	LADYSMITH	WI 54848
LADYSMITH HARDWARE HANK	503 LAKE AVE W	LADYSMITH	WI 54848
T & T SPORT AND MARINE	HWY 8 W	LADYSMITH	WI 54848
SEVEN PINE TROUT HATCHERY	BOX 15	LEWIS	WI 54851
BONE LAKE STORE	RT 2 BOX 78	LUCK	WI 54853
DENUCCI'S 35 VILLA	HWY 35 & 48	LUCK	WI 54853
DOODY'S BAIT & SPORT SHOP	RT 1 BOX 248	LUCK	WI 54853
PINE GROVE RESORT	RT 2	LUCK	WI 54853
BARB'S GENERAL STORE	120 LAKE ST BOX 109	MIKANA	WI 54857
REST POINT RESORT	RT 3	MILLTOWN	WI 54858
STU'S SPORT SHOP	BOX 224	MILLTOWN	WI 54858
FIRESIDE LAKE RESORT INC	RT 3 BOX 283	NEW AUBURN	WI 54757
ISLAND LAKE SPORT SHOP	N802 MUD LAKE RD	NEW AUBURN	WI 54757
NORTH SHORE BAR & CMPGRND	RT 3	NEW AUBURN	WI 54757
202 CHIEFTAN ST	213 CASCADE ST	OSCEOLA	WI 54020
MORK'S BIG LAKE STORE	RT 2 BOX 137C	OSCEOLA	WI 54020
OSBORNE'S BAIT	RT 2 BOX 77BB	OSCEOLA	WI 54020
PINE LAKE STORE	RT 2 BOX 121AA 45TH AVE	OSCEOLA	WI 54020
BRENT'S BAIT	36 NOBLE AVE	RICE LAKE	WI 54868
CRAYFISH EXPRESS	1111 DUKE ST	RICE LAKE	WI 54868
DBA RAINBOW HOME CENTER	1124 HAMMOND AVE	RICE LAKE	WI 54868
HUNTING & FISHING HDQTS	1822 S MAIN	RICE LAKE	WI 54868

Area Bait Shops: continued

WARDS MINNOWS	919 E SAWYER ST	RICE LAKE WI 54868
DEER LAKE BAIT	RT 2	ST CROIX FALLS WI 54024
FAMILY SPORT & MARINE	RT 2 BOX 158	ST CROIX FALLS WI 54024
HOUSE OF CHEESE & GIFTS	BOX 685	ST CROIX FALLS WI 54024
ONE STOP INC	RT 2 BOX 158	ST CROIX FALLS WI 54024
D & D SPORTS	RT 2 BOX 319A	TURTLE LAKE WI 54889
PRUNOS BAIT AN TACKLE	RT 2	TURTLE LAKE WI 54889
MIDWAY RESORT	RT 1 BOX 116	WEYERHAUESER WI 54895

Area Guides:

HANSEN	DOUGLAS	RT 4 BOX 63	AMERY	WI 54001
ANDERSON	JOSEPH	RT 1 BOX 574	BALSAM LAKE	WI 54810
DUNCAN JR	JAMES	BOX 68	BALSAM LAKE	WI 54810
HOEN	BERNARD	403 COURTHOUSE AVE BOX 56	BALSAM LAKE	WI 54810
MOLAMPHY	EDWARD	RT 1 BOX 328	BALSAM LAKE	WI 54810
SWANSON	ALICE	BOX 341 RT 1	BALSAM LAKE	WI 54810
BAUER	HARRY	1099 9TH ST	BARRON	WI 54812
BEDIENT	GARY	1762 11TH AVE	BARRON	WI 54812
BECKER	HARLAN	1354 19 1/2 ST	CAMERON	WI 54822
SHAIDE	CLARENCE	2403 14TH AVE	CAMERON	WI 54822
TOURVILLE	EUGENE	RT 1 BOX 260	CENTURIA	WI 54824
AUGUST	ROBERT	1026 2ND ST	CHETEK	WI 54728
HAWKOS	ALVIN	RT 1 BOX 920	CHETEK	WI 54728
SANDBERG	CLAYTON	BOX 618	CHETEK	WI 54728
SCHOENFUSS	EUGENE	973 23 1/2 ST	CHETEK	WI 54728
SMITH	TRACY	192 21 1/4 ST	CHETEK	WI 54728
WORDEN	CLINTON	409 DALLAS ST	CHETEK	WI 54728
ZAPPA	HERMAN	BOX 236	CUMBERLAND	WI 54829
ANDREWSON	BRIAN	RT1 BOX 216	DRESSER	WI 54009
FEIRTAG	RON	RT 1 N7798 FLAMBEAU RD	LADYSMITH	WI 54848
FISK	EARL	112 S 1ST ST #1	LADYSMITH	WI 54848
PRODEN	DAVID	N7520 PRODEN RD	LADYSMITH	WI 54848
SHIBLEY	DAVID	603 MINER AVE E	LADYSMITH	WI 54848
TUMA	LOUIE	720 SUMMIT AVE	LADYSMITH	WI 54848
TUMA	RICHARD	N5731 CEMETERY RD	LADYSMITH	WI 54848
HOEN	MARK	RT 3 BOX 151	LUCK	WI 54853
ROETTGER	RICHARD	RT 2	LUCK	WI 54853
QUILLEN	ROBERT	100 HEMLOCK ST	MIKANA	WI 54857
SEEFLUTH	GAYLE	RT 1	NEW AUBURN	WI 54757
BATHKE	RICHARD	36 W STOUT ST	RICE LAKE	WI 54868
BAUER	MICHAEL	2192 BLACKBIRD LA	RICE LAKE	WI 54868
BRAATZ	RONALD	20 W SLOCUMB	RICE LAKE	WI 54868
ELWOOD	WILLIAM	1813 19TH AVE	RICE LAKE	WI 54868
GREINER	STEVEN	2774 24TH AVE	RICE LAKE	WI 54868
HAJDASZ	WAYNE	1035 SOO BL	RICE LAKE	WI 54868
KLARE	TIMOTHY	122 MONROE AVE	RICE LAKE	WI 54868
MENSE	STEVEN	2171A MONROE AVE E	RICE LAKE	WI 54868
PETRY	GEORGE	1846 MOON LAKE LA	RICE LAKE	WI 54868
ROOSEVELT	WAYNE	230 HILLTOP DR	RICE LAKE	WI 54868
SCHERF	KEITH	903 N MAIN ST	RICE LAKE	WI 54868
SEVERSON	MICHAEL	2832 24TH AVE	RICE LAKE	WI 54868
SMETANA	THOMAS	1810 19TH ST	RICE LAKE	WI 54868
TASKER	JOHN	1112 LEE ST	RICE LAKE	WI 54868
WINNINGHAN	BRUCE	2405 15 1/4 AVE	RICE LAKE	WI 54868
HENDERSON	BARRY	BOX 184	SHELDON	WI 54766
HOEN	MICHAEL	BOX 635	ST CROIX FALLS	WI 54024
LUNDE	ALLEN	RT 1 BOX 686	ST CROIX FALLS	WI 54024
FEIRTAG	RONALD	W6560 POINT RD	TONY	WI 54563
MAKOSKY	THOMAS	W6338 LAKESHORE DR	TONY	WI 54563
DIRKES	WILLIAM	BOX 205	WEYERHAEUSER	WI 54895

CAMPGROUNDS

Dispersed Camping:

Barron County, permits dispersed camping except in special designated areas.
Polk County, does not permit dispersed camping.
Rusk County, camping restricted to designated areas.
St Croix National Scenic Riverway, does not permit dispersed camping.
WI DNR, does not permit dispersed camping on its properties.

Private Campgrounds

Chetek/Rice Lake Area:

Hemlock Heights Green Acres Resort & Campground: located 10 miles NE of Rice Lake off Hwy 48 E; water & elec, playground, boat rental; on Hemlock Lake; Hemlock Heights Green Acres Resort & Campground, 2483 28th St, Rice Lake, WI 54868; (715) 234-8232.
Hillside Resort & Campground: located on the north end of Potato Lake; water & elec, flush toilets, playground, firewood, boats; on Potato Lake; Hillside Resort & Campground, N 1250 Potato Lake Rd, Chetek, WI 54728; (715) 353-2478.
The Kamping Place on Devil's Lake: KOA Kampground; located 10 miles north of Rice Lake on Hwy 53; 124 sites, some with water & elec, flush toilets, showers, dump station, camp store, laundry, snack bar; on Devil's Lake; The Kamping Place on Devil's Lake, P.O. Box 3, Haugen, WI 54841; (715) 234-2360.
Ken's Kampsites & Resort: 45 shaded lots, 35 water front sites, water & elec, dump station, picnic tables, firewood, hot showers, flush toilets, swimming, fishing, boat, motor, paddle boat, pontoon rental; on the Chetek Chain of Lakes; Ken's Kampsites & Resort, Box 222, Chetek, WI 54728; (715) 859-2887.
Northland Resort: RV sites, water & elec, swimming beach, boat rental; on Lake Chetek, 683 acres; Northland Resort, 785 N. Lakeview Dr, Chetek, WI 54728; (715) 924-3214.
Paul Bunyan's Resort: located close to downtown Rice Lake; campground, full hook-ups, laundry, boat & motor rentals; Paul Bunyan's Resort, 939 Lakeshore Dr, Rice Lake, WI 54868; (715) 234-2996.
Six Lakes Resort & Campground: water & elec, showers, playground, basketball, rec hall, swimming, fishing, boat & motor rentals, beer bar; on Pokegama Lake, 494 acres; Six Lakes Resort & Campground, 2535 White St, Chetek, WI 54728; (715) 924-3680.
Shady Rest Campground & Bar: located 1/4 mile west of Haugen, on VV, turn right 1 mile; water & elec, showers, swimming; on Bear Lake; Shady Rest Campground & Bar, Rt 3, Rice Lake, WI 54868; (715) 234-7339 or 234-8857.
Summer Haven Resort: campground, hook-ups, flush toilets, showers, camp store, swimming beach, pontoon & paddle boat rental; on Ojaski Lake, 567 acres; Summer Haven Resort, 1106 24 3/4 St, Cameron, WI 54822; (715) 859-2918.
TJ's Timberline Resort & Campground: level lakeshore camping, liquor bar; on Potato Lake; TJ's Timberline Resort & Campground, Rt 2, Box 243, Chetek, WI 54728; (715) 834-5331.
Wildwood Resort & RV Park: located 1 mile north of Chetek on Hwy SS (old 53); spacious, full hook-up site; flush toilets, showers, picnic tables, playground, game room, horseshoes, basketball, camp store, heated swimming pool, boat launch; on Prairie Lake in the Chetek Chain of Lakes; 865 8 1/4 Ave, Chetek, WI 54728; (715) 924-3259.

Cumberland Area:

Anchor Inn Resort: located on Hwy 8 in Turtle Lake, 2 miles east of Jct of 8 & 63; camping, boats; on Turtle Lake; Anchor Inn Resort, Hwy 8, Turtle Lake, WI 54889; (715) 986-4623.
Camp Brigadoon: located north of Cumberland on Hwy 63 to Cty Hwy H, then left on H for 3.5 miles; 90 sites, water & elec, swimming beach, boat launch; Camp Brigadoon, Rt 4, Box 60, Cumberland, WI 54829; (715) 822-8561.
North Lake Campground: located west of Cumberland on Hwy 63, 2.5 miles on Hwy G; lakeside sites, fishing, swimming; North Lake Campground, Rt 1, Box 103, Comstock, WI 54826; (715) 822-2440.

St Croix Falls Area:

Pine Grove Resort: located 7 miles east of Luck on Cty Hwy I; 40 sites, most with elec, showers, game room, camp store, boats; on Bone Lake; Pine Grove Resort, Rt 2, Luck, WI 54853; (715) 857-5335.
Schillberg's Brookside Campground: located on Hwy 35 on the north edge of Osceola; 125 wooded sites, 42 elec hook, showers, dump station; Schillberg's Brookside Campground, Rt 3, Box 128, Osceola, WI 54020; (715) 294-3197.

Ladysmith Area:

Ron's Flambeau River Resort: water & elec, showers, dump station, boats, canoes; on the Flambeau River; Ron's Flambeau River Resort, N2395 Cty Trk E, Bruce, WI; (715) 868-5255.
Thornapple River Campground: located 4 miles north on Hwy 27; 25 riverside sites, some with water & elec, hot showers, dump station, hiking trails, playground; on the Thornapple River; Thornapple River Campground, 6599 Hwy 27, Ladysmith, WI 54848; (715) 532-2834.

Municipal and County Campgrounds:

Veteran's Memorial Park, Cameron: located on the west shore of Prairie Lake, 1.5 miles south of Cameron on Hwy 53 and 1 mile east; pit toilets, picnic tables, water, playground, hiking trails, boat landing; on Prairie Lake; Village of Cameron, Village Hall, 603 Main St, Cameron, WI 54822; (715) 458-2117.

Hawkins Park, Hawkins: free overnight camping with water & elec; Village of Hawkins.
Pioneer Park, Prairie Farm: located at the junction of Cty Hwy A & F, 5 miles west of U.S. 25; camping, hook-ups; village of Prairie Farm, Prairie Farm, WI 54762.
Haley Park, Sheldon: camping permitted, toilets, picnic tables; on the Jump River, Sheldon, WI 54766.
Village Park, Turtle Lake: located in Western Barron County at the intersection of Hwys 8 & 63.

County Campgrounds:

Southworth Memorial Park, (Ten Mile Park) is located south of Chetek on Cty SS, then east on 6th Ave (Partridge Ln); picnic area, drinking water, toilets and boat landing; on Ten Mile Lake.
Veterans Memorial Park, is located south of Cameron on Cty SS, then east on 12 1/2 Ave to the park; picnic area, drinking water, toilets, playground, hiking trails, boat landing; on Prairie Lake.
Waldo Carlson Park, (Red Cedar Lake Park) is located north of Mikana on Hwy 48, then east on 29th Ave (Park Rd) to Red Cedar Lake; elec, picnic area, drinking water, toilets, playground, swimming, boat landing; on Red Cedar Lake.

AREA ACTIVITIES

Boat Rentals:
Chetek Economy Marine: boat, pontoon rental; 101 Banks St, Chetek, WI 54728; (715) 924-3318.
Farrell's Resort & Bait Shop: boat, pontoon rental; 701 Park Dr, Balsam Lake, WI 54810; (715) 485-3178.
Pete's Landing: pontoons; 121 Lakeview Dr, Chetek, WI 54728; (715) 924-3100.
Quest: canoe, pontoon rental; Osceola, St Croix Falls & Wild River State Park locations; (800) 992-2692, (715) 755-2692 or (715) 294-2692.
Romar Ltd: located on Hwy 63 N in Cumberland; boat & motor rentals; (715) 822-4863.

Petting Zoo:
Fawn-Doe-Rosa: located 2 miles east of St Croix Falls on Hwy 8; petting zoo and animal park; (715) 483-3772.

Museum & Historical Sites:
Barron County Historical Museum: located 1.5 miles west of Cameron on Museum Rd or Cty Hwy W; also called the Pioneer Village Museum, tours; Barron County Historical Society, Rt 2, Cameron, WI 54822.
Clear Lake Area Historical Museum: exhibits include Sports Memorabilia, Gaylord Nelson Room, Main Street of Shops & Stores, log cabin, school room; in the Old Elementary School Building in Clear Lake.
Rusk County Historical Society Museum: located at the Rusk County Fair Grounds in Ladysmith; one room school house and two display buildings; (715) 532-6450.

Scenic Tours & Sites:
Cascade Falls: scenic waterfalls on Hwy 35 near Osceola.
Quest: Osceola, St Croix Falls & Wild River State Park Locations; canoe trips from 1 hour to 1 month; (800) 992-2692, (715) 755-2692 or (715) 294-2692.
Ten Mile Resort: pontoon cruises on the Chetek Chain of Lakes; Box 618, Chetek, WI 54728; (715) 924-4011.
Wisconsin State Fish Hatchery: located in downtown St Croix Falls on 230 River South; brook and brown trout fish hatchery; Box 397, St Croix Falls, WI 54024; (715) 483-3535.

EMERGENCY NUMBERS

Should you need help, listed below are the phone numbers for the sheriff and local hospitals.

Sheriff:

Barron County: (715) 537-3106
Polk County: (715) 485-3151
Rusk County: (715) 532-2200

Wisconsin State Road Condition Report: (800) 762-3947

Hospitals:

Apple River Valley Memorial, 221 Scholl St, Amery, WI 54001, (715) 268-7151
Barron Memorial Medical Center, 1222 E Woodland Ave, Barron, WI 54812 (715)537-3186
Cumberland Memorial Hospital, 1110 7th Ave, Cumberland, WI 54829, (715) 822-2741
Frederic Memorial Hospital, Hwy 35? United Way, Frederic, WI 54837, (715) 327-4201
Lakeview Medical Center, 1100 N Main St., Rice Lake, WI 54868 (715) 234-1515
Ladd Memorial Hospital, 301 River St, Osceola, WI 54020, (715) 294-2111
Rusk County Memorial Hospital, 900 College Ave.W., Ladysmith, WI 54848, (715) 532-5561
St Croix Valley Memorial Hospital, 204 S. Adams St, St Croix Falls, WI 54024, (715) 483-3261

OTHER INFORMATION SOURCES

County:

Barron County Forestry Office, 311 E LaSalle Ave, Barron, WI 54812 (715) 537-6295.
Polk County Parks Dept or Planning Dept, Courthouse, Balsam Lake, WI 54810, (715) 485-3161.
Rusk County, Forester, Courthouse, Ladysmith, WI 54848 (715) 532-6062.

State: WI Department of Natural Resources

WI DNR, Cumberland Area Headquarters, 1341 2nd Ave, Box 397, Cumberland, WI 54829 (715) 822-3590. Covers Barron, Burnett, Polk and Washburn Counties.
WI DNR, Park Falls Area Headquarters, Case Ave., PO Box 220 Park Falls, WI 54552 (715) 762-3204. Covers Price, Taylor, Rusk and Sawyer Counties.
WI DNR Ranger Station, 311 E LaSalle, Barron, WI 54812, (715) 537-5046.
WI DNR Ranger Station, W8945 Hwy 8, Ladysmith, WI 54848, (715) 532-3911.

Chambers of Commerce:

Balsam Lake Commercial Club, Balsam Lake, WI 54810
Barron County Clerk's Office, Courthouse Barron, WI 54812, (715) 537-6200
Chetek Chamber of Commerce, Rt 4, Chetek, WI 54728, (715) 924-4765
Chetek Resort Owners Assoc., PO Box 172, Chetek, WI 54728, (715) 924-4440
Cumberland Chamber of Commerce, PO Box 665, Cumberland, WI 54829 (715) 822-2477
Ladysmith Area Chamber of Commerce, 817 Miner Ave, Ladysmith, WI 54848, (715) 532-3561
Osceola Business Assoc., Box 251, Osceola, WI 54020, (715) 755-3300
Polk County UWEX Office, Center Building, Balsam Lake, WI 54810, (715) 485-3136
Rice Lake Chamber of Commerce, 37 South Main St, Rice Lake, WI 54868 (715) 234-2126
Rusk County Clerk's Office, 311 East Miner Ave, Ladysmith, WI 54848 (715) 532-2100
St Croix Falls, Chamber of Commerce, PO Box 278, St Croix Falls, WI 54024

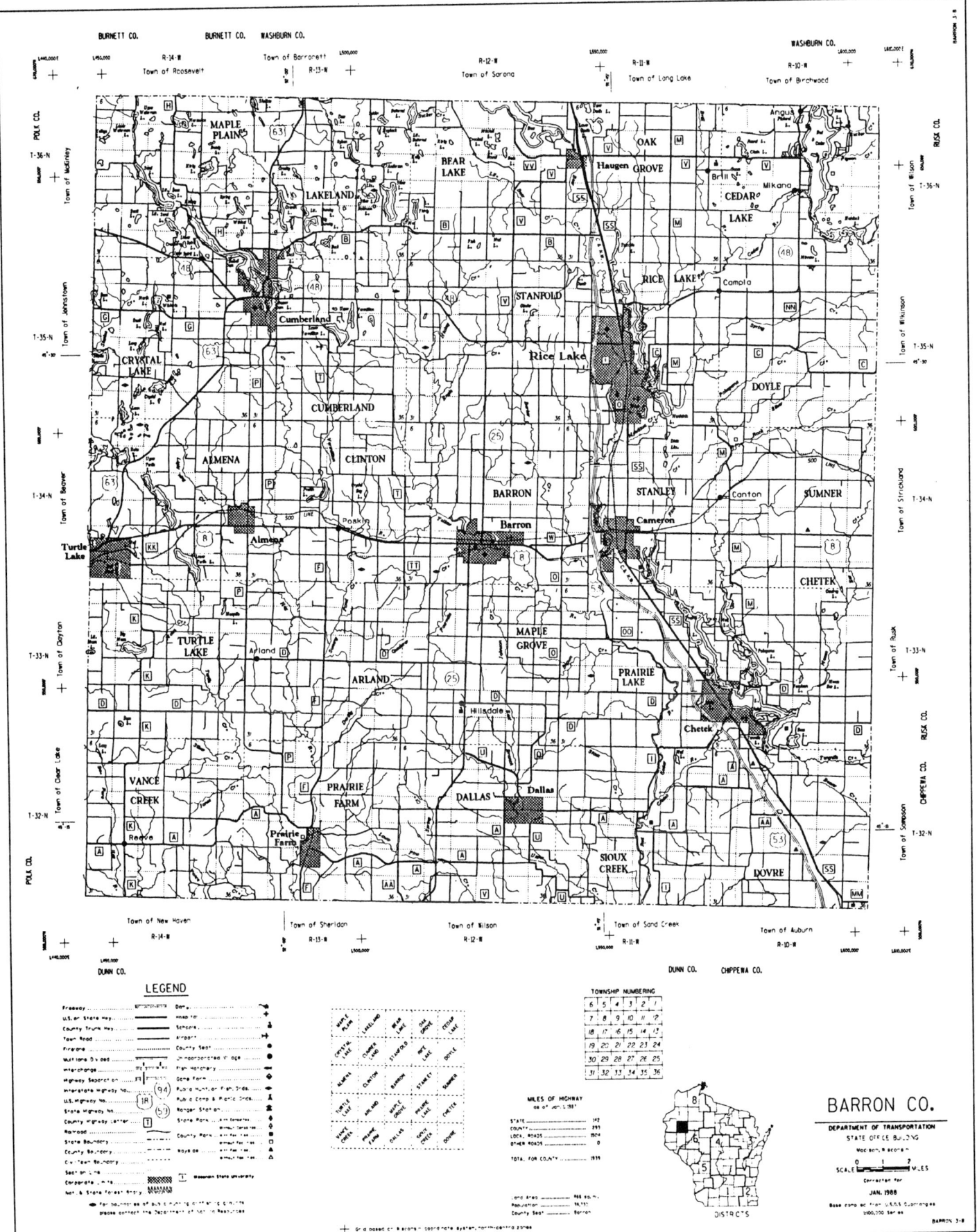

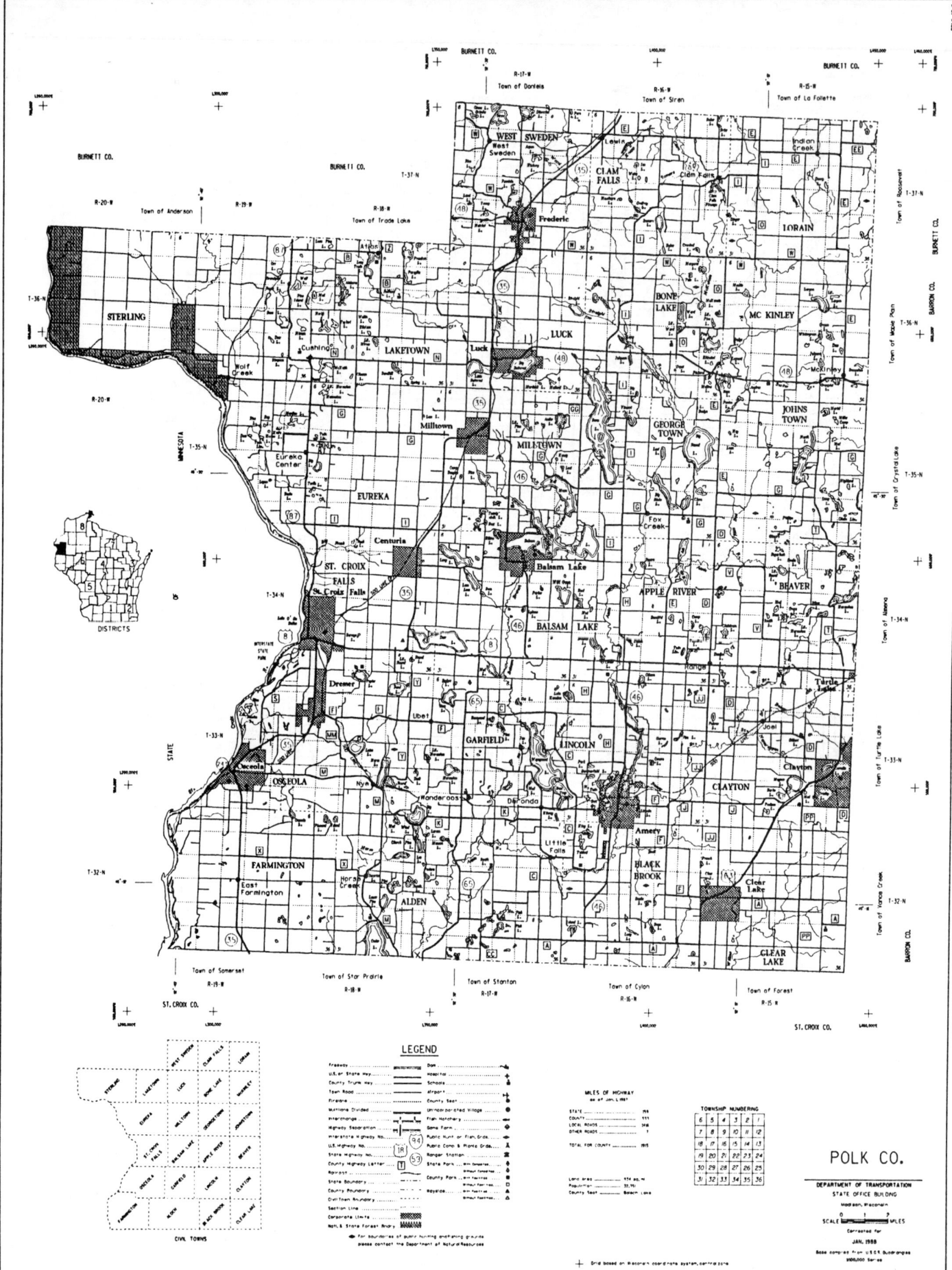

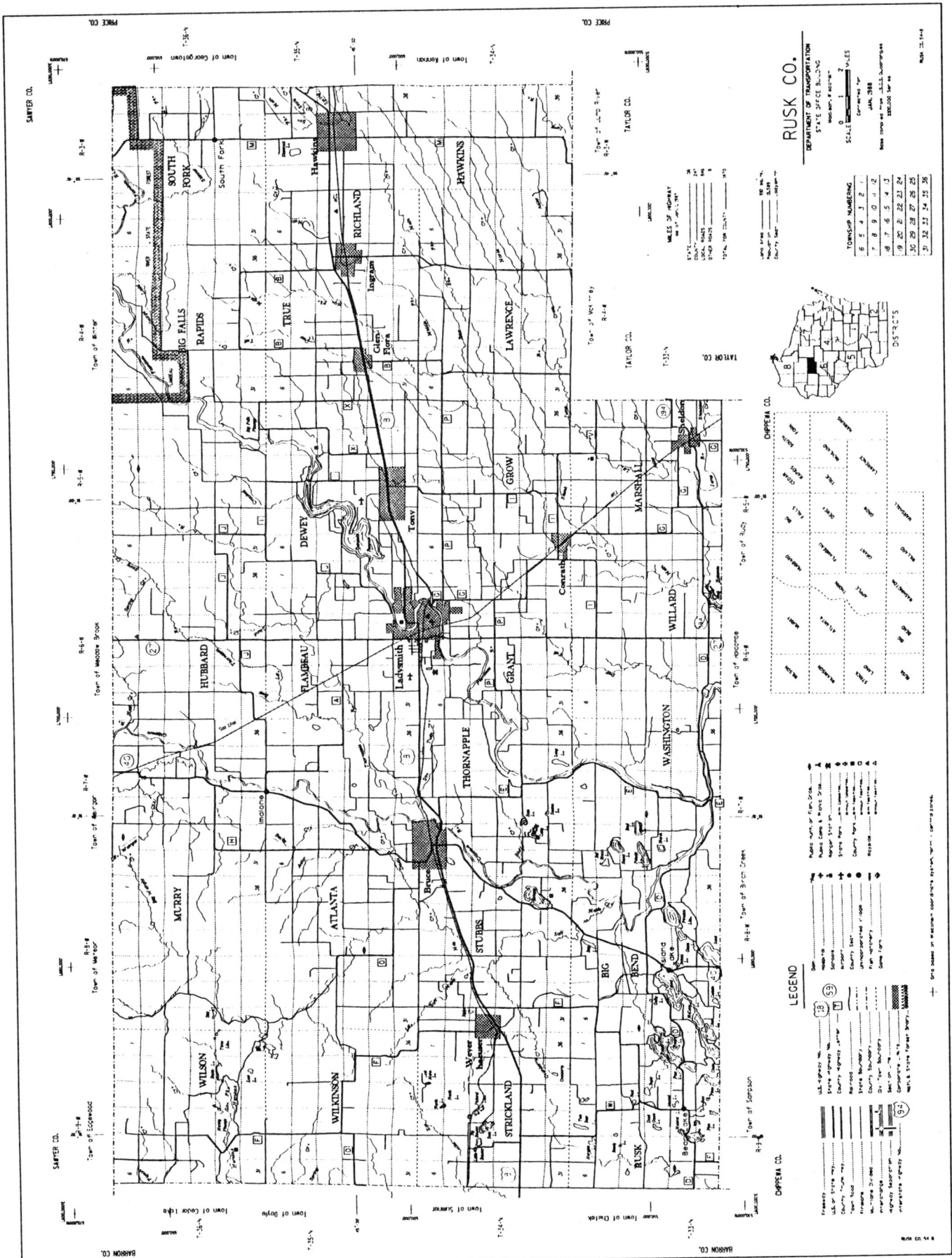

AREA 4
Western Coast Area
Dunn, Pepin and St Croix Counties

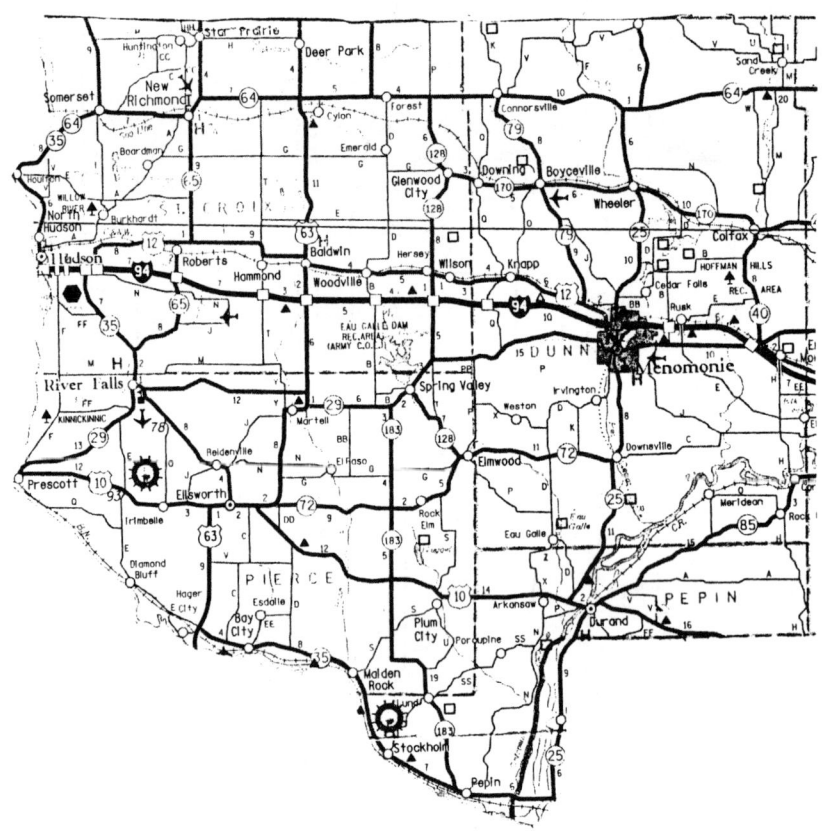

The early history of the Western Coast Area is preserved in songs and tales of the Indians, explorers and trappers who made their way through this wilderness in the 17th and 18th centuries. In later years the loggers, lumber barons and immigrants retraced the steps of the early explorers to carve a new home out of the land stretched before them. The new settlers were struck by the beauty and power of the landscape--mighty rivers, bluffs, river valleys and rolling hills, all of which escaped the last great advance of the glaciers, but not by much. Just to the north one can see the terminal moraines of the last advance.

Wisconsin's Western Coast is framed by two large river valleys of the Mississippi and St. Croix Rivers, cut by the glacial melt waters. The broad valley of the Mississippi, with its bluffs up to 300 feet tall, runs from Diamond Bluff to Iowa. This area is also the start of Coulee Country, which is another name for the many streams and river valleys located here.

There are a number of cities plus a scattering of unincorporated settlements.

In **Dunn County**, Menomonie, the county seat, is located in south central Dunn County on I-94. Elk Mound is to the east off I-94. To the north on Hwy 25 is Wheeler with Colfax to the east of Hwy 170 and Boyceville and Downing to the west on Hwy 170.

In **Pepin County**, Durand, the county seat, is located on Hwy 10. To the southwest along the Mississippi River on Hwy 35 is Stockholm and Pepin.

In **Pierce County**, Ellsworth, the county seat, is located on Hwy 10 in the center of the county. River Falls is to the northwest on Hwy 29 with Spring Valley to the northeast on Hwy 29. To the southeast on Hwy 10 is Plum City and Prescott to the west. To the south on Hwy 35 along the Mississippi River is Bay City and Maiden Rock.

In **St Croix County**, Hudson, the county seat located in the west end of the county on I-94. Ten miles to the west is Minneapolis/St Paul. To the east along Hwy 12 there is Roberts, Hammnd, Baldwin, Woodville and Wilson. To the north along Hwy 64 there is Sommerset and New Richmond. Along the northern county line is Star Prairie on Hwy 65 and Deer Park on Hwy 46.

RECREATIONAL WATERS

Lakes and Flowages:

There are 43 named (10,473 acres) and 92 unnamed (377 acres) lakes in the region, including several man-made flowages. This accounts for 0.9 % of the total number of Wisconsin lakes, covering 1.1 % of the state's total inland surface water. As we go farther south out of the glaciated areas there are more rivers, but fewer lakes. The older, ancient glacier lakes have disappeared with many rivers developing well defined river valleys. Many of the rivers have fluctuating water levels, making them difficult to canoe.

Dunn County has 7 named (3,595 acres) and 10 unnamed (34 acres) lakes; larger ones are flowages.

Tainter Lake, 1,752 acre flowage, starts about 4 miles northeast of Menomonie. It can be reached by Hwy 25 and Cty BB, D and G. Landings can be found on both the north and south sides and at a county park. The area is more scenic, with less development than surrounding lakes. Fishing is for walleye, large and smallmouth bass, northern pike, crappies and white bass.

Menomin Lake, 1,405 acres, located on the northeast side of Menomonie, is a flowage of the Red Cedar River. The southwestern shore is well developed. A city park is on the south shore with a county boat landing and park on the north shore. The lake provides good fishing for walleye and bluegills. The back waters north to Tainter Lake also provide good fishing. Spring white bass runs can be found just below the Cedar Falls Hydro Dam and Rapids.

Pepin County has 5 named (221 acres) and 20 unnamed (52 acres) lakes. The more noted ones include:

Lake Pepin, which in reality is a natural flowage on the Mississippi River. The lake's dimensions have changed over time due to sifting sediments and water levels. Presently the lake is about 30 miles long and 3 miles wide, at the widest point, with a depth from 20 to 35 ft. There is a mix of shoreline types framed against the high bluff. The fishery is a good mix of warm water species. There are other recreational opportunities including boating.

Pierce County has 5 named (238 acres) and 28 unnamed (149 acres) lakes. The more noted ones include:

Nugget Lake, 116 acre flowage, is located north of Plum City in the southeast area of the county. The lands around this flowage on the Plum Creek are county owned and have been developed into a park. This has helped in maintaining an undeveloped look. There is a good bass and bluegill fishery.

St Croix County has 26 named, (6,629) acres and 34 unnamed, (143 acres) lakes.

St Croix Lake, 4,668 acres, is a natural widening of the St Croix River. It is located at Hudson on the Wisconsin/Minnesota state line. Being one of the few large lakes in the area, it is heavily used for sailing, boating, water skiing and fishing. Fisheries are a good mix of warm water fishes like walleye, catfish, sturgeon, panfish and more. The area is well developed, even though it is still part of the National Scenic Riverway. Access can be found in the settlements along the river.

Cedar Lake, 1,107 acres, is located on the Polk County line. Go north of New Richmond on Hwy 65 to Star Prairie, then west on Cty H and around the lake on Cty H, HH or M. As with many of the area's lakes, it is well developed with access on the north and south ends. Fisheries are primarily walleye and white bass with a mix of other game species.

Bass Lake, 293 acres, is located north of Hudson on Hwy 12 east, then north on Cty A, then north on Cty I and east on 153rd Ave to a landing at a county park. Fisheries include largemouth bass and bluegills. The area around the lake is well developed.

Perch Lake, 43 acres, is a smaller lake which is stocked with trout. It is a deep lake, 63 ft, with clear waters. The shoreline is about 50% developed. It is located north of Hudson on Hwy 35, then east on Cty E and north 1/2 mile on 130th Ave to the landing.

Rivers:

St Croix River, is a 164 mile river that extends well into northern Wisconsin. It is also a National Scenic Riverway. For more information please see Area 2, page 47 for more information.

Kinnickinnic River, has its start in central St Croix County and flows south and west to River Falls through several small flowages, through a narrow river valley with a gorge into the St Croix River. The river is noted for its trout fishing. However it cannot be canoed, especially below River Falls. Normally the water levels are too low; however when there is high water these sections become very dangerous. Canoeing at that time is not recommended by the WI DNR.

Mississippi River, is this country's longest river, which stretches from Upper Minnesota to the Gulf Coast below New Orleans. In this area the river begins its passage between bluffs which extend down to Iowa. Between the main river channel and the bluffs are railroads, cities, wetlands, backwaters and more. The river is used for barge transportation, fishing, hunting, boating and other recreation. These waters provide good fishing for many species of fish including catfish, panfish, walleye and bass. Such a large river as the Mississippi will have very dangerous currents, especially during periods of high water. Care must be taken when boating or swimming.

Red Cedar River, has its start just south of Hwy 8 near Cameron where several creeks and the Yellow River join. It flows south through Sand Creek Village to Colfax, then southeast into Tainter Lake, then south over Cedar Falls Hydro Dam and Rapids and into Lake Menomin. South of Menomonie the river flows through farm lands and broad river valleys into the Chippewa River. The river also provides good fishing along the way. Access points are provided at county parks and picnic areas.

Rush River, flows from Eastern St Croix County south through Pierce County into Lake Pepin. Though it is 124 miles long, only the lower portions can be accessed by boat due to size and water level fluctuations. The upper reaches are trout waters.

Apple River, has its start at Wapogasset Lake in central Polk County. From there it flows south through farm and wooded lands to Star Prairie. It continues southwest over several dams and flowages to Somerset. From this point the river is used for tubing, down to the Apple Falls Flowage. From the flowage, the river drops through a canyon and into the St Croix River. Much of the river is shallow, sandy and meandering.

Chippewa River, completes its journey to the Mississippi River. The river flows through broad timbered river bottoms and valleys with its slow moving, meandering waters. There are many sloughs, islands and backwater areas, providing a wilderness look. Waterfowl and furbearers are present plus a good fishery of walleye and small mouth bass. The bottom is sifting sands and gravels. Much of this section of the river is part of the Tiffany Wildlife Area.

Trout Streams:

There are 108 streams classed as trout waters, covering 419 miles. There are 32 miles of Class I, 260 Miles of Class II and 127 miles of Class III. Several of the noted streams include the Willow and Kinnickinnic River in St Croix County; Rush and Eau Galle Rivers and Trimbelle Cr. in Pierce, and in Dunn County, many of the smaller streams provide good fishing.

Public Lands

County:

Dunn County, has no county forest; however there are a number of parks.
Pepin County, has no county forest or recreational lands; however there are several parks.
Pierce County, has no county forest. There is one county park on Nugget Lake.
St Croix County, has no county forest; however there are three county parks.

State:

Dunn County:
Muddy Creek Wildlife Area, 5,400 acres of state owned and leased lands, is located between Menomonie and Elk Mound. I-94 is on the north border, Hwy 12/29 passes through the property, and Iron Cr Rd and Waneka Rd, north of Cty E, also provide access. The lands are a mix of farm lands, small wood lots, marsh and stream. This is primarily a public hunting grounds for stocked pheasants. Other small game, waterfowl and deer are also present.

Dunnville Wildlife Area, 5,200 acres of state owned and leased lands, is located about 10 miles south of Menomonie on Hwy 25, then east 2 miles on Cty Y. The Chippewa River forms the eastern boundary. The property is a mix of farm lands, river bottoms and oxbow lakes. It is managed as a public hunting grounds for pheasants and waterfowl with small game, dear and furbearers present.

Many of the smaller properties listed below were acquired to improve fishery habitat and provide access to area streams and rivers. As an additional benefit, these lands provide good wildlife habitat for watching and hunting. These lands are a mix of farm lands, river bottoms, marshes and brush.
Big Beaver Creek, 954 acres, is located 3 miles east of Boyceville on Hwy 170, then 5 miles north on Cty F, then west on Big Beaver Rd. The property is to the south along the creek.
Bolan Cr, is located north of Boyceville on Hwy 79, then 1 mile west on Hwy 64 and just north on Cty Q. The property is to the west of Cty Q and north of Old Hwy 64.
Eau Galle River, 237 acres, is located 13 miles southwest of Menomonie on Cty D, then west 1.5 miles on Cty C.
Gilbert Cr, 120 acres, is located 7 miles west of Menomonie on Hwy 29, just before Cty Q, north.
Hay Cr, 375 acres, located about 8 miles east of Hwy 25 on Hwy 64, then north 1/4 mile on Sunnyside Rd. The property is to the east along the creek.
Hay River, 122 aces, is begins 1 mile east of Wheeler on Hwy 170. The property is east and south to the river.
Otter Cr, 402 acres, is located 4 miles north of Hwy 64 at Wheeler on Hwy 25, then 1 1/4 mile east on Clover Swamp Rd. The property is to the north, south and east along the creek.
Lambs Cr, 895 acres, is located 5 miles north of Menomonie on Hwy 25. The property is to the west on Woods Rd. The properties are scattered along the creek between Cty F and Hwy 25.

Pierce County:
Rush River Wildlife Area, 119 acres, is located at Maiden Rock, south of Hwy 35 where the Rush River enters the Mississippi River. This is a delta area and river bottoms with timber. The primary wildlife species include waterfowl, deer and furbearer.
Pierce County Islands, 831 acres, is a group of islands and shoreline along the Mississippi River between Hwy 63 and Bay City. The property is a mix of river bottoms, sloughs and timber with deer, waterfowl and furbearers present.

Pepin County:
Tiffany Wildlife Area, 12,300 acres, is located west of Durand on Cty P and south on Cty N. The property will be to the east on town roads all the way to the Mississippi River. A second route would be to continue south on Hwy 25. After crossing the Chippewa River the property will be west of Hwy 25. Located in both Pepin and Buffalo Counties, the Chippewa River passes through the middle of the project. It is an area of river bottoms, backwater channels and sloughs. It is primarily a waterfowl and furbearers area. It is a great area to observe wildlife in a river environment.
Thompson Slough, 233 acres, is located 1 mile west of Durand on Cty P. The property is on the south side of the road. This is mainly farm lands and river bottom, offering a variety of small game species.

St Croix County:
St Croix Islands, 1,046 acres, is located west of Somerset and Cty I. The property is made up of islands in the St Croix River, Apple River and adjacent shoreland. The area is managed for pheasant and deer. The last mile before the Apple River enters the St Croix is called the Apple River Canyon Natural Area for its unique and still natural state. This area can be reached by Rice Lake Rd, 210th Ave and 192nd Ave west of Cty I.
Cyclon, 1,849 acres, & Cyclon Marsh, 513 acres, are located in northeast St Croix County. From Hwy 64, go north on Hwy 63, then west on Cty H, then north 1 mile to the marsh, which is to the west. If you stay on Cty H and south on 250th St the project is to the west. 222nd Ave is on the north and 220th St is on the west. 240th St runs into the project. Cylon is a mix of marsh and farm lands managed as public hunting grounds for pheasant and deer. Cyclon Marsh is all leased lands in a marsh/lowland/brush area for stocking and hunting pheasants.

Federal:

Federal Waterfowl Production Areas, 1,000 acres, are small scattered parcels throughout the county. These areas are owned by the federal government and managed by the WI DNR primarily for the production of waterfowl. Wetlands, grassy cover areas and good quality water is maintained to produce waterfowl. These would be good spots to observe ducks and other waterfowl species.

PARKS, LANDINGS AND OTHER THINGS:

Dunn County:

County Parks:

Boyceville Village Park, is located north of the Hay River on Hwy 79. There is a picnic area with playground, drinking water and toilets.
Caddie Woodlawn Park, is located south of Downsville on Hwy 25. This park has the home of Caroline Woodhouse, whose life story was novelized by her granddaughter in "Caddie Woodlawn". Facilities at the park include picnic area with shelter, drinking water and toilets.
Champney Park, is located north of Menomonie on Cty B. The park is on the south shore of Upper Lake Tainter. Facilities include boat landing, picnic area, drinking water and toilets.
Dr Felland Park, is located on Hwy 170 just west of Colfax. There is a picnic area with drinking water and toilets.
Eau Galle Dam Park, is located at the dam on Cty D in town. There is a picnic area with toilets.
Lambs Creek Park, is located north of Menominie on Hwy 25, then east on Cty D and south on Cty G to the bridge. The park is on the south shore at the narrows between Upper and Lower Lake Tainter. Facilities include boat landing, picnic area, drinking water and toilets.
Myron Park, is located on Cty I north of Sand Creek in the northeast corner of the county. There is a campgrounds with picnic area, boat landing, drinking water and toilets.
Northwest Landing, is located north of Menominie on Hwy 25, then east on Cty D. The park is to the south on the north shore of Upper Lake Tainter. Facilities include boat landing, picnic area, drinking water and toilets.
Pineview Park, is located is located south of Menominie on Hwy 25, then south on Cty Z at Downsville. The park is on the east shore of Lake Eau Galle. There is a picnic area with boat landing, swimming, drinking water and toilets.
Sand Creek Park, is located is on the north side of Cty V in Sand Creek. The park, on the west shore of the Red Cedar River, has a boat landing with swimming and toilets.
Thatcher Park, is located in the northwest corner of the county, north of Hwy 64 at Cornersville on Cty K. Facilities include picnic area and toilets at the south branch of Hay River.
22 mile Ford Park, is located just east of Colfax on Hwy 40, then north on Cty M. The park is on the west side on the Red Cedar River. There is a boat landing, picnic area, toilets and drinking water.
Lake Menomin County Park, is located on the east side of Menomonie off Hwy 12/29, follow the signs. Several organizations are developing hiking and ski trails. There are hiking trails plus a picnic area, shelter and handicap fishing.

Municipal Parks:

Andy Pafko Park, is located on Hwy 170 in Boyceville. There is a picnic area with drinking water and toilets.
Boyceville Airport Trailer Park, is located on Hwy 78 south of Hwy 170. Facilities include camping, picnic area, drinking water and toilets.
Colfax Memorial Park, is located east of Hwy 40 on Railroad Ave, then north on a short side road. Located on Eighteen Mile Cr, there is a picnic area with playground and toilets.
Knapp Village Park, is located in Knapp on Hwy 12. Facilities include a picnic area with swimming, drinking water and toilets.

City of Menomonie:

Cedar-Rama Park, located on Lake Menomin on Stout Rd (Hwy 29), just east of Main St, has a picnic area & water.
Point Comfort Park, located on the east side of town, is east on Stout Rd (Hwy 29), then north on 21st St. There is a picnic area with boat landing, playground, swimming, drinking water and toilets.
Wakanda Park, located on the north side of town, and east of Hwy 25/12 on Pine St. There is a boat landing, picnic area, playground, drinking water and toilets plus the Lions Club Game Park (buffalo, elf & deer) and nature trails.
Riverside Park, is located south of Hwy 29 and on the west shore of the Red Cedar River. This is the start of the Red Cedar State Park Trail. There is a picnic area with playground, drinking water and toilets.

State Parks:

Hoffman Hills State Park, is located east of Menomonie on Hwy 12, then north on Cty E, then north on Cedar Valley Rd to the park, which is also just west of Hwy 40. This is a 656 acre park with 8.5 miles of trails for hiking and cross country skiing. There is a shelter, observation tower, drinking water, toilets and organized youth group camping.

State Waysides:

Hwy 12, located 0.1 miles west of Cty K east of Knapp, has a picnic area with drinking water.
Hwy 12, located .75 miles west of Cty B east of Menomonie, has a picnic area with drinking water and toilets.
Hwy 64, located 0.5 miles west of Cty M on the Red Cedar River, has a picnic area, boat landing, drinking water & toilets.
I-94, east bound, located 5.6 miles east of Hwy 25, has a picnic area, drinking water and toilets.
I-94, West bound, located 9.1 miles east of Hwy 25, has a picnic area, drinking water and toilets.

Pepin County:

County Parks:

Silver Birch & Holden Parks, are located west of Durand on Cty P, then 1 mile south on Cty N and east on Cty NN. These parks are on Birch Lake. There is camping, with water and toilets.

Municipal Parks:

Pepin City Beach is located south of First St, on Lake St. The beach is on Lake Pepin.
Sportmen's Landing, Pepin, is located at the east end of First St. The landing provides access to Lake Pepin.
Stockholm Village Park, is located south of Hwy 35 in Stockholm. Facilities include a picnic area, shelter, drinking water, toilets, boat landing, camping, playground and fishing.
Deer Island Boat Landing is located about 3 miles south of Stockholm on Hwy 35. The landing is on a side road, south of the highway.

City of Durand:

Memorial Park, is located in downtown Durand, two blocks north of the jct of Hwy 25 & 10 and one block west. The park has a picnic area, toilets, playground, a small wading pool, and open shelter.
Tarrant Park, located on the north and west side of Hwy 85, on the north side of town, has a picnic area with shelters, swimming pool, concession stand, toilets, playground, organized sports, drinking water and toilets.

State Waysides:

Hwy 35, located 2.7 miles north of Cty J on Lake Pepin, has a scenic overlook, picnic area, drinking water and toilets.
Hwy 10, located 0.7 miles southeast of Cty V, has a picnic area, drinking water and toilets.
Hwy 25, located 1.75 miles southwest of the northern county line, has a scenic overlook, picnic area, drinking water & toilets.
Hwy 35, located at Cty JJ, has a picnic area, drinking water and toilets.

Pierce County:

County Parks:

Nugget Lake County Park, 752 acres, RR1, Box 213 B, Plum Lake, WI 54761, (715) 639-5611, is the county's only park. It is located east of Ellsworth on Hwy 72, then south on Hwy 183 and east on Cty HH. The park has a 116 acre lake with beach and changing house. There is a boat landing, camping, dumpstation, hiking and ski trails, picnic area, shelters, canoe and boat rentals, playground and drinking water. A entrance fee is charged.

City of River Falls:

Glen Park, is located west of Main St (Hwy 29) on Park St, on the Kinnickinnic River. Facilities include organized sports, open fields, hiking and ski trails, picnic area and playground.

City of Prescott:

Freedom Park, is located south of Hwy 10 on Broad St to Jefferson St. The park is to the south on the Mississippi River. There is a picnic area, camping, playground, drinking water and toilets.
City Beach, is located on Lake St, west of Hwy 10 on Lake St Croix. There is a beach with bathhouse.
Mercord Mill Park, is located just south of where Hwy 10 crosses the Mississippi River on Front St. Facilities include picnic area with shelter.
Boat Landing, on the Mississippi River, is located south of where Hwy 10 crosses the Mississippi River on Front St.

Municipal Parks:

Spring Valley Municipal Park, is located on Hwy 29 on the west side of town. There is a picnic area, shelter, drinking water, playground and toilets.
Village Park, Plum City, located on Main St south of Hwy 10, has a picnic area with shelter.
Village Park, Maiden Rock, located on Lake St west of Hwy 35, has a picnic area with camping and boat landing on Lake Pepin.
Butternut Park, Elmwood, is located south of Hwy 72. There is a picnic area, camping, toilets, drinking water, playground, organized sports and hiking.
Ellsworth Community Park, Ellsworth, is located north and east of Main St (Hwy 10) on Grant St. There is a picnic area with shelter, toilets, drinking water and playground.
Triangle Park, Ellsworth, is located on Main St (Hwy 10) and Walls St. There is a picnic area with toilets, drinking water and playground.
Bay City Village Park, Bay City, is located south of Hwy 35 on Wabash Ave, then south on Lake Pepin Blvd. Located on Lake Pepin, this park has a picnic area, camping, toilets, drinking water, beach and boat landing.

State Parks:

Kinnickinnic State Park, Rt 3, Box 262, River Falls, WI 54022, (715) 425-1129, is located just north of Prescott on Hwy 10, then 1 mile east on Hwy 29, then about 4.5 miles north on Cty F. The park is still in the development stage. The main use and access is by boat, due to the parks location on the Kinnickinnic and St Croix Rivers. There is almost a mile of beach for picnicking, swimming and hiking. Boat camping is permitted for a fee.

State Waysides:

Hwy 35, located 3 miles west of Maiden Rock has a picnic area, drinking water and toilets.
Hwy 10, located 0.7 miles east of Cty D, has a picnic area, drinking water and toilets.
Hwy 29/63, located at the jct of Hwy 63 & 29, has a picnic area, drinking water and toilets.
Hwy 63, located on the Mississippi River at the Wisconsin Channel Fisherman's Lot, where there is a boat landing.

Federal Recreation Site:

Eau Galle Lake Recreation Site, operated by the Corp of Engineers, is located just north of Spring Valley on Hwy 183. The west area can be reached off Cty B and the campgrounds and boat landing are off Cty NN. This recreation area is on Eau Galle Lake, an impoundment of the Eau Galle River. There are three different recreation areas which are located in both Pierce and St Croix counties. The Main Day Use Area, just north of town, has beach with bathhouse, toilets, boat landing and picnic area. The Northwest Area offers hiking trails and toilets. The Campground Area has backpack and drive-on camp sites plus toilets, dumpstation, fire wood, drinking water, playground, overlooks and 6 trails. There is also a boat landing further south on Cty NN.

St Croix County:

County Parks:

Glenn Hills County Park Ski Trails, Rt 1, Box 111, Glenwood City, WI 54013, (715) 265-4613, is located north of I-94 on Hwy 128, then east on Cty E and north on Rustic Road #3. Located on Glen Lake, an impoundment, the facilities include picnic area, boat landing, beach, bathhouse, campground, showers, drinking water, toilets, scenic overlook, golf course and trails.

Pine Lake County Park is located north on Baldwin on Hwy 63, then west about a mile on 110th St and 1 mile north on 205th St. The park with picnic area, shelter, toilet and boat landing are on the west shore of Pine Lake.

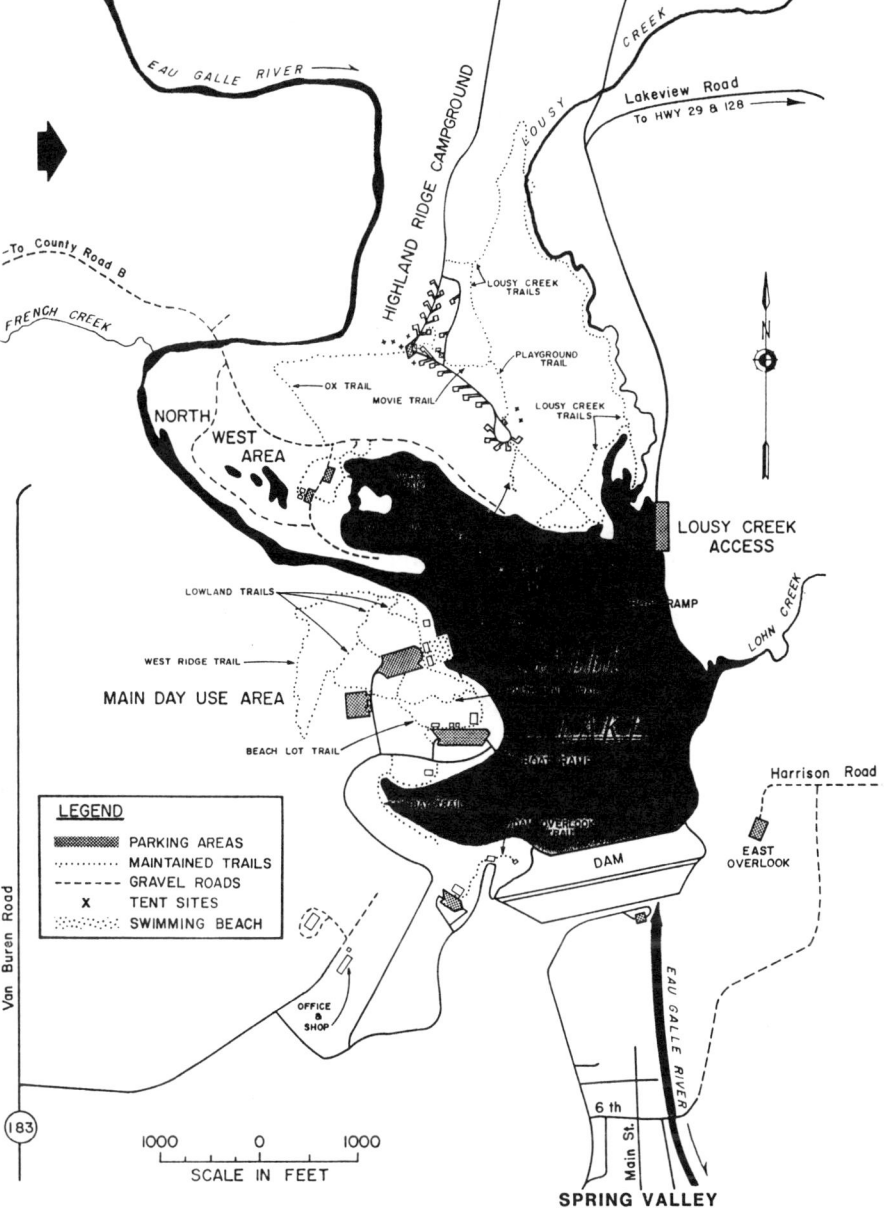

Troy County Beach, is located 1 mile south of Hudson on Cty F and west on Cty FFF. The park, located on the St Croix River, is open from June 1st to Sept 1st. There is a beach with changing room and toilets.

Municipal Parks:

Steven Memorial Park, Woodville, is located south of Hwy 12 on Lockwood St, then just east on River St. The park, to the north on the East Branch of the Eau Galle Cr, has organized sports, picnic area, shelter, and restrooms.

Mill Pond Park, Baldwin, is located in the eastern part of town between the railroad tracks and East Maple St. Facilities include organized sports, restrooms and picnic shelter.

Somerset Village Park, is located on River St just west of the river and north of Hwy 64. The park is used as a starting point for tubers on the river. Other facilities include picnic area, toilets and drinking water.

Veteran's Memorial Park, Somerset, is located west of the river and north of Hwy 64 on Hud St. Facilities include picnic area, shelter and playgrounds.

Mary Park, New Richmond, is located east of Hwy 65; take the first street south of the river to the east, then take the second street to the north. The park is on a mill pond on the Willow River. Facilities include picnic area, pool, shelter buildings, drinking water, restrooms, boat landing and organized sports.

New Richmond Nature Center, is located south of the jct of Cty A and Hwy 64. In this 16 acre wooded area there is the nature center, picnic area, toilets and 1 mile nature trail. No camping or motorized vehicles are permitted.
Hatfield Park, New Richmond, is located west of Hwy 65/64 on the north end of town on Hatfield Lake. Facilities include organized sports, shelters, picnic area, restrooms and a canoe landing.
Hinman Park, Glenwood City, is located on Hwy 170 between 6th and 7th St. Facilities include swimming beach, shelter, picnic area and playground.

City of Hudson:

Prospect Park, is located north of I-94 on Hwy 35, then take the first through road to the east. Facilities include shelters, picnic area, playground, toilets and nature area with wildflower trail.
Lakefront Park, is located north of I-94 on Hwy 35, take the first road to the west to Lake St Croix. Facilities include swimming, bathhouse, boat landing, bank fishing, sea wall for walks, picnic area, restrooms, drinking water and play area.

State Parks:

Willow River State Park, Rt 2, Hudson, WI 54016, (715) 386-5931, is located east of Hudson on I-94, then north on Hwy 12 1 3/4 miles, at Sono Jct continue north to Cty A, then north several miles to the park. Located along the Willow River Valley, the park offers many different sights, including a 200 ft gorge on the river, rolling terrain from the last glacier and more. Facilities include three camping areas, 8 miles of trails, three lakes, the Willow River, a nature center, beach, drinking water, toilets and picnic area.

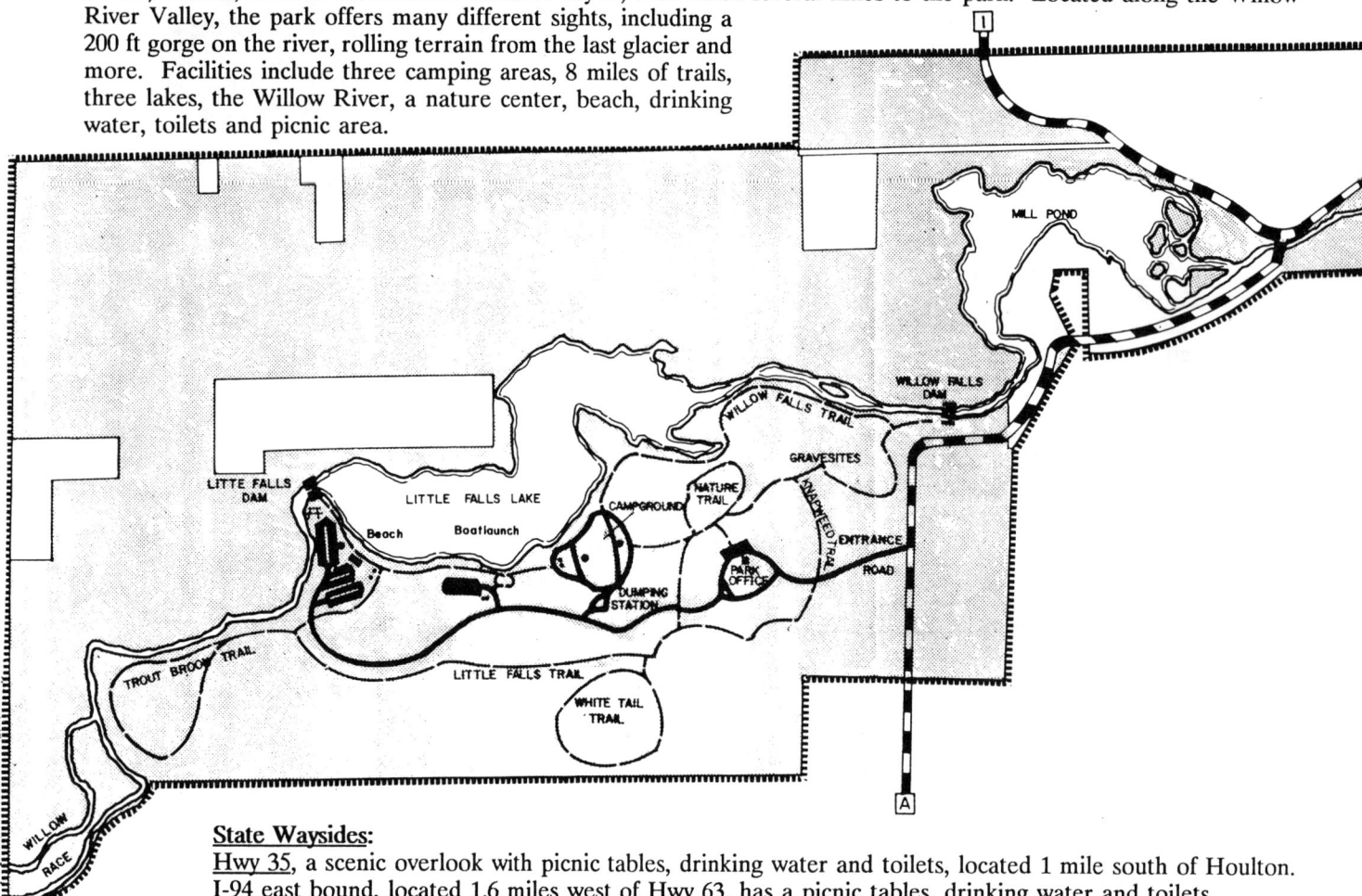

State Waysides:
Hwy 35, a scenic overlook with picnic tables, drinking water and toilets, located 1 mile south of Houlton.
I-94 east bound, located 1.6 miles west of Hwy 63, has a picnic tables, drinking water and toilets.
I-94 west bound, located 1.5 miles west of Hwy 128, has a picnic tables, drinking water and toilets.
I-94, located at Hudson, has a tourism center with picnic area, drinking water and toilets.

St Croix National Scenic Riverway, is discussed in Area 2, page 47 of this book.

TRAILS

Mountain Bikes:

Dunn County, are permitted.
Pepin County, there are no trails.
Pierce County, lands are open for bike use.
St Croix County, there are no trails.
Wisconsin DNR, does permit the use of these bikes on selected trails managed by the Department. It is best to contact the property manager to get the latest information.
National Park Service, does not permit bikes off the paved surfaces.

All Terrain Vehicles:

Dunn County, are not permitted on county property.
Pepin County, there are no trails.
Pierce County, lands are not open for ATVs.
St Croix County, there are no ATV trails.
Wisconsin DNR, does not permit the use of these vehicles on any of the trails managed by the Department.
National Park Service, does not permit ATVs on their property.

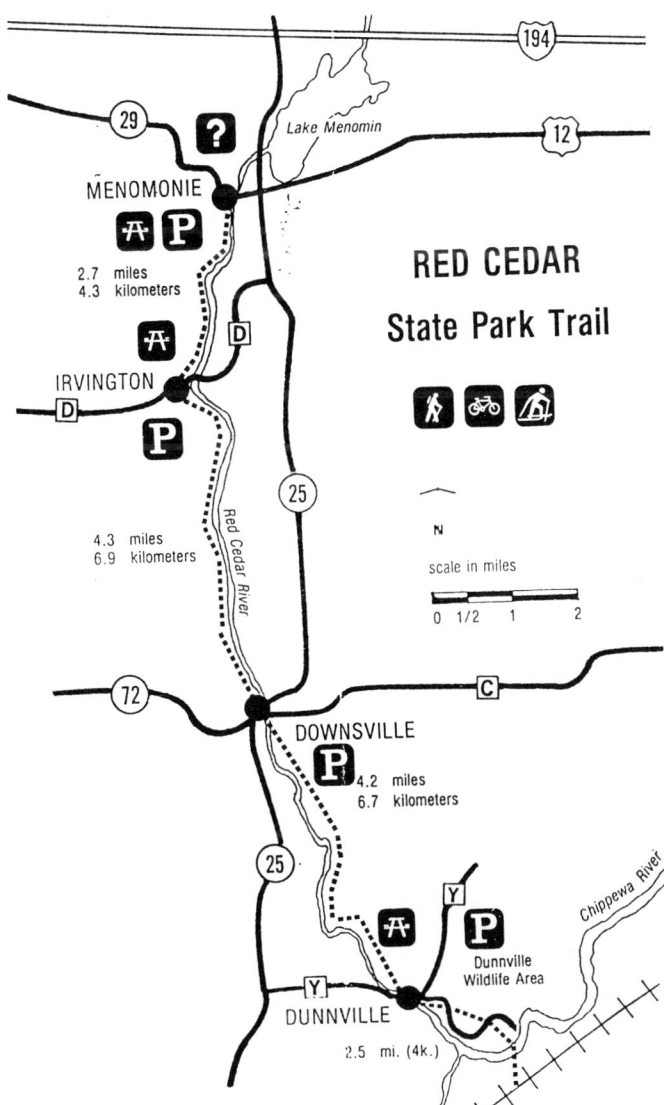

Horses:

Dunn County, does not permit horses on their properties.
Pepin County, there are no trails.
Pierce County, lands are not open to horses.
St Croix County, the only land that is open to horses is the Woodville Multi Use Trail.
Wisconsin DNR, policies vary with the properties; it is best to contact the property manager for the latest information.
National Park Service, does not permit horses on their trails.

Hiking, Hunting and Cross Country Ski Trails

Dunn County:

Red Cedar River State Park Trail, is a 14.5 mile long trail which starts on the south side of Hwy 29 at Riverside Park, Menomonie, which is on the west bank of the Red Cedar River. The trail extends south along the river through Irvington, Downsville and Dunnville to the Chippewa River. The trail surfaced with limestone screening, is flat with eleven bridges, making it ideal for biking, hiking, cross country skiing and more.

Lake Menomin County Park, is located on the east side of Menomonie off Hwy 12/29, follow the signs. Several organizations are developing hiking and ski trails. Presently there are 10 miles of trails and a picnic area.

<u>Hoffman Hills State Park</u>, is located east of Menomonie on Hwy 12, then north on Cty E, then north on Cedar Valley Rd to the park. There are 8.5 miles of trails for hiking and skiing, plus a shelter, observation tower, drinking water and toilets.

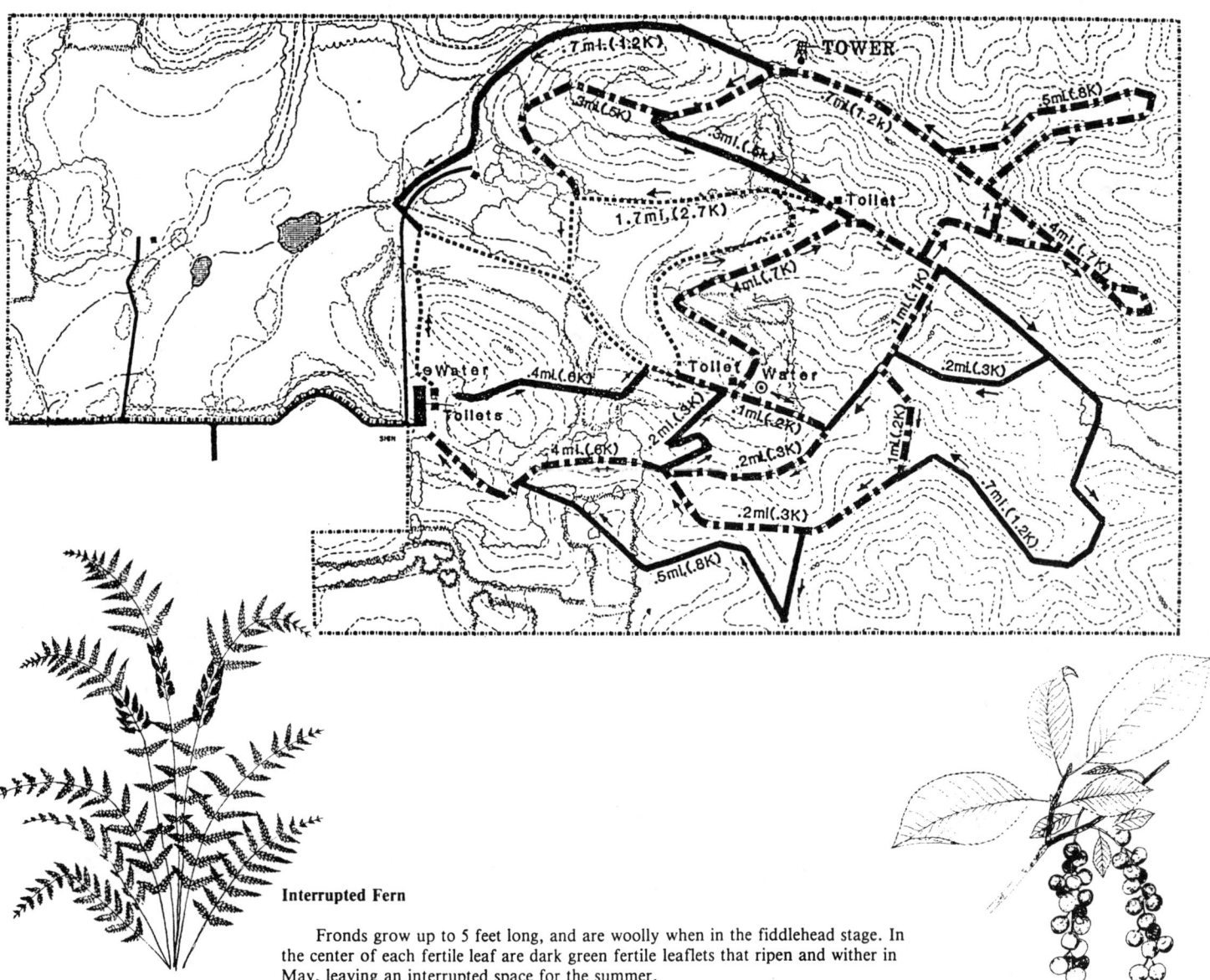

Interrupted Fern

Fronds grow up to 5 feet long, and are woolly when in the fiddlehead stage. In the center of each fertile leaf are dark green fertile leaflets that ripen and wither in May, leaving an interrupted space for the summer.

Interrupted fern. GK

Choke Cherry

This is usually a shrub or small tree with egg-shaped, sharp-toothed leaves. The bark is gray-brown and smooth. Flowers, usually white, appear between April and July.

Purplish fruits appear between July and October. The tart berries can be made into jellies, pies or wine. Many species of birds feed on the berries and animals such as deer and rabbits eat the tender bark and twigs.

Leaves and twigs, like those of the black cherry, may cause serious cyanide poisoning if eaten. Crushed leaves and broken twigs smell like burnt almond.

Choke cherry. GK

Pepin County: There are no official trail systems in the county.

Pierce County:

Nugget Lake County Park Ski/Hiking Trails, are located east of Ellsworth on Hwy 72, then south on Hwy 183 and east on Cty HH. There are 6 miles of trails open for hiking and intermediate cross country skiing.
Eau Galle Lake Recreation Site, operated by the Corp of Engineers, is located just north of Spring Valley on Hwy 183. The west area can be reached off Cty B and the campgrounds is off Cty NN. Trails can be found at the Main Day Use Area and Highland Ridge Campground.

St Croix County:

Glenn Hills County Park Ski & Hiking Trails, Rt 1, Box 111, Glenwood City, WI 54013, (715) 265-4613, is located north of I-94 on Hwy 128, then east on Cty E and north on Rustic Road #3. The park is on the east side. There are several loops, with one for beginners.
Willow River State Park, (715) 386-5931, is located east of Hudson on I-94, then north on Hwy 12 1 3/4 miles, at Sono Jct continue north to Cty A, then north several miles to the park. There are 6 trails covering 8 miles. These include Burr Oak Nature Trail (with 35 stations), Little Falls, Trout Brook, White Tail, Knapweed and Willow Falls Trail.
Woodville Multi-Use Trail, is an abandoned railroad acquired by the county, from Woodville south to the county line. The trail, used by hikers, bikers, horseback riders and others, extends about 7 miles south, crossing I-94 and parallels 250th St. At the county line the old railroad turns east into Spring Valley.
Wisconsin's Great River Road, follows the Mississippi River along the 250 miles of Wisconsin's west coast. Located between the bluffs and the river, this scenic route starts at Prescott were the St Croix River joins the Mississippi. It then follows Cty E and Q south to Hager City, where it follows Hwy 35 south to Prairie Du Chien in southern Wisconsin. The route takes you through small villages, past scenic overlooks and provides excellent views of the river and the happenings along it. The section from Maiden Rock to Alma is considered one of most scenic in America.

Canoe Trails:

There are many rivers in this area of Wisconsin. However due to the shallow, meandering nature of many of these rivers, they are not easily canoed. In addition, spring and summer flash floods may occur, giving way to dangerous conditions. Please check with local authorities or the WI DNR about the canoeing conditions on these rivers.
Willow River, due to fluctuating water levels, river valleys and its shallow, meandering course, is not considered to be canoeable.
Rush River, Pierce County, is canoed in the spring time or when there is high water. There are no rapids but there may be riffle areas. You can put in at Cty A & Hwy 10, canoe south about 7 miles to Hwy 35 & the Mississippi River.
Red Cedar River, is canoed from Chetek to Sand Creek Park and on to Colfax off Hwy 170. This is considered a nice float trip with no rapids. The river provides good fishing along the way. There are access points provided by county parks and picnic areas.
St Croix River, is canoed throughout its entire length, however, the lower sections are heavily used by power boats. Caution must be used in the large and more open areas of the river. For more information please see section 2, page- - for more information.
Kinnickinnic River, due to its size and fluctuating water levels, is not a good canoeing river, especially the section below River Falls. Normally the water levels are too low for canoeing. However, when there is high water, these sections become very dangerous. Canoeing at that time is not recommended by the WI DNR.
Apple River, has its start at Wapogasset Lake in central Polk County. From there it flows south through farm and wooded lands to Star Prairie. Sections of the upper river to Star Prairie are canoed. Again, the water levels are important on just how canoeable the various sections really are.
Chippewa River, completes its journey to the Mississippi River. The river flows through broad timbered river bottoms and valleys with its slow moving, meandering waters. The many sloughs and backwater areas lend the river a more untamed, wilderness appearance. Canoeing provides an opportunity to see more waterfowl and furbearers.

GUIDES AND BAIT SHOPS

Area Bait Shops:

ARCHIE BAR	BOX 397	ARKANSAW	WI 54721
BALDWIN AUTO PRO	980 MAIN	BALDWIN	WI 54002
FARMERS COOP PROD ASSOC	930 10TH AVE	BALDWIN	WI 54002
GREAT RIVER ROAD GARAGE	BOX 33	BAY CITY	WI 54723
RIVER ROAD GARAGE	101 E HWY 35	BAY CITY	WI 54723
TAINTER LAKE BAIT & GUN SH	RT 2 BOX 199	COLFAX	WI 54730
LARRYS BAIT	RT 1 BOX 214	DEER PARK	WI 54007
DICK'S SPORTING GOODS	406 W MAIN ST	DURAND	WI 54736
OLLIES SPORT SHOP	301 MENOMONIE ST	ELK MOUND	WI 54739
BARBS' DAM RESORT	RT 1 BOX 1095	HAGER CITY	WI 54014
EVERT'S RESORT	BOX 1097	HAGER CITY	WI 54014
GENES TACKLE	RT 2 BOX 2006	HAGER CITY	WI 54014
ISLAND CAMPGROUND	RT 2 BOX 2124	HAGER CITY	WI 54014
BOAT-TIQUE/TOON FISHIN CHARTERS	501 2ND ST	HUDSON	WI 54016
BURKHARDT COOP	RT 2	HUDSON	WI 54016
HANSEN'S TEXACO	I94 & HWY 35	HUDSON	WI 54016
GREAT RIVER GIFT & TACKLE	HWY 35 MAIN ST BOX 236	MAIDEN ROCK	WI 54750
BIG JOES SPORT CENTER	513 N BROADWAY	MENOMONIE	WI 54751
TWIN SPRINGS CAMPGROUND	3010 CEDAR FALLS RD RT 7	MENOMONIE	WI 54751
WOLSKE BAY MARINA	900 WOLSKE BAY RD	MENOMONIE	WI 54751
BRETZ'S BAIT & BOAT	RT 2 BOX 95A	NEW RICHMOND	WI 54017
DOSTAL'S BAIT	RT 2 BOX 62	NEW RICHMOND	WI 54017
BERG'S SPORTING GOODS	BOX 3	PEPIN	WI 54759
SMITH BROTHERS LANDING	1ST ST BOX 122	PEPIN	WI 54759
SMITH BROTHERS LANDING INC	E FIST ST	PEPIN	WI 54379
LEO'S LANDING INC	137 FRONT ST	PRESCOTT	WI 54021
TOMS STORE	RT 1	RIDGELAND	WI 54763
FOUR SEASON'S SPORT & WORK	703 N MAIN	RIVER FALLS	WI 54022
JOEL'S BAIT & TACKLE	BOX 548	SIREN	WI 54872
RUSSELL'S SPORT 'N BIKE	730 JEWELL ST	STAR PRAIRIE	WI 54026
WILSON GEN STORE		WILSON	WI 54027

Area Guides:

BECKWITH	WAYNE	RT 3 BOX 124	COLFAX	WI 54730
CHRISTIANSON	DALE	RT 2 BOX 368	COLFAX	WI 54730
LUHMAN	STEVEN	BOX 181	DEER PARK	WI 54007
WIDMAR	JOHN	HWY C BOX 20	DOWNSVILLE	WI 54735
KRAFT	JAMES	RT 2 BOX 19	DURAND	WI 54736
LANGLOIS	THEODORE	854 E MADISON ST	DURAND	WI 54736
WHEELER	DONALD	RT 4 BOX 117B	EAU CLAIRE	WI 54701
WIINAMAKI	ROBERT	504 WINTER AVE	ELMWOOD	WI 54740
VOKES	EUGENE	RT 1 BOX 1081	HAGER CITY	WI 54014
VOLENEC	DOUGLAS	RT 1 BOX 1571	HAGER CITY	WI 54014
STEINMETZ	ROBERT	1442 E OAK TRL	HOULTON	WI 54082
ANDERSEN	THOMAS	985 SCOTT RD	HUDSON	WI 54016
BAUER	TERRY	327 3RD ST	HUDSON	WI 54016
BECKEN	HARVEY	1090 S FRONT ST	HUDSON	WI 54016
BECKEN	REBECCA	1090 S FRONT ST	HUDSON	WI 54016
BLEMKE	DANIEL	1103 6TH ST	HUDSON	WI 54016
HANSON	JEFFREY	327 1/2 DIVISION ST	HUDSON	WI 54016
PARK	ALAN	1029 SOMMER ST N	HUDSON	WI 54016
SCHILLING	JOHN	405 BROOKWOOD DR	HUDSON	WI 54016
ALLEGAR	LAWRENCE	350 PARK AVE	NEW RICHMOND	WI 54017
HESSELINK	LARRY	RT 1 BOX 70B	NEW RICHMOND	WI 54017
GRAY	MICHAEL	157 ELM ST	PRESCOTT	WI 54021
LIVINGSTON	LEONARD	1357 WALNUT ST	PRESCOTT	WI 54021
BECK	DAVID	450 W JOHNSON #6	RIVER FALLS	WI 54022
LOVICK	THOMAS	RT 2 BOX 240C	SOMERSET	WI 54025

CAMPGROUNDS

Dispersed Camping:

Dunn County, does not permit dispersed camping.
Pepin County, does not permit dispersed camping.
Pierce County, does not permit dispersed camping.
St Croix County, does not permit dispersed camping.
WI DNR, does not permit dispersed camping on its properties.
National Park Service, does not permit camping at non-designated sites.

Private Campgrounds:

Apple River Campground: located just north of Somerset on Hwy 35; 500 campsites (100 with water and elec), picnic tables, firewood, dump station, hot showers, restrooms, laundry, camp store, two game rooms, two swimming pools, concession stand, tubing; Apple River Campground, Box 307, Somerset, WI 54025; in Wisconsin - (800) 472-6803, outside Wisconsin - (800) 637-8936.

Edgewater Acres Campground: located on Cedar Falls Rd, 3 miles N.E. of I-94; wooded, lakeview sites, hot showers, heated pool, boat launch, rec hall, volleyball, horseshoes, dump station; on upper Lake Menomin; Menomonie, WI 54751; (715) 235-3291.

Float-Rite Park Campground: located off Hwy 64 in Somerset; tent & RV camping; restrooms, showers, picnic area, camp store, tubing, playground, dump station, laundry; Box 276, Somerset, WI 54025; in Wisconsin (715) 247-3453, outside of Wisconsin (800) 826-7096.

Gasper's Bar & RV Camp: located 2 miles north of Somerset on Hwy 35; RV camp, indoor volleyball, shuttle bus to tubing on the Apple River, food & liquor; Gaspers RV Camp, P.O. Box 50A, Somerset, WI 54025; (715) 247-3868.

Island Campground: located on the Mississippi River across the river from Red Wing, MN; 30 campsites, water, electricity, flush toilets, hot showers, dump station, laundry, boat launch, boat rentals, groceries; Island Campground; P.O. Box 256, Red Wing, MN 55066; (715) 792-2502.

KOA Campground: located in Menomonie; grassy level sites, restrooms, game room, swimming pool, mini golf, volleyball, Kamping Kabins; KOA Campground, Rt 7, Box 1, Menomonie, WI 54751; (715) 235-0641.

Pepin Ozarks Campground: located north of Pepin, turn right off 183 at cemetery; water, elec, showers, wooded sites, playground, hiking area; (715) 442-2600.

Sunrise Park: located 1/4 mile south of Somerset on Cty Hwy I; family camping, water, elec, picnic area, restrooms, showers, dump station, rec hall, playground, tubing; on the Apple River; Sunrise Park, P.O. Box 136, Somerset, WI 54025; (715) 247-5258.

Twin Spring Resort Campground: located on the north edge of Menomonie; 75 sites, 51 with water & elec, pull-through sites, showers, firewood, laundry, swimming pool, playground, mini golf, ball diamond, horseshoes, rec hall, trails, boat launch, bait; Twin Springs Resort Campground, 3010 Cedar Falls Rd, Menomonie, WI 54751; (715) 235-9321.

Yogi Bear's Jellystone Park Camp-Resort: located at River's Edge Tubing Park, 2 miles east of Somerset on Hwy 64; water & elec, hot showers, restrooms, laundry, camp store, playground, picnic area, dump station, swimming pool, tubing, water slides; River's Edge Camping, Box 67, Somerset, WI 54025; (715) 247-3305, outside WI (800) 826-7328.

Riverdale Campground: located at River's Edge Tubing Park, 2 miles east of Somerset on Hwy 64 (away from main portion of river); free shuttle service, water, elec, hot showers, picnic area, dump station, shaded sites, daily canoe trips, tubing, water slides; River's Edge Camping, Box 67, Somerset, WI 54025; (715) 247-3305, outside WI (800) 826-7328.

Municipal Campgrounds:

Butternut Park, Elwood: 15 campsites, water, a few electric hookups; Elmwood Village Hall; (715) 639-3792.

Village of Pepin Campground: located on Hwy 35 in Pepin; camping with water and restrooms, no fee; Pepin Municipal Campground, 1000 3rd St, Pepin, WI; contact Mrs James (Cindy) Fayerweather, Village Clerk, (715) 442-3171.

Freedom Park, Prescott: 12 campsites, open during the summer only; Prescott City Hall, (715) 262-5544.

Stockholm Village Park: no reservations needed; campsites include water and elec, toilets, picnic area, boat launch; Short Stop Grocery/Cafe, Merle Stewart, Stockholm, WI 54769; (715) 442-2023.

County Campgrounds:

Glen Hills County Park Campground: follow I-94 to the Glenwood City exit, go north approx 3 miles on Hwy 128, watch for signs; operated by St. Croix County; 61 campsites (34 with elec), clean toilets, drinking water, dump station, hot showers, swimming beach, picnic area, hiking trails, boat launch, canoe & boat rental, playground, scenic overlook, golf course; Glen Hills Park Manager, Rt 1, Box 111, Glenwood City, WI 54013; (715) 265-4613.

Nugget Lake County Park: located in Pierce County; 55 unit campground with elec on some units, water, toilets, picnic area, dump station, hiking and x-country ski trails, boat launch, swimming, bath changing houses, canoe and boat rental; open year round; on Nugget Lake, 116 acres; Nugget Lake Park, Plum City, WI 54761; (715) 639-5611.

Holden Park: located 4.5 miles southwest of Durand on Cty Hwy N; water, electricity and toilets; Pepin County.

Myron Park: located on Cty I north of Sand Creek in the northeast corner of the county; Dunn County; picnic area, boat landing, drinking water and toilets.

Silver Birch Park: located 4.5 miles southwest of Durand on Cty Hwy N; water and toilet facilities; Pepin County.

State Campground:

Willow River State Park: located east of Hudson on I-94, then north on Hwy 12 1 3/4 miles, at Sono Jct continue north to Cty A, then north several miles to the park; three camping areas; trails, three lakes, the Willow River, a nature center, beach, drinking water, toilets and picnic area; Rt 2, Hudson, WI 54016, (715) 386-5931; Willow River.

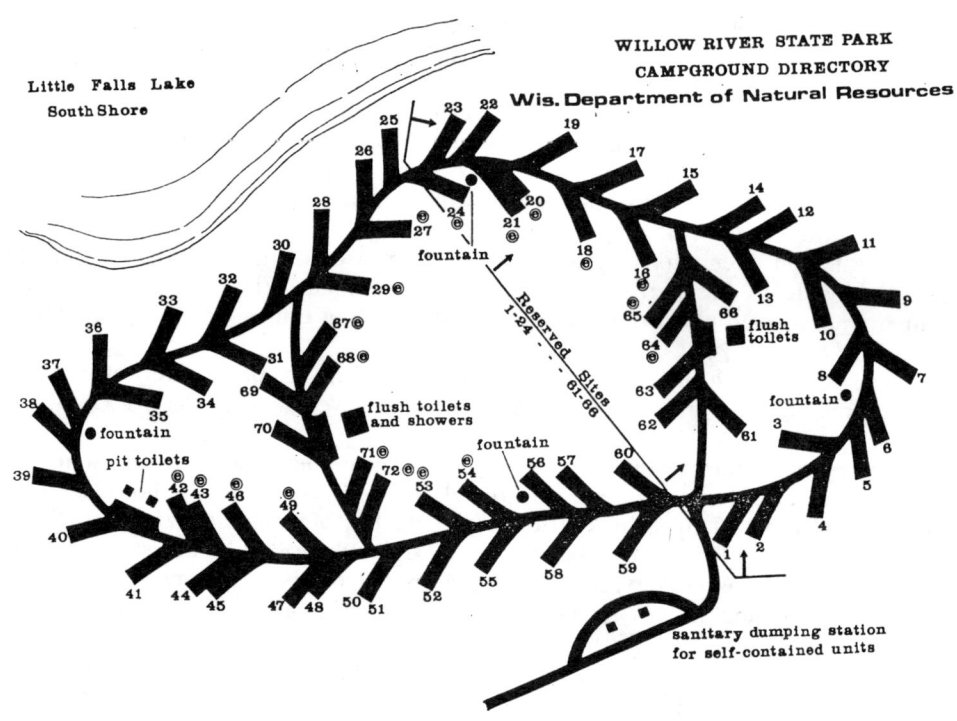

Federal Recreation Site:

Eau Galle Lake Recreation Site: located just north of Spring Valley on Hwy 183. The west area can be reached off Cty B and the campgrounds and boat landing are off Cty NN; 30 sites; Main Day Use Area, beach, bathhouse, toilets, boat landing, picnic area, toilets, backpack and drive-on camp sites, dumpstation, fire wood, drinking water, playground, overlooks and trails; US Army Corps of Engineers, Park Manager, Eau Galle Lake, P.O. Box 190, Spring Valley, WI 54767, (715) 778-5562; on Eau Galle Lake, an impoundment of the Eau Galle River.

Area Activities

Attractions:

<u>Apple River Grand Prix</u>: located 1 mile west of Somerset on Hwy 64; go karts, bumper boats, pitching machine; (715) 247-5621.
<u>Star Prairie Trout Farm</u>: located 15 min N.E. of Somerset, on Cty Hwy H, in the Village of Star Prairie; trout fishing in a Class A hatchery; bait & tackle furnished; RR1, Box 264, Star Prairie, WI 54026; (715) 248-3633.
<u>Wild Waters Water Park</u>: located at the junction of Hwys 35 & 64 in Somerset; water slides, tube slides, kiddie area, mini golf, picnic area, concessions; open daily from Memorial Day to Labor Day; Apple River Wild Waters Water Park, P.O. Box 148, Somerset, WI 54025; (715) 247-3363 or (715) 246-2178.

Bike Rentals:

<u>Red Cedar Trail Outfitters</u>: located at the Red Cedar Trail Head and Hwy 29, 1/2 mile from downtown Menomonie; bike rentals, tours, instruction; 910 Hudson Road, Menomonie, WI 54751; (715) 235-5431.

Boat Rentals:

<u>Big Joe's Sport Shop</u>: located just north of the Lake Menomin Bridge in Menomonie; canoe rentals; 513 N. Broadway, Menomonie, WI 54751; (715) 235-5431.
<u>Red Cedar Trail Outfitters</u>: canoe rentals, bus to drop you off and pick you up; see information under bike rentals.

Charters:

<u>Toon Fishin Charters</u>: chartered pontoon fishing on the St Croix River; fishing equipment, bait, music, coffee, ships store; Toonfishin' Charters, c/o The Boat-tique, 501 Second St, Hudson, WI 54016; (715) 386-3032.

Inner Tube Rentals:

<u>Big Joe's Sport Shop</u>: see information under boat rentals.
<u>Jim's Taxi</u>: located in Menomonie; (715) 235-1154.
<u>Red Cedar Trail Outfitters</u>: see information under bike rentals.

Museums:

<u>Caddie Woodlawn Park</u>: located several miles south of Downsville on Hwy 25; The novel **Caddie Woodlawn** is the real-life story of Caroline Woodhouse, who grew up on the banks of the Red Cedar River 8 miles south of Menomonie in the 1860's. The actual home of Caddie Woodlawn is found in the park. Dunn County Historical Society, Box 437, Menomonie, WI 54751; (715) 235-3862 or (715) 235-3653.
<u>Durand Railroad Depot</u>: depot built in 1882 has exhibits from Pepin County history: 407 W. Wells St, Durand, WI.
<u>Empire In Pine Lumber Museum</u>: located in Downsville; blacksmith shop, cook's shanty, lumbermen's sleeping bunks, old time jail and post office, period furnishings, logging history program, free admission; Dunn County Historical Society, P.O. Box 437, Menomonie, WI 54751; (715) 235-3862 or (715) 235-3653.
<u>The Heritage Center</u>: located on the corner of Wilson Ave and 7th St in Menomonie; owned by the Dunn County Historical Society; three floors of exhibits reflecting various aspects of Dunn County history; Dunn County Historical Society, P.O. Box 437, Menomonie, WI 54751; (715) 235-3862 or (715) 235-3653.
<u>Little House Wayside</u>: located 7 miles northwest of Pepin on Hwy 183; reconstructed log cabin and picnic facilities mark the birthplace of Laura Ingalls Wilder. A museum is also maintained in the Village of Pepin.
<u>Mabel Tainter Memorial Theatre</u>: located in downtown Menomonie, at 205 Main St.; houses a free library, large meeting hall, 314 seat theatre, gay nineties museum; Mabel Tainter Memorial, P.O. Box 250, Menomonie, WI 54751; (715) 235-9726.
<u>Octagon House</u>: located just 1 mile off Hwy I-94 and within 1 block of Hwy 35; museum complex maintained by the St Croix County Historical Society; includes Octogan House, the Garden, and Carriage Houses; 1004 Third St, Hudson, WI 54016.

Old Courthouse Museum: located in Washington Square in Durand, 1/2 block west of Hwy 10; on the National Register of Historic Places and one of only two surviving wooden courthouses in the state; site of the only lynching to occur in Pepin County and probably the last one in the state; Pepin County Historical Society; (715) 672-8673.
Wilson Place Museum: located at the south end of the highway 12/25 bridge over Lake Menomin in Menomonie; former mansion of lumber baron Capt. William Wilson; seasonal tours, guided tours, gift shop; Wilson Place, 101 Wilson Circle, Menomonie, WI 54751; (715) 235-2283 or (800) 826-6970, outside of Wisconsin.

Scenic Areas:

Crystal Cave: located 2 miles west of Spring Valley on Hwy 29; an underground wonderland of stalactites, stalagmites and fossils; hour long walking tours, gift shop; open weekends only in April, May, Sept, and October, daily from Memorial Day to Labor Day; (715) 778-4414.
The Great River Road: follows the Mississippi and is marked on both sides of the River. There are historical markers and scenic overlooks along the way between charming river towns.
Rustic Road R3-4:located south of Glenwood City on Hwy 128, south on Jerdheim Rd.
Rustic Road R13: located on Cty A, east of Hudson, then onto Trout Brook Rd north.

Tubing:

Apple River Hideaway: located on 170th St in Somerset, just off Hwy 64; inner tube rides on the Apple River, concessions, showers, game room, picnic area, shuttle bus service; Somerset, WI 54025; (715) 247-3230.
Apple River Tubing: located on the Apple River, just north of Somerset on Hwy 35; 10 minute "Rapid Ride", 2 hour "Relax-A-Float", or 4 mile "Marathon Float"; free parking and shuttle bus, free use of swimming pools with tubing ticket, campground; Box 307, Somerset, WI 54025; (715) 247-3378, in Wisconsin - (800) 472-6803, elsewhere - (800) 637-8936.
Floaters Haven Park: located on the Apple River, off Hwy 64, 1 1/2 miles east of Somerset; 2 and 3 hour tube rides, shuttle bus, picnic area, bathhouse, group rates; open 7 days a week; Box 173 A, Somerset, WI 54025; (715) 247-5215.
Float-Rite Park: located off Hwy 64 in Somerset; tubing on the Apple River; 2 and 3 hour trips, shuttle bus, mini golf, amusement center, concessions, campground; Bx 276, Somerset, WI 54025; (715) 247-3453.

River's Edge: located on the Apple River, 2 miles east of Somerset on Hwy 64; tube rides, shuttle service, picnic area, concessions, souvenirs, bathhouse, restrooms, water slides, hot showers, fun center, canoe rental, campground; open daily; Box 67, Somerset, WI 54025; in Wisconsin - (715) 247-3305, elsewhere in U.S. - (800) 826-7328.
Somerset Camp: located on Hwy 64 in Somerset, across the street from Dairy Queen; 45 minute and 3 hour tube rides on the Apple River, shuttle bus service, picnic area, campground; Rt 2, Box 537, Somerset, WI 54025; (715) 247-3728.
Sunrise Park: located 1/4 mile south of Somerset on Cty Hwy I; tubing on the Apple River, shuttle bus service, change rooms, restrooms, showers, camping; Box 136, Somerset, WI 54025; (715) 247-5258.

*SAFETY TIPS FOR TUBING

   *Tennis shoes recommended

   *Wear shorts, jeans, or swimsuit

   *If you wear glasses, tie them securely

   *Young children should wear life jackets and their tubes can be tied to yours

   *Take no valuables (purses, watches, jewelry, etc.) Keys can be left at tube rental

   *Rapids area-non swimmers and children can walk around the area and then continue on

   *No styrofoam or glass containers allowed on the river

Zoos & Wildlife Displays:

Deer Park: located on Hwy 46 near the north boundary of St. Croix County; live deer display in a scenic park.
Lion's Club Game Park: located 5 minutes south of exit 41 on I-94 in Menomonie; game park featuring buffalo, elk, white and brown deer, reindeer; nature trail.

EMERGENCY NUMBERS

Should you need help, listed below are the phone numbers for the sheriff and local hospitals.

Sheriff:

Dunn County: (715) 232-1348
Pepin County: (715) 672-5944
Pierce County: (715) 273-5051
St Croix County: (715) 386-8251

Hospitals:

Baldwin Community Hospital, 950 Curtis St, Baldwin, WI 54002, (715) 684-3311
River Falls Area Hospital, 550 N. Main St, River Falls, WI 54022, (715) 425-6155
Chippewa Valley Hospital, 1620 3rd Ave West, Durand, WI, (715) 672-4211.
Myrtle Werth Medical Center, 2321 Stout Rd, Hwy 29/12 East, Menomonie, WI 54751, (715) **235-5531**
Hudson Memorial Hospital, 400 Wisconsin St, Hudson, WI 54016, (715) 386-9321
Holy Family Hospital, 535 Hospital Rd, New Richmond, WI 54017, (715) 246-1201

OTHER INFORMATION SOURCES

County:

Dunn County Recreation Dept. Courthouse, Menomonie, WI (715) 232-1651
UW EX. Pepin County, Courthouse, Durand, WI 547, (715) 672-5214
UW Extension Pierce County, Courthouse, Ellsworth, WI 54011, (715) 273-3531, ext 243
St Croix County Parks Dept, Glenwood City, WI 54013 (715) 265-4613

State: WI Department of Natural Resources

WI DNR, Eau Claire Area Headquarters, 2004 Highland Ave. Eau Claire WI 54701 (715) 839-3777. Covers Dunn, Eau Claire, Pepin, Pierce and St Croix Counties.
WI DNR Ranger Station, Hwy 29 W & Brickyard Rd, Rt 6, Box 1, Menomonie, WI 54751, (715) 232-1242.
WI DNR Ranger Station, St Croix & Pierce County, DNR, AG Center, Box 61 Baldwin, WI 54002, (715) 684-2914.

Federal:

US Army Corps of Engineers, Park Manager, Eau Galle Lake, P.O. Box 190, Spring Valley, WI 54767, (715) 778-5562.

Chambers of Commerce:

Baldwin Chamber of Commerce, 1040 12th Ave, Baldwin, WI 54002
Dunn County UWEX Office, Courthouse, Menomonie, WI 54751, (715) 232-1636
Durand Commercial Club, Box 156, Durand, WI 54736
Ellsworth Commercial Club, Box 737, Ellsworth, WI 54011
Hudson Chamber of Commerce, Po Box 438, Hudson, WI 54016, (715)386-8411
Knapp Village Office, PO Box 86, Knapp, WI 54749
Menomonie Chamber of Commerce, 335 Main St, Box 246, Menomonie, WI 54751, (715) 235-9087
New Richmond Chamber of Commerce, 156 E 1st St. PO Box 42, New Richmond, WI 54017, (715) 246-2900
Pepin County, UWEX Office, 550 West 7th Ave, Box 39, Durand, WI 54736, (715) 672-5214
Pierce County, UWEX Office, 414 West Main St, Ellsworth, WI 54011, (715) 273-3531, ext 243
Prescott Chamber of Commerce, PO Box 244, Prescott, WI 54021
River Falls Chamber of Commerce, 115 East Elm, Box 172, River Falls, WI 54022
St Croix County, Clerk's Office, 911 4th St, Hudson, WI 54016 (715) 386-5581, ext 218
St Croix County, UWEX Office, Agriculture Center, Baldwin, WI 54002, (715) 684-3301
Somerset, Chamber of Commerce, Box 357, Somerset, WI 54025, (715) 247-3366

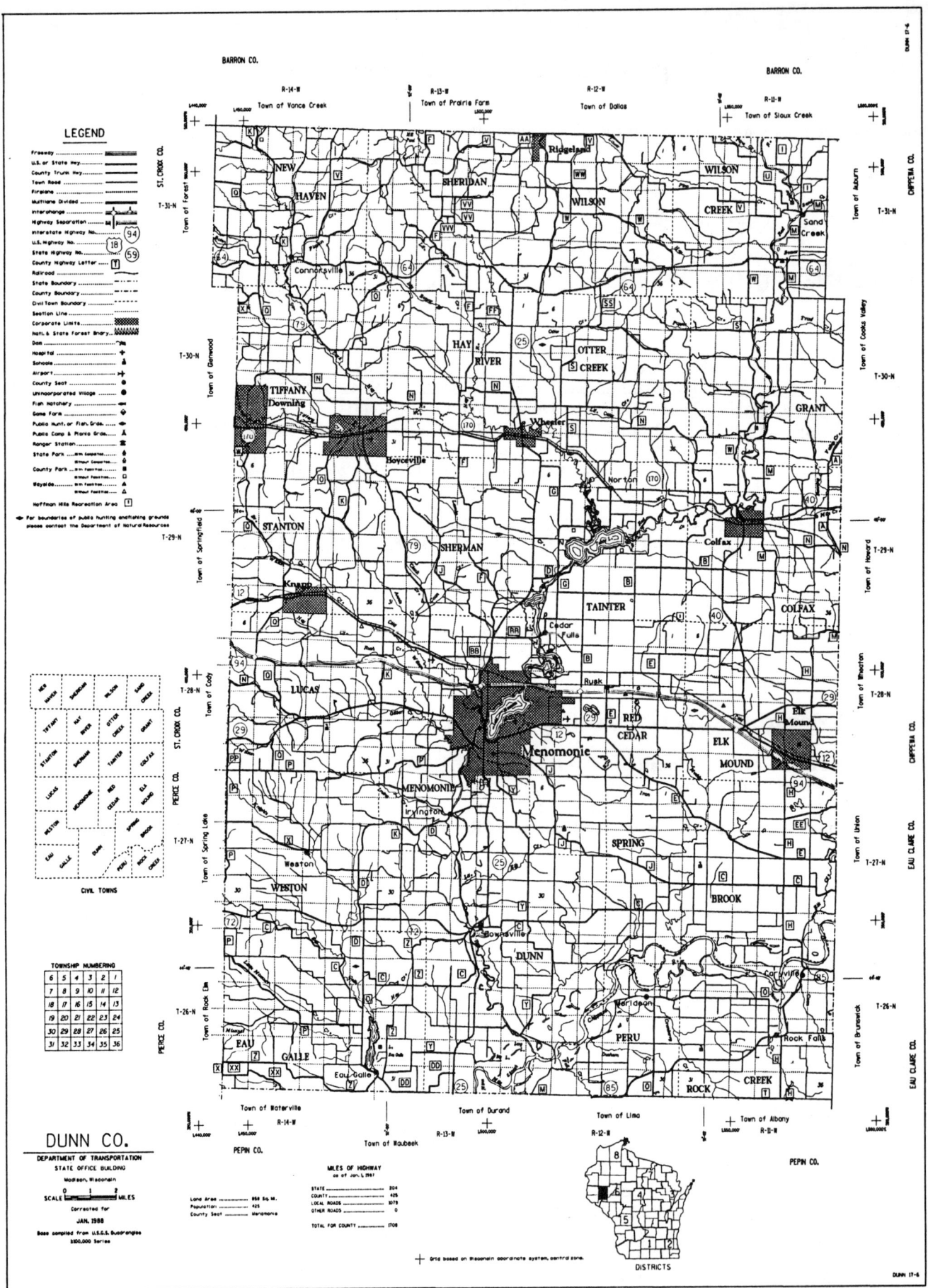

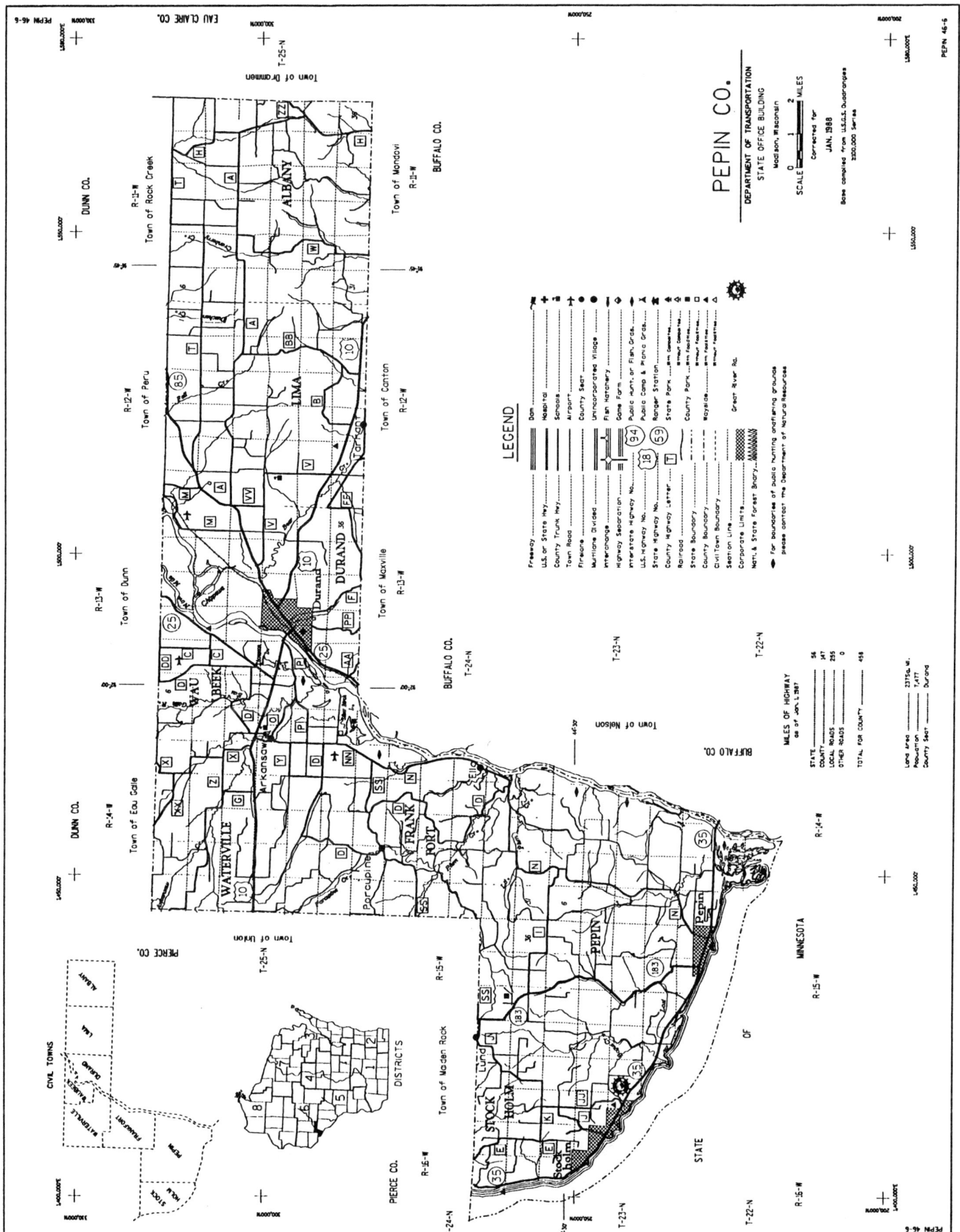

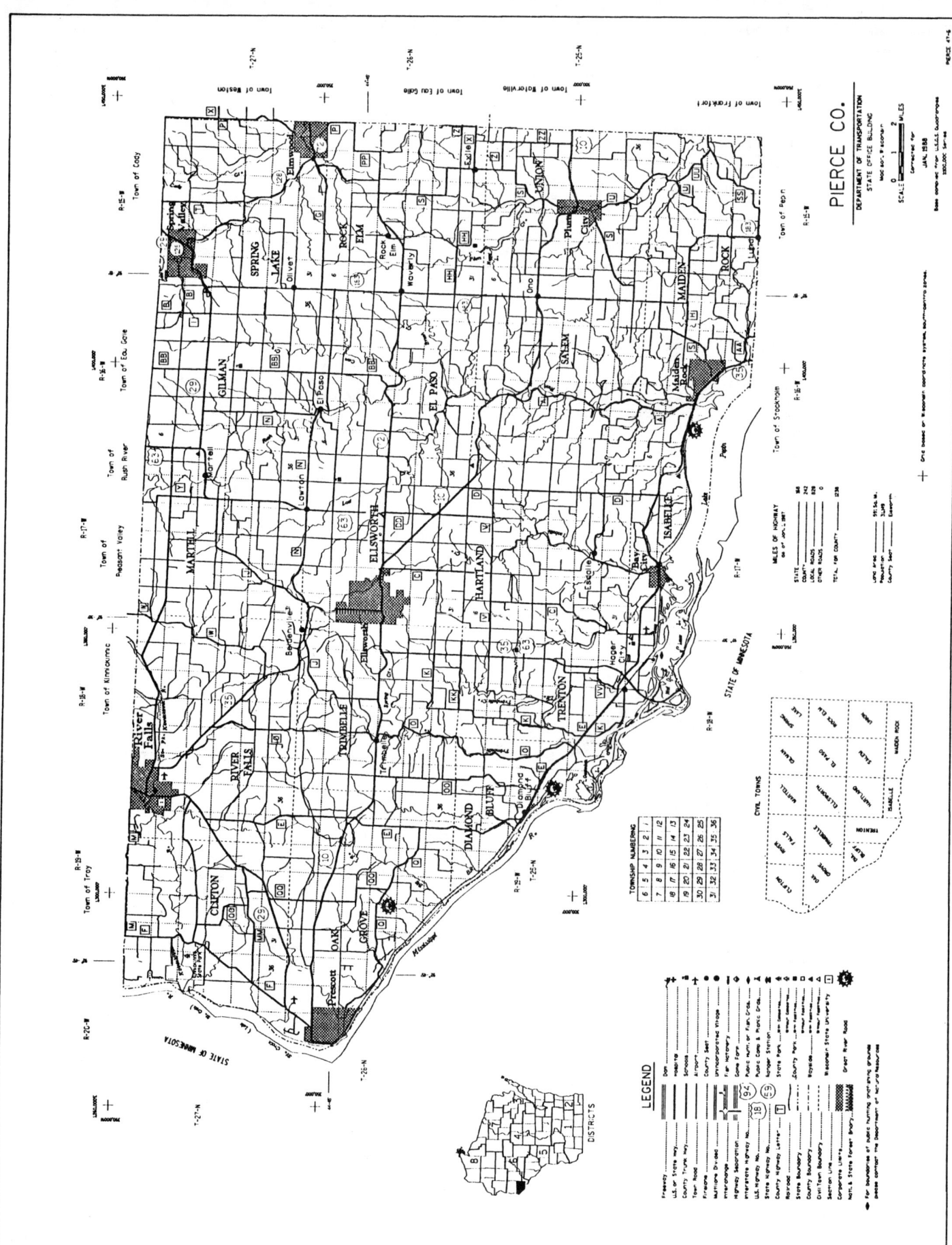

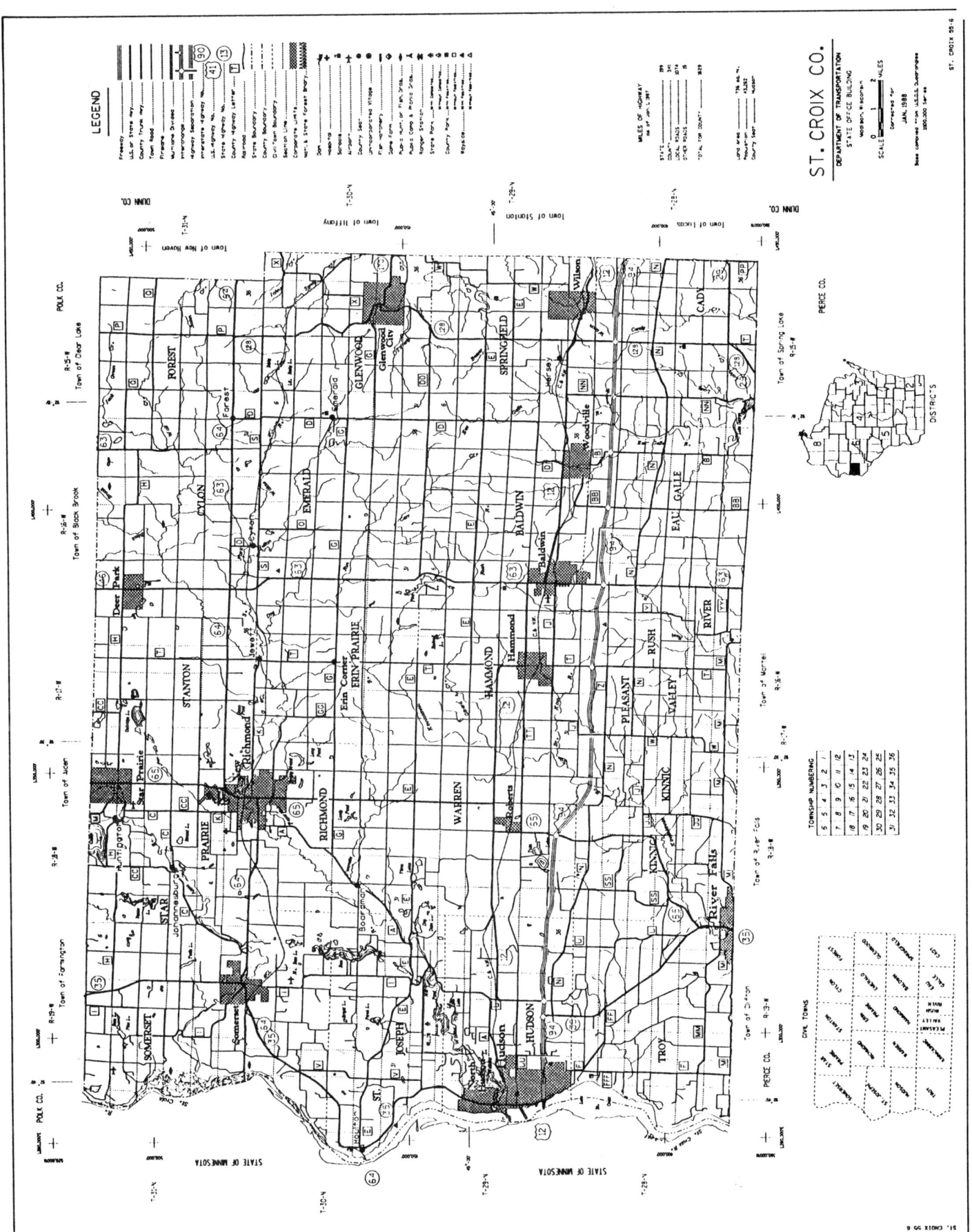

AREA 5
Transitional Area
Chippewa, Clark, and Eau Claire Counties

Tens of thousands of years ago the last advance of the Wisconsin Glacier moved across the state, carrying with it tons of ice, rock and sediment, reshaping the landscape. When the glacier finally stopped and slowly melted, it left a trail of ridges (moraines) and hills (drumlins), formed by the new debris. South of the glacial advance lie the dry uplands of southwestern Wisconsin known as the Driftless Area. Here, the unglaciated hills and valleys were formed by eons of erosion. In between is an area where ancient glaciers, depositing their glacial till, formed small lakes and hills. Over time, erosion has modified this landscape to the point where glacial landforms have almost disappeared and there is little distinction with the southern Driftless Area. This is known as the Transitional Area.

Today the outwash plains and oak and pine forests of southern Clark County, the driftless hill country of southwestern Eau Claire County and the end moraines and glacial lakes of northeastern Chippewa County provide many interesting recreational opportunities for all to enjoy.

There are a number of cities plus a scattering of unincorporated settlements.

In **Chippewa County**, Chippewa Falls, the county seat, is located at the south central end of the county on the Chippewa River. Cadott, Boyd and Stanley are to the east on Hwy 29. To the northeast on Hwy 178 is Cornell; with Bloomer And New Auburn to the northwest on Hwy 53. The City of Eau Claire just enters the county to the south on Hwy 124.

In **Clark County**, Neillsville, the county seat, is located on Hwy 10 and 73 in the south central area of the county. Thorp, Withee, Owens, Curtiss and Abbotsford are along the northern border on Hwy 29.

In **Eau Claire County**, Eau Claire, the county seat located in the north west corner of the county with I-94 heading northwest to Minneapolis/St Paul. The City of Altoona borders Eau Claire on the east; while along Hwy 12 to the east and south is Fall Creek, Augusta and Fairchild.

RECREATIONAL WATERS

Lakes and Flowages:

There are 209 named (23,312 acres) and 306 unnamed (1,129 acres) lakes in the region, including several man-made flowages. This accounts for 3.5 % of the total number of Wisconsin lakes, covering 2.5 % of the states total inland surface water. Farther south out of the glaciated areas there are more rivers but fewer lakes. Most of the larger lakes are flowages.

Chippewa County has 193 named (19,085 acres) and 257 unnamed (913 acres), lakes. The vast majority of lakes are in the glacial moraine areas in the northwestern corner of the county, north of a line from New Auburn to Cornell.

Lake Wissota, 6,300 acres, is formed by a dam on the Chippewa River northeast of Chippewa Falls. The lake can be reached by Cty S and X with landings on these roads and at the state park. There is a good fishery present in the lake, however there are many other recreational demands. These include water skiing, sailing and boating.
Holcombe Flowage, 3,890 acres, formed by a dam on the Chippewa River, is located north of Cornell on the Rusk and Chippewa County line. The flowage can be accessed off Hwy 27 and 194 and Cty M. An irregular shore line provides bays and islands for quiet fishing and canoeing and open water for other recreational activities. Fishing is good with a nice mix of game and panfish.
Marsh Miller Lake, a 436 acre flowage, is located east of Bloomer on Hwy 64, then 2 miles north on Cty AA and east on Birch Point Rd. There is good panfishing with a nice mix of other game fish. The lake has relatively little development around it due to the lowlands.
Otter lake, a 673 acre flowage, is located east of Cornell on Hwy 64, then south 5 miles on Cty G and east on Otter Lake Leja Rd. There are access points on both ends of the lake and at the county park. This is a long, narrow, scenic lake with several islands and bays. A mix of panfish, walleye, bass and northern pike are present.

Clark County has 6 named (1,447 acres) and 24 unnamed (191 acres) lakes. The more noted ones include:

Mead Lake, 320 acres, is located on Hwy 73 north of Neilsville to Greenwood, then west 7 miles on Rocky Run Rd, 1 mile north on Bachelors Ave, then west on a town road 1 mile. There is a county park on the west end of the lake. Walleye, bass and panfish are present.
Arbutus Lake, 839 acres, is formed by a dam on the Black River and straddles the county line. Three county parks and many homes surround the lake. There is a mix of game and panfish present.

Eau Claire County has 10 named (2,780) acres and 10 unnamed (25 acres) lakes.

Lake Altoona, a 840 acre flowage, is located on the east side of Altoona. The lake is formed by a dam on the Eau Claire River. There is a mix of fish present. A county park is located on the south side. Being this close to an urban setting, there are many demands and much development placed around the lake.
Lake Eau Claire, a 860 acre flowage, is located 5 miles north of Augusta on Hwy 27 in the eastern end of the county. There is development on the lake and a county park with access on the north side. The county forest and 17 islands provide a more scenic setting. Again there is a mixed fishery of panfish and walleye.

Rivers:

Black River, has its start in southern Taylor County and travels south through Clark County and into Lake Arbutus. Below the lake, it turns southwest and flows to the Mississippi River. In the upper regions the character of the river is a mix of deep gorges, swift rapids and granite boulders with flowages and impoundments. During low water levels it is difficult to travel, while in high waters it can be dangerous. In the sections below Black River Falls, in Jackson County, the river is canoeable to the Mississippi River. There are access points at bridges.
Chippewa River, the character is that of a large, slow moving river with several impoundments. The river bottom is mostly sand with some rocky areas. Dams can be found at Holcombe (Holcombe Flowage), Cornell (Cornell Flowage), Jim Falls (Old Abe Lake), east of Chippewa Falls (Lake Wissota), in Chippewa Falls and in Eau Claire (Dells Pond). Portages around these dams can be over 1/2 mile long. The fishery include walleye, catfish, panfish and northern pike. On the majority of the river boats can be used; however, water levels fluctuate, depending on the amount of water being released at the hydroelectric dams. The sections from Holcombe Dam to Cornell are scenic, with a flowage type environment and not a lot of development. The section just below Jim Falls only can be canoed at times. A 12 miles section below the Chippewa Falls Dam to Eau Claire can also be boated but the lower 1/2 can only be canoed due to rock shelf, boulders and riffle areas in the upper half.

Trout Streams:

The area has 71 streams classed as trout waters, covering 257 miles. There are 193 miles of Class I, 90 Miles of Class II and 74 miles of Class III. Several of the noted streams include Dickinson Cr, Clark County and Duncan Cr, McCann Cr and Elk Cr in Chippewa County,

Public Lands

County:

Eau Claire County, has 50,000 acres of forest located in eastern Eau Claire County plus scattered sections along the Eau Claire River from Altoona to the Eau Claire Lake. General boundaries are Cty MM & D on the north; Cty N and G on the west and Hwy 12/27 along the southeast. The county line is along the east side. Hunter walking trails, canoe landing on the Eau Claire River, ski trails and county parks can also be found.

Clark County, maintains 133,000 acres of county forest. These lands are located along the lower two thirds of the western county line and along the southern county line. The forest is to the west of a general boundary of Cty M south, then Cty I east, then Cty G south, Hwy 10 east, Hwy 73 south and Cty Z south to the county line. There are numerous roads passing through the area to provide easy access to over 70 miles of walking trails.

Chippewa County, has 31,000 acres in two units. The larger unit is located at the northern county line and halfway between New Auburn and Cornell. A general boundary would be Cty AA on the west, Hwy 64, Cty E & Z on the south and Cty Z on the east. Cty E & M split the property. The second unit is in the northeast corner with Cty M on the north and Cty W on the south and Cty G splitting the property. The county has forest roads through these properties to provide easy access.

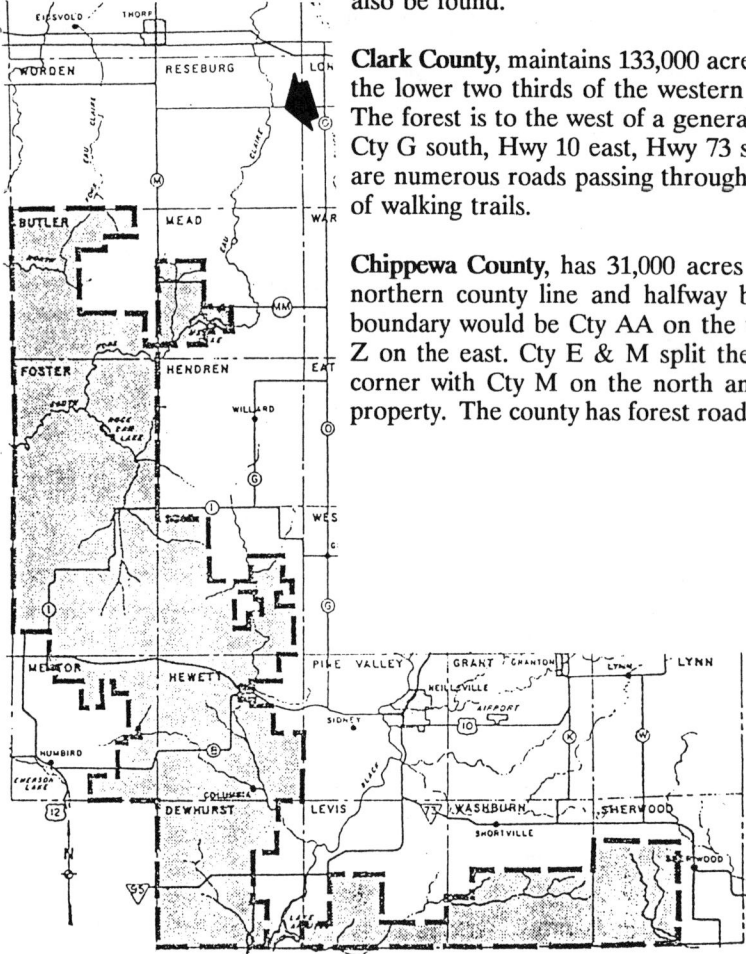

State:

Chippewa County:

Jim Falls Wildlife Area, 5,000+ acres of leased lands, is located about 3 miles south of Cty Y at Jim Falls on Cty S, then 1 mile east on Weimer Rd. These lands are primarily public hunting grounds for pheasants. Waterfowl, deer and small game and nongame species are also present. The area is a mix of farm fields, timber, wetlands and brush.

Hallie Wildlife Area, 600+ acres of leased lands, is located 3 miles west of Hwy 53 between Eau Claire and Chippewa Falls on Cty OO. These lands are managed primarily as public hunting grounds for pheasants. Again waterfowl and small game and nongame species are also present. The area is a mix of farm fields, wood lots, wetlands and brush.

The following small project areas are designed to provide public access to these waters. These areas also provide habitat for both game and non-games species of wildlife.

McCann Creek, two properties. First is located just north of the airport on Hwy 64, east of Bloomer. The second one is 4 miles north of Hwy 64 on Hwy 40, opposite W Long Ln.

Sand Creek, is located 2.5 miles west of New Auburn on Cty M. Property is on the west & north sides of Cty M.

Duncan Creek, 214 acres, is located 2 miles east of New Auburn on Cty M, then south on Baldry Ln.

Elf Creek, is located west of Chippewa Falls on Hwy 29, 1 mile west of Cty M.

Eau Claire County:

Pleasant Valley Wildlife Area, 1,700 acres, is located 8 miles south of Eau Claire and I-94 on Cty F. Cty F passes through the project with Cty WW on the southern fringe. This area is primarily a public hunting ground with a mix of farm lands and small woodlots for pheasant hunting.

Augusta Wildlife Area, 2,100 acres, is located north of Augusta on Cty G, with Cty GG on the north side. This is primarily a habitat area of flowages, ditches and dikes with millet plantings to promote the production of waterfowl. Pheasants are also planted for hunting.

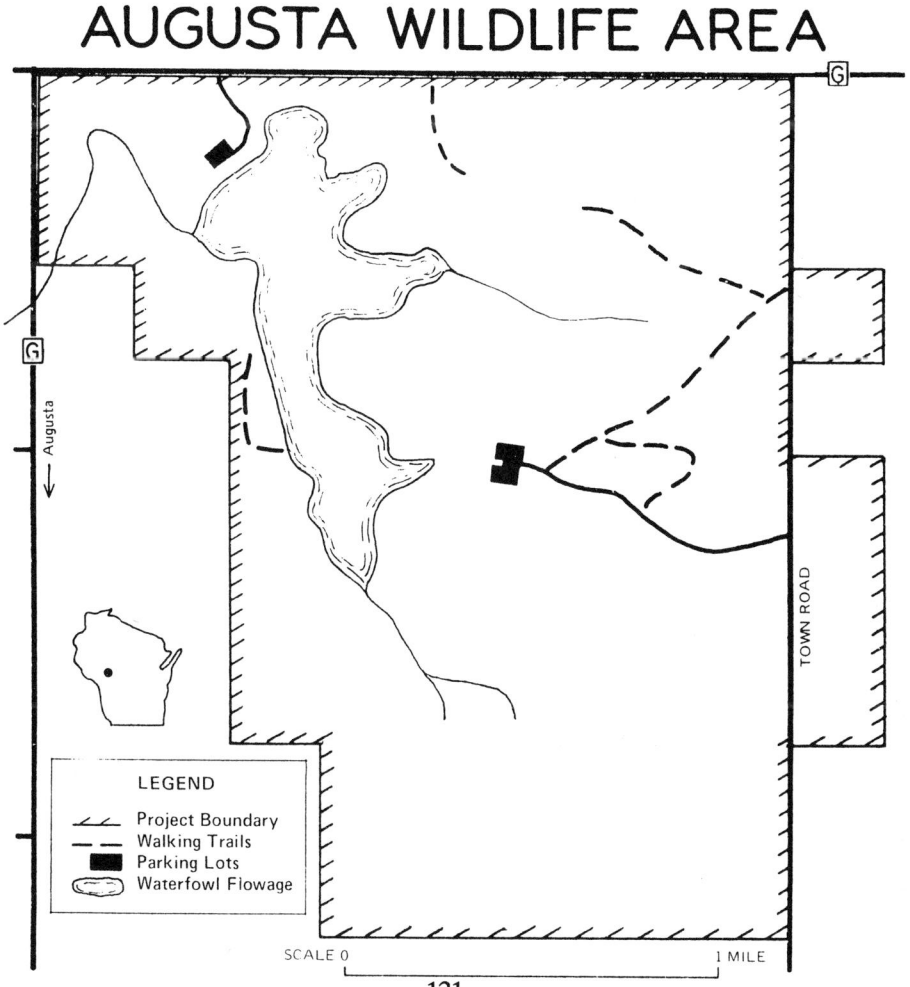

PARKS, LANDINGS AND OTHER THINGS:

Chippewa County:

County Parks:

Morris-Erickson County Park, is located in the northwest corner of the county. Take Hwy 53 north to New Auburn, then east on Cty M, then north on Hwy 40 about 2 1/2 miles north to the park. Facilities include camping, swimming, playgrounds, picnic area, shelters, toilets and boat landing on Long Lake.
Pine Point County Park is located in the northeast area of the county. Take Cty M 2 1/2 miles west of Hwy 27, the park is to the north after crossing the Holcombe Flowage. Facilities located on a point in Holcombe Flowage include camping, swimming, playground, picnic area, shelter and boat landing.
Round Lake County Park is located north Hwy 53 to New Auburn, then east on Cty M, then north on Hwy 40 about 1 3/4 miles, continue north on a town road. The park and boat landing are about a mile down the road and on the west side.
Otter Lake County Park is located in eastern Chippewa County north of Hwy 29 on Cty G, then east on Otter Lake Leja Rd. Located on Otter Lake, park facilities include camping, swimming, drinking water, toilets, boat landing and picnic area.

Municipal Parks:

Anson Park is located 1 mile north of the City of Chippewa Falls on Hwy 124, then about 8 miles east northeast on Cty S. The picnic area and boat landing are on the Chippewa River, which is just south of Jim Falls.
Chapman Park, Stanley, is located north of Hwy 29 on Cty X/H then west on 4th Ave. The park will be to the north. Facilities include camping, swimming, toilets, picnic area, drinking water, and a deer yard.
Fandrey Park, Stanley, is located north of Hwy 29 on Cty X/H, then west on 4th Ave. The park is to the north before crossing the river. It is on the east shore of Chapman Lake. Site of an old lumber mill, there is a picnic area with open shelter, drinking water and toilets.
Cornell Municipal Boat Landing is located north of Hwy 64 on Brunet Park Rd. There is a landing to the Chippewa River plus a picnic area and toilet.
Cadott Community Park is located north of Hwy 29 on Hwy 27 and to the west. The park, on the Yellow River, has a beach and picnic area.
Birch Creek Town Park is located 3 miles west of Hwy 27 on Cty M, then north 1 1/4 miles on Range Line Rd and east on town road. It is located on the west shore of Holcombe Flowage. Facilities include a swimming and picnic area.
Bloomer City Beach is located east of Hwy 53 on Hwy 40 on Lake Como.

City of Chippewa Parks:

Irvine Park and Zoo is located on the north side of town. One way to get there is from Jefferson St north of Hwy 29, then west on Bridgewater Ave. The park is on the north side of the road. This 400 acre complex includes a zoo, campgrounds, hiking trail, picnic area, playground and open playfield.

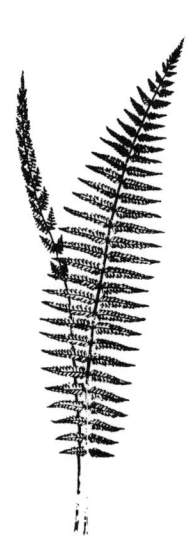

Cinnamon fern. GK

Cinnamon fern

The cinnamon fern is common in the northern sections of North America, it has twice-divided narrow sterile fronds and is about 3 feet tall. Fertile stalks appear in early spring are at first green and then turn cinnamon in color. The stalk base is very hairy.

State Parks:

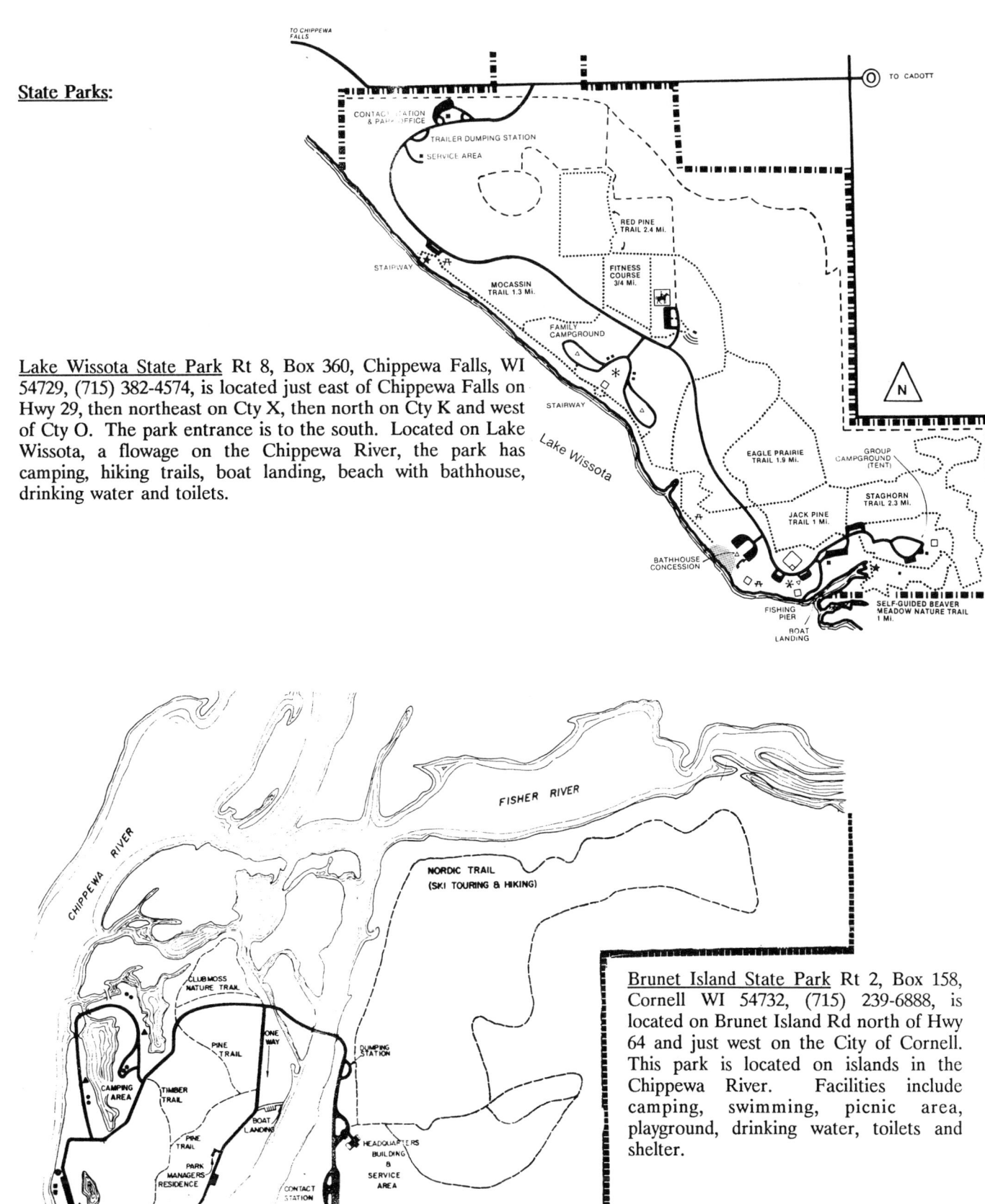

Lake Wissota State Park Rt 8, Box 360, Chippewa Falls, WI 54729, (715) 382-4574, is located just east of Chippewa Falls on Hwy 29, then northeast on Cty X, then north on Cty K and west of Cty O. The park entrance is to the south. Located on Lake Wissota, a flowage on the Chippewa River, the park has camping, hiking trails, boat landing, beach with bathhouse, drinking water and toilets.

Brunet Island State Park Rt 2, Box 158, Cornell WI 54732, (715) 239-6888, is located on Brunet Island Rd north of Hwy 64 and just west on the City of Cornell. This park is located on islands in the Chippewa River. Facilities include camping, swimming, picnic area, playground, drinking water, toilets and shelter.

Ice Age Scientific Reserve Park:

Chippewa Moraine Ice Age Scientific Reserve Park, is part of the Ice Age Trail System. This park will be 4,000 acres of noted Ice Age features like ice walls, lake plains, outwash plains and kettle lakes. The park will be made up of 1,000 acres of county forest and 3,000 acres of lands to be purchased. The project, located east of New Auburn, is 1 mile east of Hwy 40 on Cty M. County M passes through the north portion of the proposed park.

State Waysides:

Hwy 178, located 0.2 miles north of Cty S, has a picnic area.
Hwy 53, located 2.5 miles north of Eau Claire, has a picnic area.
Hwy 27, North, located 0.5 mile south of county line at Holcombe Flowage, has picnic area, boat landing to the flowage, drinking water and toilets.
Hwy 27, located 3 miles north of Hwy 29, has picnic area, drinking water and toilets.
Hwy 64, 1 mile north of Bloomer, has a picnic area, drinking water and toilets.
Hwy 178, located 4 miles south of Cornell, has a boat landing, picnic area, drinking water and toilets.
Hwy 29, located 5 miles east of Chippewa Falls, has a picnic area, drinking water and toilets.

Clark County:

County Parks:

Bruce Mound Winter Sports Area, is located south of Neillsville on Hwy 73, then continue south and west on Hwy 95. Take a town road south 1 mile east of the county line. Facilities include downhill skiing, tubing, hiking and snowmobiling.
Black River Park, is located 3 miles west of Withee on Hwy 29, then north on Cty O. Located on the Black River, park facilities include picnic area, shelters and hiking.
Humbird Park, is located at Hwy 12 and Cty B & F in the southwestern corner of the county. There is a small picnic area with swimming and boat access to Emerson Lake.
Russell Memorial Park is located in the extreme southwestern corner of the county on Beach La, just east of Cty J at the Jackson County line. This well developed park is adjacent to the Jackson County Park and on Lake Arbutus. Facilities include swimming, camping, picnic area, shelters, telephone, concessions, laundromat, showers and more.
Rock Dam Park, is located 7 miles west of Greenwood, Hwy 73, on Cty G, then west on Cty GG, continue west on Willard Rd, then south on Butler Rd to the park. The park, located on Rock Dam Lake, has a picnic area, campgrounds, swimming, shelter, hiking trails, dump station, drinking water, playground, laundromat and country store.
Sherwood Park, is located in the extreme southeast corner of the county. Take Cty Z south of Hwy 73 for 2 miles, then west on town road 1 mile, then south into the park. There is a picnic and camping area with shelter, playground and swimming on Sherwood Lake.
Mead Lake Park, is located 10 miles south of Hwy 29 on Cty O, then 5 miles west on Cty MM. Facilities include camping, picnic area, swimming, dump station, drinking water and playgrounds.
Greenwood Park, is located on the north end of Greenwood, west of Hwy 73 and on the Black River. Facilities include picnic area, shelters, campground, toilets and playgrounds.
Snyder Park is located 6 miles west of Neillsville on Hwy 10, then north on Arndt La. Keep to the left to the park. Facilities include campgrounds, swimming, picnic area, shelter, toilets and landing on Wedges Cr.

City of Neillsville:

Listeman Arboretum, is located south of Hwy 10 on Sunset St. The entrance is on 2nd Street. With extensive frontage on the Black River, the area is used for interpretive and nature education programs. There are hiking trails throughout the arboretum.
Schuster Park, is located north of Hwy 10 on the southeast side of town. Facilities include picnic areas, shelters, toilets, open area, organized sports area, and informal cross country ski area.

Municipal Parks:

Thorp City Park is located in town. Facilities include playground, toilets, picnic area, shelter and tennis courts.
Owens City Park, is located north of Hwy 29 on Cty D, then east on Third St, south on Oak to Second St. The park is adjacent to the Poplar River. There is a picnic area, shelters, campground (6 trailer sites), fishing and restrooms.

Dorchester Village Recreation Park, is located north of Hwy 29 on Hwy 13, then west on Cty A into town, then south on Linden St and east on Third St. This 40 acre park is located on an impoundment on the Poplar River. Facilities include picnic area, camping and swimming. There are shelters, organized sports area, playground and walking trails.
Granton Community Park, is located east of Neillsville on Hwy 10 then north on Cty K. The park is on the north side of town. This 40 acre park on O'Neill Cr has a picnic area, shelter and concession stand, playground, organized sports area, toilets and a half acre fishing pond.

State Waysides:

Hwy 10, located 3 miles west of Neillsville, has a scenic overlook with picnic area, drinking water and toilets. It is located next to the Viet Nam War Memorial.
Hwy 10, located at Hwy 12, has a picnic area, drinking water and toilets.
Hwy 73, is located at the Poplar River Bridge north of Greenwood with a boat landing to the river and a picnic area.
Hwy 29, located 2 miles west of Thorp on the North Fork of the Eau Claire River, has a picnic area, water and toilets.

Eau Claire County:

County Parks:

Big Falls Park, is located about 9 miles east of Eau Claire on Cty Q, then south on Big Falls South Forest Road. Facilities include picnic area, drinking water and toilets plus access to Eau Claire River.
Coon Fork County Park, is located 1 mile east of Augusta on Hwy 12, then 3 1/2 miles northeast on Cty CF. Facilities include camping, nature trails, picnic area, shelters, swimming, canoeing, boat landing, playground, drinking water, toilets and skiing.
Harstad County Park, located 3 miles east of Fall Creek on Hwy 12, then 1 3/4 miles east on Cty HH, then north on Cty HHH. Facilities include camping, picnic area, shelter, canoeing, drinking water, playground and toilets.

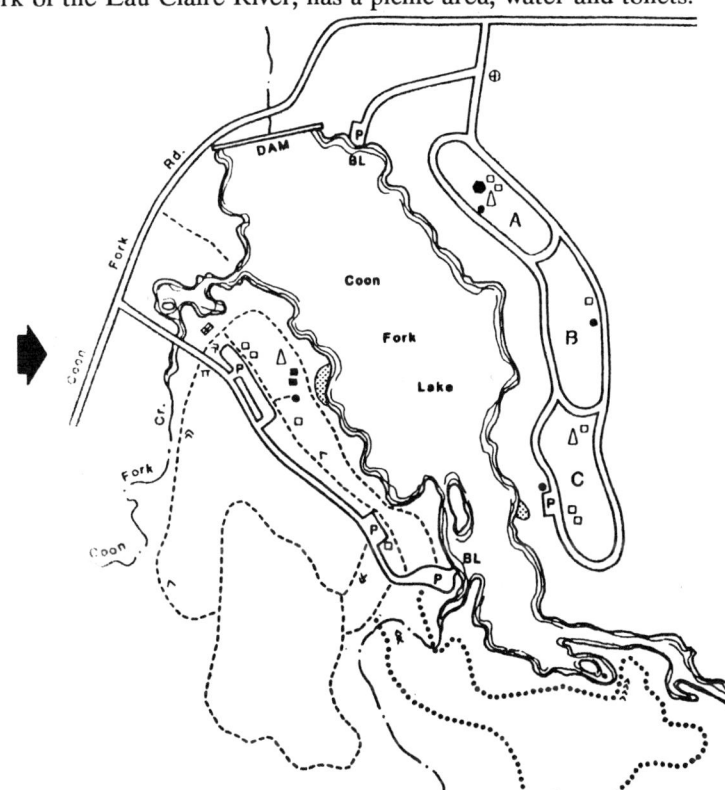

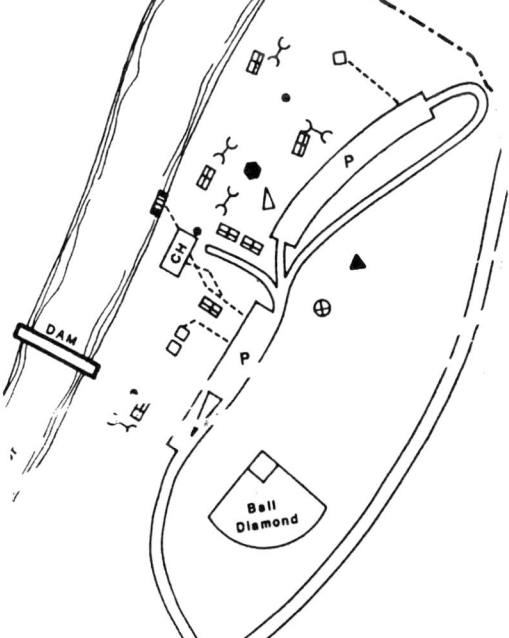

Lake Eau Claire Park, (715) 286-2681, is located 5 miles north of Augusta on Hwy 27. Facilities include picnic area, shelter, canoeing, boat landing, playground, drinking water and toilets.
North Shore Lake Eau Claire Beach, is located north of Augusta on Hwy 27, after crossing the river turn east on North Shore Dr, continue east on Cty N. Beach is on the south side of the road.
L.L. Phillips Park, is located about 5 miles east of Eau Claire on Cty Q, then Cty QQ. Facilities include picnic area, shelter, drinking water, nature trail, ski trails and toilets.
Lowes Creek Park, located just south of Eau Claire. It can be reached by Hwy 93 or S Lowes Cr Rd. Facilities include drinking water and skiing.
Beaver Creek Reserve, (715) 877-2212, is located about 10 miles east of Eau Claire on Cty Q, then 1 mile south on Cty K. This property includes Hobbs Observatory, Eau Claire Youth Camp and Wise Nature Center. Facilities include camping, nature trail, playground, canoeing, skiing, lodge and cabins, drinking water and toilets.

Lake Altoona Park, (715) 834-9042, located on the northeast side of town, on the south shore of the lake. Facilities include picnic area, shelter, swimming, canoeing, boat landing, playground, drinking water and flush toilets.

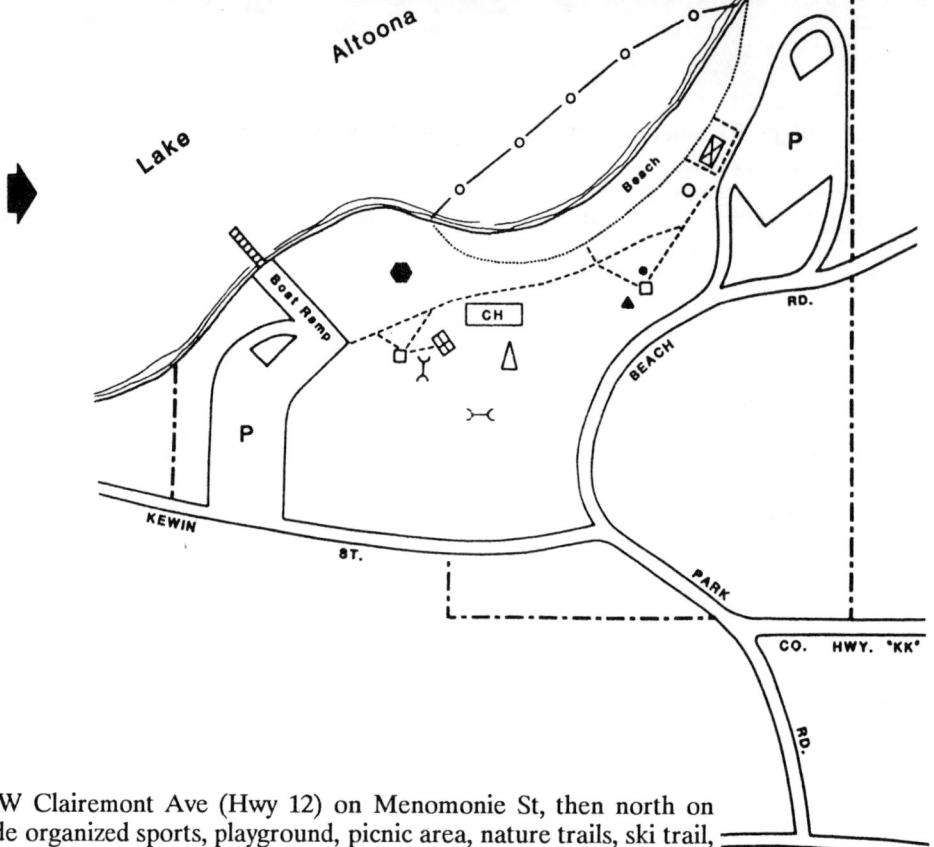

City of Eau Claire:

Carson Park is located east of W Clairemont Ave (Hwy 12) on Menomonie St, then north on Carson Park Dr. Facilities include organized sports, playground, picnic area, nature trails, ski trail, shelters and toilets.
Paul Bunyan Logging Camp, Carson Park, (715) 836-7680, is a visitor/interpretive center for an authentically recreated logging camp of the 1890's.
Mt Simon Park, is located on the south shore of Dells Pond. Take Main St west of Hwy 53, then right on Harding Ave, left on Madison St, right on Forest St to the park. Facilities include organized sports, boat landing, playground, picnic area, shelters and toilets.
Riverview Park, is located on the north side of town. Take Eddy La west of Hwy 53, then south on Starr Ave and west on Riverview Dr, which is on the east shore of the Chippewa River. There is an island picnic area along with boat landing, toilets, shelters, playground and ski trail.
Rod & Gun Club Park, is located on the west side of town. Take Park Ridge Dr north of W Clairemont Ave. There is a picnic area with shelter, toilets and playground.
Half Moon Beach is across from Carson Park. It is south of the intersection of Cameron and Madison St. There is a beach with picnic area, playground and toilets.

Nature Center:

Ralph H Wise Nature Center, (715) 877-2212, is located east of Eau Claire on Hwy 12, then north at Fall Creek about 3 miles on Cty K. Located at the junction of Deinhammer Creek and Eau Claire River, facilities include a center, nature trails, interpretive programs and ski trails.

Municipal Parks:

Altoona City Park, is located between 10th and 8th St at Garfield. There are organized sports, open area, picnic area and toilets.
Augusta's North Side Park, is on Cty G at the northern city limits. Facilities include organized sports, picnic area, playground and shelter.
Fairchild's Foster Park, is located north of Hwy 10/12 on Center St (Cty H) at Main St. There is a picnic area, shelter, toilets, water and open space.
Randall Park, Fall Creek, is on Hwy 12 at the western village limits and has a picnic area, toilets, shelter & open space.
Keller Park, Fall Creek, is located north of Hwy 12 on Cty K. Facilities include organized sports, playground, picnic area, shelter, toilets, water and open spaces.

State Waysides:

Hwy 93, a scenic overlook with picnic tables is located 0.2 miles north of Cty F.
Hwy 12, located 4.5 miles southeast of Hwy 53. Facilities include picnic tables, drinking water and toilets.
Hwy 85, located 1 mile west of Hwy 37, has a picnic area, drinking water and toilets.

TRAILS

Mountain Bikes:

Clark County, permits the use of bikes on county trails.
Chippewa County, lands are open for bike use.
Eau Claire County, has some question if they are permitted where vehicles are prohibited. It is best to call the Forester's office first.
Wisconsin DNR, does permit the use of these bikes on selected trails managed by the Department. It is best to contact the property manager to get the latest information.

All Terrain Vehicles:

Clark County, has an ATV trail which connects with Jackson County Trail. This 56 mile long county operated ATV trail is west of a line that starts at Hwy 10 and Cty B and extends north on Ziegler Rd, then west on Cty G, north on Cty M to Cty GG. There are parking lots at Hwy 10 & Cty B and south of Cty M/G. The trail extends west to the county line.
Chippewa County, does not have any ATV trails & does not encourage unrestricted use.
Eau Claire County, does not permit ATVs on any county lands.
Wisconsin DNR, does not permit the use of these vehicles on any of the trails managed by the Department.

Horses:

Chippewa County, lands are presently open for horseback riding.
Clark County, does permit horses on county land. There is bridle trail At Wildrock Parklot, see below.
Eau Claire County, permits horses on county forest lands, except in parks or where posted, such as newly seeded trails.
Wisconsin DNR, policies varies with the properties, therefore it is best to contact the property manager to get the latest information.

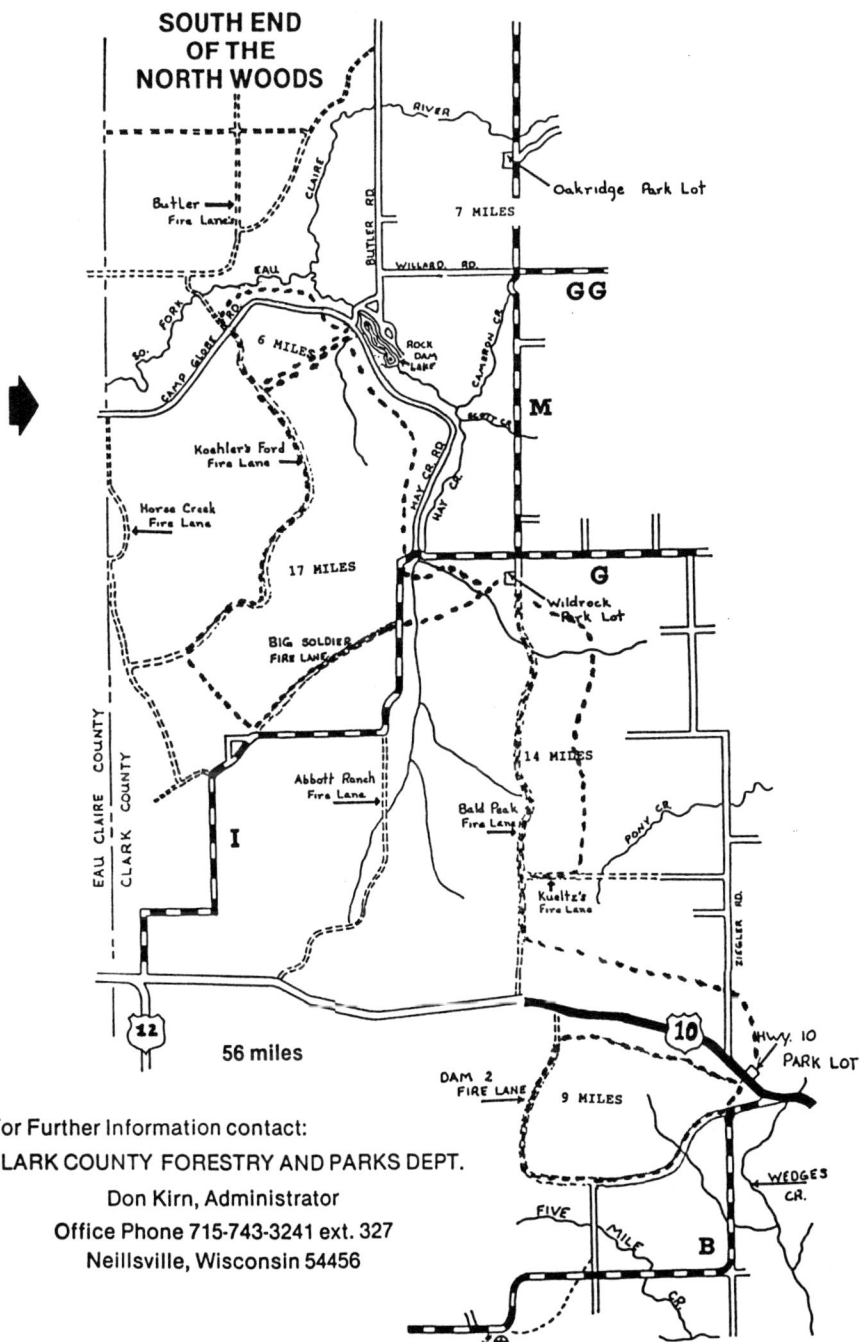

For Further Information contact:
CLARK COUNTY FORESTRY AND PARKS DEPT.
Don Kirn, Administrator
Office Phone 715-743-3241 ext. 327
Neillsville, Wisconsin 54456

Hiking, Hunting and Cross Country Ski Trails

Eau Claire County:

Carson Park, city of Eau Claire is located east of W Clairemont Ave (Hwy 12) on Menomonie St, then north on Carson Park Dr. Facilities include ski trail and toilets.

Fairfax City Park, City of Eau Claire, is located east of Hwy 93 on Golf Rd. Park is to the north. This undeveloped park has a hiking and ski trail.

Tower Ridge Ski Area, is located east of Eau Claire on Cty QQ 5.5 miles, then north on S. 82nd Ave. There are 11.2 miles of trail in 7 loops. There are trails for beginner, intermediate and experts.

Lowes Creek County Park Trails, located just south of Eau Claire can be reached off Hwy 93 or S Lowes Cr Rd. The parking lot is east on Palomino Rd. There is a 2.4 west loop for beginners and a 2.5 mile east loop for intermediate skiers.

Coon Fork Park Ski Trails, is located 1 mile east of Augusta on Hwy 12, then 3 1/2 miles northeast on Cty CF. The trail head is east of Coon Fork Rd. There are 3.2 miles of beginner and intermediate trails through the park and along the lake.

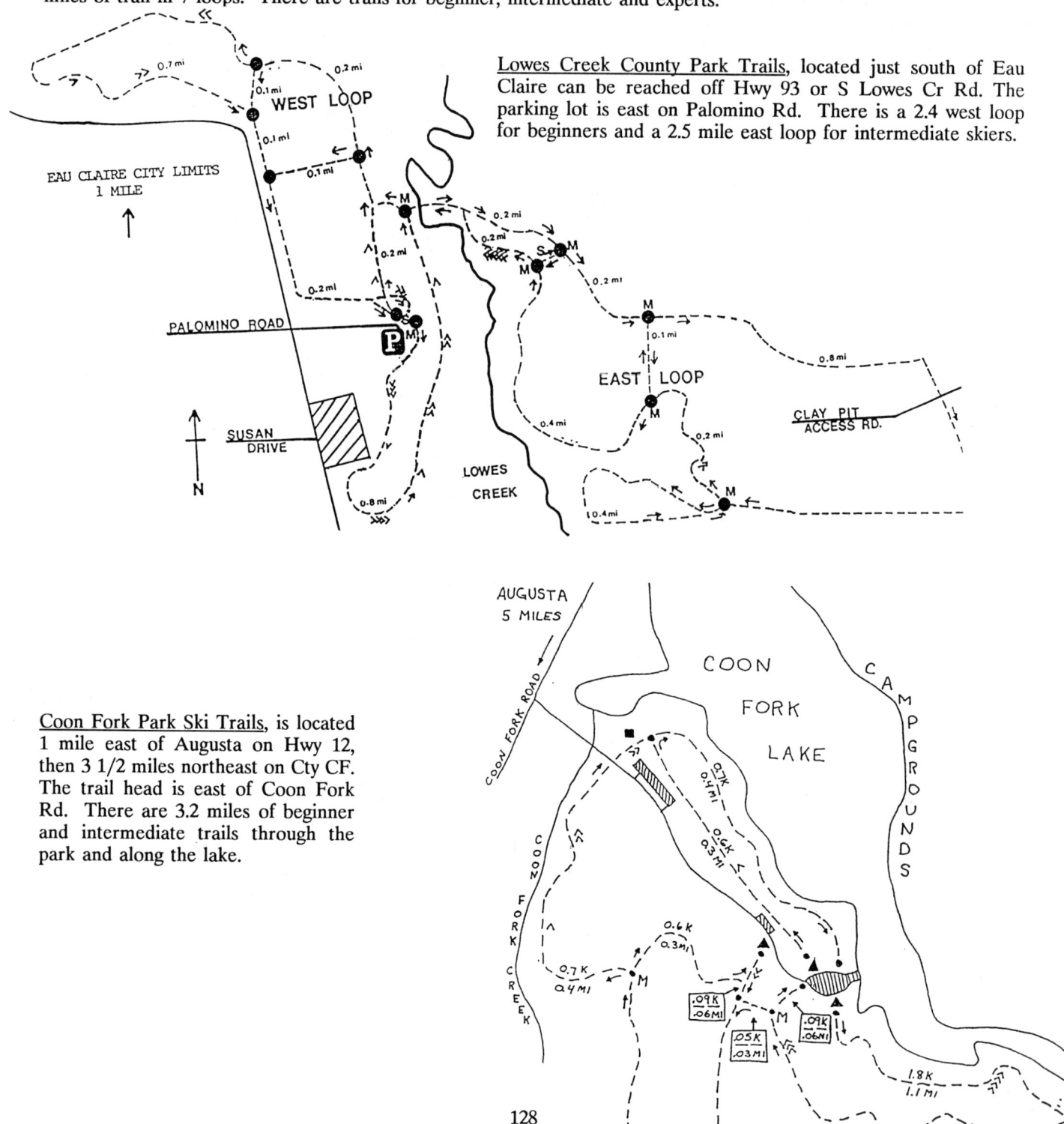

Eau Claire County Forest Hunter Walking Trails can be found on Forest Roads #3, #2 and #1 and on Park Rd off Cty MM.

Buffalo River State Trail passes just south of Eau Claire County and terminates at Fairchild. This 36.4 mile trail starts at Mondovi and parallels the Buffalo River and Hwy 10. The trail surface is not developed and therefore not suited for most bikes. It is open from May 25 to Oct 31 for ATV, horse, hiking and mountain bike use.

L.L.Phillips Park Ski Trails, is located about 5 miles east of Eau Claire on Cty QQ. The parking lot is on the south side of the road. There are 2.9 miles of trails west of S 82nd St. This trail system connects with the Tower Ridge trails to the west.

Clark County:

Levis Ski Trail, operated by Clark County, is located 12 miles west of Neillsville on Hwy 95. The parking lot is just west of Cty J. There are 4 trail loops around Levis Mound which cover 9 miles. The trails are classed as intermediate to advanced.

Bruce Mound Ski Trails, operated by Clark County, is located 3 miles east of Merrillan on Hwy 95, then south on Bruce Mound Road to the parking lot. There is a north and south loop covering 4 miles. The trail is rated as easy. Tubing and down hill skiing are also available.

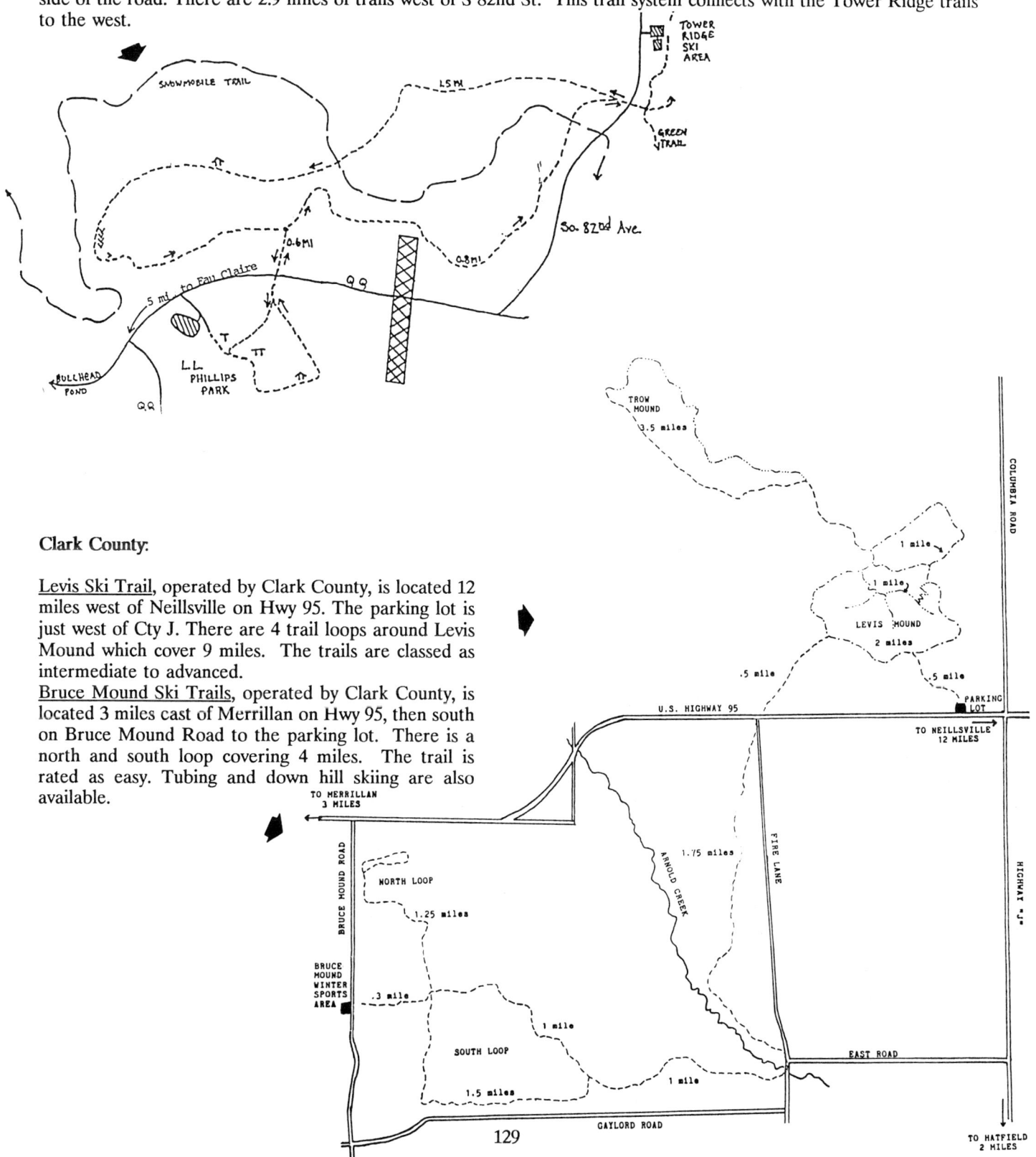

Rock Dam Cross Country Ski Trail, is located 7 miles west of Greenwood and Hwy 73 on Cty G, then west on Cty GG, continue west on Willard Rd, then south on Butler Rd to Rock Dam Road. The trail starts at the county park. There are two loops each, 2 miles long.

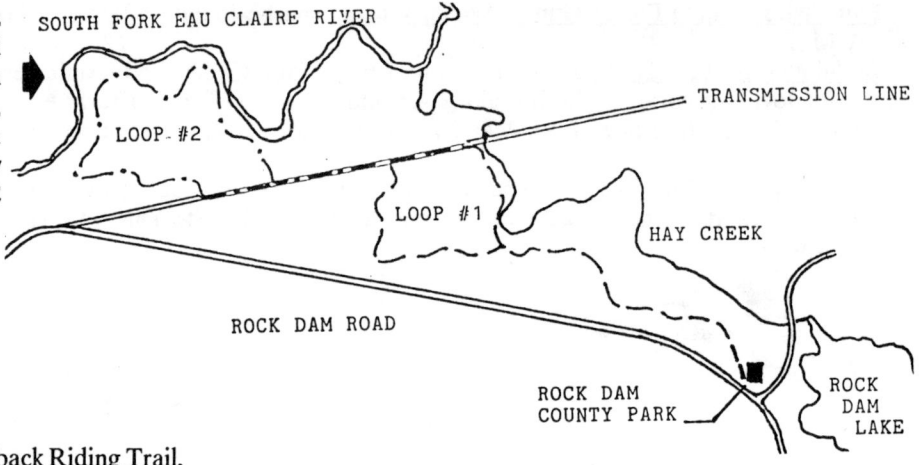

Wildrock Parklot, Clark County Horseback Riding Trail, is located 22 miles north west of Neillsville. Take Hwy 10 west of Neillsville, then north on Cty I to Cty M. At that intersection go south on Bald Peak Rd. The trail is a 14 mile loop to the south and west. It crosses Cty I several times as it follow logging roads.

Clark County Hunter Walking Trails, are located throughout the forest. There are over 90 miles of trails. Please talk to the county forester for exact locations.

Chippewa County:

Brunet Island State Park Rt 2, Box 158, Cornell WI 54732, (715) 239-6888, is located on Brunet Island Rd north of Hwy 64 and just west on the City of Cornell. There are four trails which include: Clubmoss Nature Trail, a 3/4 mile self-guided walking trail; Pine and Timber Trails 2 miles of trails through pine plantations and mature hemlock on the island, and Nordic Trail, a 3 mile cross country ski trail on the mainland.

Cedar Inn Ski Trails, Rt 1, Bloomer, WI 54724, (715) 568-1174, is located east of Bloomer on Hwy 64, then north on Cty AA, then east on Hungry Run Dr. After crossing O'Neil Cr turn south. There are 14 miles of groomed trails.

Deer Fly Trail Area, Chippewa County, is located either east of Bloomer on Hwy 64, then north on Cty E or east of New Auburn on Cty M. Between these two roads are a number of game trails through 8,500 acres of county forest. The area is a portion of the terminal moraine and features sharp ridges, rolling hills, lakes and streams.

Hickory Ridge Trail, Chippewa County, is located north of Chippewa Falls on Hwy 124. At Hwy 64 you can go east, then northeast on Cty E and then north on Bob's Lake Rd. Or you can go west on Hwy 64, then north on Cty AA, then east on Hungry Run Dr/Bob's Lake Road. It offers over 7 miles of ski trails through scenic areas, over steep hills and around many lakes. The trail, rated for intermediate and advanced skiers, goes through a more remote forest area.

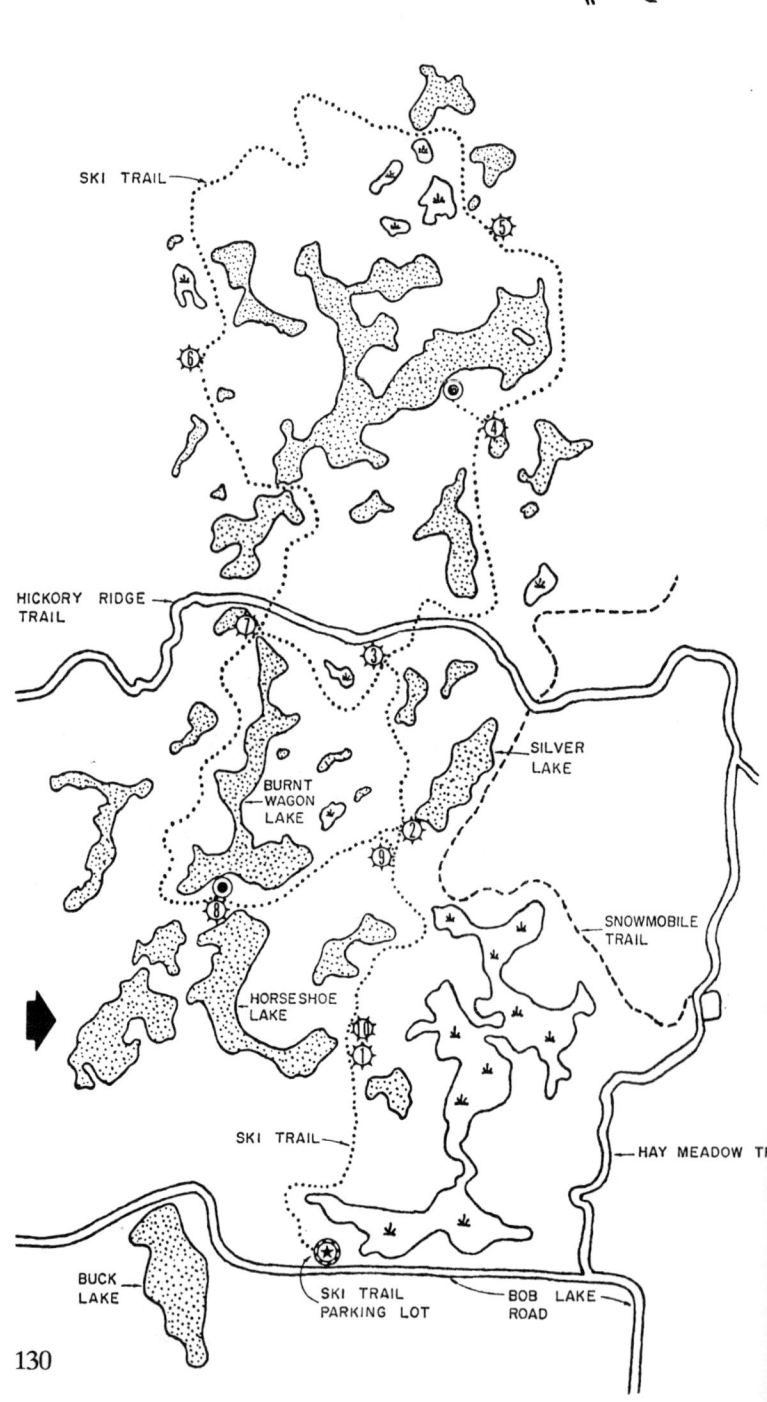

Lake Wissota State Park Ski Trail, R 8, Box 360, Chippewa Falls, WI 54729, (715) 382-4574, is located just east of Chippewa Falls on Hwy 29, then northeast on Cty X, then north on Cty K and west of Cty O. The park entrance is to the south. There are 4 trails ranging from 1 to 3 miles long, designed for the beginner. The trails pass through pine forest, mixed hardwoods and along the lake.

Otter Lake Interpretive Trail, located at Otter Lake County Park, is north of Hwy 29 on Cty G, then east Otter Lake Leja Rd. This is a 1/2 mile nature trail.

River Road Ski Trail, Chippewa County, is located 2 1/2 miles north of Cornell on Cty CC, then east on the first town road which follows the river. There are two loops. The Blue Trail is 2 1/2 miles long with steeper downhill and uphill grades. The Yellow Trail, 1.5 miles, is more gentle but is still difficult with some steeper areas to be classed as intermediate.

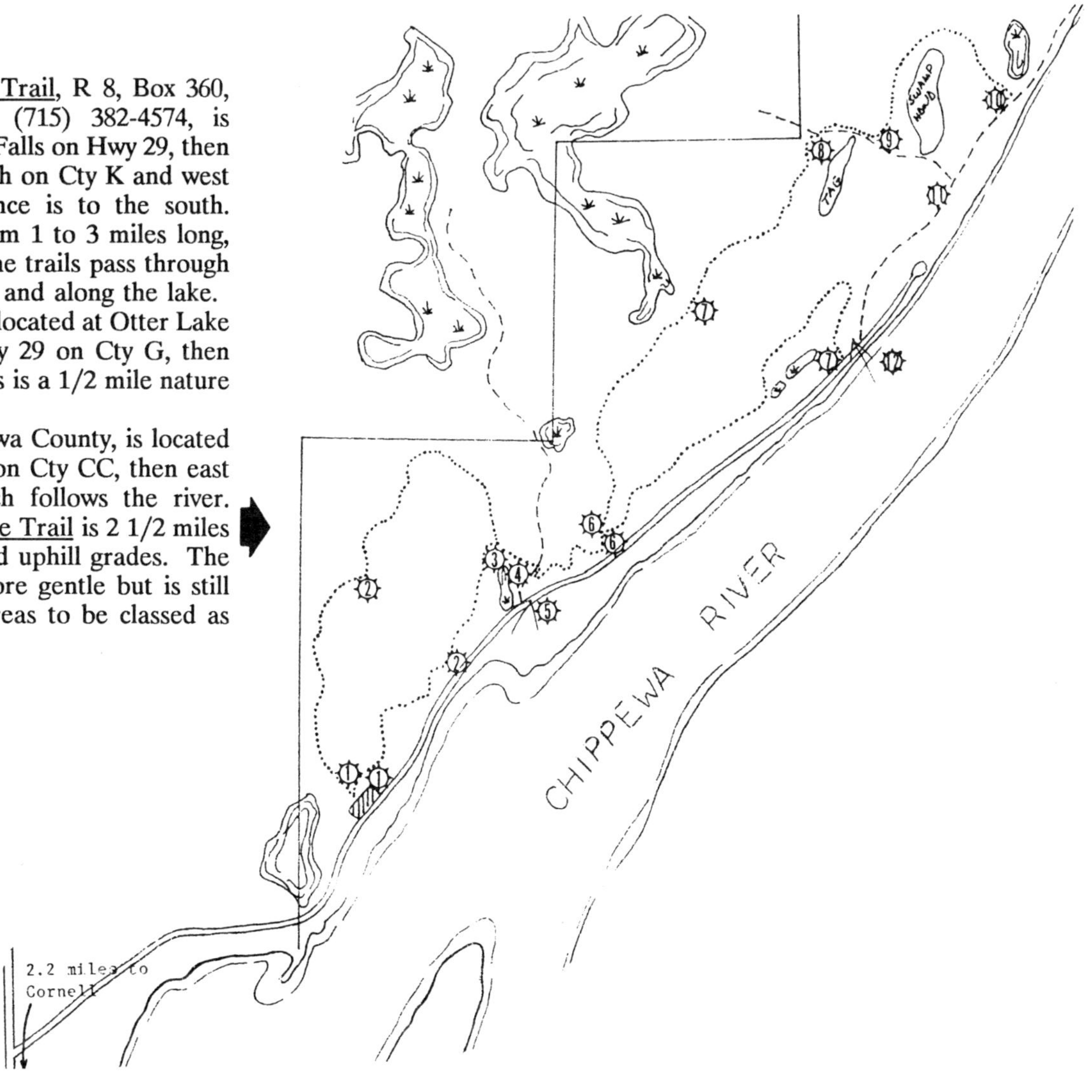

Ice Age National Scenic Trail System:

Chippewa County Segment is a 20 mile long trail through a terminal moraine of gentle hills, sharp ridges, pot hole lakes and interglacial lake beds. The trail extends from the Ice Age Park at Shattuck Lake east to Cornell. The trail starts at Shattuck Lake parking lot, about 16 miles west of Holcombe and Hwy 27, heading south and then east, weaving between 21 small lakes to Plummer Lake Rd parking area, which is just south of Cty M. This first segment is 6 miles long. From here the trail again heads 6 miles to the east, crossing Deer Fly Trail, and ending at Cty E. Part of the trail passes through private lands, so please stay on the trail. The last segment is 8 miles from Cty E to Cty CC and the Chippewa River. This section follows forest lanes and hunter walking trails, crossing fields and woodlands over beaver dams to Cty CC. Parking is permitted along a gravel side road. Camping is only permitted along the trail when on county lands.

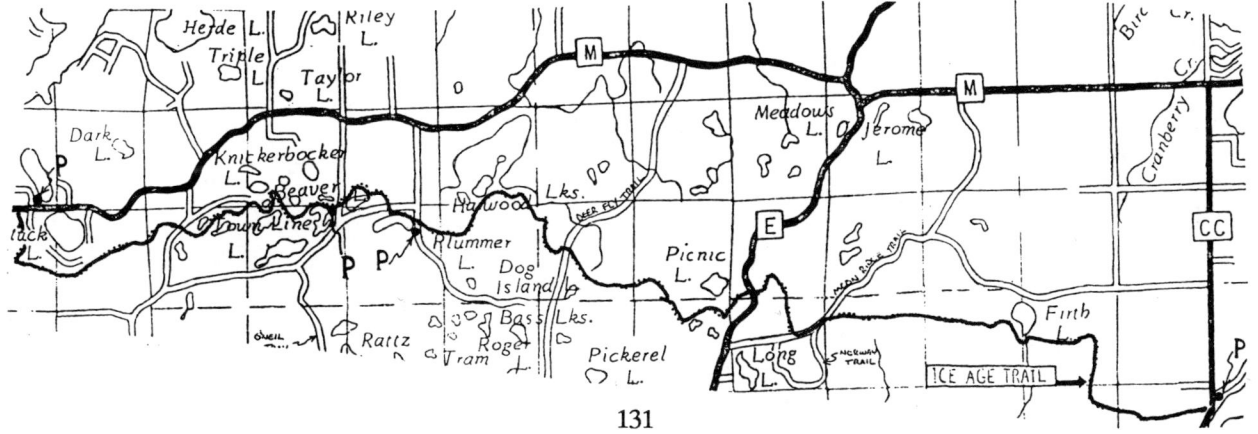

Canoe Trails:

<u>Chippewa River</u>, can be canoed throughout the region. The river character is that of a large, slow moving river with several impoundments. The river bottom is mostly sand with some rocky areas. In several sections there will be heavy power boating. Other sections are quiet where the canonist will have it for oneself. The upper sections will have a more wilderness appearance while the lower sections go through farm lands and urban development. Waters around the dams can be dangerous.

<u>Eau Claire River</u>, named by a French voyager in 1767 (means clear water), can be both challenging and easy depending on the water levels and section of the river. The upper reaches from Cty MM and Cty H to Cty G have rapids and boulder fields. On the north fork, 2 miles south of Cty MM, there is a falls that must be portaged. From Cty G to the Flowage, there should be no problems. It is 15 miles from Cty H to the dam on Lake Eau Claire. At the dam there is a 3/4 mile portage back to the river west of Hwy 27. From the dam, past Harstad Park to Cty K, is 14 1/2 mile, with only 1 rapids, just west of Cty K. From here to Big Falls and a portage is 1 1/4 miles. Then it is 8 3/4 miles to Lake Altoona and a landing on the south shore. If you continue down to the Chippewa River there is a 5/8 mile portage on Indian Hills Dr to below the dam.

<u>North & South Forks of Eau Claire River</u>, Clark County, with their slow moving water and sand bottom, are suited for family canoeing. The north fork may have log jams and downed trees which must be portaged. The Eau Claire County sections can be dangerous, please see the river description above.

<u>Black River</u>, Clark County section, is 54 miles long which ends at Lake Arbutus. The character of the river is one of deep gorges, swift rapids and granite boulders, and may provide challenging canoeing during high water only for the experienced. During low water there can be a lot of walking. There are access points at bridges.

<u>Townline/Knickerbocker Canoe Trail</u>, in located in Northern Chippewa County. Take Cty M east of New Auburn, then about 5 miles east of Hwy 40 take Town Line Rd to the south. There are landings on Town Line Lake and Horseshoe Lake. The trail then goes through six small lakes with portages to end at Knickerbocker Lake. There is no development on the lakes, making it a wilderness experience. There is fishing along the way. Camping is permitted. During dry weather you may have to drag your canoe through the smaller seepage lakes.

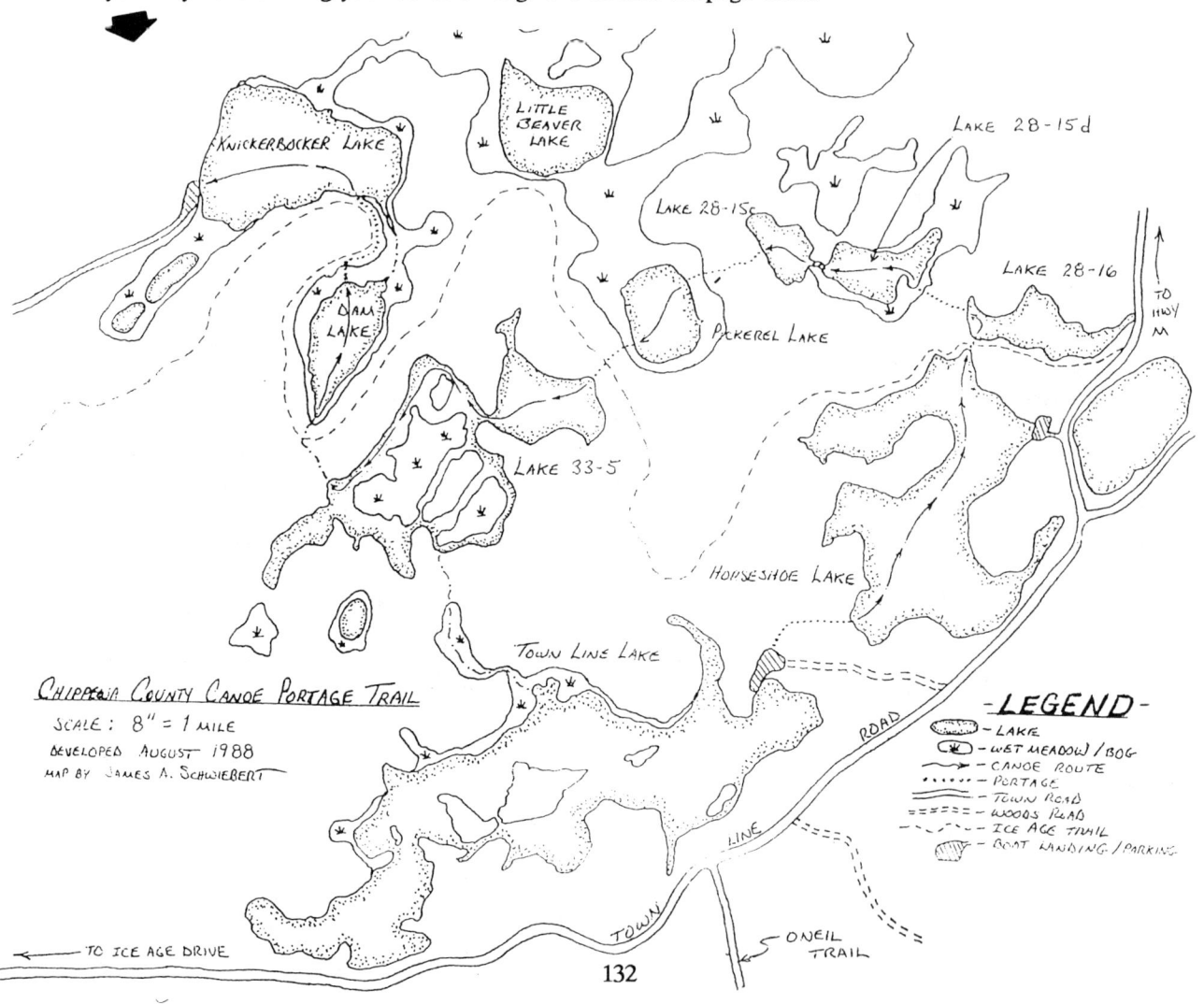

GUIDES AND BAIT SHOPS

Area Bait Shops:

SUN RAY LIQUOR & SPORTS	3628 SPOONER AVE	ALTOONA	WI 54720
RICK'S HWY 27 BAIT & SPORT	RT 1 BOX 74	AUGUSTA	WI 54722
BIRCH POINT RESORT	RT 1	BLOOMER	WI 54724
YVONNES SPORT & GIFT	RT 1 BOX 30	BLOOMER	WI 54724
TRUE VALUE HARDWARE	BOX 52 257 MAIN ST	CADOTT	WI 54727
BELOW DECK BAIT SHOP	RT 6	CHIPPEWA FALLS	WI 54729
BILLS SPORT SHOP	620 N BRIDGE ST	CHIPPEWA FALLS	WI 54729
ESLINGER'S SERVICE & SPORT	205 JEFFERSON AVE	CHIPPEWA FALLS	WI 54729
GORDY'S HARDWARE HANK	5501 VALLEY RD	CHIPPEWA FALLS	WI 54729
O-FISH-ALL SPORTS SHOP	4711 S PRAIRIE VIEW RD	CHIPPEWA FALLS	WI 54729
WALLY'S BAIT SHOP	RT 5 BOX 45	CHIPPEWA FALLS	WI 54729
WISSOTA BAIT	RT 8 BOX 339F	CHIPPEWA FALLS	WI 54729
MINNOWS ARE US	1904 S 8TH ST	CORNELL	WI 54732
STACKER CITY SPORTS	BOX 852 111 MAIN ST	CORNELL	WI 54732
KALEPP FISH FARM	RT 1	DORCHESTER	WI 54425
T AND S BAIT AND TACKLE	BOX 402	DORCHESTER	WI 54425
BUROKERS TAXIDERMY BAIT &TACKLE	1721 BIRCH ST	EAU CLAIRE	WI 54703
E C SPORTS	2000 HIGHLAND D30	EAU CLAIRE	WI 54701
INDIANHEAD SPORTSMAN CENTER	2104 CAMERON ST	EAU CLAIRE	WI 54703
NORTH SHORE LANDING	4315 17 NORTHSHORE DR	EAU CLAIRE	WI 54703
M-T MUG	117 S MAIN	GREENWOOD	WI 54437
EWERS STORE	RT 1	HOLCOMBE	WI 54745
FLATER'S RESORT	270 N CO E	HOLCOMBE	WI 54745
LAKE HOLCOMBE SPORT SHOP	RT 2 BOX 300	HOLCOMBE	WI 54745
LARRYS SOUTH SHORE RESORT	26064 CTH M	HOLCOMBE	WI 54745
JUNCTION BAIT SHOP	MAIN ST	JIM FALLS	WI 54748
WINDMILL RESORT INC	RT 1 BOX 161A	JIM FALLS	WI 54748
WOODY'S BAIT	RT 1 BOX 75	JIM FALLS	WI 54748
BRUCE'S TROPHY & TACKLE	RT 1 BOX 2	NEILLSVILLE	WI 54456
HOLIDAY STATION STORE	106 E DIVISION ST	NEILLSVILLE	WI 54456
ROBIN'S NEST	RT 2	NEILLSVILLE	WI 54456
MAX'S RESORT-GEORGE'S LIVE	RT 3	NEW AUBURN	WI 54757
MICK & DICK'S GENERAL	RT 3 BOX 44	NEW AUBURN	WI 54757
MIKES PLACE	RT 3	NEW AUBURN	WI 54757
TOM PLUMMER CONST	RT 3	NEW AUBURN	WI 54757
OEMIG'S SPORT SHOP	115 N BROADWAY	STANLEY	WI 54768
CARDINAL CORNERS BAIT	100 E STANLEY	THORP	WI 54771
COZY CORNER	RT 3	THORP	WI 54771
BAR TWO	RT 1	WILLARD	WI 54493

Area Guides:

EASTMAN	STEVEN	637 RED OAK DR	ALTOONA	WI 54720
COLVIN	MELVIN	225 HUDSON ST	AUGUSTA	WI 54722
FITZMAURICE	DENNIS	RT 1	AUGUSTA	WI 54722
RAYKOVICH	CHARLES	214 17TH AVE	BLOOMER	WI 54724
ARBUCKLE	DAVID	RT 5 BOX 516	CHIPPEWA FALLS	WI 54729
BRIST	KENNETH	RT 5 BOX 261	CHIPPEWA FALLS	WI 54729
BURSAW	JEFFREY	424 GOLDSMITH ST	CHIPPEWA FALLS	WI 54729
CHRISTENSON	ROBERT	RT 8 BOX 375	CHIPPEWA FALLS	WI 54729
DULIAN	DONALD	RT 6 BOX 369A	CHIPPEWA FALLS	WI 54729
FRANSWAY	JEFFREY	1116 WATER ST	CHIPPEWA FALLS	WI 54729
GASSEN	GREGORY	400 PUMPHOUSE RD #56	CHIPPEWA FALLS	WI 54729
KING	C	1050 W SPRUCE	CHIPPEWA FALLS	WI 54729
MICHELS	PAUL	914 FRONT ST	CHIPPEWA FALLS	WI 54729
STELTER	DICK	RT 5 BOX 552	CHIPPEWA FALLS	WI 54729
SMITH	TERRY	RT 2 BOX 179B	CORNELL	WI 54732
ANDREWS	LARRY	1222 E LEXINGTON BL	EAU CLAIRE	WI 54701
BECKWITH	BRIAN	2575 9 MILE CREEK RD	EAU CLAIRE	WI 54701
BRITTEN	ROGER	3447 HALLIE LA	EAU CLAIRE	WI 54702
CANDELL	WILLIAM	RT 4 BOX 244	EAU CLAIRE	WI 54701
CLARK	GEORGE	RT 1 BOX 128	EAU CLAIRE	WI 54703
DORN	CHARLES	3607 PATTON ST	EAU CLAIRE	WI 54701
HOCH	DALE	3252 MARS AVE	EAU CLAIRE	WI 54703
KAUFMAN	KERRY	717 BOLLES ST	EAU CLAIRE	WI 54701
KRAUSE	FLOYD	2615 FAIRFAX ST	EAU CLAIRE	WI 54701
KUMFERMAN	GEORGE	2333 11TH ST	EAU CLAIRE	WI 54703

Area Guides: continued

LABLANC	RONALD	1507 FRISBIE LA	EAU CLAIRE	WI 54703
MADSON	DARRYLL	1911 FOLSOM ST	EAU CLAIRE	WI 54703
OLSON	LAVERNE	661 WIS ST	EAU CLAIRE	WI 54703
REABE	WILLIAM	421 MAPLE ST	EAU CLAIRE	WI 54703
REITER	DANIEL	6992 TIMBER RIDGE	EAU CLAIRE	WI 54701
WASHBURN	ADOLPH	3611 PINE PLACE RD	EAU CLAIRE	WI 54701
WISNER	DONALD	110 GARFIELD AVE	EAU CLAIRE	WI 54701
GRANT	THOMAS	10165 HILLVIEW RD	FALL CREEK	WI 54742
VOLD	GARY	RT 3 BOX 44	FALL CREEK	WI 54742
BORGESON	ALLEN	208 E CENTRAL ST	GREENWOOD	WI 54437
BURPO	WILLIAM	BOX 210	HOLCOMBE	WI 54745
EWER	ROBERT	RT 1 BOX 149	HOLCOMBE	WI 54745
GLENCKE	BRUCE	BOX 306A RT 1	HOLCOMBE	WI 54745
SITLER	HAROLD	RT 1 BOX 335	HOLCOMBE	WI 54745
WENDELL	ROBERT	RT 2 BOX 300	HOLCOMBE	WI 54745
STEPHENSON	STEPHEN	RT 1 BOX 163	JIM FALLS	WI 54748
BUTTERFIELD	BRIAN	RT 3 BOX 124	NEW AUBURN	WI 54757
BURBEY	MARK	612 W 3RD ST	OWEN	WI 54460
SATONICA	RODNEY	RT 1	OWEN	WI 54460
HARYCKI	SYLVESTER	RT 2	THORP	WI 54771
MILLER	RAY	RT 1	UNITY	WI 54488
BAEHR	WALTER	RT 1	WITHEE	WI 54498
NORDLOF	ROBERT	RT 2 BOX 133	WITHEE	WI 54498

CAMPGROUNDS

Dispersed Camping:

Chippewa County, permits dispersed camping outside of designated camping areas.
Clark County, permits dispersed camping.
Eau Claire County, permits dispersed camping on forest lands from Sept 16 to April 30th for up to two weeks.
WI DNR, does not permit dispersed camping on its properties.

Private Campgrounds:

Bloomer/New Auburn Area:

Birch Point Resort: campground & cabins; open year round; boat launch, boat rental, bar & dining room; on Marsh Miller Lake; Rt 1, Bloomer, WI 54724; (715) 568-1525.
Clyde & Mary's North Shore Bar & Campgrounds: overnight and seasonal camping, swimming, boats, bait, groceries; Rt 3, New Auburn, WI 54757; (715) 868-2504.
Loon Lake Camping: family camping, fishing, swimming, wooded campsites; Rt 1, Box 140, New Auburn, WI 54757; (715) 967-2148.
Princes Resort: campground & cabins; open year round; boat rental, fishing; bar & dining facilities; Rt 3, Bloomer, WI 54724; (715) 288-6550.
R & R Bar: campgrounds, boat rental, fishing, mini golf, bar; Rt 3, Bloomer, WI 54724; (715) 288-6800.
Rock Lake Resort & Campground: open year round; showers, dump station, ski & snowmobile trails, fishing, boat & pontoon rental, bar, pizza; Rt 1, Bloomer, WI 54724; (715) 568-4370.
Salisbury Resort: located on Hwy 40 on Salisbury Lake; overnight trailer camping; open year round, swimming, Rt 3, New Auburn, WI 54757; (715) 967-2584.
Sand Lake Shores: camping, hook ups, fishing, swimming, bar & grill; on Sand Lake; Hwy 40, New Auburn, WI 54757; (715) 967-2534.
Willie's Overnight Campground: drive thru sites, dump station, RV sales; Bloomer, WI (715) 568-4947.

Chippewa Falls/Eau Claire Area:

Duncan Creek Campground: natural, quiet setting; bathrooms, showers, elec, water, playground, fishing; Rt 3, Box 21, Chippewa Falls, WI 54729; (715) 723-3825.

Kamp O'Klare: located 3 miles SE of Eau Claire at the jct of I-94 and Hwy 53; wooded, level sites, water & elec, toilets, showers, laundry, dump station, heated pool; Kamp O'Klare, 4000 House Rd, Eau Claire, WI 54701; (715) 832-7379.
Mallard Resort: located 8 miles north of Chippewa Falls on Hwy 178; campground & cabins; showers, elec, picnic tables, boat launch, fishing, boat rentals, swimming beach, store; on Lake Wissota and Chippewa River; Rt 3, Box 168, Chippewa Falls, WI 54729; (715) 288-6511.
O'Neil Creek Campground: located 4 1/2 miles north of Chippewa Falls on Hwy 124; campground with complete facilities, rec hall, canoeing, fishing, swimming; on O'Neil Creek with access to Lake Wissota; Rt 5, Chippewa Falls, WI 54729; (715) 723-6581.
Pine Harbor Campsite: Rt 8, Chippewa Falls, WI 54729; (715) 723-9865.
Woodland Motel & Campgrounds: located 6 miles north of Augusta on Hwy 27; 50 sites, water & elec, showers, restaurant, playground, mini golf, volleyball, trails, boat, bike rental; Woodland Motel & Campground, Box 73, Hwy 27, Augusta, WI 54722; (715) 286-2112.

Holcombe Area:

Flater's Flambeau Point Resort: camping, cottages, swimming beach, fishing, river trips, playground, ski & snowmobile trails, food; N270 Cty E, Holcombe, WI; (715) 595-4771.
Kostick's Resort: camping area, cabins, live bait, boat rental; on Lake Holcombe; (715) 532-5032.
Little Tee Pee Campground: take Hwy 27 to Lake Holcombe; seasonal campsites, LP gas; (715) 595-4732.
Paradies Recreation Area, Inc: camping with showers, elec, arcade, bar, ATV trails; Rt 2, Box 60, Holcombe, WI 54745; (715) 447-8774.
Pleasant Acres Campground: located 4 miles north of Holcombe on Hwy 27, 1 1/4 miles west on N. Shore Dr; 45 sites, 34 with water & elec, playground, heated pool, firewood, dump station; Rt 1, Holcombe, WI 54745; (715) 595-4464.
Ward Flambeau Resort: located 5 miles west of Hwy 27 on Cty D; campground & cottages; hook ups available, dump station, showers, docks, game room, bait, groceries; W103 55W. Cty D, Holcombe, WI 54745; (715) 595-4738.
Windmill Resort: located 3 miles north of Jim Falls on Hwy 178; campground, cabins, bar, boats, food; on Chippewa River; Rt 1, Jim Falls, WI 54748; (715) 382-4349.

County Campgrounds:

Chippewa County:

Morris-Erickson County Park, is located in the northwest corner of the county. Take Hwy 53 north to New Auburn, then east on Cty M, then north on Hwy 40 about 2 1/2 miles north to the park; Chippewa County; swimming, playgrounds, picnic area, shelters, toilets; on Long Lake.
Pine Point County Park is located in the northeast area of the county. Take Cty M 2 1/2 miles west of Hwy 27, the park is to the north after crossing the Holcombe Flowage; Chippewa County; swimming, playground, picnic area, shelter, boat landing; on Holcombe Flowage.
Otter Lake County Park is located in eastern Chippewa County north of Hwy 29 on Cty G, then east on Otter Lake Leja Rd.; Chippewa County; swimming, drinking water, toilets, boat landing, picnic area; on Otter Lake.

Clark County:

Russell Memorial Park is located in the extreme southwestern corner of the county on Beach La, just east of Cty J at the Jackson County line: Clark County; 188 sites; swimming, picnic area, shelters, telephone, concession, laundromat, showers; Lake Arbutus.
Rock Dam Park, is located 7 miles west of Greenwood, Hwy 73, on Cty G, then west on Cty GG, continue west on Willard Rd, then south on Butler Rd to the park; Clark County; 100 sites; picnic area, swimming, shelter, hiking trails, dump station, drinking water, playground, laundromat and country store; on Rock Dam Lake.
Sherwood Park, is located in the extreme southeast corner of the county. Take Cty Z south of Hwy 73 2 miles then west on town road 1 mile, then south into the park; Clark County; 38 sites; elec, water, toilets, picnic area, shelter, playground, swimming; on Sherwood Lake.
Mead Lake Park, is located 10 miles south of Hwy 29 on Cty O, then 5 miles west on Cty MM; Clark County; 60 sites; elec, water, picnic area, swimming, dump station, drinking water and playgrounds; on Mead Lake.
Greenwood Park, is located on the north end of Greenwood, west of Hwy 73 and on the Black River; Clark County; 14 sites; elec, picnic area, shelters, toilets and playgrounds; on the Black River.
Snyder Park is located 6 miles west of Neillsville on Hwy 10, then north on Arndt La. Keep to the left to the park; Clark County; 32 sites; camping $5.00, elec $1.50, water $1.50; swimming, picnic area, shelter, toilets, elec, water hookups; on Wedges Cr.

Eau Claire County:

Coon Fork County Park, is located 1 mile east of Augusta on Hwy 12, then 3 1/2 miles north east on Cty CF; Eau Claire County; nature trails, picnic area, shelters, swimming, canoeing, boat landing, playground, drinking water, toilets.
Harstad County Park, located 3 miles east of Fall Creek on Hwy 12, then 1 3/4 miles east on Cty HH, then north on Cty HHH; Eau Claire County; picnic area, shelter, canoeing, drinking water, playground and toilets.

Municipal Campgrounds:

Irvine Park: located on Bridgewater Ave in Chippewa Falls; 55 campsites; elec, flush toilets, firewood, showers, tennis courts, playground, public swimming pool, golf course, zoo, biking trails; (715) 382-4574.
Dorchester Village Recreation Park, is located north of Hwy 29 on Hwy 13, then west on Cty A into town, then south on Linden St and east on Third St. This 40 acre park is located on an impoundment on the Poplar River.

State Campgrounds:

Brunet Island State Park: located just north of Cornell, where the Fisher River joins the Chippewa; 69 campsites in a 1,030 acre park; elec, flush toilets, playgrounds, swimming beach, hiking trails, shelter, picnic areas, x-county ski trails.

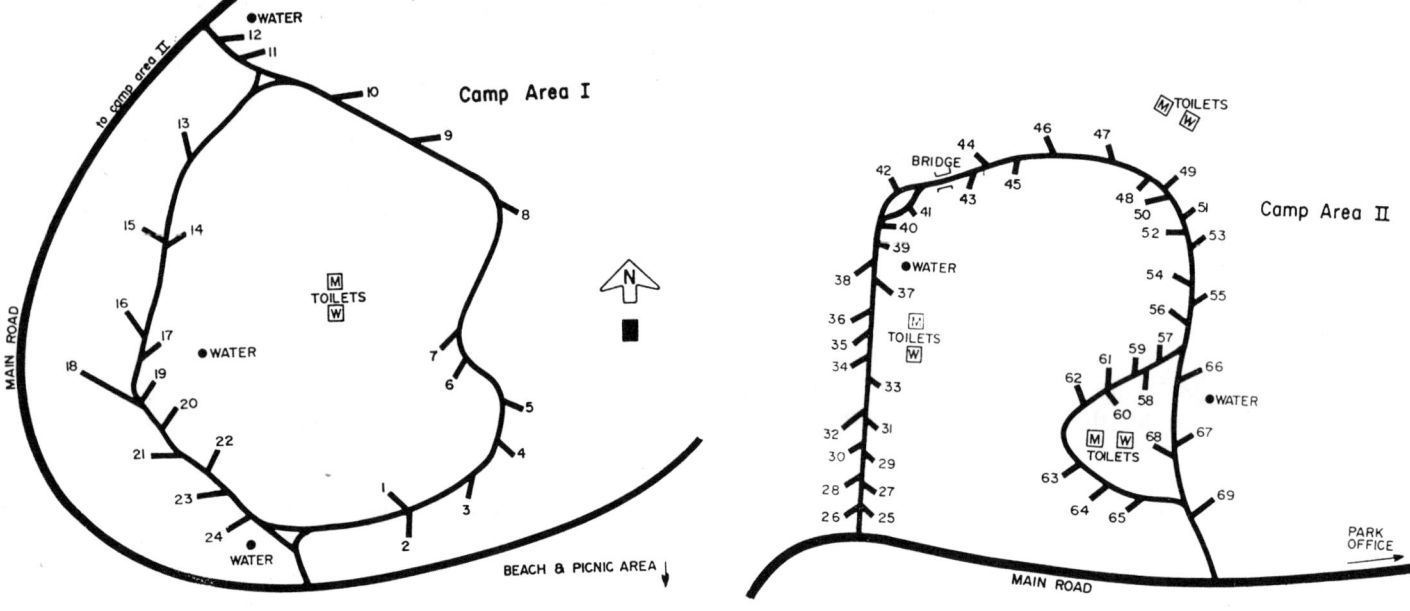

Lake Wissota State Park: located on Cty trunk O; 76 campsites on 1,044 acres; 300 ft sandy beach, hiking, skiing, and snowmobile trails, elec, flush toilets, playground, shelter; Rt 8, Chippewa Falls, WI 54729; (715) 382-4574.

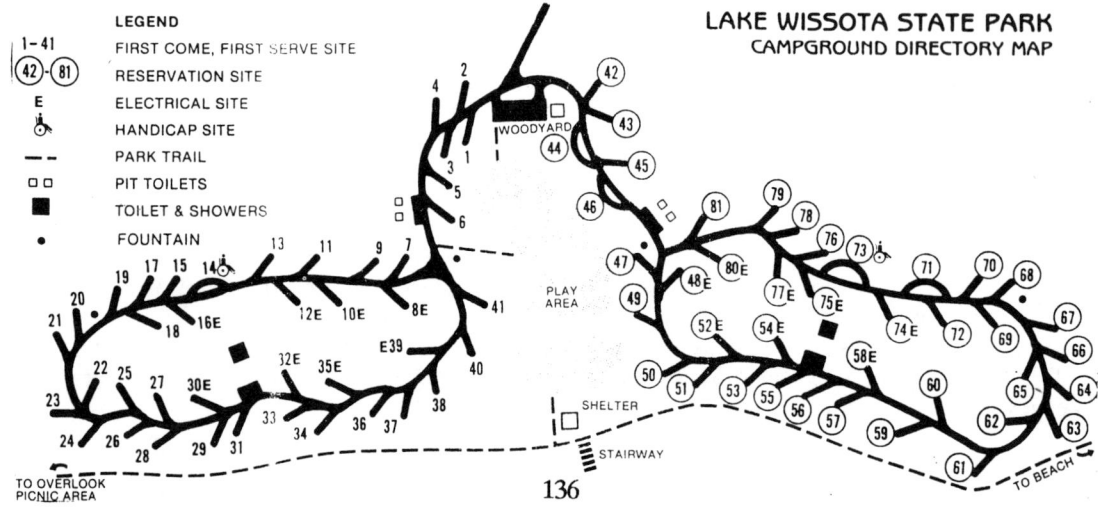

AREA ACTIVITIES

Boat Rental:

Birch Point Resort: boat rental; Rt 1, Bloomer, WI 54724; (715) 568-1525.
Cedar Inn: located, north end of Marsh Miller Lake; boat & pontoon rental; Rt 1, Bloomer, WI 54724; (715) 568-1174.
Kostick's Resort: boat rental; (715) 532-5032.
Lake Aire Resort: boat & motor rental; Rt 1, Box 337, Holcombe, WI 54745; (715) 595-4422.
Lake Holcombe Marina: located 2 miles west of Hwy 27 on M; pontoon & paddleboat rentals; (715) 595-4633.
Lake Holcome Sport Shop: located 1/4 mile west of Hwy 27 on Cty M; canoe rental; (715) 595-4293.
Larry's South Shore Resort: canoe rentals; Rt 2, Holcombe, WI 54745; (715) 595-4424.
Prentice Bros. Our Own Hardware: sporting goods, canoe rental; Main St, Cornell, WI.
Princes Resort: boat rental; Rt 3, Bloomer, WI 54724; (715) 288-6550.
R & R Bar: boat rental; Rt 3, Bloomer, WI 54724; (715) 288-6800.
Rock Lake Resort: boat & pontoon rental; Rt 1, Bloomer, WI 54724; (715) 568-4370.

Ski Rental:

Cedar Inn: located at the north end of Marsh Miller Lake; ski rental, 14 miles of groomed trails; Rt 1, Bloomer, Wi 54724; (715) 568-1174.

Ski Hills:

Bruce Mound: located 3 miles east of Merrillan or 15 miles SW of Neillsville, on Hwy 95; groomed downhill runs, beginner to intermediate, night skiing; x-country skiing on well marked scenic trails; inner tubing; rental of equipment; Clark County Forestry & Parks Dept., Neillsville, Wisconsin 54456; (715) 743-3241 or 743-2296.

Tours:

Leinenkugel Brewery: located in Chippewa Falls; Hospitality Center open 9am to 4pm daily; tours available Monday-Friday during summer months; (715) 723-5557.
Cook-Rutledge Mansion: located in Chippewa Falls; one of the finest examples of High Victorian-Italianate architecture in the midwest; tours available through special appointment; 505 W. Grand Ave, Chippewa Falls, WI 54729; (715) 723-7181.
Wisconsin World's Fair Pavilion: located in Neillsville; open to tours daily.

Museums:

Chippewa Valley Museum: located in Carson Park in Eau Claire. Take I-94 to Hwy 37 North, turn left onto Hwy 12, follow signs into Carson Park; one of Wisconsin's largest regional museums; open year round, Tues-Sun, 1:00-5:00 pm; P.O. Box 1204, Eau Claire, WI 54702; (715) 834-7871.
Clark County Historical Society Fine Arts Museum: open May through October.
The 1897 Jail Museum: located in Neillsville; operated by the Clark County Historical Society; artifacts from Neillsville's past; 215 East Fifth Street, Neillsville, WI 54456; (715) 743-3655 or 743-2694.
Thunderbird Museum: located in Hatfield, take I-94 exit Black River Falls, north on Hwy 12 to Hwy E; rare sea shell collection, Indian artifacts, antique collectibles and much more; guided tours, gift shop; Rt 1, Merrillan, WI 54754; (715) 333-5841.
Tufts' Museum: located in Neillsville; an interpretive restoration of a turn of the century home filled with antiques and mementos; open weekends May through September; 26 Hewett St, Neillsville, WI 54456; (715) 743-3000.

Zoos:

Irvine Park Zoo: located in Chippewa Falls; zoo provides viewing of deer, elk, bear, buffalo, lions and other animals.

EMERGENCY NUMBERS

Should you need help, listed below are the phone numbers for the sheriff and local hospitals.

Sheriff:

Clark County: (715) 743-3157; emergency (715) 743-3224
Chippewa County: (715) 723-8511; emergency (715) 723-4441
Eau Claire County: (715) 839-4701

Hospitals:

Community Memorial Hospital, 1501 Thompson St. Bloomer, WI 54724 (715) 568-2000.
St. Joseph's Hospital, 2661 Cty I, Chippewa Falls, WI 54729 (715) 723-1811.
Luther Hospital, 1221 Whipple St. Eau Claire, WI 54702 (715) 839-3311.
Sacred Heart Hospital, 900 W. Clairemont Ave. Eau Claire, WI 54701 (715) 839-4121.
Memorial Hospital, 216 Sunset Place, Neillsville (715) 743-3101.
Victory Memorial Hospital, 230 E. 4th Ave, Stanley, WI 54768 (715) 544-5571.

OTHER INFORMATION SOURCES

County:

Clark County Forestry & Parks Dept, Courthouse, Neillsville, WI 54456 (715) 743-3241 ext. 327.
Chippewa County Forestry & Parks Dept., 711 N Bridge St, Chippewa Falls, WI 54729, (715) 723-1831 ext 226.
Eau Claire County Parks & Forest, 3015 E Hamilton Ave, Eau Claire, WI 54701, (715) 839-4738.

State: WI Department of Natural Resources

WI DNR, Black River Falls Area Headquarters, Hwy 54 E, R 4, Box 18 Black RIver Falls, WI 54615 (715) 284-1400. Covers Clark, Buffalo, Trempealeau and Jackson Counties.
WI DNR, Eau Claire Area Headquarters, 2004 Highland Ave, Eau Claire, WI 54701 (715) 839-3777. Covers Eau Claire, Chippewa, Dunn, St Croix, Pepin and Pierce Counties.
WI DNR Ranger Station, Rt 2, Box 163 Cornell, WI 54732, (715) 239-6355.
WI DNR Ranger Station, Courthouse, Neillsville, WI 54456, (715) 743-3961.
WI DNR Ranger Station, Hwy 29 W & Brickyard Rd, Rt 6 Box 1, Menomonie, WI 54751 (715) 232-2631.

Chambers of Commerce:

Bloomer Chamber of Commerce, Box 136, Bloomer, WI 54724, (715) 568-3339.
Chippewa Falls Chamber of Commerce, 811 N Bridge St, Chippewa Falls, WI 54729, (715) 723-0331.
Eau Claire Convention & Tourism, 2129 Brackett Ave, Eau Claire, WI 54701, (715) 836-7680; 1-800-344-FUNN.
Eau Claire Lakes Business Assoc, Rt 1, Box 156 Gordon, WI 54838.
Lake Holcombe Resorts Assoc. Box 264 Holcombe, WI 54745.
Neillsville, Chamber of Commerce, Box 52, Neilsville, WI 54456, (715) 743-6444.
New Auburn, Blue Diamond Resort Assoc., Rt 3, New Auburn, WI 54757, (715) 967-2584.

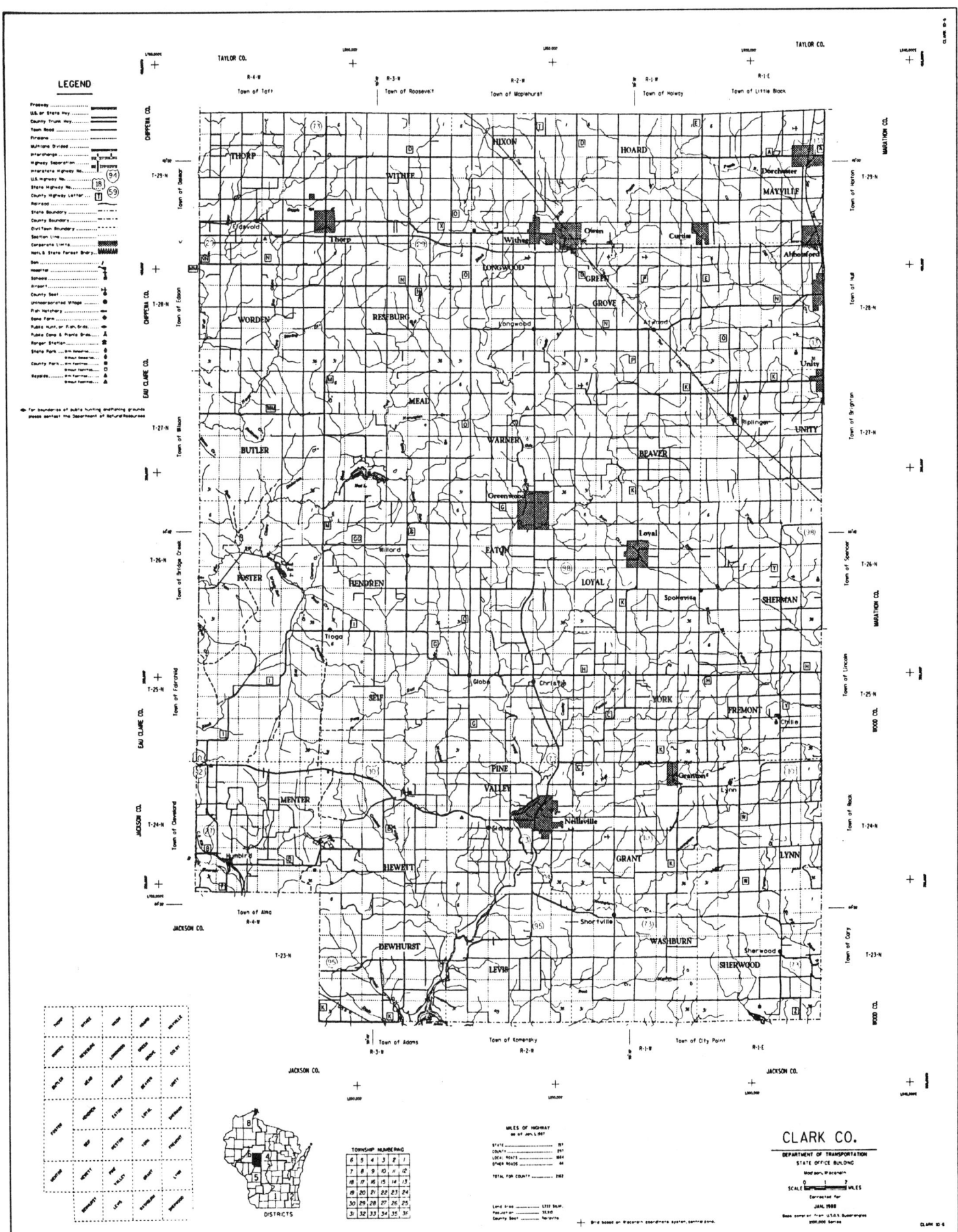

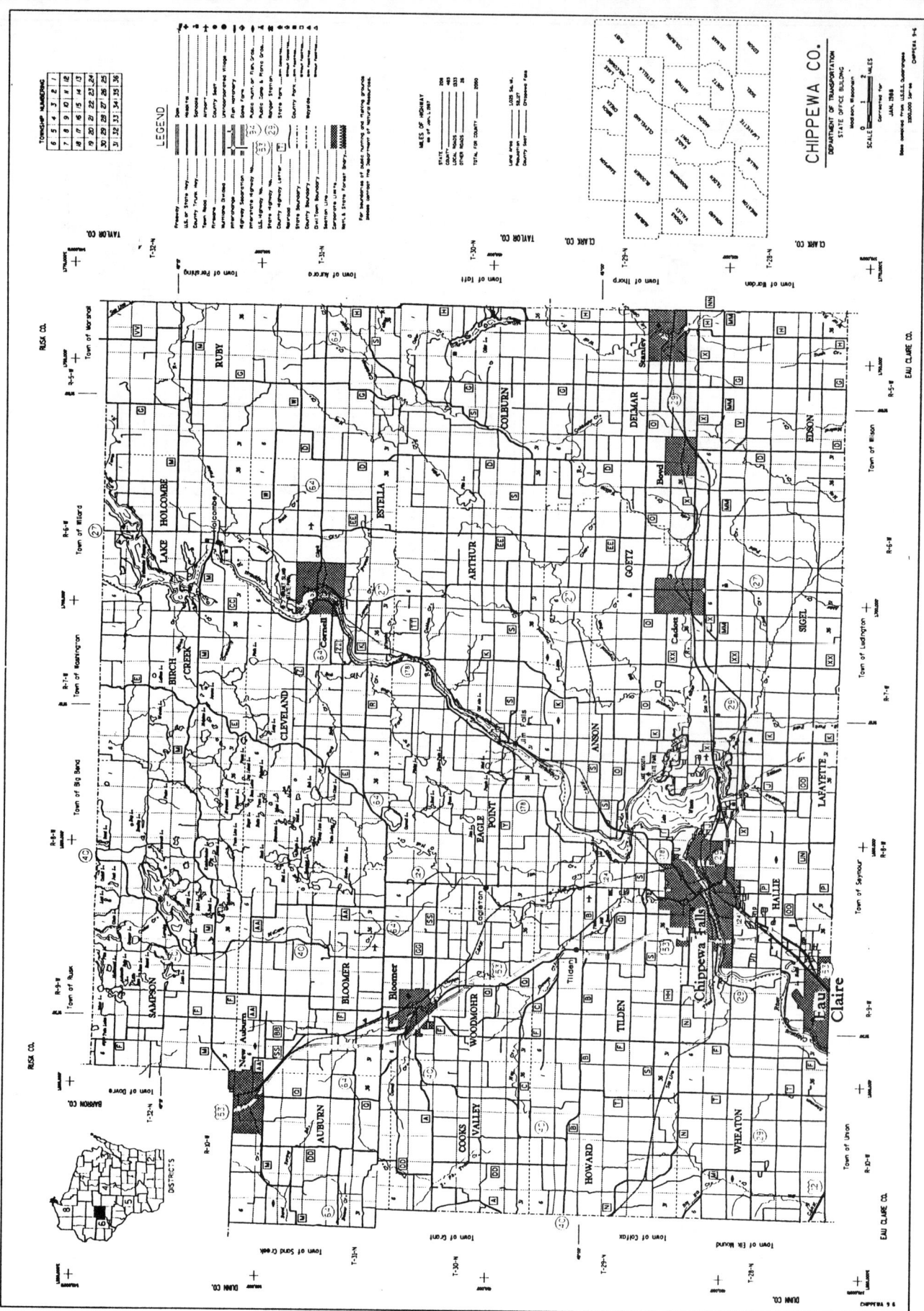

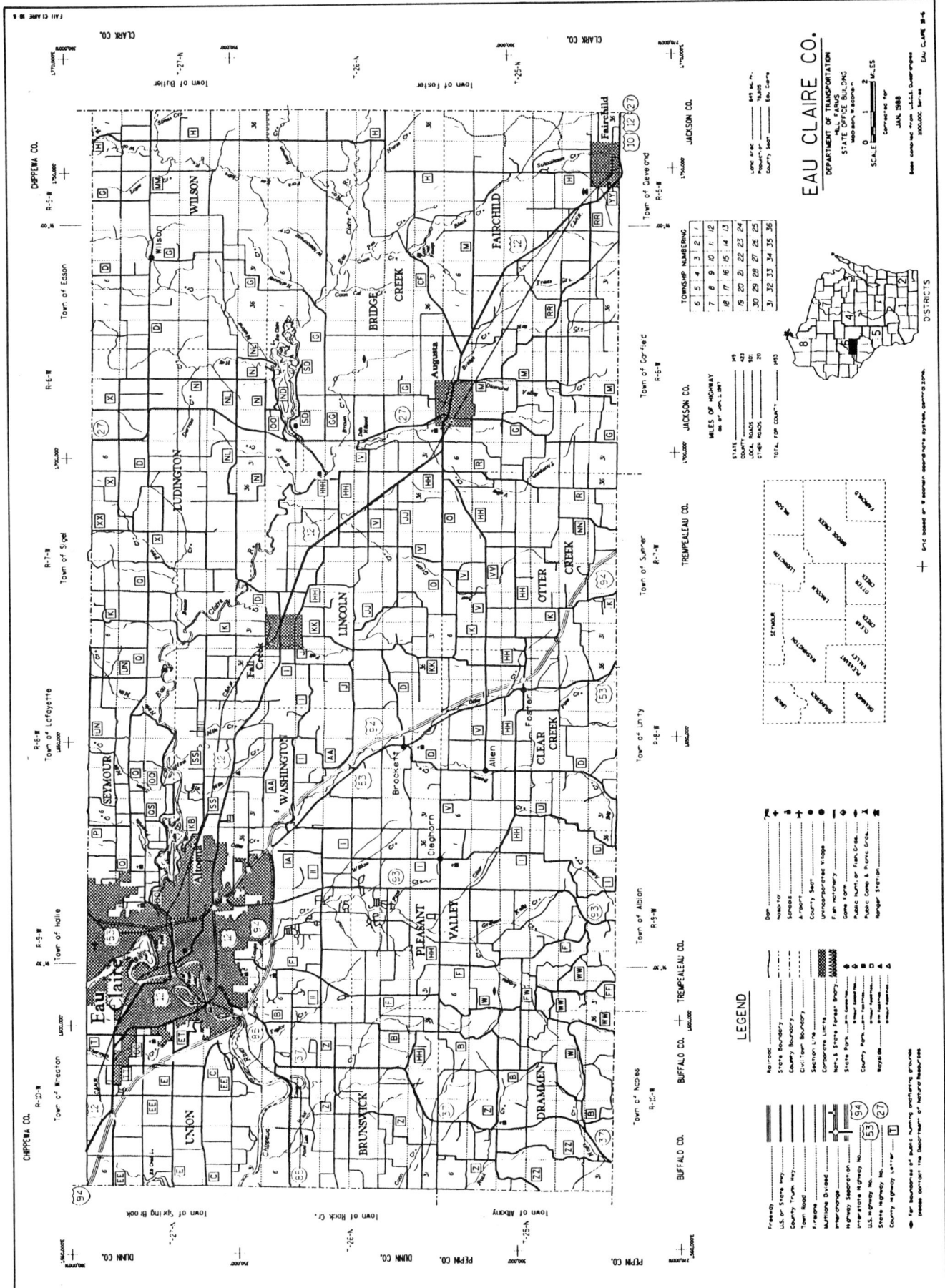

INDEX

ALL TERRAIN VEHICLES:
(See Trails)

AREA ACTIVITIES:

Ashland, 30
Barron, 91
Bayfield, 30
Burnett, 66
Chippewa, 137
Clark, 137
Douglas, 30
Dunn, 111
Eau Claire, 137
Pepin, 111
Pierce, 111
Polk, 91
Rusk, 91
St. Croix, 111
Sawyer, 66
Washburn, 66

BAIT SHOPS:

Ashland, 22
Barron, 88
Bayfield, 22
Burnett, 60
Chippewa, 133
Clark, 133
Douglas, 22
Dunn, 108
Eau Claire, 133
Pepin, 108
Pierce, 108
Polk, 88
Rusk, 88
St. Croix, 108
Sawyer, 60
Washburn, 60

CAMPGROUNDS:
Private

Ashland, 25
Barron, 90
Bayfield, 25
Burnett, 66
Chippewa, 134
Douglas, 25
Dunn, 109
Eau Claire, 134
Pepin, 109
Pierce, 109
Polk, 90

Rusk, 90
St. Croix, 109
Sawyer, 64
Washburn, 65

CAMPGROUNDS:
Municipal/State

Amnicon Falls, 27
Ashland, 27
Big Bay, 27
Barron, 90
Bayfield, 26
Bois-Brule, 27
Burnett, 66
Burnett Island, 136
Chippewa, 135
Clark, 135
Copper Falls, 27
Copper Range, 27
Douglas, 26
Dunn, 109
Eau Claire, 136
Lake Wissota, 136
Pattison Falls, 27
Pepin, 109
Pierce, 109
Polk, 90
Rusk, 90
St. Croix, 109
Sawyer, 66
Washburn, 66
Willow River, 110

CAMPGROUNDS:
Federal

Apostle Islands NL, 16
Chequamegon NF, 27
Eau Galle Rec Site, 110
St Croix NSR, 50

CANOE TRAILS:

Apple, 107
Bois-Brule, 8
Chippewa, 58, 107, 132
Eau Claire, 132
Flambeau, 58
Loyhead Lake Canoe Area, 57
Namekagon, 47
Red Cedar, 107
St Croix, 47
Sawmill Canoe Area, 57
Totagatic, 58

Townline/Knickerbocker Canoe Trail, 132

COUNTY MAPS:

Ashland, 33
Barron, 93
Bayfield, 34
Burnett, 70
Chippewa, 140
Clark, 139
Douglas, 35
Dunn, 114
Eau Claire, 141
Pepin, 115
Pierce, 116
Polk, 94
Rusk, 95
St. Croix, 117
Sawyer, 71
Washburn, 72

EMERGENCY/ INFORMATION:

Ashland, 31
Barron, 92
Bayfield, 31
Burnett, 68
Chippewa, 138
Clark, 138
Douglas, 31
Dunn, 113
Eau Claire, 138
Pepin, 113
Pierce, 113
Polk, 92
Rusk, 92
St. Croix, 113
Sawyer, 68
Washburn, 68

GUIDES:
By County

Ashland, 23
Barron, 89
Bayfield, 23
Burnett, 61
Chippewa, 133
Clark, 133
Douglas, 23
Dunn, 108
Eau Claire, 133
Pepin, 108

Pierce, 108
Polk, 89
Rusk, 89
St. Croix, 108
Sawyer, 61
Washburn, 61

LAKES & FLOWAGES:

Arbutus Lake, 119
Balsam Lake, 75
Bass Lake, 97
Bone Lake, 75
Cedar Lake, 97
Chetek, 75
Chippewa Flowage, 37
Clam Lake, 37
Dairyland Flowage, 75
English Lake, 7
Grinding Stone, 37
Holcombe Flowage, 119
Island Lake, 75
Lake Altoona, 119
Lake Eau Claire, 119
Lake Namekagon, 7
Lake Pepin, 97
Lake Wissota, 119
Long Lake, 7
Long Lake, 37
Marsh Miller Lake, 119
McKenzie Lake, 37
Mead Lake, 119
Menomin Lake, 97
Mineral Lake, 7
Minong Flowage, 37
Nelson Lake, 37
Nugget Lake, 97
Otter lake, 119
Perch Lake, 97
Red Cedar, 75
St Croix Flowage, 7
St Croix Lake, 97
Shell Lake, 37
Tainter Lake, 97
Wapogasset Lake, 75
Yellow Lake, 37

PARKS:

Apostle Island NL, 15
Ashland, 14
Barron, 80
Bayfield, 12
Burnett, 45
Burnett Island State Park, 123
Chequamegon NF, 17
Chippewa, 122
Clark, 124

Douglas, 12
Dunn, 100
Eau Claire, 125
Eau Galle Lake Rec. Site, 103
Hoffman Hills State Park, 101
Interstate State Park, 82
Kinnickinnic State Park, 102
Lake Wissata State Park, 123
Pepin, 101
Pierce, 102
Polk, 81
Rusk, 80
St. Croix, 103
St Croix NSR, 47
Sawyer, 45
Washburn, 46
Willow River State Park, 104

PUBLIC LANDS:
By County

Ashland, 8
Barron, 76
Bayfield, 8
Burnett, 38
Chippewa, 120
Clark, 120
Douglas, 8
Dunn, 98
Eau Claire, 120
Pepin, 99
Pierce, 99
Polk, 76
Rusk, 76
St. Croix, 99
Sawyer, 39
Washburn, 40

PUBLIC LANDS:
Federal

Apostle Islands NL, 15
Chequamegon NF, 10
Eau Galle Rec Site, 103
St Croix Riverway, 47

PUBLIC LANDS:
State
Amsterdam Sloughs WA, 42
Augusta WA, 121
Bark Bay Preserve, 8
Bean Brook, 43
Bear Lake WA, 43
Beaver Brook WA, 43
Behning Cr, 77
Big Beaver Cr, 99
Bolan Cr, 99
Brule River SF, 8

Chief River WA, 43
Clam River, 41
Crex Medow WA, 41
Cyclon, 99
Cyclon Marsh, 99
Danbury WA, 42
Douglas County WA, 9
Duncan CR, 121
Dunnville WA, 99
Eau Galle River, 99
Elf Cr, 121
Flambeau River SF, 44
Fish Lake WA, 42
Grassy Lake WA, 77
Gov. Knowles SF, 44
Hallie WA, 121
Hay Cr, 99
Hay River, 99
Jim Falls WA, 121
Joel Marsh WA, 77
Kiezer Lake WA, 42
Kissick Swamp WA, 43
Lambs Cr, 99
Lighting Cr, 77
Loon Lake, 77
McCann Cr, 121
McKenzie Cr WA, 77
Muddy Cr WA, 98
Namekagon Barrens, 42
Namekagon River, 43
New Auburn, 77
Parker Cr, 77
Pierce County Islands, 99
Pleasant Valley WA, 121
Port Wing Preserve, 9
Potato Cr WA, 78
Quaderer Cr. 77
Otter Cr, 99
Rice Beds CR, 77
Rush River WA, 99
St Croix Islands, 99
Sand Cr WA, 41
Sawyer Cr, 43
Snake Cr, 77
Sweeny Pond, 77
Tenmile Cr WA, 79
Tiffany WA, 99
Thompson Slough, 99
Totagatic River WA, 43
Totagatic Lake WA, 9
Washington Cr WA, 78
Weirgor Springs WA, 44
Whalen Cr, 43
White River, 9
Yellow River, 77

RIVERS:

Apple, 98
Black, 119
Bois-Brule, 7
Chippewa, 38, 75, 98, 119
Flambeau, 38, 75
Kinnickinni, 98
Mississippi, 98
Namekagon, 47
Red Cedar, 75, 98
Rush, 98
St Croix, 47
Totagatic, 38

TRAILS:
All Kinds
By County

Ashland, 18
Barron, 83
Bayfield, 18
Burnett, 51
Chippewa, 130
Clark, 129
Douglas, 18
Dunn, 105
Eau Claire, 128
Pepin, 107
Pierce, 107
Polk, 86
Rusk, 86
St. Croix, 107
Sawyer, 51
Washburn, 51

TROUT STREAMS:

Ashland, 7
Barron, 76
Bayfield, 7
Burnett, 38
Chippewa, 120
Clark, 1
Douglas, 7
Dunn, 98
Eau Claire, 120
Pepin, 98
Pierce, 98
Polk, 76
Rusk, 76
St. Croix, 98
Sawyer, 38
Washburn, 38

Campground Cookery

The Most Indispensable Item In Your Campground Kitchen!

A complete guide to outdoor cooking. A handy book for everyone, from the novice camper to the experienced outdoor cook. Campground Cookery leads you through the steps in building a campfire, cleaning fish and poultry, and demonstrates seven different methods of cooking food outdoors. This book also features suggested menu plans and a camper's kitchen checklist.

*Snacks * Breakfasts * Salads * Stews * Main Dishes *
*Vegetables * Deserts * Kid's Recipes *

ISBN 0-962-3430-2-1 - 160 pages - 220 recipes - $8.95

(5% Tax, Wis Residents) & $2.50 Shipping per order.

Explorer's Guide Publishing,
4843 Apperson Dr.
Rhinelander, WI 54501
(715) 362-6029